10/14

Praise for *The Collapse*

"The fall of the Berlin Wall was one of the landmark events of the twentieth century, but this great change involved accidental and non-violent causes. In wonderfully readable prose, Mary Elise Sarotte tells a compelling story of how history works its surprises."

—Joseph S. Nye, Jr., Harvard University Distinguished Service Professor
and author of *The Future of Power*

"In *The Collapse*, Mary Elise Sarotte provides a needed (and highly readable) reminder that the peaceful culmination to 1989's dramatic developments was in no way inevitable."

—General Brent Scowcroft, former National Security Advisor

"Meticulously researched, judiciously argued, and exceptionally well written, *The Collapse* describes the fall of the Berlin Wall from an unprecedented perspective. Mary Elise Sarotte weaves together numerous German, American, and Soviet accounts, allowing the reader to crisscross the Berlin Wall on the eve and in the course of its collapse. It will come as a surprise to many that this climactic event in Cold War history resulted not from agreements reached in Washington, Berlin, Moscow, or Bonn, but from the uncoordinated actions of people on both sides of the Berlin divide. *The Collapse* makes it possible for those who made history in 1989 to speak in their own voices."

—Serhii Plokhy, author of *The Last Empire:*
The Final Days of the Soviet Union

"From a remove of 25 years, the fall of the Berlin Wall seems foreordained. In fact, as Mary Elise Sarotte shows, this historic moment was an improbable concatenation of events and decisions triggering in perfect if accidental sequence. Catastrophe at times was just seconds away. As someone who was in Leipzig and Berlin as the crucial events unfolded, I can say that Sarotte gets it exactly right, capturing the fear, confusion, courage, and growing excitement as hitherto ordinary people peacefully toppled the deadly barrier that symbolized the Cold War."

—Mike Leary, Pulitzer Prize–winning journalist

"In her compelling and fast-paced narrative, Mary Elise Sarotte reminds us that the end of the Cold War was not foreordained, but that courageous acts by East German dissidents, offhand comments by GDR officials, and the actions of one perplexed border-guard changed the course of twentieth-century history. This is essential reading for those who want to understand the role of contingency and human agency in the unexpected opening of the Berlin Wall."

—Angela Stent, author of *The Limits of Partnership:*
US-Russian Relations in the Twenty-First Century

THE
COLLAPSE

THE
COLLAPSE

The Accidental Opening
of the Berlin Wall

MARY ELISE SAROTTE

BASIC BOOKS

A Member of the Perseus Books Group
New York

Published by Basic Books, a Member of the Perseus Books Group

Books published by Basic Books are available at special discounts for bulk
purchases in the United States by corporations, institutions, and other
organizations. For moreinformation, please contact the Special Markets
Department at the Perseus Books Group, 2300 Chestnut Street, Suite 200,
Philadelphia, PA 19103, or call (800) 810-4145, ext. 5000, or e-mail
special.markets@perseusbooks.com.

Library of Congress Cataloging-in-Publication Data
Sarotte, Mary Elise.
The collapse : the accidental opening of the Berlin Wall / Mary Elise Sarotte.
pages cm
Includes bibliographical references and index.
ISBN 978-0-465-06494-6 (hardback) — ISBN 978-0-465-05690-3 (e-book)
1. Berlin Wall, Berlin,
Germany,1961-1989. 2. Germany (East)—Politics and government—1989-1990.
3. Berlin (Germany)—
History—1945-1990. I. Title. II. Title: Accidental opening of the Berlin Wall.

DD881.S213 2014

943.087'8—dc23

2014026435

10   9   8   7   6   5   4   3   2   1

For Dianne and Al, Steve, and Mark

It is not always going from bad to worse that leads to revolution.

What happens most often is that a people that puts up with the most oppressive laws without complaint, as if it did not feel them, rejects those laws violently when the burden is alleviated. . . .

The evil that one endures patiently because it seems inevitable becomes unbearable the moment its elimination becomes conceivable.

—ALEXIS DE TOCQUEVILLE[1]

Contents

Maps and Photos

MAPS

PHOTOS

Abbreviations in the Captions, Maps, and Text

ABC   US broadcast network

ADN   East German news service

ARD   West German broadcast network

CBS   US broadcast network

CDU   Christian-Democratic Union (political party in West Germany; separate political party in East Germany; merged in 1990 in united Germany)

CIA   US Central Intelligence Agency

CSCE   Conference on Security and Cooperation in Europe

CSSR   Czechoslovak Socialist Republic

DM   Deutschmark (the currency of West Germany in 1989)

DPA   German Press Agency (West German news service, initials in German)

EC   European Community

EU   European Union

FDP   Free Democratic Party (West German, then German; also known as the Liberals)

FRG   Federal Republic of Germany (generally known in English as West Germany; see note on names)

GDR   German Democratic Republic (generally known in English as East Germany; see note on names)

ID   Personal identity paperwork

MfS   East German Ministry for State Security (also known as the Stasi)

NATO   North Atlantic Treaty Organization

NBC   US broadcast network

NSC   US National Security Council

RHG   Robert Havemann Society (initials in German)

SBM   Berlin Wall Foundation (initials in German)
SED   East German Socialist Unity Party (the East German ruling
         party, initials in German)
UK   United Kingdom of Great Britain and Northern Ireland
US   United States
USSR   Union of Soviet Socialist Republics
ZDF   West German broadcast network

Note on Names

Writing a book in English based on audio and video recordings, documents, and interviews that were mostly in languages other than English creates a challenge in the use of certain names. For example, this book uses the common English-language terms "East Germany" and "West Germany" despite the fact that those precise names are used only rarely in German-language sources from the time period, which generally refer instead to East Germany as the German Democratic Republic, or GDR, and West Germany as the Federal Republic of Germany, or FRG. The exact names are not trivialities, given that what, exactly, the two Germanys called themselves and each other was a constant source of contention. In the interest of producing a clearly written text for the English-language reader, however, I have adopted the common English terms despite their differences from the original sources, as well as using the acronyms GDR and FRG for variety. It is additionally worth noting that, starting on October 3, 1990, the newly reunified Germany kept the former West German name of "Federal Republic of Germany" for itself, so references to the FRG after that date describe all of the united country instead of just the western half of the divided one. Similar to my use of East and West Germany is my use of "East Berlin" for clarity, even though the GDR regime generally avoided referring to its half of divided Berlin by that name. Instead, it preferred to use either "Berlin"—thus implying, incorrectly, that it held sway over the entire city—or the more formal "Berlin Capital of the GDR." Finally, I have relied on common English-language names of not just places but also people, such as "Joseph Stalin" for the former leader of the Soviet Union.

Introduction

Discovering the Causes of the Collapse

To put it in a nutshell, causes cannot be assumed in history any more than in any other field. They must be discovered.
—MARC BLOCH[1]

O N NOVEMBER 9, 1989, AT 6:30 P.M. Eastern Time, television viewers tuned to NBC were about to see an amazing sight. The network's anchorman, Tom Brokaw, was just beginning to broadcast the *NBC Nightly News* live from West Berlin. Two days earlier, he and his producers had decided that the show's staff should travel to the divided city at the epicenter of Cold War Europe. The crew had built a high broadcast platform directly in front of the point where the Wall cut the iconic Brandenburg Gate off from the West. Brokaw and his team had also rented a cherry picker, to raise NBC's camera operators and their equipment to a height with a commanding view, and enormous floodlights, to ensure that the nighttime scene was well lit. NBC was the only television broadcaster from any country with such a setup at this location, the most visually significant site in the city. The decision to go to West Berlin and to stake out this spot was about to pay off more handsomely than the network could ever have expected.

As the *Nightly News* began, the audience got its first look at Brokaw on the raised platform. His dark blue wool coat stood out in sharp relief against the Wall behind him. Thanks to the camera angle, viewers could also see the Brandenburg Gate, partly illuminated by the lights from West Berlin and partly hidden behind the Wall in the shadows of East Berlin. On the western side of the Wall, beneath Brokaw's platform, a massive, raucous crowd filled all visible areas. Some crowd members were even taking advantage of the unusual shape of the barrier at this site—it was shorter and stockier than elsewhere, reportedly in order to prevent enemy tanks from breaking through to the gate—to climb up and to stand on it.[2] The climbers already on top were struggling to keep their footing as water cannons targeted them from the eastern side.

The overall effect was striking. The spray from the upward-gushing columns of water from the East brilliantly reflected the light from the West. It looked roughly as if someone had transported an illuminated fountain from Las Vegas to the middle of divided Berlin. Stunned viewers heard Brokaw describe the scene by saying, "What you see behind me is a celebration." The jubilation, he explained, was the result of an unexpected decision. As "announced today by the East German government . . . for the first time since the Wall was erected in 1961, people will be able to move through freely!"[3]

Brokaw and his crew could not sit back and relish the exclusive broadcast from the gate, however. Rather, his team had to stay alert as it became increasingly clear that the story was not a straightforward one. If the East German regime had announced that people could move freely across the Wall, why was it using water cannons to prevent them from doing just that? Divided Berlin was six hours ahead of New York, meaning that it was cold, dark, and late at Brokaw's location. Drenching visitors in water in the middle of a November night, or knocking them off the roughly eight-foot-high Wall altogether, did not seem to be much of a way to say "welcome." NBC's cameras also recorded images of some celebrants on the eastern side being forcibly dragged away.

Why were East German security forces using water cannons and hauling off peaceful celebrants? Why was NBC the only television network from any country with a broadcast platform set up in front of the Brandenburg Gate? Above all, why was the Berlin Wall opening in the middle of the night and in such a bizarre manner? Did the word "opening" apply at all? Until that evening, no one expected that the Wall would fall. Instead, well into 1989, escaping East Germany remained a fatal exercise. The last killing by gunshot had occurred in February of that year; the last shooting at the Wall, a near-fatality in broad daylight, had taken place in April; and the last death during an escape attempt on the larger East German border had happened just three weeks earlier.[4] And the border between the two Germanys was, of course, only a part of the larger line of division between the two military blocs in Europe, both armed with thermonuclear

The Berlin Wall in front of the Brandenburg Gate, circa November 1984, with a sign in the foreground reading, "Attention, you are now leaving West Berlin." The shape of the Wall at this location—shorter and thicker than elsewhere—was reportedly meant to deter tanks from attacking this particularly symbolic site. *(SBM, Bild Nr. 0034-09104; photo by Margret Nissen)*

weapons. Up to the night of November 9, 1989, as in the preceding years and decades, the East German ruling regime had maintained forceful control over the movement of its people.

The regime had not, in fact, intended to part with its control on the night of the ninth. The opening of the Wall was not the result of a decision by political leaders in East Berlin, even though a number of them would later claim otherwise, or of an agreement with the government of West Germany in Bonn. The opening was not the result of a plan by the four powers that still held ultimate legal authority in divided Berlin: the United States, the United Kingdom, and France in the West, and the Soviet Union in the East. The opening was not the result of any specific agreement between the former US president, Ronald Reagan, and the Soviet leader, Mikhail Gorbachev. The opening that night was simply not planned.

Why, then, was it happening? Enormous crowds were surging toward both the eastern and western sides of the Wall. The East German regime struggled to maintain order not only at the Brandenburg Gate but also at

the Wall's border crossings—for there was no crossing at the gate itself—
with armed troops, physical barriers, and other means. At some locations,
security forces succeeded in regaining control over the crowds, but the
people kept coming. Again and again, East Germans told the border officials, in so many words, *You should let us pass.* Again and again, those same
officials—who only weeks if not days before would have turned weapons
on them—let them out. Why?

I<small>N ORDER TO ANSWER</small> this question of why, it is also essential to answer
the question of how.[5] These questions are of course closely related, but
they have a sequential order: it is necessary to figure out how the Berlin
Wall opened first, before moving on to why.[6] And to understand how the
Wall fell, it is in turn necessary to go back to the original evidence, because many false claims have sprung up in the intervening years.[7] These
claims are not surprising, given that any success always has a number of
fathers. But when we reexamine the immediate causes of the collapse of
the Wall on the basis of firsthand evidence and interviews, the significance of accident and contingency—rather than of planning by political
leaders—rapidly becomes apparent. The opening represented a dramatic
instance of surprise, a moment when structures both literal and figurative
crumbled unexpectedly.[8] A series of accidents, some of them mistakes so
minor that they might otherwise have been trivialities, threw off sparks
into the supercharged atmosphere of the autumn of 1989 and ignited a
dramatic sequence of events that culminated in the unintended opening
of the Berlin Wall. This book will examine not only those sparks but also
the friction between the two competing and contemporaneous processes
in East Germany that produced them in the first place: the rise of a revolutionary but nonviolent civil resistance movement, and the collapse of
the ruling regime.[9] Put simply, the opening of the Wall represented the
moment when the movement eclipsed the regime.[10] The opposition seized
on mistakes made by the dictators themselves to end their control over the
border, and that control turned out to be the key to their power; without
it, the regime crumbled.

It is simply a remarkable coincidence that this sequence of events unfolded during the two-hundredth-anniversary year of the French Revolution. This coincidence serves to suggest, however, that we should draw
on Alexis de Tocqueville's famous account of 1789 to help us understand
what happened two centuries later. Tocqueville concluded that a loosening

of the old guard's oppressive rule in eighteenth-century France had, rather than satisfying the people, only inspired the masses to use violence to demand more changes. Previously accepted grievances had become instantly unbearable as soon as their elimination appeared possible. Tocqueville's insight suits 1989 admirably, because that autumn followed a similar period of loosening. Gorbachev, in his roughly four years in power to that point, had dramatically alleviated the burden of oppression on the residents of both the Soviet Union and its larger bloc through a number of reforms. Without this alleviation, the Wall would not have fallen. Yet Gorbachev's reforms alone were not enough to open the Wall, for they were not meant to end Communist Party control of either the USSR or Eastern Europe. Rather, they represented an acknowledgment of the failures of the Soviet Union both to provide for the needs of its citizens at home and to compete with the United States on the world stage.[11] To address these failures, Gorbachev instituted many changes to the running of his party and his state, but he did so in the hope of saving them, not of dismantling them. In other words, he did not want to betray his socialist ideals; instead, he wanted to safeguard them, by making what he felt were necessary adaptations.

He expected that his allies, the men in charge of the East European states in the Soviet bloc, would do the same, and he did not intend to empower alternative movements, such as Solidarity in Poland or the nationalist groups within the Soviet Union itself.[12] And Gorbachev's reforms were in no way intended to dissolve the Soviet military alliance, the Warsaw Pact—or to end the occupation of divided Germany. That occupation had been purchased at far too dear a price for any leader in Moscow to abandon it for nothing in exchange. Millions of civilians and soldiers had lost their lives in the unspeakably brutal struggle following Adolf Hitler's decision to invade the Soviet Union on June 22, 1941. Moscow viewed its subsequent occupation of defeated Germany as wholly legitimate, given all the blood that had been shed to repulse and to conquer the Nazis after that invasion. Even after the Soviet occupation zone was notionally declared to be an independent state called the German Democratic Republic, or GDR, on October 7, 1949, the new state remained de facto under the control of Moscow, and the Soviet troops stayed.[13] At no point was this control more apparent than in 1953, when an unexpected revolt broke out in many parts of the GDR following the death of Communist leader Joseph Stalin. It was Soviet tanks that ultimately ended the revolt and reasserted order.[14]

The construction of the Wall in 1961 further solidified the division of Berlin and, by extension, of Germany. Even decades later, the most famous call for an end to that division—delivered by Reagan himself on June 12, 1987—did not result in any opening of the barriers. Reagan made this call in a speech delivered at the same location in front of the Berlin Wall from which Brokaw would broadcast the actual, chaotic opening two and a half years later. In his address, Reagan challenged the Soviet leader personally: "General Secretary Gorbachev, if you seek peace . . . come here to this gate! Mr. Gorbachev, open this gate! Mr. Gorbachev, tear down this wall!"[15] Despite these dramatic lines—which some of Reagan's own advisors had attempted to cut from the speech because they found them too confrontational—no opening of the gate, or even tentative agreement or provision for a future opening, resulted. Gorbachev and Reagan met at a number of summits, agreed on arms control measures, and ratcheted down Soviet-US hostility, but they did not produce a plan for the end of the German division, either before or after Reagan left office in January 1989 and his successor, former Vice President George H. W. Bush, became president.[16] As a result, while the actions of Moscow and Washington provided the overall context in which the Wall could open—and have rightly been the subject of extensive study already—we cannot understand the immediate causes of the collapse of the Berlin Wall by looking solely at what the superpowers did.[17] We must look elsewhere, and that is the purpose of this book: to investigate the crucial short-term reasons that the potential for the opening of the Wall turned into the reality of its collapse.

The wisdom of yet another great French thinker, Marc Bloch, is illuminating on this count. Bloch suffered grievously at the hands of the Nazis after the Germans successfully conquered France in a matter of weeks in spring 1940. Bloch, a First World War veteran and the father of six children, became an active member of the French resistance in response to that invasion. Bloch's last writings were published posthumously, for he was caught by the Gestapo, subjected to torture, and executed by firing squad on June 16, 1944, just days after the Allies successfully landed on the beaches of Normandy and began to free Europe from the brutality of the Germans.

Writing after the fall of France, Bloch drew not only on his scholarship but also on the tragedy that his country was experiencing to issue a warning about causality in history. Causes, he cautioned, are not to be assumed—in history, politics, or any other field. Instead, they must be searched for and discovered.[18] And in searching, we must not fall prey to the bias of hindsight, the assumption that what happened had to happen. Events such as the French Revolution of 1789, or the swift fall of France in 1940, appear inevitable in hindsight, even though they were not. If we assume the inevitability of events, we ignore the agency of people forced to make far-reaching decisions under immense pressure, the core of the story told here.[19]

Following Bloch's suggestion, this book will move beyond assumptions about the opening of the Berlin Wall by searching for causes in the evidence from the time. It will explore first how, then why, the Wall opened in the course of a narrative based on sources from multiple countries. Fortunately, such evidence is now abundantly available. Many of the relevant archival materials have become accessible, and, crucially, it is still possible to pair these sources with interviews of the people who were there. Such interviews have to meet a high standard: they must stand up not just to the interviewer's estimate of their veracity but also to the written historical record itself.[20]

That historical record is an extremely detailed one, due largely to the decades-long work of the East German secret police, known formally as the Ministry for State Security and informally as the Stasi. After German unification in 1990, the legislators of newly united Germany decided to make Stasi files available to former targets of surveillance and to researchers alike, rather than locking them away. Thanks to the law that they put in place, it is possible to view the daily paperwork of dictators with minimal restrictions.[21] Since the files of the Stasi's political master—the Socialist Unity Party, universally known by its German initials, SED—are nearly all available as well, it is possible to fill the gaps in the Stasi records by using these party sources. Many files from the ruling parties of East Germany's former Warsaw Pact allies are also open, as are state sources from various former Soviet bloc countries.[22] Western sources are now available in large amounts as well. Last but not least, since the events are recent enough, audio and video clips from the time serve as additional evidence. In short, the sources available on this topic are diverse and plentiful to the point of being overwhelming.[23]

This evidence not only makes the accidental and contingent nature of the opening of the Wall plain but also reveals that the people who brought about the fall of the Wall on November 9 were, by and large, not internationally known politicians. Rather, they were provincial figures, deputies rather than bosses, and even complete unknowns. Roughly a dozen of them will loom large in the pages to follow: they were individuals such as Katrin Hattenhauer, a teenage rebel thrown into solitary confinement for her political views; Uwe Schwabe, a former soldier turned public enemy number one; Christoph Wonneberger and Hans-Jürgen Sievers, two ministers at Protestant churches in the Saxon region of the GDR, convinced that change had to come and that they could help to usher it in; Roland Jahn, a very well-connected staffer at a West Berlin TV station; Aram Radomski, an East German drifter brutally forced apart from his girlfriend and seeking revenge; his friend Siggi Schefke, dreaming of forbidden travel to the West; Marianne Birthler, a youth counselor in East Berlin; and mid-level loyalists such as Helmut Hackenberg, one of the party's many second secretaries; Gerhard Lauter, an ambitious young department head in the East German Interior Ministry; Igor Maximychev, the deputy Soviet ambassador in East Berlin; and, finally, Harald Jäger, a second-tier passport control officer running the night shift at an East Berlin border checkpoint. Most of these people were little known beyond their immediate communities, if even that, but they would all contribute significantly—and at times unintentionally—to the collapse of the Berlin Wall. They would become the catalysts of the collapse.[24] The story of these people and their struggles amid the tide of larger historical changes is at the heart of this book.[25]

Although the details of 1989 in divided Germany are unique, these individuals and their broader experience have a significance that transcends their own time and place. Even though this book focuses on the specific story of one dictatorial state, it also tells a more general tale of an extremely rare and heartening event: a citizenry that peacefully overcame an abusive regime. It is all the more astonishing that this peaceful success culminated in Berlin, a city steeped in a militarism that had inflicted so much suffering on the world.[26]

The dozen or so individuals featured in the story told here experienced 1989 in their own personal ways, yet they also serve as representative examples of dissidents, loyalists, and chroniclers in a time of successful revolution. Their histories show that passage through a time of upheaval such as they collectively experienced is anything but a smooth process. The GDR opposition movement in particular was small, fragmented, and quarrelsome. Human frailties were all too often apparent within it. Yet that movement's members were ultimately able to rise to the occasion. Inspired by the Solidarity movement in Poland, by Gorbachev, by the mistakes of their own rulers, and by each other, they became able in 1989 to do what for so long had eluded them: motivate the broader population of East Germany to join them. Once they did, the revolution that resulted was able to breach an armed border without violence and to produce the single event that, above all others, still symbolizes the end of the Cold War.

The fall of the Wall may have been just one event in the larger collapse of the Cold War, but it was the event that forever ended the possibility of a return to the past.[27]

Learning the story of the rise of the peaceful revolution, the collapse of the East German regime, and the opening of the Berlin Wall therefore means learning about more than one particular country or event. It involves understanding the larger challenges inherent in making a nonviolent struggle against dictators succeed. This book shows how much has to go right—and it is a lot—to achieve such a success.[28] By examining how it happened in East Germany in 1989, we can learn how and why dictators' subordinates choose to disobey orders, and so do not use violence against unarmed protestors even though they have instructions to do so, or how and why oppressed people choose to extend trust to total strangers in crises, and so begin to form large, durable communities of protest. The latter point is particularly important, and surprising. As we will see, dictatorial leaders who had worked together for decades had no trust whatsoever in each other, while dissident leaders in groups riddled with secret police spies exhibited a startling openness to, and confidence in, outsiders willing to help.

We can also perceive in this story the costs of triumphalist assumptions made by outsiders about what happened in divided Berlin in 1989. In the United States, the opening of the Wall lent credibility to the unfortunate motto "From Berlin to Baghdad."[29] In other words, the opening contributed to a mistaken belief that Washington was the sole author of the collapse of the East German dictatorship, and that the United States could duplicate that success in other locations around the globe at little cost. Certainly the freedoms of the Western countries played a profoundly motivational role in 1989, but the story told here shows the need for a more nuanced understanding of the significance of accident, contingency, and, above all, the agency of local actors.

IN SUMMARY, IT is worth spending time looking at the details of how and why the Berlin Wall opened on November 9, 1989, because they add up to larger lessons that matter. That night represented the moment when a peaceful civil resistance movement overcame a dictatorial regime. It is all too seldom that such a peaceful success happens at all, let alone leaves a magnificent collection of evidence and witnesses scattered broadly behind itself for all to see. By looking at this evidence, listening to these witnesses, and learning this story—as it actually unfolded, not as we assume it did—we gain new respect and understanding for people who try to promote peaceful change in the face of dictatorial repression, for the odds that they face, and for the ways in which outsiders can actually help to promote their success instead of merely assuming that they have done so.[30] A blunter way of putting this is that it was not a given that Brokaw would be broadcasting good news from his perch in front of the armed border on the night of November 9. Twentieth-century Berlin was a city with a history of brutality. The events of the late 1980s had indeed given those Berliners living behind the Wall the inspiration needed to challenge their repressive rulers, as Tocqueville's analysis suggested they might. But Tocqueville's writings also suggested that, in rising up, East Germans would reject the regime's laws and borders with violence.[31] How and why that violence did not occur are what makes the story of the opening of the Berlin Wall at once unique and universally significant.[32]

PART I

The Struggle Within
the Soviet Bloc and Saxony

Chapter One

A Brutal Status Quo

THE SOUND OF GUNFIRE carried a long way, especially at night, after the noise of the day had receded, and in the winter, when the trees had no leaves to muffle the shots. At such times, the residents of the divided city of Berlin could hear the shootings a mile or more away from their origin at the Wall. The gunshots did not happen every week, or even every month, but by 1989 they were a regular and recognizable occurrence. Everyone knew what the noise meant. In the West, it caused concern and revulsion. In the East, it caused fear.

Karin Gueffroy, a divorced mother of two sons, lived in Johannisthal, a part of East Berlin near the Wall and opposite the West Berlin district of Neukölln. Whenever she awoke to the sound of gunfire, she invariably had the same thought. Someone, usually young and usually male, was trying to escape the GDR by fleeing across the Wall, and someone else, usually parents, would soon receive horrible news. Maybe their son would be imprisoned for trying to escape, maybe he would be injured, or maybe worse. Gueffroy generally found it impossible to go back to sleep after hearing the noise. She listened instead to West Berlin broadcasters, since they always tried to report as much as they could about any shooting. Sometimes, she also spent the remaining night hours imagining how it would feel to receive such news about one of her sons.[1]

Gueffroy's experience revealed a central truth about the state in which she lived, a truth that had not changed in 1989 despite all of Gorbachev's reforms: the East German ruling regime's authority still rested on its ability to control the movement of its people. That control, in turn, rested on the use of force. Of course, the control often took more complex and subtle forms as well, resulting in adaptation, complicity, and participation on the part of those living in East Germany. Out of necessity, East Germans found ways to come to terms with dictatorial control and, despite it, to make their lives as satisfying as possible.[2] When Karin's younger son, Chris, demanded of his mother that they try to move to the West, she responded that she was too scared to start again in a new place and too comfortable with what she had. She had an apartment and a job, and could put up with the rest. Chris became incensed: "That cannot be enough for a life. You can always start again!" Then he complained, not for the first or last time, about how much he wanted to see the world, especially the United States.[3]

His mother's response was an understandable one, since the political forces that had created the division of Germany were ultimately beyond the control of the people of the GDR or even the leaders of the country. That division was a consequence of the way that the Second World War had ended and of the emergence of a standoff between a military alliance headed by the United States, the North Atlantic Treaty Organization or NATO, and the Soviet alliance, the Warsaw Pact.[4] The division of Germany was also, in a conceptual sense, an expression of a long-term historical competition between Communist and democratic visions for organizing modern societies. The confrontation between these two visions had a profoundly distorting effect throughout the twentieth century. Around the globe, it led both Western and Communist leaders to engage in imperialistic behavior even as they denounced such behavior. Residing in what was essentially the frontline state of the broader Soviet empire, East Germans such as the Gueffroys felt the consequences keenly. The ruling regime of their country believed that it had not only to defend itself against enemies of the Soviet bloc but also to keep its own people in. The armed barriers and the sound of gunshots at night were the results.[5]

The division of defeated Germany after the end of the Second World War, and a similar subdivision of the city of Berlin, had not originally been intended to last for decades. Rather, both sets of divisions were initially short-term responses to the chaos across postwar Germany. Buildings were in ruins and hunger was rampant.[6] These divisions were meant to split the tasks associated with occupying the devastated country and city among the four major victorious powers—Britain, France, the United States, and the Soviet Union—until a peace conference could put permanent rules in place at some later date. However, tensions between the superpowers rendered a peace conference impossible. There were endless disagreements

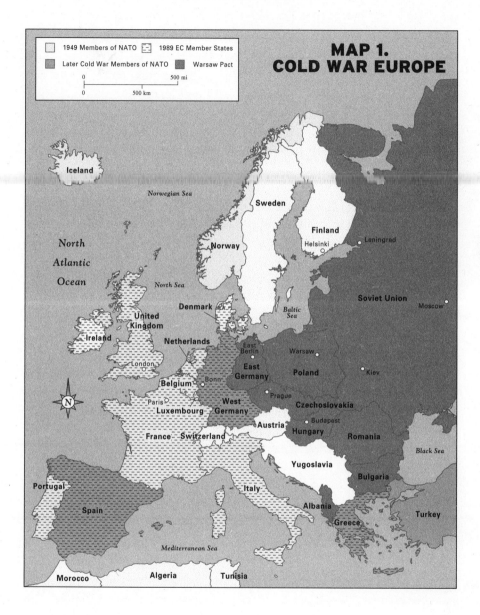

over multiple aspects of the occupation. To cite just one example, Soviet occupation forces raped women on a massive scale, and there was little the Western allies could do to stop them short of using force.[7]

Conflicts with the Soviets in divided Germany and elsewhere culminated in the decision of the Western allies, working with local leaders, to turn their occupation zones into a state, the Federal Republic of Germany (FRG) or West Germany, in May 1949. In order to make clear that unifying all of Germany remained a desired goal, however, the newly minted West Germans took a number of steps to show that their state was a provisional one. They chose the small town of Bonn as their capital rather than a major city such as Frankfurt. They declared that Germans, broadly defined, had rights of citizenship in the new state, which meant as a practical matter that any German who could reach FRG soil had the right to a passport and social services almost immediately, rather than having to go through lengthy asylum or emigration application procedures. Finally, legal experts drafted the so-called Basic Law, rather than a constitution, as the foundation of the new state. The Basic Law's Article 146 stated that a constitution would take its place at some unspecified future date, when "the German people" could freely decide upon it. Until then, the Basic Law would serve as the legal backbone of the FRG.[8]

The irony was that under this Basic Law, West Germany developed the most durable political institutions in German history. For much of the late nineteenth century and the first half of the twentieth, Germany had been cursed with political institutions that had failed to provide real stability or safeguards against dictators. Now the supposedly provisional institutions of the FRG were doing the trick, at least in the western part of the divided country.[9] The stability provided by the Basic Law contributed to, among other things, a resounding economic recovery in West Germany. The FRG developed a successful "social-market" economy and overcame the physical destruction and chaos left behind by two world wars more quickly than anyone had expected. West Germany also benefited, as did other Western European states, from extensive Marshall Plan aid from the United States.[10]

To the east, the Soviet Union supervised the process of turning its zone into another new state, the GDR, also in 1949. Despite having a democratic state structure and even a multiparty system on paper, the GDR became an entity ruled de facto by the Politburo of its Socialist Unity Party (usually known by its German initials, SED). To control the GDR's state institutions, East German party leaders claimed nearly all significant state posts for themselves in parallel to their party leadership posts. When either party or state decisions of any significance needed to be made, the Politburo would seek direction from Moscow.[11] This guidance was often transmitted to East Berlin by the Soviet ambassador, who thus became the political éminence grise in the capital city.

The two new German states soon became part of the Western and Eastern military alliances. In 1955, in close consultation with the Western allies, the democratically elected government of West Germany brought the FRG

MAP 2.
DIVIDED GERMANY
IN 1989

DENMARK

Baltic Sea

North Sea

SCHLESWIG-
HOLSTEIN

Rostock

Hamburg

Bremen

GERMAN
DEMOCRATIC
REPUBLIC

Oder River

NETHERLANDS

LOWER SAXONY

Weser

West
Berlin

East
Berlin

Warta R.

NORTH RHINE-
WESTPHALIA

River

Merseburg

Leipzig

Oder R.

Elbe River

Neisse River

Cologne

Erfurt

Jena

Region
Historically
Known As Saxony

Dresden

Bonn

HESSE

Koblenz

Main

River

RHINELAND-
PALATINATE

SAAR

BAVARIA

Prague

CZECHOSLOVAKIA

FEDERAL REPUBLIC
OF GERMANY

Danube River

BADEN-
WÜRTTEMBERG

Mosel River

Rhine River

FRANCE

Munich

N

SWITZERLAND

AUSTRIA

0   100 mi

0   100 km

into NATO.[12] The GDR became part of the Warsaw Pact, although the ruling regime had no electoral mandate for that membership decision, unlike in the West. Elections did take place regularly in the GDR, but the tallies were clearly fraudulent—the SED regularly won around 99 percent of the vote—and in any event did not matter, since East Germany would not have been able to get rid of Soviet troops even had its leaders wished to do so.

As a result, the sheer number of foreign troops and nuclear weapons present in divided Germany was enormous. In 1989, the chancellor of West Germany, Helmut Kohl, pointed out to the visiting US president, George H. W. Bush, that even though in places West Germany was only as wide as the length of Long Island, New York, there were 900,000 soldiers stationed there. Staring at them from across the border were an estimated 380,000 Soviet troops.[13]

T HE GUNS AND fortifications at the border that ran between the two Germanys were thus physical manifestations of a division that had emerged unexpectedly and for multiple reasons. These fortifications made crossings of the border between the two Germanys difficult, but as late as 1961 movement within all four occupation sectors of divided Berlin remained possible. On August 13 of that year, however, the SED, under the leadership of Walter Ulbricht, halted such movement by starting construction of the Wall, thereby sealing off the western sectors of the city from both East Berlin and the rest of the GDR.[14] East Germany had simply been losing too many people to the West, especially those of working age. This reason was not the public justification given for the Wall's construction, however. Not only Ulbricht but also his successor, Erich Honecker, and indeed all significant SED leaders proclaimed that the Wall was an antifascist barrier, made necessary by the actions of the Western allies. Honecker even famously predicted in January 1989 that the Wall would "still be standing in fifty and even in one hundred years."[15]

Born in 1912, Honecker had joined the German Communist Party in 1929 and spent a decade in prison for resisting the Nazis. After his release and the end of the Second World War, he became a leading figure in East Berlin, running the party's youth organization. He ousted his boss, Ulbricht, in what was essentially a palace coup, and managed thereby to become general secretary of the Politburo himself in 1971.[16] By the time of his "hundred years" remarks in 1989, he had spent his eighteen years in power running not only the country but also the SED, of which about one in five adults in the GDR were members, in a dictatorial manner.

Honecker did not seek to force more East Germans into party membership because the SED had numerous other means of extending and exerting its control. It ran not only all state institutions but also all so-called mass organizations, such as youth and labor organizations, as well as all of the country's universities. Among other things, such control meant that politically suspect schoolchildren, or the offspring of politically suspect parents, could and routinely would be barred from going to college.

The only partial exceptions to SED control were the Catholic churches and the much more numerous Protestant churches. The regime frowned upon religious activity, but churches in the GDR persisted nonetheless. They even enjoyed a limited amount of autonomy under close party and Stasi surveillance, in part due to their own efforts to maintain that freedom and in part because churches became havens for dissidents. Party leaders recognized that it was helpful to have opposition members collected at well-known, easily observable locations such as churches, and so tolerated such havens as long as dissident activity within them did not become too energetic.[17] As a result, the churches were valued by some dissidents for the shelter that they could offer, but avoided by others because of the high risk of observation.[18] One of the reasons that the East German activists Bärbel Bohley and Jens Reich, among others, helped to found a civil rights organization called New Forum in 1989—that is, a new forum independent of church-based opposition movements—was that they wanted to minimize contact with church staff in the employ of the Stasi, although of course neither they nor their organization could escape surveillance altogether.[19]

If the churches or any other institution strayed too far from party expectations for their behavior, the SED could deploy its ultimate instrument of intimidation, the formidable Ministry for State Security or Stasi. As a percentage of the population of the GDR, the Stasi was the largest surveillance organization in recorded history. In 1989, it had more than ninety thousand full-time employees and at least one hundred thousand "unofficial colleagues," or undercover agents and informants, nearly all of them men.[20] Over the lifetime of East Germany, a country of only seventeen million people, something on the order of a quarter million people had served as full-time Stasi staff. It is possible that another six hundred thousand served as informants at some point. By one estimate, there was one full-time secret police officer for every 180 citizens. By contrast, in the Soviet Union that number was roughly one to 600; in Czechoslovakia, one to about 900; and in Poland, one to 1,500.[21]

The East German regime had to pay for all of these people and their surveillance activities, of course. The regime spent so much on the Ministry for State Security that it came to rely on the ministry as a kind of "catchall" institution for any issue of importance. At times the Stasi functioned as a defense, interior, and foreign ministry all at once. Some of its branches worked as both domestic and foreign intelligence agencies, while others provided a kind of law enforcement. There were also special "branch offices" at post offices, for on-site censorship, and at border crossing points, where the Stasi oversaw passport controls and supervised the flow of traffic. The only major political institution that the Stasi did not dominate was the SED itself. Otherwise, the secret police could reach into nearly any area of East German politics, society, and life.[22]

One of the ministry's most important tasks was to control the movement of the people of East Germany. The Stasi worked together with the People's Police, under the Interior Ministry, and border soldiers, largely under the command of the Defense Ministry, in its attempts to control such movement. There was another important entity involved as well. The East German command headquarters for border troops was in Karlshorst, a region on the outer fringes of East Berlin and not coincidentally the location of the largest Soviet secret police, or KGB, station in a foreign country. The vast KGB complex in Karlshorst had more than a thousand staff members.[23] There were also KGB agents in other locations throughout the GDR, and they worked together with the East German secret police. Stasi files still contain, for example, the correspondence to and from a young Vladimir Putin, who worked at a KGB outpost in Dresden in the late 1980s.[24]

THE SINGLE MOST important physical barrier to the movement of East Germans was the Berlin Wall. By 1989, "the Wall" had become more than just a single structure; it was a barrier complex, or a death strip, consisting at some locations of multiple walls, along with ditches, dog runs, fences, lighting arrays, and tank traps and other vehicle barriers. This deadly strip stretched for roughly ninety-seven miles.[25] The security lights running the length of the Wall made West Berlin the only city on earth with a border that was, at night, fully traced in lights and visible from outer space.[26] There were about seventy miles of alarmed fence running along much of the wall complex, and almost two hundred guard towers and five hundred dogs keeping watch over it.[27]

Similar fortifications, and more, existed on the border between West and East Germany. For example, in 1972, Honecker ordered the installation of self-triggering devices called SM-70s, which used the explosive TNT to shoot more than a hundred steel projectiles once tripped. The projectiles would tear into the flesh of wild animals and escapees alike, leading to horrific and bloody scenes. The effect of these devices was so gruesome that

The death strip between East and West Berlin, undated photo. The west-ernmost wall at this location (far left) was taller and thinner than the sec-tion in front of the Brandenburg Gate, and also had a rounded top, which made it difficult for would-be climbers to surmount the barrier. East Ger-mans were still losing their lives in attempts to cross the Wall as late as March 1989. *(SBM, Bild Nr. 0015-12614; photo by Hans-Joachim Grimm)*

the SED did not install them along the Wall, where it would have been too easy for West Berliners to bear witness to their carnage.[28]

In addition to such automated devices, guards and dogs patrolled the West German–East German border. According to one former dog handler, Diet-mar Schultke, East German border guards would try to prove to each other how tough they were by abusing their service animals. Their dogs had hacked-off tails, ears lost to frostbite, and stinking coats laden with parasites as a result. Schultke also later admitted that if snow made feeding any of the far-flung dogs chained to the outer reaches of the border difficult, they would be left to freeze and to starve to death, howling in misery.[29]

If the walls, self-triggering devices, and dogs all failed, border sol-diers could also shoot would-be escapees. Over the course of the nearly three-decade history of the Berlin Wall, there were at least seventeen hun-dred known cases of shots fired at those attempting to flee.[30] Yet despite these incidents—not to mention the fact that residents near the Wall, such as the Gueffroys, could hear them—SED leaders continually denied the existence of an order to shoot.

On paper there was not, strictly speaking, an "order," since the documents in question were intentionally ambiguous, in order to provide East German leaders with plausible deniability if they were challenged by foreign supporters of human rights. The written instructions suggested that border soldiers had some discretion in deciding what to do when faced with an escape attempt. The reality was different, however. Regardless of what existed in writing, border soldiers were repeatedly told to stop escapees by all means necessary. Fleeing East Germans were to be either caught or "destroyed," nothing else. Unpleasant details, if needed, could always be manipulated for later reports. Since, for example, shooting to defend one's own life was always considered acceptable, troops could justify any gunfire by stating that they had believed their lives to be in danger. Border guards even received rewards—monetary bonuses, vacations, and promotions—for shooting would-be escapees; particularly accurate marksmen earned a "shooter's cord" to decorate their uniforms. Western human rights groups seeking to undermine the practice tried to reach out to border guards directly with the motto "Aim to miss, don't become a murderer."[31]

The gap between the ambiguous written orders and the all-too-brutal practice had a cost for the regime, however. Meant to allow regime leaders to save face, this gap created ambiguity that contributed to uncertainty on the part of border officials and a willingness to make their own decisions at key moments, such as the night the Wall would open. The ruling regime maintained the ambiguity, however, because the members of the SED elite were obsessed with how foreign government leaders, heads of state, and directors of international institutions regarded them and the GDR.[32] In dealing with these leaders, the party wanted to be able to deny that there was an order to shoot—such as when the GDR was seeking membership in international organizations, or financial support from Bonn. Honecker, especially, seems to have been deeply and personally concerned with the GDR's reputation abroad. He pursued all forms of foreign recognition, whether in the form of international conferences or sporting events such as the Olympics, always hoping to present himself and his country as equals to leaders and states in the West.

This sensitivity to outside opinion put the Politburo in a tricky position. As the GDR's economy declined and it became increasingly dependent on various forms of support from West Germans, it had to pay more attention to Bonn's revulsion at killings on the border. Sometimes that revulsion could lead to major changes. In the mid-1980s, Honecker ordered the removal of the gruesome SM-70s from the border between the two parts of

Germany, largely due to international condemnation of them.[33] And the publication of an Amnesty International report in January 1989, accusing the GDR of grievous human rights violations, brought the SED more unwelcome attention.[34] At other times, however, Honecker and his comrades would simply stonewall on the issue of violence at the border, since it represented an essential component of their power and control. For example, the East German defense minister, Heinz Kessler, assured journalists at a major West German newspaper, *Die Zeit,* in an extended interview in 1988 that "there has never—never!—been an order to shoot."[35]

S INCE TELEVISION AND radio broadcasts from West Berlin and West Germany could be received in the GDR, comments such as Kessler's seeped back into East Germany. They gave rise to popular rumors that the shootings had, in fact, stopped. One such rumor reached the ears of Karin Gueffroy's younger son, Chris, at the start of 1989. The twenty-year-old man felt that he could no longer accept the constraints of life in the GDR. He was young, ambitious, and athletic; he had shown an unusual skill at sports as a child and had been sent to a specialized training school, where he had become a talented gymnast. Chris had wanted to go on to study at a university and to take up a career as a pilot, but his politically suspect attitude meant that the state blocked his access to higher education. Instead, he held a job as a waiter at a restaurant catering to Western visitors. As a friend and fellow waiter in a similar situation, Dirk Regel, later remembered, the constant interaction with foreign guests, particularly with Americans, was an unwelcome reminder of how trapped he and Chris were.[36]

When Chris heard a false rumor that the shootings on the border had stopped, he and a friend decided to try to escape to the West. Chris felt confident that his strength and gymnastic skills would enable him to make it across the Wall. Even if he did not succeed, he figured that at worst he would be arrested, spend some time in jail, and get out before too long.[37]

Late on the night of February 5, 1989, without his mother's knowledge, Chris Gueffroy and a friend scaled an outer barrier wall roughly a mile from where she lived, and entered the border complex proper. They then crossed a signal fence by pulling apart some barbed wire, not realizing that this action set off alarms. The young men were heading for another barrier when suddenly two guards opened fire, shortly followed by two more. One of the guards, wearing a shooter's cord on his uniform to signal his accomplishments as a marksman, braced his weapon on an electrical housing box in order to improve his already excellent aim. From a distance of approximately one hundred feet, he shot Chris Gueffroy in the heart. Gueffroy died within a few minutes. His friend was injured but survived and was taken into custody.[38] After the corpse and the injured man were hauled away, the guards shared a celebratory drink with their commanding officer. In the days that followed, they received special decorations, extra leave, and a dinner in their honor. The marksman received a promotion as well.[39]

As it always did, the noise from the shooting startled Karin Gueffroy out of her slumber. She worried, as usual, about how some other parents would deal with the bad news that would surely follow. The next day, when Chris failed to stop by for breakfast as he had promised, it struck her as strange, but she pushed her anxiety aside. Her concern grew when a neighbor came to her door with a confession: Chris had asked the neighbor to join in an escape attempt, but the neighbor had refused out of fear. Now panicked, Karin went to Chris's apartment, where she found his papers and cash in a small neat stack on top of his desk. She was certain at that point that something was seriously wrong. Instinctively she opened the top drawer of Chris's desk and slid the cash and papers into it, trying to make the scene look less strange in the event that she would not be the only one viewing it.

She was too late. Chris's apartment and Karin herself were already under Stasi observation, and there was worse to come. On February 7, there was a knock on Karin's door. A Stasi officer took her to a building where, she guessed, her son was being held after his escape attempt. At first Karin had a feeling of relief, despite her Stasi escort. She assumed that, whatever she had to endure at the hands of the secret police, she could at least expect to see her son in detention or, at a minimum, find out where he was. A bizarre two-hour session of small talk with Stasi officers over coffee followed. Karin was surprised by how many details the agents knew about her and Chris.

Suddenly a uniformed officer appeared and abruptly spoke two sentences: "Ms. Gueffroy, I would like to tell you here and now that your son attacked a military unit and died. Do you need a doctor?" In response, she started repeatedly screaming, "You murdered him!" The men hustled her out of the building.

Karin's surreal experience on February 7 represented only the beginning of her ordeal at the hands of the Stasi. The secret police were convinced that she had known of her son's escape attempt and were relentless in their efforts to punish her and to extract more information from her. Her ex-husband, Chris's estranged father, did not contact Karin at any time after their son's death; she assumed that he was afraid of being implicated.[40] Over Karin's objections, the body of her son was cremated, and she received an invoice for the cost. She was allowed to hold a memorial service, but the Stasi insisted on making all of the arrangements, including the choice of the flowers—and then sent her another invoice.

Meanwhile, the ministry interrogated her for five or six hours a day, three or four times a week, for months. Gueffroy was allowed to go home at night but knew that she was on a short leash. The ministry commandeered her neighbors' apartment in order to maintain its surveillance of her and at times simply sent a car with agents to park right in front of her building. She fought back as best she could. The East German ruling regime let the elderly make visits to the West, in the hope that they would stay there and drain Western health care resources rather than Eastern ones. Knowing this, Karin asked the grandmother of a friend for help. On a visit to a relative in West Berlin, the grandmother smuggled a passport photo of Chris, hidden in a box of matches, across the border. The relative took the photo to a Western television station, which broadcast it and identified Chris as the victim of the February shooting. This action earned Karin, back in Berlin, even more fury from the Stasi.[41]

At the end of a long day of interrogation, Karin would often ask herself, *Can this really still be happening in 1989?* [42] In an attempt to understand why it could, Karin, drawing on her involuntary but extensive dealings with the security forces, eventually concluded that about three-quarters of the members of the regime and its security forces felt some sense of restraint, but the remaining quarter were thugs who knew no limits and were worthy heirs to the Nazis. On the night of his death at the Wall, she believed, her son had fallen prey to the brutal quarter.[43]

Chris Gueffroy bore the tragic distinction of being the last person to die by gunfire while trying to climb over the Wall. He was not the last person to die in an escape attempt, however. In March 1989, another East German, Winfried Freudenberg, fell to his death as he tried to flee in a balloon over the Wall. Nor were Chris and his friend the last to become the targets of a shooting. In April 1989, a border official shot at two would-be escapees in broad daylight. One of the targets later said that he considered it a miracle that he was still alive, since a bullet had passed very close to his head; he guessed that it had been meant to hit him between the eyes. The two would-be escapees had instantly halted their attempt to flee, and survived the ordeal as a result.[44] There were no more shootings at the Berlin Wall after that, but they did continue elsewhere. As late as August 22, 1989, a Hungarian border officer shot and killed an East German, Werner Schultz, as he tried to flee from Hungary together with his wife and child. And the final fatality in an escape attempt occurred on the night of October 18–19, 1989, when another East German, Dietmar Pommer, drowned as he tried to swim across the Oder River to Poland, by then partly under the control of Solidarity.[45] In other words, up to three weeks before the opening of the Wall, East Germans still felt compelled to take the risk of fleeing, despite the odds of a fatal injury.

The international revulsion at both Chris Gueffroy's February 1989 death—generated in no small part by his mother's efforts to publicize it abroad—and the April shootings, coming as they did four years after Gorbachev had risen to power in Moscow, was so profound that even Honecker realized that he would have to give some ground on the question of gunfire at the border. Westerners had been able to snap photographs of the April shooting incident, capturing the border guard firing at escapees with a cigarette dangling from his lips. An internal Stasi report concluded that "the enemy"—apparently meaning Western politicians—could use this unfortunate photograph "to discredit the policies of the party."[46]

In April 1989, Honecker told Egon Krenz, his fellow Politburo member and heir apparent to the leadership of the party, to issue instructions that "one should not shoot." Instead, border officials should do a better job of preventing escapes in the first place with "more and deeper ditches [and] more and better obstacles . . . that are not visible to the opponent" in the West.[47] The practical effect of Honecker's words at the implementation level—namely, what instructions the border officials who had access to weapons actually received—was that they should use those weapons to stop escapes only if their "own life is under threat."[48] Given the practice of the preceding decades, however, this was a standard that would not be hard to reach. And the head of the Stasi, the octogenarian Erich Mielke, revealed the hypocrisy of these instructions when, two weeks after they were issued, he pointedly told Stasi subordinates that the use of firearms by border guards was "completely justified." For good measure he added, "If you are going to shoot, then you must do it so that the target does not then get away."[49]

Fʀᴏᴍ ᴛʜᴇ ᴏᴛʜᴇʀ side of the armed border, Bonn did what it could to provide ways for East Germans to leave their country without having to run the risk of being shot. West Germany's ability to do so came from the GDR's need for economic support. This support usually bore a face-saving name for East Germany—such as "transit sum," meaning a lump sum ostensibly intended to defray the costs of travelers transiting across GDR territory—but it created a condition of dependency nonetheless. Bonn used this dependency to twist the arms of Politburo members on human rights and other issues. For example, Bonn was able to convince the GDR to allow family members separated by the division of Germany to reunite in the West, or to get political prisoners released from Eastern jails and transferred to West German territory. Between 1963 and 1989, Bonn essentially purchased the freedom of an estimated thirty-three thousand such individuals. An internal document from the office of the West German chancellor in February 1989 summarized the decades-old practice and indicated what had become the established "payment" amounts, although payment usually took some form other than direct cash payouts. Still, the "prices" had become largely fixed: approximately 4,500 Western Deutschmarks (DM) per person for members of a family to be reunited and 96,000 DM for the release of a political prisoner. Individuals who had managed to take refuge in an embassy, however, earned only 10,000 DM for the East German regime, thus creating an incentive for East Germany to keep such individuals out of embassies and get them into prisons, where they would realize their full earning potential for the regime.[50] On top of this practice, a number of accords struck in the 1970s between the two Germanys also created, among other things, predictable means for West Germans to cross the border between the two Germanys or the Berlin Wall. After the implementation of these accords, the number of Stasi workers doubled; there were many more Western travelers to watch.[51]

This status quo in divided Germany might have continued much longer but for the effects of the Conference on Security and Cooperation in Europe, or CSCE, and the dawn of the Gorbachev era in the Soviet Union.[52] Before these developments, East Germans who were not elderly, separated from family, or imprisoned had little hope of leaving the GDR. Some business trips or visits for birthdays or funerals were allowed, but only under certain conditions. In one unusually blunt memo, for example, Krenz wrote to Honecker that "underage children should not be allowed to go along on trips," and Honecker wrote "agreed" on the memo. In other words, travel would be possible only if young children or spouses stayed behind, essentially as collateral.[53] Other than these limited options, most East Germans had no ability to travel or to emigrate. Some expressed their dismay by applying for approval to leave the GDR, even though there was no clear procedure for dealing with such "applications."[54]

The CSCE helped to create change. Participants in the initial CSCE session came from both sides of the Iron Curtain and included the United States and the Soviet Union. They signed the CSCE's so-called Final Act in Helsinki in 1975, providing guarantees of certain basic human rights. The Soviet Union and its allies signed this act because it contained something else that Moscow badly wanted: language to the effect that the post–World War II borders in Europe were inviolable. The Soviet Union had hoped to receive such guarantees at a peace conference to mark the end of the Second World War, but since that had never come about, by 1975 Moscow was willing to settle for the CSCE as the next best option. Accepting some unimportant rhetoric (from the Soviet point of view) on human rights seemed to be a small price for it and its allies to pay in exchange for the long-sought guarantees.

The Soviet Union significantly underestimated the power of that rhetoric, however. Throughout the 1970s and the 1980s, activists in both the East and the West pressed members of the Warsaw Pact to live up to the Helsinki human rights clauses. Moreover, the CSCE process did not end with Helsinki, despite the fact that the conference had produced a document called the Final Act. Instead, a series of lengthy follow-up CSCE meetings—most notably an extended session held in Vienna between 1986 and 1989—expanded upon the Final Act's provisions. One of the prime movers at the end of the Vienna conference was George Shultz, the US secretary of state, who pushed hard for a successful outcome before the end of the Reagan administration's second term (and his time in office) on January 20, 1989. Whereas, for example, initial CSCE documents had emphasized family reunions and thus were of little help to those in the East who did not have relatives in the West, the agreements emerging from the Vienna talks brought a sea change. They explicitly created a right to leave a country, and not just for family reunions. Shultz achieved his goal: CSCE members applied their signatures to the Concluding Document in Vienna on January 15, just five days before Shultz left office.[55]

In addition to the pressure from the CSCE, the ascent of Gorbachev in the Soviet Union brought yet more headaches for the hard-liners in East Berlin. Gorbachev believed that the Soviet Union needed an era of restructuring and reform in order to compete better with the United States.[56] He decided not only to reduce what his country spent on armaments but also, using the catchphrase "new thinking," to begin liberalizing Moscow's relations with its allies. As the Soviet Union gradually allowed some freedom of speech and assembly, East Germans' expectations rose— following the pattern discerned by Tocqueville—in the hope that they might enjoy similar freedoms at home.[57]

In 1988, the East Berlin regime responded to the prevailing winds in Vienna and Moscow by instituting, if not a right to leave the GDR, at least a right to apply to leave, which had not previously existed. Of course, the state still had the authority to decide whether to approve an application.[58] This move was not enough; the SED, under threat of international isolation and Soviet disapproval, was still forced into signing the detested Vienna Concluding Document in January 1989. After the signing, Mielke made clear to his Stasi subordinates that they should hinder implementation of this document in the GDR as much as possible.[59] And an internal analysis for the East German Politburo concluded that "every state could decide for itself" on the degree to which the Vienna accord would actually be implemented; in East Germany there would be hardly any implementation at all. The SED also chose to ignore calls for the "legalization of political opposition."[60] The hopes of reformers inside the party were likewise discouraged; regional party and Stasi leaders received a warning in February 1989 that "those who think 'we must change our politics' no longer belong in our party."[61] East Berlin also worried that Bonn would use the Vienna accord to damage the GDR's reputation on the international stage. Even worse, Bonn might make its financial support contingent upon the terms of the accord. Internal West German documents did indeed suggest that Bonn saw ways of using the Vienna Concluding Document as a means of pressuring East Germany.[62]

O NE OF THE people who did manage to take advantage of the new right to apply was Karin Gueffroy. Though emigration would mean leaving her other adult son behind, she believed that she had to escape the Stasi, which, she worried, would have her classified as mentally ill and lock her in a facility for the rest of her life.[63] She filed an application to emigrate to the FRG. Despite various delaying tactics and tricks—the relevant office refused to accept the application at first—she pressed on. Perhaps because of the ever present concerns about the GDR's reputation abroad and the damage the Gueffroy case was doing to it, or perhaps because the Stasi had realized that the months of interrogation were not yielding any useful information, the Ministry for State Security finally gave in and approved her application to emigrate. She could take only two suitcases, however, and was forbidden to take Chris's ashes. As a silent protest, Karin held a conversation in her head with Chris at the very moment she crossed over to the West, the goal her son had not realized. In her own mind, she apologized to her son for ignoring his insistence that they should try to emigrate to the West: *Chris, I was wrong and you were right—you can start again. You just have to prevent yourself from getting to be too cowardly, or too comfortable.* Karin eventually found a job with a West Berlin broadcaster and dedicated herself to the daunting task of seeking some kind of justice for her dead son.[64]

Her chances of success were small as long as the East German ruling regime remained in power. In the summer of 1989, however, those chances improved dramatically when an unexpected breach occurred on the Hungarian border of the Soviet bloc. This development became the first significant incursion into the SED's control over the movement of its people, although the party was initially slow to recognize it as such. Despite the fact that this breach happened at a distant point on the Austro-Hungarian border, however, its tumultuous consequences would soon sweep across the Soviet bloc, into the Saxon region of the GDR, on to East Berlin, and finally up to the Berlin Wall itself.

Chapter Two

Marginal to Massive

THE RULERS IN EAST BERLIN did not realize at first that developments on the border between Austria and Hungary in the spring and summer of 1989 would pose a massive challenge to their own authority. Hungary was a fellow member of the Warsaw Pact, and the SED trusted it enough to allow East Germans to travel there with relatively little paperwork. As a result, large numbers of GDR residents did so, particularly during holiday periods. Of course, there was always a potential risk from the point of view of the Politburo in East Berlin: given that Hungary had a direct border to Austria, residents of the GDR could try to escape while on vacation. To prevent this, the East German ruling regime had signed a treaty with Budapest in 1969, obliging Hungary to stop East Germans from leaving for Austria without permission, should any try to do so. East Berlin could take comfort from the fact that Budapest had fulfilled the treaty's terms for two decades. Hungarian leaders had not only prevented escapes but also, in many cases, identified the would-be escapees and handed them over to the Stasi, in violation of international norms for the treatment of refugees.[1]

Cooperation among Soviet bloc members began to break down, however, after Mikhail Gorbachev came to power, since the leaders of the various countries disagreed about how to respond to the reforms in Moscow.[2] In East Berlin, Erich Honecker personally took a number of steps to show his disapproval of such reforms. On Honecker's orders, the GDR postal service started forbidding distribution of a German-language Soviet magazine called *Sputnik* in November 1988. The SED's top man did not like the tone of the articles appearing in it.[3] Honecker also made clear at a party plenary session in December 1988 that there would be no Soviet-style *glasnost* (openness) or *perestroika* (restructuring) in East Germany of the kind that Gorbachev had promised to institute in the USSR. Nor was East Berlin's displeasure limited to public gestures. When a senior KGB officer, Leonid Shebarshin, visited East Berlin in April 1989, he had to endure an uninterrupted hour-long tirade by Erich Mielke. The East German complained about insufficient decisiveness in response to "attacks by the enemy," by which he apparently meant the party leaders in Hungary and Poland who were showing sympathy with Gorbachev. Mielke also expressed astonishment that criticism of Joseph Stalin based on archival documents had recently appeared. The head of the Stasi demanded to know why such documents, along with the people who knew about them, had not been "liquidated." When finally allowed to respond, Shebarshin remarked that Mielke was speaking to him as if Shebarshin were "an accused man."[4] Mielke would not be mollified, and his confrontational Cold War mind-set remained firmly in place throughout 1989. This worldview was apparent, for example, in the fact that as late as May 5, 1989, his ministry was still working on a plan under which contingents of the East German People's Army, with the support of the Stasi, would march into and then occupy West Berlin.[5]

Mielke's strategy of holding on to a hard-line approach, thereby following the instructions of his political master, Honecker, was a risky one in the changing climate of the late 1980s. One person who saw the risks of this strategy was Helmut Kohl, who said as much to Gorbachev when the latter visited Bonn in June 1989. During a one-on-one conversation, the West German chancellor complained that, while Honecker might suppress calls for change for a time, in the end his hard-line stance would make matters worse. According to the Russian summary of the conversation, Kohl told Gorbachev that "Honecker is not trying any reforms, and, because of this, he is destabilizing the situation."[6]

In contrast to East Berlin's chilly response, in both Warsaw and Budapest Gorbachev's actions provoked real change. In Poland, the independent Solidarity labor movement seized upon the new era of openness to convince the Polish ruling party to meet for roundtable talks and to discuss possibilities for gradual democratization.[7] The talks began on February 6, 1989, the very same morning that East German border guards carried away the lifeless body of Chris Gueffroy after killing him during his escape attempt the night before. The attitude of the ruling regime in Poland could not have been more different from the brutality of the SED,

however: Polish party leaders agreed to hold a semi-free, two-round election in June 1989.[8]

When the first votes from that election were counted, the magnitude
of Solidarity's victory caught nearly everyone by surprise. Poles had given
Solidarity all but one of the seats in the lower house of parliament that it
had been allowed to contest, and ninety-two out of a hundred in the upper
house. By the end of the second round, Solidarity had won all but one of
the upper house seats as well. The victory was so great that observers both
in Poland and abroad, most notably in Washington, worried that the hu-
miliation might cause either the Polish or Soviet party leaders to annul the
results of the elections, but they did not. Although the Polish party leader,
Wojciech Jaruzelski, was able to remain as president after the elections, a
Solidarity leader, Tadeusz Mazowiecki, became his prime minister.[9]

Following the Polish example, Hungarian roundtable sessions between
the ruling party and members of the opposition began in June 1989.[10] Budapest and Moscow also began working out a plan for Soviet occupation
troops to leave Hungary.[11] A ceremonial reburial of Imre Nagy, leader of
the Hungarian uprising of 1956 that had, like the East German revolt of
1953, been put down by Soviet forces, took place on June 16 as well. An
activist group called the Committee for Historical Justice had organized
this dramatic event, but Hungarian party leaders tolerated it, and some
even took part personally. The ceremony drew an estimated two hundred
thousand people and represented a major snub to the Soviet Union.[12]

The Hungarian prime minister, Miklós Németh, who was also a party
leader, told Gorbachev that he hoped to see a real multiparty system develop. Németh also explained to Gorbachev that he and his colleagues had
decided "to remove completely the electronic and technological protection
from the western and southern borders of Hungary." Hungarian enforcement of restrictions on crossing the border—at least as applied to Hun-
garians—had long been erratic, and now Németh was making clear to
Gorbachev that he and his colleagues had decided their country had "out-
lived the need for" such border fortifications. The armed border, as he put
it, "now serves only for catching citizens of Romania and the GDR who
try to escape illegally to the West through Hungary"—in other words, the
citizens of the countries that took the hardest line about restricting unapproved emigration. Németh promised Gorbachev that, of course, he would
"talk to the comrades from the GDR" about this step, and had Hungarian
Interior Ministry officials advise the Stasi of what was going on. These officials reassured the secret police in East Berlin that, despite the upcoming

changes, Hungarian security forces would still ensure that East Germans would not get out. They would intensify policing to compensate for the dismantling of the barriers at the border. The Stasi, taking these promises at face value, seems to have let its guard down and did not take any dramatic action to intervene or to prevent this breach in the border of the Soviet bloc from arising.[13]

Initial demolition of Hungarian fortifications on the border to Austria began in the spring with relatively little fanfare, but gained increasing public attention after a symbolic event on June 27 at which both the Hungarian and Austrian foreign ministers, Gyula Horn and Alois Mock, wielded wire cutters for reporters' cameras. As promised, Budapest continued to prevent East Germans from leaving despite the demolition. A worrisome development from the viewpoint of East Berlin, however, was new Hungarian interest in fulfilling the terms of the UN Convention on Refugees. If fully implemented, this development could mean that Hungary would no longer force individuals classified as refugees back to their country of origin. The open question was whether Budapest would start classifying East Germans as refugees and cease returning them.[14]

Hoping that the days of being stopped by Hungarian border guards were over, large numbers of East Germans took advantage of their ability to travel to Hungary in the summer of 1989 to head for the Austro-Hungarian border. The Stasi prepared a surprisingly honest internal summary of the reasons behind what soon became a mass exodus to Hungary. The East German Ministry for State Security concluded that the main motivations were a lack of consumer goods and services in the GDR, the poor state of medical care, the limited possibilities for travel, the sorry workplace conditions, the bureaucratic attitude of the state, and the lack of a free media.[15]

From their partners in Hungary, Stasi officials urgently sought clarification of what Budapest's new interest in UN commitments meant for the citizens of the GDR. They soon got their answer. By July, Budapest began diverging more and more from its long-standing practice. Hungarian border officials were still hindering escape attempts by East Germans—including with firearms, as happened in August 1989—but, as the Stasi noted, the number of such people returned to the East German security forces, or even simply identified by name to East Berlin as having made an escape attempt, was dwindling.[16] The decreasing cooperation between the Stasi and the Hungarian security forces paralleled a decrease in cooperation between the Stasi and its Polish equivalent.[17]

Would-be escapees to the West became increasingly caught in limbo. Unable to cross into Austria, but not forcibly turned over to East German security forces as in previous years and unwilling to go home, they were stuck in Hungary. Many ended up seeking asylum on the grounds of the West German embassy in Budapest. Some would-be refugees even decided to abandon the escape attempt across the border altogether and simply headed directly for that embassy—and, increasingly, for the embassies in Prague and Warsaw as well.[18]

The West German Foreign Ministry in Bonn had to scramble to provide for such people. Normally it was the chancellery, under Kohl, that took the lead on questions of relations between the two Germanys. Since the would-be escapees were not only in third countries but also on embassy grounds, however, the Foreign Ministry had to be involved. Heading the Foreign Ministry was Hans-Dietrich Genscher of the Liberal Party, or FDP. It was only due to a coalition with this party that Kohl—the leader of the Christian Democratic Union, or CDU—could serve as chancellor, so Kohl had to tolerate a certain amount of independence on the part of his "kingmaker," Genscher.[19] In contrast to Kohl, a Catholic who had been born in 1930 in the western town of Ludwigshafen, Genscher had been born in 1927 in a town that became part of East Germany and so had a personal interest in the GDR above and beyond his official duties.

Kohl and Genscher carried out a two-track response to the refugee crisis in the summer and fall of 1989. The chancellery handled East Berlin, and Kohl wrote to Honecker to ask for his assistance.[20] The Foreign Ministry handled Budapest, and Genscher reached out to the Hungarian foreign minister, Horn.[21] Meanwhile, Bonn's pseudo-embassy in East Berlin, the "permanent representation," closed, partly due to overcrowding by more would-be escapees within its walls and partly to forestall a rift over the fate of those escapees while the leaders of West Germany sought to find a solution with Honecker.[22]

Honecker's ability to respond to these events in the summer of 1989 became limited, however, because he began feeling seriously unwell. Learning of his infirmity, Gorbachev and his chief foreign policy advisor, Anatoly Chernyaev, expressed hope that the seventy-seven-year-old Honecker—whom Gorbachev reportedly called an "asshole" in private—would use his illness as a reason to step down.[23] Honecker had no such intent. Instead, he underwent an aggressive series of tests, treatments, and surgery in an effort to get back to work as soon as possible. Such was Honecker's desire to resume control that when his physicians discovered that he had cancer, they decided not to inform him of the real cause of his pain, fearing his anger.[24]

Honecker was thus sidelined in summer 1989. Since ultimately he had to decide on all matters of consequence, without him the Politburo was frozen with indecision in the face of the mounting refugee crisis in Hungary. Honecker even made matters worse through his own insecurity, effectively rendering the Politburo lame during his unexpected three-month absence by appointing the lethargic sixty-two-year-old Günter Mittag as his temporary replacement. Usually in Honecker's absence that job went to Honecker's "crown prince," the ambitious fifty-two-year-old Egon Krenz, but Honecker did not want Krenz taking advantage of the sick leave, and so sent him on an involuntary "vacation."[25] Krenz, who could only seethe as the Politburo failed to take decisive action in response to the developing crisis in Hungary in summer 1989, began plotting to oust Honecker.

By August 14, the Hungarian foreign minister estimated the number of East Germans at large in Hungary to be over two hundred thousand.[26] Despite this daunting figure, Hungary still hesitated to break its treaty obligations to East Germany entirely. Foreign Minister Horn kept resisting pressure by the West Germans to recognize the East Germans as refugees and to call in either the UN High Commission on Refugees or the International Red Cross to deal with them. Facing a litany of requests from a subordinate of Genscher's along these lines, Horn threw up his hands. "Hungary is in a precarious situation," he admitted, and "relations with the GDR are bad." But turning the matter over to the Red Cross or UN was still too dramatic a step for Horn at that point.[27]

It would take the personal intervention of Kohl to convince the Hungarian prime minister, Németh, to break with the East German ruling regime altogether. Joining forces, Kohl and Genscher invited Németh and Horn to visit the FRG. The West Germans organized a secret meeting at lovely Gymnich Palace, a restored castle near Bonn used as a guesthouse by the FRG's government. In a two-and-a-half-hour meeting followed by a luncheon on August 25, Kohl and Genscher convinced their Hungarian counterparts that the most sensible way forward was cooperation with the West on the issue of East German refugees. Németh's main concern was not to endanger "the success of Gorbachev's policies." But Hungary was facing a severe economic crisis, and Németh agreed that he would need the help of the West to master it. Doing as Bonn wanted with regard to the East Germans would, Németh seems to have hoped, encourage not only

Bonn but also Washington to offer financial support and to develop fuller trade relations with Hungary.[28] For his part, Kohl said he would speak to West German bankers who could provide assistance to Budapest. By the end of the visit, Németh had made a decision: Hungary would fully open its borders to the West for the citizens of East Germany.[29]

Budapest informed Moscow of its decision. Horn also told Oskar Fischer, the East German foreign minister, of the plan on August 31, 1989, explaining that Budapest had decided to open its borders fully on September 11.[30] The choice of this date was partly to give East Berlin advance notice and partly to have the dramatic opening happen during a convention of the West German CDU, Kohl's party. Kohl apparently wanted to use the sensation to fend off a possible leadership challenge that was likely to emerge at that convention.[31] The gambit would work for Kohl, but members of the East German Politburo, still essentially leaderless, were flabbergasted and unsure how to respond. Panicky SED appeals to Moscow to put pressure on Budapest proved unavailing.[32] As the clock ran out, East German party leaders could do little other than express their outrage.

Just after midnight on September 11, the Hungarian borders opened for East Germans as promised. Scenes of massive hordes crossing into Austria appeared on television screens worldwide. Kohl sent Németh a telegram the next day, thanking him for "this generous act of humanity."[33] According to a Hungarian estimate, after September 11 a total of six hundred thousand East Germans used Hungary's borders to head west in the autumn of 1989.[34] Back in the GDR, it seemed as if everyone knew someone who had headed to the West from Hungary.[35] Privately, the Hungarian ambassador to West Germany, István Horváth, communicated to the chancellery in Bonn that Budapest was shocked by the sheer size of the wave of East Germans flowing across its borders. Hungarian leaders were also amazed by the extent of global media interest in the event.[36]

THE REFUGEE CRISIS was not over, however. On September 18, a week after the Hungarian border opening, Western journalists reported that GDR security forces had started physically preventing East Germans from crossing into Hungary in the first place.[37] The SED regime would soon end travel to Hungary altogether. Since it was still possible to exit the GDR for Czechoslovakia, however—the ruling regime in Prague disapproved of Gorbachev as well, so East Berlin still felt that it could trust its Czech comrades—would-be refugees now concentrated on the West

German embassies in Prague and Warsaw instead of the Austro-Hungarian border.

At the end of September 1989, there were thousands of East Germans living in miserable conditions on the grounds of the FRG embassy in Prague in particular—and those numbers kept rising. Genscher, in New York City to attend the UN General Assembly, took advantage of the presence of multiple other foreign ministers to have conversations not only with his East German opposite number, Fischer, but also with his Soviet counterpart, Eduard Shevardnadze. Genscher's description of the plight of East German children stuck living outdoors appears to have struck a chord with Shevardnadze. As a result of Genscher's pleas, the Soviet foreign minister urged East Berlin to "do something."[38]

By that point, Honecker had recovered enough to return from his extended sick leave. Back on the job in late September, he offered Bonn a one-off deal, presumably under Soviet pressure: he would "expel" the embassy-squatters from East Germany. In other words, it would be Honecker who would decide that their leaving the GDR was a necessity. The embassy-squatters had already left, of course, but not on Honecker's terms. Such was Honecker's mania for control that he would have sealed trains—a mode of transport with tragic historical significance, given their previous use to transport the targets of Nazi persecution to internment and death—bring the embassy-squatters back through the GDR. Once the squatters' identities were recorded, thereby enabling the GDR to confiscate their property, the individuals were then to be "expelled" directly to West Germany, still on the same trains. Honecker had the Politburo approve a resolution to this effect on September 29, and Bonn agreed to it.[39]

Genscher departed from New York in order to manage implementation of this plan, but not without first sending Shevardnadze a note thanking him.[40] After a stop in Bonn, Genscher, together with Rudolf Seiters of the chancellery and a number of his and Seiters's aides, headed for Prague. Other diplomats departed on a similar mission for the FRG's Warsaw embassy.[41] They had all initially received East Berlin's permission to ride on the sealed trains along with the refugees, but Honecker had second thoughts about the wisdom of letting senior West German officials appear to lead East Germans out of their dire situation. By the time Genscher and Seiters landed in Prague, the terms of the deal had changed. Their less-famous aides could ride on the trains, but the two prominent politicians would not.[42]

This late change did not stop the overall plan from taking effect, however. On the evening of September 30, Genscher, with Seiters at his side, dramatically announced the deal from a balcony of the Prague embassy to the well over four thousand East Germans there. After tense delays, lower-level West German officials rode with the squatters on six trains out of Prague on the night of September 30–October 1. There were similar arrangements in Warsaw as well, where about eight hundred people had taken refuge in the FRG's embassy.[43] The West Germans on board the trains worked to prevent any unfortunate incidents during the unnerving journey back through the GDR. Particularly frightening moments ensued when the trains stopped in East Germany and security officials boarded to record the identities of those leaving, but these moments passed without confrontations and the trains were allowed to roll onward.[44] Seiters later estimated that about fifty-five hundred East Germans made it to West Germany by this means.[45]

Instead of ending the crisis, however, matters went from bad to worse when Honecker made another fateful decision on October 3. Effective that day, he sealed East Germany entirely—and even before the public announcement of the sealing, GDR security officials on the Czech border turned back fourteen hundred would-be travelers.[46] Honecker's unprecedented act had far-reaching consequences. For the first time, crossing any border at all required both a passport, which only a minority of residents of the GDR had, and specific approval for each trip—even for a visit to another Warsaw Pact state. In the tense days of October 1989, such approvals seemed unlikely.[47]

To make matters even worse, a fall holiday period had just started, and thousands of people had already booked trips either to or through Czechoslovakia. Angry East Germans, many of them now stuck at the GDR-Czech border in the southeastern region of divided Germany historically known as Saxony, made their rage about their cancelled trips known.[48] In the wake of the border sealing, the number of demonstrations in Saxony would become the largest of any region of the GDR.[49] The growing Saxon crisis was a sign of a dangerous development: by closing all escape vents, Honecker had increased the pressure inside the GDR to dangerous levels. According to one analysis of dictatorships, people living under dictators have essentially three choices: to remain loyal, to find some means of exit, or to voice their discontent.[50] Denied the possibility of exiting the GDR, the citizens of East Germany found their choices limited to expressing loyalty or voicing discontent, and an increasing number chose the latter in October 1989.

Honecker faced another problem as well. In the brief interval between when the first set of trains full of embassy-squatters from Prague left on October 1 and the closing of the border on October 3, more East Germans had managed to get into the Prague embassy. Another set of sealed trains out of Czechoslovakia and through East Germany was organized as a result.[51] This time, however, the Prague trains would cross through the GDR after it had ceased allowing any other possibilities for exit. As a result, not only those stuck in Saxony but thousands of other East Germans as well rushed to train tracks and stations when what became known as "the last trains to freedom" approached.

Chaotic and violent scenes occurred in various locations in Saxony, particularly in the city of Dresden, where the trains were scheduled to pass through the GDR en route to the West.[52] The East German secret police estimated that, by the evening of October 4, as a second set of eight trains departed Prague, more than twenty-five hundred people were blocking Dresden's main train station itself and another twenty thousand people were mobbing the streets outside the station. The KGB outpost in Dresden presumably observed developments closely as well, and given that Vladimir Putin was on the staff of that outpost at the time, he may have witnessed the chaos with his own eyes. The blockage forced the trains from Prague to sit for hours on the tracks south of Dresden. Panicked, the GDR leaders contacted their Czech comrades to see if they would take the trains back, but the Czechs refused, so East German security forces fought to clear the Dresden train station. It took until the early morning hours of October 5 to get at least three of the trains through. The rest were rerouted through other cities.[53]

According to an internal report, forty-five policemen were injured in the course of that evening (the number of injuries among protestors was not noted) and at least one police car was turned over and set on fire. There was widespread destruction of the main train station building both inside and out.[54] Western journalists managed to report on some of the turmoil; Gorbachev's advisor, Chernyaev, noted in his diary that there were "terrible scenes" broadcasting everywhere.[55]

Upheaval in Saxony continued even after the last "trains to freedom" passed. On October 5, more than four hundred People's Army soldiers, armed with machine guns, were sent to Dresden to stand in reserve under the leadership of the People's Police.[56] Protestors would later recount

Stasi photo of cars abandoned by their owners in Czechoslovakia, October 1989. East German refugees left behind their vehicles (which they had often waited years to purchase) in large numbers during the mass exodus to the West in autumn 1989. The Stasi collected them at sites such as this one before bringing them back to East Germany. *(MfS, from collection of RHG, Fo HAB 24051)*

multiple incidents of police abusing protestors and detainees throughout the first week of October, both on the streets and at hastily organized detention centers.[57] What Karin Gueffroy had called the brutal quarter was clearly giving vent to its worst instincts in Saxony. East Germany, the state on the front line of the Cold War division of Europe, seemed to be on the verge of a descent into violent chaos.

THE VIOLENCE IN Saxony and the massive and chaotic wave of emigration out of East Germany that had preceded it were traumatic events for the residents of the GDR remaining behind. Acres of abandoned autos belonging to émigrés stood in rows after having been towed away to depots. Sales of furniture from abandoned apartments started taking place. Televised Western images of the emotional scenes of thousands upon thousands of East Germans who had left everything behind to get to the West made those still in the GDR reconsider the costs of remaining in their own country. Nearly everyone knew a colleague, a neighbor, or even a child who had departed, or who had tried to flee. The exodus was impossible to ignore, and so demanded reactions from the many millions left behind.[58]

Expressing discontent about the running of the GDR was one obvious way to react. The question was whether that expression of discontent would continue to take the violent form that it had assumed in Dresden. In an effort to prevent that from happening, a group of twenty protestors convinced Dresden party and state authorities to begin a dialogue with them on October 8, after days of chaotic street scenes, but the threat of mass violence remained.

It was in the neighboring Saxon city of Leipzig, however, that the threat of violence would become most dangerous. The people who would ultimately face this threat and take on the ruling regime in Leipzig were, at first, a marginal crowd. They were an embattled set of dissidents, mainly active within that city's centrally located Nikolai Church, particularly at the Nikolai peace prayers held every Monday at 5:00 p.m.

Activist groups used this regular prayer service as a chance to gather at the Nikolai's central location, but they faced an uneven response from church leaders. Some Leipzig church elders supported their use of the prayer session, while others were hostile. The activists also faced external pressures in the form of constant Stasi surveillance and infiltration by undercover agents. At times the Stasi considered driving the group members out of the Nikolai Church altogether, thus denying them their only reliable gathering point other than their own apartments. The secret police refrained from doing so, however, reportedly on the advice of Matthias Berger, a Protestant minister in Leipzig who was also an undercover Stasi operative. Berger argued convincingly that it made surveillance easier if all of the activists were mostly gathered in one location. The Stasi continued to tolerate the dissidents' activities at the Nikolai.[59]

Foreign observers did not think, before the autumn of 1989, that such activist groups posed much of a threat to the regime in any event. The West German equivalent of an ambassador to East Germany, Franz Bertele—called the "permanent representative," to emphasize Bonn's view that East Germany was not a foreign country and therefore did not need an ambassador—explicitly bet on the Stasi. In a report to his superiors in Bonn, Bertele announced in September 1989 that the "state security service will continue to ensure that the atmosphere of upheaval does not develop into actual upheaval."[60] In his view, "the regime is threatened neither by the criticism of the church nor by that of the opposition groups" because the church "does not understand its role as being primarily a political one." Instead, the church saw its role as being merely "pastoral, that is, helping people who are unable to come to terms with the condition of the state and society."[61] At times, it seemed as if Bertele might be right. The activists affiliated with the Nikolai Church struggled to survive.[62]

Despite the odds against them, these church activists transformed themselves in the late 1980s from a marginal movement into a massive one. To understand how they succeeded, it is essential to understand their distinctive context: the Saxon city of Leipzig. Saxony as a whole had a storied religious history, since it had been the home of Martin Luther and at the forefront of the Protestant Reformation. Within Saxony, Leipzig had long been an important center of learning. By 1989, the theology department of the University of Leipzig had been in existence for six centuries.[63] In the war-torn twentieth century, however, Leipzig's tracts of once-handsome buildings had suffered both damage and extended neglect. Nearby chemical and industrial plants spewed toxic waste into the region's air and water, blackening not only the buildings but also the skin and lungs of area residents. The village of Mölbis, on the southern outskirts of Leipzig, was by some accounts the dirtiest city in Europe. Visibility could be so miserable that residents had trouble seeing their own hands at times.[64] Leipzigers complained that their problems were routinely forgotten and ignored by the party leaders in East Berlin.[65]

Yet Leipzigers found ways to rise above the grime. When the ruling regime inflicted more architectural damage on the already wounded city by tearing down its historic University Church in 1968, there were protests rather than silent acquiescence.[66] Leipzigers also took pride in their impressive musical heritage. Their city was both the former home of Johann Sebastian Bach and the current home of the internationally acclaimed conductor Kurt Masur, who had presided over the city's renowned Gewandhaus Orchestra since 1970.[67] The Nikolai activists drew on this musical heritage in their efforts, organizing an unapproved street music festival in the summer of 1989. Although it was broken up by security forces, the would-be festival generated a great deal of public sympathy for the activists involved.[68]

Leipzig was also a provincial city unusually familiar to foreigners because it had long held major trade fairs every spring and fall. They continued into the 1980s, and the media attention that they generated would come to play a significant role in the peaceful revolution of 1989. The fairs brought visiting business figures, journalists, and politicians not only to the city but also into the homes of Leipzigers on a regular and predictable basis, since Leipzig residents were given permission to rent out rooms to them. These brief visits by foreigners opened up direct connections between Leipzigers' living rooms and the wider world.[69] In short, Leipzig was an unusual city, at once provincial and cosmopolitan—and remote enough from the power center in Berlin for its residents to run a few risks.

A small group of dedicated activists had been running those risks for years, using the peace prayers as their base. The use of a church was not unusual; a Stasi overview of opposition activity countrywide in May 1989 concluded that protestors were "almost exclusively active in the structures of the Protestant churches of the GDR."[70] But the Nikolai peace prayers were unusual in that they had a particularly long history, having taken place regularly since 1982 and irregularly even before that.[71] One of their early sources of momentum was opposition to the so-called dual-track decision of 1979, the key result of which was the modernization of NATO's nuclear missiles in the West in the early 1980s.[72] Since the East German regime approved of criticism of NATO, it initially tolerated these prayers—only to regret it later when participants also criticized Soviet missile emplacements as well. It was acceptable to oppose the enemy's missiles, but not the ones inside East Germany.

There was no hiding the fact, however, that residents on both sides of the Iron Curtain worried that the two superpowers would fight *in* Europe, rather than *for* Europe—meaning that Europeans would be the ones to suffer the consequences of any conflict between the United States and the Soviet Union.[73] On one day in October 1983 alone, disarmament rallies in various West German cities had attracted a total of a million protestors. That same year, the issue had also helped the Green Party to win seats in the parliament in Bonn for the first time.[74] East Germans, in contrast, lacking free elections, instead used the shelter of the church to raise their voices on this issue, and the Nikolai peace prayers became the most important venue in the GDR for doing so. Before long, critics of more than just NATO began attending and using this venue to air various grievances. Politics gradually came to edge out prayers altogether, leading to a conflict between those Nikolai Church staff anxious about preserving the measure of apolitical autonomy that their church enjoyed in the face of state pressure and those who wanted to encourage political protest by all means.[75]

One religious leader comfortable with the politicization of the prayers was the Reverend Christoph Wonneberger, who had moved to Leipzig in 1985 to work in a run-down church on the eastern side of the city. A native Saxon, born in 1944, he had been in the West when the Wall went up but had chosen to return to East Germany, and had even worked briefly for the Stasi in the late 1960s. He had soon transformed himself into one of the Stasi's biggest enemies, however. Over the course of the 1970s, he had become an outspoken critic of not only the East German government but also other Warsaw Pact regimes, taking part in protests in Prague and making contacts in the Polish opposition movement as well. At home in the GDR, he had called for the creation of real alternatives to mandatory military service for East Germans who wanted to be conscientious objectors. By 1989, the Stasi considered Wonneberger to have developed into one of the country's most dangerous dissidents.[76]

In Leipzig, the senior administrator responsible for the Nikolai Church, Superintendent Friedrich Magirius, invited Wonneberger to coordinate the Nikolai's peace prayers, even though Wonneberger worked at another church and not the Nikolai. Wonneberger had experience in organizing similar events, however, so Magirius thought that his help might be useful.[77] Once the outsider began organizing the peace prayers, Nikolai activists such as Katrin Hattenhauer and Uwe Schwabe quickly saw that they had gained a crucial new ally in their fight against the state.[78]

Hattenhauer, nineteen years old in 1989, had come to the attention of the Stasi at a young age due to her habit "of asking provocative questions."[79] Denied the opportunity to go to a university, she had started studying at the theological seminary in Leipzig, one of the few educational opportunities open to those who had fallen out of favor. She found herself drawn into the protest movement and persecuted even more by the Stasi. Under pressure from the state, she was forced in 1989 to leave her seminary program, and so she threw herself into oppositional activities.[80]

She worked closely with Schwabe, a twenty-seven-year-old former soldier who had become a dissident after his application to join the merchant marine had been denied. The relevant office had informed Schwabe that he was politically unreliable and therefore "not suitable for border-crossing traffic." Instead, he was given various kinds of work, including as a caregiver in a nursing home. Thanks to a like-minded friend from his time in the military, he gradually became involved with the Nikolai community. Even though he himself was not religious, it meant a great deal to Schwabe to discover a place in the GDR where people seemed to say what they actually thought. He became an outspoken leader of the Nikolai-based opposition movement, focusing on civil rights and environmental issues.[81] When the Stasi produced a ranked list of the most dangerous dissidents in Leipzig in 1989 as part of a plan for a wave of arrests, Schwabe topped that list as the number-one enemy of the state.[82]

Luckily for Schwabe, he was also recognized in more positive ways beyond his state's borders. When he was detained in January 1989, friends and supporters in the Solidarity movement got word to the office of the US secretary of state, George Shultz, who was then involved in the final days of CSCE negotiations in Vienna. After ten days in detention, Schwabe was suddenly set free. He later heard that Shultz had pressured the ever status-conscious East German leaders at the Vienna talks into releasing him.[83]

Though Hattenhauer and Schwabe had admirers and powerful friends abroad, the overall size of their movement at home was tiny. The Stasi estimated that there were, at most, only a few hundred opposition activists in all of Leipzig before the autumn of 1989.[84] Wonneberger, together with a fellow minister, Michael Turek, decided to help this small circle of activists by all means, whether by letting them use the Nikolai peace prayers to plan protests or by providing space and supplies for underground publications. Hattenhauer, Schwabe, and their friends began to organize events such as the illicit street music festival, even though Stasi agents kept close tabs on them and regularly detained and interrogated them. Undeterred, Wonneberger would take part openly in such events, at times as the only minister involved.[85] He became, as a result of his cooperation with Hattenhauer, Schwabe, and others, an even higher priority for the Stasi. As a senior Stasi officer in Department XX, the counterterrorism unit, tersely summarized the anti-Wonneberger mission in March 1989: "Wonneberger: discredit him, grind him down, instruct church to discipline him. Goal: away from Leipzig."[86]

One of Wonneberger's "crimes" in the eyes of the Stasi was his display of sympathy for East Germans who wanted to flee to the West, a burning issue in 1989.[87] Even among dissidents and those who sympathized with them, emigration inspired mixed feelings. Some understood the desire, but others condemned those who sought to emigrate, arguing that they should stay and work to improve the GDR instead.[88] The senior minister of the Nikolai Church and sometime opponent of Wonneberger, Christian Führer, would say that the thought of émigrés was painful to him and that he admired instead the people who decided, "We are not going to leave our land in the lurch."[89]

Führer's attitude toward those not sufficiently loyal to their country (in his view) reflected a larger conflict between church leaders and activists. Popular sayings from the late 1980s captured this tension. Later, after the peace prayers had given rise to a massive movement, the most famous sayings would become "We are the people" and "We are one people," the latter a call for the rapid reunification of Germany.[90] But there was also a saying that is less remembered. Outside of the Nikolai Church stood—and still stands—a sign reading "Open to all." As late as the beginning of 1989, activists would complain that there was an unwritten second half to that saying: *But not open to everything.* In other words, the church was open to people like Wonneberger, but not open to all that he wanted to do, such as helping émigrés.[91]

For their part, the leaders of the Nikolai Church worried that a crackdown could ensue if Wonneberger allowed the activists to go too far. The cautious Führer wanted the peace prayers to contain more religion and less politics, in part because of his own personal religious fervor and in part to preclude attacks by the state. Führer also dismissively assumed that, in the unlikely event of the Stasi withdrawing all of the agents that it had infiltrated into the ranks of the activist groups, those groups would no longer be able to function, since their membership would practically vanish.[92] But Führer's overall attitude was ambivalent, and he did not take steps to end the peace prayers even when it would not have been difficult for him to do so. At one peace prayer session in which he personally took part, a woman asked Führer whether he was going to let the prayers die out, since there were only six people attending. Führer, initially uncertain how to respond, did what any minister would be expected to do in such a situation: he turned to the Bible for guidance. He responded to the woman by explaining that wherever two or three people were gathered in Jesus's name, Jesus was present; since they were twice as many, they should clearly go on.[93]

To UNDERSTAND THE tensions between the activists and the church leadership over the politicization of the peace prayers, it is necessary to go back a year, to 1988, when matters came to a head at a prayer session in June. The immediate cause was a wish expressed by the activists to make a gesture of support for a young man who had spray-painted quotations from Gorbachev on a Leipzig wall. The young man was being punished, and the activists took up a collection to help pay the fines being imposed on him by the ruling regime. This was the tipping point for Führer, who saw the collection as too direct an attack on the state.[94] He sent Wonneberger a letter saying that in light of the "numerous expressions of dissatisfaction that we have received"—without mentioning from whom they had been received—church leaders wanted to reassess the conduct of the peace prayers when they resumed in late August 1988 after their traditional summer break.[95] On August 25, however, Führer saw himself unexpectedly upstaged by Superintendent Magirius, who had come to regret asking Wonneberger to coordinate the peace prayers in the first place. The superintendent felt that "the church is not an underground organization, not even a helper of such organizations," and so should not be condoning the activists' plans. Magirius believed that the position of the church in the GDR was too precarious to run the kind of risks in which Wonneberger was indulging, and so he removed Wonneberger from the job of coordinating the peace prayers altogether, giving him written notice that "you have been relieved of your duty."[96]

This sequence of events produced a fiasco at the first prayer session of the fall. Unwisely, Magirius decided to make himself one of the speakers. He used his time in front of the microphone to criticize the would-be émigrés who saw the church as the one place they could turn for support. Since those who wanted to emigrate "had taken their leave, whether internally or physically, from their part in our living together," they had, in Magirius's opinion, little claim to any kind of aid from the church. He declared that the church would not make special efforts to accommodate them. While they would not be locked out of the building, which would remain open to all, the church would give them only limited leeway in the future—it would not be open to everything.[97]

Magirius's criticism did not go down well. Moreover, the activists present thought that they had received a promise from Magirius to make public at the prayers some of the paperwork associated with the "firing" of Wonneberger. When Magirius failed to do so, a dissident with a resounding voice, Jochen Lässig, seized the microphone and started reading some of these papers, which presumably had been given to him by Wonneberger. Magirius signaled that the microphone should be turned off. It was, but Lässig's strong voice still carried. Undeterred, Magirius had the organist start playing. The organist did, but someone suddenly turned off the organ's motor, silencing it and allowing Lässig to be heard clearly once again.[98]

At this point, Führer could bear no more. He was ostensibly the se-nior religious figure in the Nikolai Church, yet Magirius had removed Wonneberger without his knowledge; Führer had heard about it as a fait accompli. A Stasi agent attending that day noted in his report that there was obviously some kind of power struggle unfolding between Führer and Magirius.[99] Führer climbed up on a pew and issued something between a command and a plea: "Dear listeners, if you stay, it will mean that the peace prayer will not go forward. . . . If you stay here, we will just be play-ing into the hands of the state. . . . If you do not leave the church now, there will assuredly be consequences."[100] He indicated that the activists should leave the church.

The prayer session thus came to an abrupt end. Activists exited into the courtyard in front of the Nikolai. They were both livid and afraid. They were being driven out of their safe haven and had no idea what future awaited them outside. Two hundred activists signed a letter of protest im-mediately afterward.[101] Many appeared at the next peace prayer anyway, but with their mouths symbolically bound shut.[102] A dissident organization in East Berlin that circulated an intermittent, semi-tolerated newsletter ran an article entitled "Leipzig Peace Prayers Choked Off."[103] Activists com-plained that the Nikolai Church's leaders, who enjoyed a certain amount of de facto immunity from state persecution, should be willing to shelter those more marginalized, instead of driving them out.[104]

It was hard to see much of a future for the Nikolai activists after this miserable event in the autumn of 1988. Yet their expulsion from the church gradually revealed itself as a blessing in disguise. As Schwabe later remarked: "It was the best thing that could have happened to us. Today I am grateful to the church for it."[105] Because Führer told the activists to take their anger outside, they did just that. Denied the space inside, they decided to continue congregating on the space outside for a regular forum on Monday evenings, despite the presence of secret police and the lack of church shelter. "We were forced to break out," Schwabe recalled. The re-sult of their move outside, Schwabe came to realize, was a new "symbiosis between the critical people from inside the church and the critical people outside of the church." Over the course of late 1988 and 1989, "it turned out to be a wonderful thing: people were interested!"[106] Partly, he came to realize, this was because of the examples set by Gorbachev and Solidarity abroad. Then the emigration crisis of 1989 swelled their ranks even more. Schwabe concluded that the "most important reason" he and his friends had come to enjoy massive support by the autumn of 1989 was "the mass emigration and the trains from the embassies, where thousands of people tried to jump on," and the violence in nearby Dresden. These events had been so traumatic that they drove many people in the GDR to political engagement, often for the first time.[107] The activists, by having the courage to stage events outside of the Nikolai in late 1988 and early 1989 after their expulsion rather than simply giving in to fear of the Stasi and giving up, started offering a venue for civil engagement at just the right time in a society critically short of such opportunities.[108]

Truncated prayer sessions continued inside the church every Monday, but the main event had moved outside. Members of the public who were too timid to enter the Nikolai, since religious activity was frowned on in the GDR, could stay safely outside but still hear what was going on. Hattenhauer and her friend Gesine Oltmanns would, for example, stand on a pile of construction materials outside the Nikolai Church and use it as a stage to address the crowds with radical calls for change.[109] It was only a matter of time before the outdoor events became mobile as well and began including short protest marches by small groups into the side streets surrounding the church.[110]

Attendance grew from week to week. The predictability of the event combined with the new outdoor venue meant that interested parties could turn up at the right time and place, but also pretend to be innocent passersby, heading for the nearby shops of the city's center. As Pastor Turek explained to Mike Leary, an American journalist visiting Leipzig at the time, "The regular rhythm of these services, the fact that you could come every Monday at 5:00 p.m. and find people who shared your concerns and gather strength from them," helped to ensure that large numbers participated in the new outdoor forum.[111] The ruling regime understood this dynamic too, and pressured church administrators to change the time and location of the event, but the administrators would not.[112]

The blessing in disguise of the expulsion had yet another benefit: it brought Führer more firmly over to the activists' side. He worked to forge a compromise whereby the dissidents could come back into the church if they wished. Part of the reason that Führer had felt uncomfortable with the activists was that they attracted media coverage, which, he had long worried, could have unfortunate consequences. As he put it, "How long would Honecker listen to such coverage before he has tanks plow into our church?"[113] So Führer had long been opposed to letting Western journalists, both German and foreign, cover events inside the Nikolai itself. But now that the activists were outside of the church, he had little control over the coverage of their actions. Führer was also deeply unhappy at the ongoing conflict within the church community to which he had devoted his life.[114] With the help of a Catholic priest acting as a moderator, Führer and dissident leaders agreed that the activists could resume their participation in the peace prayers inside the church again under new guidelines ensuring a certain religious component to the proceedings.[115]

The ruling regime did not, of course, ignore these dramatic developments inside and outside the Nikolai. Senior city officials, who were also senior party leaders, pressured Johannes Hempel, the bishop of the Evangelical and Lutheran Churches of Saxony, to rein in the activists and to block them from resuming leadership of the peace prayers. Hempel had mixed feelings but resisted the interference.[116] A showdown gradually became more likely, because if the party and state could not shut down the Nikolai protests with words, it would have to find some other way to do so.

By the late spring of 1989, the Nikolai dissidents were once again organizing the peace prayers inside the church while still coordinating events outside. That year, the May 1 holiday—Labor Day in much of the world and a particularly important holiday in Communist countries—fell on a Monday. After the peace prayers on May 1, about a hundred people subsequently held a small, unofficial May Day march as well. A West German television station was able to broadcast images of it.[117]

Incensed by the dissidents' usurpation of a prominent holiday, East German officials continued to pressure church authorities to stop them. Efforts by the Leipzig city mayor to halt the prayers altogether were unsuccessful, though party leaders did achieve one change.[118] They insisted that the name "peace prayers" was an insult. Given that the GDR defined itself as the peaceful half of Germany—in contrast to the past fascism of the Nazis and the present fascism of the West Germans—the name was unacceptable. Why should residents of a peaceful state have to pray for peace? The church gave in on this minor point and switched the name to "Monday prayers."[119] But church leaders also, unusually, issued a protest of their own. Bishop Hempel wrote to the city authorities on May 31 to complain about the massive police presence that had grown up around the Nikolai Church on a more or less permanent basis after the unexpected May Day march.[120] The activists were winning over not only the public but also church officials.

B Y THE AUTUMN of 1989, the Monday demonstrations in Leipzig had
become a serious worry for Mielke, the Stasi minister in East Berlin.
He asked his subordinates if "another June 17 is going to break out," by
which he was referring to the dramatic events of 1953 when Soviet tanks
had put down an uprising. In response, his subordinates reassured him
that "it will not happen, that is what we are here for."[121] The head of the
Stasi district in Leipzig, Manfred Hummitzsch, was not as optimistic as
the group around Mielke in Berlin, however. At the beginning of September, Hummitzsch told his men at a briefing that "the situation has
hardened and will not change." Even worse, "every condition for further
provocations is in place." He concluded that events "cannot be allowed to
get out of our control."[122]

The consequences for activists such as Hattenhauer were grim. For the
Monday night event on September 4, 1989—the Monday of the fall trade
fair, when large numbers of foreign journalists were in the city—Hattenhauer and her friend Oltmanns displayed a large banner reading "For an
open country with free people."[123] Security forces tore the banner out of
their hands immediately but did not arrest Hattenhauer or Oltmanns right
away because of the presence of the foreign journalists. After the end of
the fair, however, they came for Hattenhauer and a large number of other
activists. She was pulled down suddenly by her long hair from behind so
hard that she passed out, and she awoke to find herself in the hands of
the Stasi. It was the start of a month of imprisonment, most of which she
would spend in a cell alone. She was subjected to repeated interrogations
and threats that she would be shot. She even had to endure a simulated
execution: the teenager was forced to stand facing a wall with her hands
raised, awaiting shots that never came.[124]

Despite all of this, Stasi protocols of her interrogations show that she refused to be rattled and even criticized her interrogators. Her self-confidence
arose in part from the fact that by the fall of 1989 she already had extensive
experience with such interrogations. Surviving Stasi records show that she
resisted efforts to force her to betray her friends. "Who else took part?"
interrogators demanded to know about one event she had planned. "Ask
your colleagues about that," Hattenhauer responded. Then they asked how
she had gotten to the site of the event. Wasn't finding out how she'd gotten
there, Hattenhauer replied, "your job and not mine?"[125]

Hattenhauer and many of her fellow dissidents had been arrested, but
the number of people attending both the Monday prayers themselves and
the protests outdoors kept rising. By September 18 it was in the thousands.

Heavy-handed police responses again caused Führer to complain to the city authorities.[126] One September prayer session even included suggestions from activists to the assembled on how to behave in case of arrest. Protestors who were grabbed should "shout your own name loudly" as they were being taken away so that bystanders could note it and get word to the protestors' next of kin, since the names of those detained were not always known or released to family. If forced into a vehicle, demonstrators should "shout the number of other people in the truck with you" so passersby could also note how many other people were being taken away. If they were interrogated, they should provide only their name and address and not sign anything. These suggestions were transcribed, presumably by a Stasi agent in attendance, and sent to Honecker personally.[127]

Still the attendance at the Monday demonstrations grew. Führer began reaching out to other churches in Leipzig to see if they would hold Monday prayer sessions as well, since the Nikolai Church was becoming overwhelmed. Some of his colleagues, such as Hans-Jürgen Sievers of the Reformed Church, agreed to hold prayers at the same time as the ones at the Nikolai. But Hans-Wilhelm Ebeling, a minister at the Thomas Church, where Bach had worked centuries earlier, was unwilling to provoke the state, and so he demurred. Members of the Thomas Church's congregation would later bitterly recall that as people were being beaten in the streets in autumn 1989, the doors of the Thomas Church stayed locked to prevent protestors from fleeing inside.[128]

As Leipzig simmered with tension, the GDR state media ensured that the entire country knew that Krenz was spending the end of September and beginning of October in Beijing. The Chinese regime's deployment of the People's Liberation Army against unarmed students and other protestors in Tiananmen Square on June 4, 1989, had appalled nearly all foreign observers—except the East German Politburo. East Berlin had earned the gratitude of Beijing by praising the Chinese for their decisive action. The Politburo had also instructed the East German parliament, the Volkskammer, to issue a resolution in support of the Chinese Communist Party's actions.[129] This "approval" from the legislature stood in stark contrast to the reaction of average East Germans, however, many of whom sent letters to their leaders expressing horror at the regime's support for such violence. Some people even protested in front of the Chinese embassy in East Berlin. The Stasi kept detailed records on all of them.[130] Undeterred, in September 1989 Honecker sent Krenz to celebrate the fortieth anniversary of the founding of the PRC and to meet with the Chinese leaders responsible for the massacre. The extensive coverage of Krenz's visit and continuing praise for the Beijing leaders in the media of the GDR were clearly meant to send a message for domestic consumption.[131]

Building on the Chinese example, Honecker wrote on September 22 to all of his party's first secretaries, the leaders of the party's local organizations throughout the GDR. He informed the secretaries that the time had come to "choke off" the "hostile actions" taking place in the GDR.[132] This decisive attitude was put to the test in Leipzig on Monday, September 25. On that day, protestors began for the first time to march on the modern, multilane ring road circling the old medieval core of Leipzig; the busy ring became the march route by default, after police had blocked earlier attempts to protest in the side streets around the Nikolai.[133]

The use of Leipzig's ring road represented a fateful development. A contest emerged in which the marchers would seek to get farther and farther around the circular route and the security forces would seek to block them. The loyalist in charge of the regime's side in the developing fight for the ring was Helmut Hackenberg, a sixty-three-year-old second secretary in the Leipzig party organization. Known as a hard-liner, he had fought in the Second World War and spent time as a Soviet prisoner of war. He was standing in for his boss, the first secretary of the district, sixty-five-year-old Horst Schumann. Schumann was ailing, had repeatedly taken extended sick leave, and had even asked to be relieved of his duties entirely, but the seventy-seven-year-old Honecker would hear nothing of it. Thinking of himself, Honecker did not want to set any kind of precedent whereby a party leader could be dismissed because he was elderly and sick.[134] Schumann stayed in office as a result, but with frequent absences at a critical time, absences that contributed to the inability of the local party leaders to quash the Nikolai protests effectively.[135]

Schumann's illness was not the only hindrance that Hackenberg and other Leipzig loyalists faced. On October 7, 1989, the GDR would celebrate the fortieth anniversary of its own founding. Ever eager to seize an opportunity to trumpet the GDR on the world stage, Honecker had invited many foreign dignitaries and journalists to East Germany to attend a series of parades, meals, and speeches. The upcoming anniversary placed security forces around the country in a tricky position, however. On the one hand, East Berlin pressured Hackenberg to keep a lid on the protests before the anniversary on October 7. On the other hand, too large a crackdown might cause invited dignitaries to cancel their trips and visiting journalists to report on the violence instead of the anniversary. As one member

Security deployment in East Berlin on the evening of October 7, 1989, the fortieth anniversary of the founding of East Germany. Political leaders were attending anniversary celebrations inside the large building at the left. Later that night, security forces and demonstrators clashed violently not only in East Berlin but also in numerous other locations around the country. *(RHG Fo Ni Be 009 15; photo by Nikolaus Becker)*

of the Politburo later explained, "We hesitated to take any steps, because we didn't want any clashes on the fortieth anniversary, which wouldn't have been a very good thing internationally."[136]

On Monday, October 2, roughly ten thousand marchers set out to claim the ring, and Hackenberg had to figure out a way to disperse them without endangering the anniversary celebrations scheduled for five days later. He deployed the security forces under his command, equipping them with clubs, dogs, helmets, and shields, but did not use more drastic measures. The Politburo later received word that this level of intimidation had worked; Hackenberg had halted the progress of the October 2 march around the ring.[137] His limited escalation still had a cost, however. Members of a party paramilitary unit who had been called up for this effort on October 2 refused to appear for duty.[138]

To motivate the men and to intimidate the protestors in the future, on October 6 the party had the local paper, the *Leipziger Volkszeitung,* print a "letter to the editor," ostensibly from a commander of one of the party's paramilitary organizations. This letter, bearing the headline "No More Tolerance for Hostility Toward the State," announced that security forces were ready to defend socialism in the GDR "with weapons in our hands."[139] For the October 7 anniversary itself, Honecker ordered an "exactingly organized and coordinated cooperation as well as a reliably functioning provision of information between the protective and security organs with their other partners."[140] These instructions translated into violence in multiple cities across not only Saxony but also all of the GDR, resulting in many severely injured protestors; in one case in East Berlin, an activist nearly died.[141]

In Leipzig itself, security measures were in place well before the anniversary and included both the detention of dissidents and prevention of travel to the city by suspect nonresidents.[142] Surrounding districts received instructions not to allow their own troublemakers to leave for Leipzig.[143] Such events did not receive media coverage in the GDR, since there was no form of free press. Rather, newspapers carried congratulatory coverage of the GDR's scripted fortieth-anniversary celebrations. State-controlled media also printed even more praise for the decisive Chinese actions in Tiananmen Square and noted that Chinese leader Yao Yilin had honored the GDR by attending the October 7 anniversary in person.[144]

ALL MATTERS WOULD come to a head on October 9, the first Monday after the anniversary. Contrary to Honecker's expectations, the regime's escalation of the use of violence in September and early October had actually created an increased desire on the part of Leipzigers to claim the ring once and for all on that night. One Leipzig housewife later explained why she decided to join the October 9 march: "Every Monday was worse than the one before. There was more and more violence on the part of the state. The security forces got more and more brutal. It was clear that it was coming to a tipping point."[145] She felt that the time had come for her to get involved. Another woman decided to go to the October 9 march precisely because the October 7 anniversary violence had been so awful: "I was horrified, because I would never have thought that the 'Workers' and Farmers' State' would beat up workers like it did on October 7 and 8. It made me furious."[146] This rising anger was even apparent to outside observers. Diplomats from the United States, reporting on events to Washington not only from the embassy in East Berlin but also from Leipzig itself, concluded that there would be an enormous crowd on October 9 after the use of force on the anniversary two days earlier.[147]

Leipzigers' long-term frustrations over the decay of their city and the pollution of their immediate environment had combined with their shock at the massive emigration crisis and at the violence in Saxony's streets. The protest movement in Leipzig had gone from marginal to massive. The small group of activists, by involuntarily but then bravely taking their protest outside the Nikolai Church, had created a public venue for grievance at their open-air Monday night events, and these in turn had given rise to the massive Monday marches. The ruling regime, by responding with violence and fulsomely praising the Tiananmen Square crackdown at every opportunity, had not only failed to suppress the growing movement but also created new converts to it. The question now was what the regime would do during what would clearly be the definitive fight for the ring on October 9.

Chapter Three

The Fight for the Ring

REVOLUTIONS CAN BE HARD not only on dictators but also on documents. After the East German regime's collapse, investigations into its abuses began. Researchers scoured former GDR archives, only to find that files related to the use of violence had disappeared. Among the archives with noticeable gaps were ones detailing the official planning for the night of October 9 in Leipzig.[1] Enough evidence survives, however, to sketch at least the outlines of the party's plan to stop the Monday march and to maintain control over the ring road on that night.

By October 9, three more churches within walking distance of the ring—the Michaelis, Reformed, and Thomas Churches—had all agreed to hold Monday prayers at the same time, 5:00 p.m., as the original Nikolai session. The expansion of the prayers meant more marchers.[2] The October 9 demonstration thereby promised to reach an unprecedented size, but no one knew how large it would be. Monday, September 25, had seen possibly as many as six to eight thousand march. Monday, October 2, had seen closer to ten thousand.[3]

The party ramped up its preparations accordingly. Before the GDR's fortieth anniversary on October 7, the Leipzig Stasi chief, Manfred Hummitzsch, had complained to his subordinates about how the anniversary was "hindering our ability to make decisions. We cannot act the way that we want. We cannot use all available means" to stop marchers.[4] The center of East Berlin had become a battle zone, however, almost as soon as the scripted events on October 7 had ended. Security forces had used force to disperse unapproved demonstrations there and throughout East Germany. In the first eight days of October alone, more than three thousand people had been arrested.[5] Now, on the eve of the first Monday march after the anniversary, West German television channels noted an even more "raw" tone of authority in East Germany toward foreign journalists.[6] The goal was clearly to get all prying eyes out of the GDR, and out of Leipzig in particular, before what could potentially become the German Tiananmen.

That the SED regime had the capability to carry out a Tiananmen-level event was not in doubt. There were an estimated six hundred thousand men in the armed forces ultimately under the control of the ruling party. Even if some of those armed men disobeyed orders and refused to attack protestors, the odds remained daunting. If fifty thousand people took to the streets on the night of October 9—the highest internal party prediction—the regime could still, in theory, field multiple armed men for every single protestor.[7] The question was not if the SED regime could crush the Monday march but whether it would choose to do so.

For the fateful night, the regime did indeed position portions of its armed forces in Leipzig with instructions to prevent the protestors from circling the ring road by force. The goal was to quell the rising revolution in as much secrecy as possible, in order to limit the damage to the GDR's international reputation. Keeping the domestic media quiet would be no problem, as they were all still firmly under the regime's control at the start of October.[8] If evidence from the fight for the ring was going to make it out—most importantly to Western television stations—it would have to be through surreptitious photos and videos, made at great risk and smuggled out of the country, so the regime also focused on keeping anyone with a video camera or even simply connections to Western media away from Leipzig on October 9. As a result, not only outside reporters but also foreign journalists based in the GDR were intimidated into avoiding Leipzig on October 9— or, if they went anyway, found themselves escorted out of the city.[9]

THE REGIME'S PLANS for stopping the protests had four major components. The first, the National People's Army, readied itself to fight the people in Leipzig after having already functioned as a reserve force in Dresden.[10] The precise details are difficult to pin down, but soldiers apparently received live ammunition and gas masks as part of the preparations.[11] The police chief in Leipzig, Gerhard Strassenburg, would later say that he did not know exactly how or why the army got involved and that he himself did not request its presence; indeed, his only goal that night, he later insisted, had been to prevent violence. Strassenburg's claim matched a similar assertion by another of the second party secretaries in Leipzig, Roland Wötzel, according to whom no one in the district had the authority to command army units to move in. Their presence in Leipzig must have been ordered by someone in Berlin, he concluded.[12]

The second component, the Stasi, also made extensive preparations both at its headquarters in Berlin and at its district office in Leipzig. The Stasi minister himself, Erich Mielke, personally supervised a strategy session in Berlin on Sunday, October 8.[13] After this meeting, he sent a long telegram to the relevant subordinates with instructions. Mielke instructed Stasi employees authorized to carry weapons to start doing so immediately and to keep doing so until told otherwise. He called up various groups of the Stasi's euphemistically named "unofficial co-workers," or agents, to duty en masse. He also instructed the relevant offices to update the Stasi's lists of names of political undesirables, meaning people who were to be watched and most likely prevented from participating in the march.[14] The list for Leipzig represented a who's who of the local protest movement. Names of Nikolai Church activists were plentiful on this list and included those of both Uwe Schwabe and Christoph Wonneberger. Katrin Hattenhauer was already in jail, so the Stasi did not think it necessary to have her name on the list.[15] Mielke was still not done. He addressed the risk that demonstrators might gain access to Stasi weapons by instructing that necessary precautions be taken to prevent unapproved access to them. He also told his ministry to block the work of foreign correspondents. Getting wind of this, the West German television channel ARD reported that the city of Leipzig was completely closed to journalists.[16] On top of all of Mielke's instructions, a live video feed from rooftop cameras in Leipzig was prepared, in order to allow the party bosses in East Berlin to watch the events on the streets of Leipzig in real time as they unfolded.[17]

The third and fourth components, the police and the paramilitaries, also made their own plans for October 9. The distinction between police and paramilitary is not always meaningful, since the party ultimately controlled both, just as it ultimately controlled the army and the Stasi.[18] In the field, however, the organizational structures were at least somewhat separate; the People's Police, an established force, reported to the Ministry of the Interior, headed by Friedrich Dickel (who was of course also a party member). In contrast to the standing police forces, the paramilitaries, called "fighting groups," had to be called up in an ad hoc fashion. There were internal concerns over how many of their members would actually appear for duty and how well trained they really were.[19]

Finally, above and beyond these four armed branches of the GDR's own security forces, there were the roughly 380,000 Soviet troops stationed in the country. By October 1989, Gorbachev had established himself as a supporter of peaceful reform. There was, however, no small number of Soviet party and army leaders who disagreed with his hands-off approach to change in Eastern Europe. Later, many of them would be involved in a coup against him.[20] Thus on October 9 it was unlikely, but not impossible, that the Soviet troops in East Germany would intervene in events, possibly against Gorbachev's wishes. Indeed, the Soviet ambassador and de facto proconsul in East Germany, Vyacheslav Kochemasov, later claimed that he was concerned enough that day to call the commander of the Soviet forces in the GDR, Boris Snetkov. The ambassador reportedly told Snetkov to make certain that his troops stayed in their barracks that night. Kochemasov said that Moscow later backed him up, but only the next day.[21] And even though Gorbachev was not in a bellicose frame of mind, he was hardly willing to abandon his German ally.[22] In short, it was assumed that the Soviets would stay out of the Leipzig conflict, but that was not a given.

For his part, Erich Honecker gave clear overall instructions to his security forces about what they were to do. He informed his party's first secretaries, which included Helmut Hackenberg as acting first secretary in Leipzig, that "we should expect that there will be further riots. They are to be choked off in advance."[23] The day before the march, Sunday, October 8, Honecker met with senior party leaders to finalize the plans for accomplishing that goal.[24] Their meeting appears to have brought together all SED leaders in the realm of security, including the still-resentful Egon Krenz. From indirect evidence, it seems that Honecker asked Krenz, the head of security questions for the party's central committee, to go to Leipzig. This request appears to have caused Krenz to panic and to call Kochemasov for confidential advice. Krenz allegedly said he feared that he was being set up as the scapegoat. After the German Tiananmen, Honecker then could presumably rid himself of his troublesome former crown prince by blaming Krenz and stripping him of his power, in order to curry post-bloodshed public favor. Although Kochemasov was vague in his account of this conversation, he did note that "I understood why he [Krenz] called me . . . he understood well that the main blow was being aimed at him."[25] Honecker was right to be wary of Krenz. Krenz apparently used the "face time" with all of his significant fellow party leaders at the October 8 meeting to begin talking about a potential coup against Honecker.[26]

Lacking the resolve to launch a coup immediately, however, and perhaps not seeing a way to refuse Honecker without coming under suspicion, Krenz avoided going to Leipzig but still handled various security questions from his office in East Berlin. He received, for example, a summary of preparations from Hackenberg, who, because of the Leipzig first secretary's sick leave, would have operational control on the ground as the man in charge of the party's "district deployment command" that night.[27] Hackenberg told Krenz that he had decided to implement a new idea. On top of all of the other preparations, up to five thousand "societal forces," meaning party members and trusted sympathizers, would be instructed to pack the Nikolai Church early on the afternoon of October 9. The goal was to prevent the activists and their sympathizers from attending the 5:00 p.m. prayer session at all.[28]

In short, because of the preparations of the army, Stasi, police, paramilitaries, and party leaders themselves, a large armed force under the command of the party was ready and waiting on October 9. The exact number of armed men involved is not known but was clearly in the thousands. Fifteen hundred army soldiers appear to have been present. An unclear number of Stasi agents and employees had been activated. More than three thousand police officers would be on duty. More than half of them were not from Leipzig and therefore were more likely to attack the demonstrators, a sign that SED leaders had absorbed the lessons of Tiananmen, where local troops had refused to fire on crowds that might contain friends or family. Troops from other regions had been brought to Beijing to replace them, with bloody results.[29] Finally, about six hundred members of the party's armed paramilitary organizations were present, in addition to the five thousand party members and sympathizers who were supposed to pack churches.[30] These forces had an array of equipment and weapons at their disposal: armored vehicles, dogs, heavy machine guns, live ammunition, tear gas, and water cannons. A spray with a long-lasting color tint was also prepared, so that it could be shot by some of the water cannons on to demonstrators for their later identification and arrest.[31] In order to deal with the consequences of the crackdown, hospitals were reportedly told to make appropriate preparations.[32] Horse stalls on a large property in nearby Markkleeberg, used as holding pens for detainees on the October 7 anniversary, were once again readied to hold humans instead of horses.[33] On the night of October 7–8, the security forces had jammed ten prisoners into each narrow horse stall and left them there overnight.[34]

The overall plan was apparently as follows: According to Strassenburg, the chief of Leipzig police, his forces would break up any gathering of people starting at 10:00 a.m.[35] If that failed to work, police should clear any demonstration that formed in the area around the Nikolai Church immediately after the Monday prayers ended at approximately 6:00 p.m. If a group of people formed and made it to the ring road nonetheless, security forces should "not allow any more movement in the direction of the main train station" but instead "force this movement of people back."[36]

Strassenburg confirmed on October 9 that the police were authorized "to commence all measures" necessary to carry out this mission.[37] Written instructions confirmed by the interior minister, Dickel, reiterated that the "disruptions from the starting point of the Nikolai Church are to be blocked, along with other provocations and disruptions," and that the police should "fight them with no compromises." The distribution of live ammunition, the provision of medical treatment, and the locations to which detainees should be taken were all spelled out as well.[38] On top of these written instructions, individual policemen heard their superiors say, in essence, *Today it will be decided, it is either them or us.*[39]

Among those hearing such words were draftees, because young men who had been drafted could perform their mandatory service as so-called riot police. Some were so upset at what was happening that they found ways either to leave their barracks despite a lockdown or to get messages out, all in order to warn family and friends in the area. For example, one draftee, Silvio Rösler, later described how he had heard at an assembly at 11:00 a.m. on October 9 that the day would be "comparable with Tiananmen Square in China." As motivation, the draftees at this assembly were forced to look at photos of a badly burned policeman, presumably from the Dresden violence. "The motto was, it's us or them. They really used fear propaganda" to make us afraid, Rösler recounted.[40] He warned his family members in Leipzig "that the order to shoot had been given out" and that his relatives should "stay back." Uwe Chemnitz, also a draftee in Leipzig, got word to his brother that "things looked really serious."[41] And Leipzig residents Gisela and Wolfgang Rähder received a warning from their son by phone that "the artillery is rolling" and there was "an order to shoot."[42] Similarly, Jens Illing, a draftee who helped to dispense weapons and ammunition, warned his parents that "today on October 9 the worst will happen, stay home." His unit had gotten "an order not to allow a demonstration to take place, to break it up," and that "tonight it will be decided, them or us." Following orders, Illing had subsequently issued 9 mm Makarov pistols with at least two magazines of live ammunition per weapon to officers.[43] There was a rumor that these officers would aim their pistols at the heads of draftees who refused to do their duty that night.[44] Illing was also ordered to load numerous cases of Kalashnikovs onto trucks, and did so.[45]

Fear gripped the city. A church administrator who was number six on the Stasi's Leipzig most-wanted list, Johannes Richter, wrote a note in his calendar on October 9: "Fear. What will happen? Chinese solution."[46] Führer later described the dominant feeling of that day as "similar to a civil war."[47] In an effort to head off the bloodshed, a Leipzig professor with personal ties to Krenz, Walter Friedrich, decided to drive to East Berlin to try to convince Krenz to take action. The professor carried with him a twenty-page letter that he had written to Krenz, arguing that the time had come for Honecker to go.[48] Friedrich hand-delivered the letter to Krenz partly because of its urgency and partly because such information could hardly be trusted to the mercies of the Stasi agents in post offices who read the mail.[49] The letter predicted that "if the wrong decisions are made today . . . they could lead to the rapid decline of socialism in the GDR." Krenz received Friedrich on the morning of October 9 and indicated that, in fact, an unspecified "we" was indeed already thinking of "introducing a change in the leadership of the GDR."[50]

Friedrich was not the only prominent Leipziger who actively tried to head off bloodshed. Handmade banners calling for nonviolence began appearing in the city, such as a yellow cloth that was tacked on the outside of the Nikolai Church at about 3:30 p.m. The words on the yellow cloth called for the crowds to stay calm: "People, no senseless violence, pull yourself together, leave the stones on the ground."[51] In a similar spirit, Kurt Masur, the conductor of the Gewandhaus Orchestra, reached out to local party leaders. The musician organized a meeting on that fateful Monday with three of the party's secretaries—Hackenberg's colleagues, but on this night his subordinates, since he was the acting leader—along with the actor Bernd-Lutz Lange and the theologian Peter Zimmermann. Masur apparently did not know at the time that Zimmermann was a Stasi agent.[52] The six men, including Zimmermann, agreed to issue a public call for dialogue.[53] Their hope was to convince Leipzigers with their appeal for nonviolence, which became known as the "Appeal of the Six," to refrain from the use of force on the streets that night.

The most sustained effort on behalf of nonviolence, however, came from Wonneberger and the activists with whom he worked. Dreading the threat of violence, and inspired by the example of the American civil rights leader Martin Luther King Jr., whom Wonneberger greatly admired, they tried to figure out what they could do to prevent bloodshed. They decided to print tens of thousands of leaflets, exhorting everyone to refrain from the use of force, on a hand-cranked mimeograph machine in Wonneberger's parish office.[54] The text of the leaflet lamented that "in the past weeks, repeatedly and in multiple cities of the GDR, demonstrations have ended in violence." Admitting that "we are afraid," the authors of the leaflet nonetheless called for demonstrators to remain peaceful. "Violence only ever yields violence. Violence solves no problems." Pledging to hold "the party and state responsible" for their actions, the appeal concluded with these words: "Tonight it is on us to stop a further escalation of the violence." To bypass church rules prohibiting use of its printing equipment for non-church-related purposes—a rule meant to prevent exactly what they were doing—Wonneberger put a laughably inaccurate note at the bottom saying the memo was "church internal." Wonneberger and the dissidents then cranked out leaflets by hand for forty hours straight, producing more than thirty thousand. Since the last demonstration had included ten thousand participants, it seemed as if three times that number of appeals would be enough. The activists then started handing out leaflets on the street, despite the massing security forces and the risk of arrest.[55]

J UST ABOUT THE only certainty in Leipzig on October 9 was that there would be a showdown that night. What its outcome would be, and whether people beyond city limits would have the chance to see any images from it, remained open questions. Just as the party made its preparations, so too did a very small, clandestine band of smugglers make theirs. For years they had run risks to record, and then to smuggle out of East Germany, audio and video recordings of the crimes of the regime, whether against the environment or against its people. They knew that October 9 represented their biggest challenge yet.

The organizer of this band of "information smugglers" was not in Leipzig, or even in East Germany, but in West Berlin. His name was Roland Jahn. From the West, Jahn had organized what was essentially an underground journalistic network. The East German regime would not let him in, and his main sources of photos and videos from the GDR, the East Berliners Aram Radomski and Siggi Schefke, could not get out.[56] Jahn, a former East German himself, had never met Radomski and Schefke in person. Rather, they had been connected through mutual acquaintances, and had found trusted couriers to ferry their materials back and forth across the Iron Curtain. The best couriers came from groups that enjoyed a legal status enabling them to cross borders without a search; for some, that privilege was a result of a diplomatic posting, but for others, such as Western journalists working in the Warsaw Pact countries, it was a result of the human rights provisions of the CSCE. In addition to this covert courier service, Jahn had camera teams from the West on assignment in East Berlin "forget" to bring their equipment home with them. Radomski and Schefke, who would miraculously happen to be in the area where the expensive equipment was left behind, would quickly grab it for themselves.[57]

The two East Berliners would then, at times with the help of others but often by themselves, use the equipment to film, record, or otherwise collect material from locations all over the GDR, particularly from Leipzig. One of their greatest successes had unintentionally been made possible by Honecker personally. In a moment of hubris, Honecker had once speculated about proposing Leipzig to host the Olympic Games. This statement would have been risible had Honecker not been serious. Jahn, Radomski, and Schefke decided that Honecker's unwise proposal provided an excellent opening to alert the world to the environmental and urban decay in Leipzig. Radomski and Schefke grabbed the video cameras smuggled to them by Jahn and headed south from East Berlin to Leipzig to film an undercover mini-documentary. Their video included not just images of crumbling buildings blackened by pollution but also interviews with brave, disbelieving Leipzigers willing to say on camera that it was unthinkable that the city could host an Olympics. When the video reached Jahn in West Berlin, he ensured that it appeared on the television show *Kontraste*, to the embarrassment of the would-be Olympic host Honecker. Leipzig, of course, did not go on to host the Olympics.[58] In addition to this mini-documentary, Radomski and Schefke repeatedly filmed in Leipzig during the trade fairs. They knew that it was harder for the Stasi to crack down either on protestors or on the two of them personally when foreign reporters were in the city.[59]

By the night of October 9, 1989, because of their many contacts and trips there, Jahn, Radomski, and Schefke were all familiar with Leipzig.[60] Jahn had taken pains to develop connections to the Leipzig dissident scene in particular. He was in close contact with Jochen Lässig, the man with the strong voice who had read aloud over organ noise at the watershed Nikolai prayer session in June 1988, as well as with Gesine Oltmanns and

Three images from a longer sequence of Stasi surveillance photographs taken of Siegbert "Siggi" Schefke (the tall, bearded man with long hair) on the day of June 3, 1989. The Stasi spied on Schefke for years in an effort to uncover all the members of the dissident ring in which he was involved. *(MfS, from file BStU, BV Bln Abt. XX 4948, 1/1,2; 5/2)*

Uwe Schwabe. Jahn had even arranged (as the Stasi learned) to meet with the Leipzig activists in Czechoslovakia.[61] Now he, Radomski, and Schefke wanted to ensure that, regardless of the risks, they filmed video of the events of October 9 and then smuggled the footage out. The two East Berliners had taken their video camera to the Monday march a week earlier, on October 2, but had felt so threatened by the armed forces that they had returned to East Berlin without ever taking the camera out of the shoulder bag that concealed it.[62]

The two East Berliners and Jahn had deep-rooted motivations for their work, although it was not as if they had all been born enemies of the state, plotting away in their cribs as infants. Rather, as Jahn would later explain, life had started normally for them and "the sun had shone, even in a dictatorship."[63] As young men, however, they had all suffered the experience of being "shoved into a corner" by the state, often with violence. Such "shoving" was yet another way that the ruling regime "created its own enemies," Jahn believed.[64]

The shoving of Radomski had come while he was still a young man. Born in 1963, Radomski was the son and grandson of writers. His grandmother's writings had been favored by the regime, but his father's had not, so as a child Radomski had experienced the surveillance of his father.[65] When he was a teenager, the relevant officials refused to let Radomski study at any institute of higher education, so he found another way to spend time at one in Plauen—as a heating maintenance worker. There, in the early 1980s, he had met his "princess," a Mongolian exchange student. They fell in love; he asked her to move in with him, and she did.

One day in January 1983, his boss called Radomski into his office, saying, "You will separate yourself from this woman." Shocked, Radomski responded, "I do not think that I will do that. I do not think that you can dictate to me whether or not I have to do that." His boss responded, "Nonetheless, Aram, I recommend that you do so." His boss concluded the interview by telling him, "I am giving you four weeks. Say goodbye." Radomski left the conversation thinking, *What kind of conditions am I living under here, if my employer can tell me whether I can be together with a woman or not?* He and his Mongolian girlfriend guessed that her politically well-connected parents, who disapproved of Radomski and his family, had used their contacts in the East German regime to attempt to separate them. The two ignored the warning.

Four weeks later to the day, as he was out at a bar with friends, Radomski was assaulted and beaten severely by unknown men. Afterward, with the outline of the boot of one of his assailants still visible on his face, he was taken into custody. A court convicted, fined, and jailed him. He realized that the state had thereby achieved by "Gestapo methods" what it wanted: he was now separated from his girlfriend. The arrest deeply unsettled his father, who blamed himself for it. Radomski's Mongolian girlfriend did not visit or contact him in prison, presumably because the state prevented her from doing either. When Radomski got out six months later, she was gone. He heard a rumor that she had been forced to end her study abroad and to leave East Germany. Instead of searching for her, however, Radomski realized that something had changed. He was now filled with a sense of rage, and what he most wanted was not his "princess," whom he never saw again, but payback.[66]

Radomski drifted from location to location over the following years, but his desire for revenge would eventually lead him to the Prenzlauer Berg neighborhood of East Berlin, the only place in the GDR where he figured he had a chance of finding like-minded souls. There, Radomski indeed found a number of them, most important among them Siegbert Schefke, known to all as Siggi. They became friends and even held a joint birthday party one year. More than two hundred people attended, not least to hear the music provided by friends who would later form the rock band Rammstein.[67] Radomski and Schefke recognized that they both had scores to settle with the state. When Schefke asked the younger man if he wanted to make and smuggle videos out of East Germany, Radomski agreed on the spot, realizing that he had found his payback.

As for Schefke, he had initially played by the rules, completing his military service and studying construction engineering in Cottbus. He came under Stasi observation, however, after the secret police became convinced that his then-girlfriend was considering an escape attempt.[68] Although she was the one initially under suspicion, Schefke became forbidden to travel at all. Out of resentment, he began to question the state that he had served, and in doing so earned his own Stasi case name: "Satan."[69] At first Schefke was a "free-time revolutionary," working on building projects for the state by day and then finding ways to protest against the state by night. The Stasi instructed his employer to assign him work that would make it difficult for him to pursue his moonlighting activities. Schefke quit in response.[70] Reduced to living hand-to-mouth by giving tours to students in East Berlin and by receiving support from his parents, Schefke became more and more involved with projects such as the East Berlin "Environmental Library," a collection of forbidden literature stored in a Protestant church in East Berlin.[71] Through the library, Schefke became better connected in the protest movement, and also more active.[72]

The shoving of Radomski had been his beating and time in jail; of Schefke, his loss of travel privileges. The shoving in Jahn's case involved a death. A close friend of Jahn's, a healthy young man named Matthias Domaschk, had been hauled in by the Stasi for questioning in 1981 and then, unaccountably, died in custody. After a series of protests by Jahn, the authorities in Jena arrested not only him but also Petra Falkenberg, the woman with whom he was living and raising their four-year-old daughter, Lina. Threatening Jahn and Falkenberg with jail terms and a lengthy separation from their child, the authorities convinced Falkenberg that she should emigrate to the West with Lina. The Stasi hoped that Jahn would follow and that the East German authorities would thereby be rid of all of them. But Jahn would not go. At the cost of his relationship with the mother of his child, who accepted the deal and moved to West Berlin with Lina, Jahn refused to leave. It was a shattering sacrifice. Decades later, his daughter Lina would still blame him, saying, "The fact that you did not come with us back then, that was really a decision against me, wasn't it?"[73]

The party then took more dramatic measures against him. On the orders of Mielke himself, Jahn received a summons from a city housing office to appear late on the afternoon of June 7, 1983, ostensibly in response to Jahn's request to move to a new apartment now that his child and her mother had moved to the West. At the housing office, the Stasi informed him that the state had rescinded his citizenship and would expel him to West Germany that same day. A police escort took him home briefly, where he was supposed to collect a few personal items, but Jahn managed to escape to the apartment of a friend. The security forces tracked him down and put him in handcuffs for the two-hour drive to the border. When Jahn made comments—written down by the Stasi in his file—such as "I demand a phone call with the interior minister of the GDR," the Stasi report noted that its men "did not let themselves be provoked and dealt with him politely and considerately."[74] Jahn remembered that, for his comments, the Stasi agents jerked and twisted the handcuffs forcefully and repeatedly until he feared that his arms and wrists would break.[75]

Jahn's transport vehicle arrived at the border at 9:00 p.m., but he was held in a room until the middle of the night, presumably in order to conceal better from the public what was going on. In the early hours of the morning, he found himself being shoved into the small entry corridor of a sleeping car on a 3:10 a.m. train to the West. The security forces then sealed the doors to the entry, which had neither a window nor an emergency brake. They told the conductor of the sleeping car that Jahn was mentally ill and should not be let out under any circumstances. With Jahn hammering against the sealed doors, the train crossed into the West, where Western authorities heard his banging and managed to pry him out.[76] Jahn moved to West Berlin, where he could at least see Lina, although he and Falkenberg never again became a couple.[77] The decision that he had made to stay in the East had ended their relationship for good.

Jahn's forcible expulsion made him a media celebrity in the West; he appeared on television and in newspapers and magazines. He skillfully capitalized on that celebrity to create his smuggling network and in the course of the 1980s enjoyed a number of successes. When, for example, the courageous East German activists Bärbel Bohley and Ulrike Poppe were arrested for protest actions in late 1983, Jahn's network informed the world of their detentions and pressured the regime to free them. Bohley and Poppe were released in January 1984.[78] Jahn could not rest on his laurels, however. Since he was always losing his "correspondents" to arrest, expulsion, or betrayal, he continually needed to add new ones.[79] By the late 1980s, he had recruited Radomski and Schefke, and they soon became his main source of video of East Germany.[80]

The Stasi were aware of Jahn's connection to Schefke by July 1987 but chose not to put either Schefke or Radomski in jail immediately.[81] The officer in charge of Schefke's case felt instead that it was essential to conduct "further investigation into the contact partners" of the two East Berliners.[82] The secret police assumed that their two targets had a vast network of helpers, and so they wanted to hold off on any arrests until enough surveillance had been carried out to catch them all. Undercover Stasi agents infiltrated Radomski and Schefke's group of friends, and the secret police interrogated the two repeatedly.[83] Not knowing at the time that the Stasi was holding back because of the search for their nonexistent horde of helpers, Radomski and Schefke lived in fear of being sent to prison.[84] But the Stasi's mistaken assumption that two men could not cause so much trouble on their own kept them out of jail during the critical months of 1989.

Jahn, Radomski, and Schefke guessed that the October 9 demonstration would surpass all others in size and significance. They also knew that there was a good chance that the German Tiananmen might unfold, and they felt a special obligation to try to record it, despite the personal risks involved. As Radomski put it, "If there are going to be pictures, then let them be ours."[85] First, Radomski and Schefke had to get from East

Berlin to Leipzig, which was no easy task on October 9. Because of the anniversary, the Ministry for State Security had been observing Schefke around the clock since October 3. The ten Stasi agents assigned to observe him around the clock did not even bother to conceal their presence. They smoked cigarettes in the courtyard of his apartment building and followed him every time he walked out the door. "They always came with me," he remembered. This was "extremely unpleasant," because it meant that Schefke could not carry the video equipment supplied by Jahn out his front door; the risk that the Stasi would confiscate it was too great.

He and Radomski devised a plan to evade the Stasi on October 9. They bought a number of timers for the lights, radio, and television in Schefke's apartment and set the devices to turn on about two hours after Schefke actually woke up and got dressed in the dark. They hoped that the Stasi would think that Schefke was still asleep and would not notice him sneaking out of his apartment via the roof of his building. At first the plan worked. Schefke climbed out on the roof, holding his equipment close to him. Managing to get from his building's roof to another and then another, he climbed down to street level about a third of a mile away, where Radomski was waiting with a car.[86]

They were spotted and followed. The two managed to evade their pursuers, but realized that they needed a different vehicle to get out of Berlin, otherwise the Stasi would find them again. They parked their car and went by tram to a friend of Schefke's, Stephan Bickhardt, a Protestant minister. Schefke told Bickhardt that he needed to use his car to get out of the city. Bickhardt agreed to lend it to him, even though he needed the vehicle that week for his own wedding.[87]

As Radomski and Schefke drove down to Leipzig in the borrowed car, they realized that even if it had been their first time making the trip, they could not possibly have gotten lost—all they had to do was to follow the convoy of armed men and vehicles also heading to Leipzig. Radomski was sure that at any moment someone from a convoy would pull them over and arrest them, but it did not happen. "I have never understood how we got through, but we got through," he would remark decades later. The two videographers got close enough to the convoys at times to see individual soldiers sitting in some of the armed transports, but the troops were apparently not charged with investigating other travelers on the way.[88]

When Radomski and Schefke arrived in the city, they were amazed at the sheer mass of people there. Security forces and onlookers were all crowded into the city's center. The two men quickly began trying to find a concealed location from which they could film. Given that at the Monday march a week before, they had never felt safe enough to take their video camera out of its bag, they decided that this week they would not fall in with the marchers again. Instead, the two decided to select a tall building overlooking the ring road. The idea was to climb up to a useful vantage point, conceal themselves, and film.

At the first tall building they chose, however, Radomski and Schefke were chased away by the building superintendent. After considering a number of other places, they tried a residential apartment building and stumbled upon a door with stickers on it. In their experience, stickers, which were officially discouraged, meant that someone sympathetic lived inside. They knocked and were delighted when a man with long hair—another sign of rebellion—answered and said that they could use his window. Radomski and Schefke thought that they were set, until they entered and noticed a child sleeping in one of the rooms of the apartment. They did not want to draw the attention of the security forces or, even worse, gunfire, especially if that endangered a child. And even if there was no gunfire, it was not uncommon for the Stasi to seize upon remarks by children to persecute their parents. An innocent word from the child in school later about the two men with the video camera might be sufficient to condemn the father. They decided to leave the apartment, even though there was no guarantee that they would find another.[89]

Eventually Radomski and Schefke ended up at Leipzig's Reformed Church, which had a tall tower and stood directly on the northern arc of the Leipzig ring road. The staff of the Reformed, unlike at the Thomas Church, left the front door to the ring road unlocked in case marchers needed refuge. The two East Berliners entered the church and, once inside, knocked on one of the internal doors, which turned out to be the entrance to the residence of Hans-Jürgen Sievers, a forty-six-year-old minister at the church, and his family. The two Berliners were lucky that they had chosen Sievers's door. Other Reformed Church staff exhibited the same kind of antipathy toward activists as some of the leaders of the Nikolai Church, but Sievers, a former mechanic who had later studied theology, was sympathetic to dissidents.[90]

Sievers recalled that when he opened the door on October 9, two very anxious young men were standing there. Intuitively, the minister did not ask their names, either then or at any other point in what was to come. It was only later that he would find out who they were. Radomski and Schefke figured there was no point making small talk and so came right out with their blunt question: could they use his church tower to film that night? Sievers, shocked, took a moment to think.[91] He was scared—the two men could be undercover Stasi agents—but he also had an inner conviction that if blood was going to flow that night on the streets in front of his church, then it should be seen. It should be broadcast as widely as possible, "seen as far away as America and Japan and everywhere else—otherwise nothing will ever change here."

Sievers, taking a significant risk, decided to trust the two strangers and to let them use the tower that night. Thinking of the potential consequences for his family, he requested that, if they were caught, they not say he had let them in. Radomski and Schefke agreed, then asked if they could hide their equipment in his home temporarily—its presence alone would be sufficient grounds for arrest on that day—so that they could assess what was already happening in the city and get some food and other supplies.[92] Sievers let them do so, as long as they promised to climb the tower well before the doors opened for the 5:00 p.m. peace prayers that would be held in the Reformed Church that night as well as at the Nikolai and other churches. The two young men vowed to return in time and departed. Sievers became petrified when one of his sons unexpectedly appeared immediately afterward, and he did his best to keep the boy away from the concealed video equipment, since he did not want his son implicated in any way.[93]

Radomski and Schefke headed toward the Nikolai Church to see if they could pick up any useful information about the coming crackdown. Although they thought they had already used up their share of luck in meeting Sievers, at the church they found that they still had some to spare: they ran into their most trusted courier, Ulrich Schwarz.[94] Schwarz was a West German who lived in East Berlin as a correspondent for *Spiegel* magazine.[95] He had first arrived in 1976, once the original CSCE Final Act had made it possible for Western correspondents to work in the GDR, but had been thrown out roughly a year later for publishing materials from dissidents.[96] However, under pressure in the Gorbachev era, East Berlin authorities had reluctantly let him return, and Schwarz had established contact with Schefke. Schwarz was particularly useful because, thanks largely to the CSCE accords, he could cross checkpoints without a search. For its part, the Stasi found that a half dozen of Schwarz's new neighbors were willing to spy on him.[97]

Schefke had not told Schwarz that they were going to Leipzig, but Schwarz had independently had the same idea: to get to Leipzig, despite the ban on any journalistic activity there. By way of subterfuge, Schwarz had driven his car to the parking lot of Schönefeld Airport, outside of East Berlin, but instead of boarding a flight, he had boarded a train to Leipzig. When he arrived in Leipzig, like Radomski and Schefke, he figured that he would head for the Nikolai Church. The church seemed to be acting like a magnet, drawing onlookers all day long—including yet another acquaintance of Radomski and Schefke, a young American woman named Belinda Cooper. The two knew Cooper through mutual friends in East Berlin who were running their own protest group, for which she was a courier.[98] These mutual friends had asked Cooper to go to Leipzig and to be prepared to provide eyewitness testimony of the Monday march and the potential bloodshed. As a US citizen, she could assume that she would be able to return to the West afterward and get the message out. Until she arrived in Leipzig, however, she had no idea of how dangerous her mission actually was.

After their chance meeting at the Nikolai Church, the four came to the conclusion that, given the massive security presence, matters looked grim and there would be safety in numbers. They agreed to meet at the end of the day in the lobby of Leipzig's Hotel Merkur, to make sure everyone was still safe, and to travel back to Berlin together in Radomski and Schefke's borrowed car. Since the hotel catered to foreigners, there was less chance of violence spilling over into it, and Cooper and Schwarz could wait there without being conspicuous.[99] When the four parted, Radomski and Schefke headed back to the Reformed Church in order to climb the tower well before the start of the peace prayers at 5:00 p.m.[100]

IT SEEMED THAT everyone had the same thought that day—go to, or call, the Nikolai Church—and so the church was frenetically busy, inside as well as out. In a city without freedom of assembly, press, or speech, Leipzigers used the church's phone lines as a kind of substitute news center. From all over the city, Führer and other church staff received calls, some anonymous, alerting them to new developments. As soon as one call ended, the telephone would immediately ring again. Führer pressed his wife into service to help with the challenge of continuously answering the phone.[101] They learned that workplaces were dismissing employees early and telling them to exit the city center as soon as possible, to go home, and to stay there. Schools let children out early as well. The Nikolai also received numerous reports of uniformed officers, including army officers, appearing and congregating in ever larger numbers throughout the city. And Führer got word that party members were being told to pack the church to keep out actual prayer participants.[102]

Führer and his Nikolai Church colleagues were thus not surprised when more than a thousand party members started arriving at their doorstep at about 1:30 p.m. for a prayer service that would not start until 5:00 p.m. Later, Helmut Hackenberg would recognize that this action had backfired. The crowd of loyalists cramming into the Nikolai Church only served to keep more people out on the street, where they became harder to contain than if they had been inside.[103] As Hackenberg admitted at the end of October: "We went into the church, comrades, and I have to say, it was wrong. We sat inside and they stood outside."[104] It backfired in another way as well. Thanks to some quick thinking by Führer, it produced new converts to the cause—from within the party's own ranks.

Führer saw the church filling up with a large, grim-faced crowd reading multiple copies of the party's newspaper, *Neues Deutschland.* There were not five thousand loyalists, as Hackenberg had ordered, but it was still a good-sized crowd, already well on its way at 2:00 p.m. to filling the church.[105] Führer thought he could not allow such tension to last for three hours, because it might escalate to something worse. He decided that he had to do something to decrease the chances of a confrontation. Indicating that he knew who the early arrivals were, he announced, "You are welcome here." He informed the group that he was going to close off parts of the church to ensure that there would be room for "workers and a few Christians" to fit in once they got off work, since "the working proletariat can only arrive, at the earliest, at 4:00 p.m."[106] One of the party members present reported that after these remarks the tension decreased, and during the roughly three-hour wait that followed, party members remained seated and spoke quietly to one another.[107] Führer later remembered that party members seemed moved by his words and by the experience of spending time in the church. Some contacted him later to thank him for his handling of the potentially explosive situation. Führer recalled it as "an unbelievable event. We could never, with letters or any other way, have reached so many of the comrades" and shown them that they were not the "criminals" that their party made religious leaders out to be.[108]

By 5:00 p.m., not only the Nikolai but also the other three churches that had agreed to hold peace prayers were all packed and ready to begin. The Leipzig police estimated that there were two thousand attendees in the Nikolai Church, fifteen hundred in the Thomas Church, and a thousand

**MAP 3.
LEIPZIG CITY CENTER
AND RING ROAD**

at the Michaelis Church and Sievers's Reformed Church combined, but
staff members at the Reformed Church put the numbers at closer to double that.[109] The police also did not know about two extra attendees at the
Reformed Church, hunching down in the open-air tower. Radomski and
Schefke were doing their best to get comfortable in the damp and to avoid
the worst of the pigeon dung.

Beneath them, Sievers prepared to speak to what he counted as 1,500
people jammed into a space built for 450.[110] He opened his remarks with a
famous passage from Corinthians: "When I was a child, I spoke as a child,
I understood as a child, I thought as a child." He then told the assembled,
in simple but powerful words, that the time had come for them to put away
childish things and to become adults. Sievers knew that the two men in the

tower above his head—the two men he had let in—would do their best to
ensure that, whatever happened, the world would see that Leipzigers would
no longer allow the dictatorial regime to treat them like children.

The East German minister then invoked the American civil rights
leader Martin Luther King Jr., since Sievers, like Wonneberger, admired
him deeply. In 1964, Sievers had even enjoyed the privilege of singing in a
choir at a service King attended during his visit to both halves of divided
Berlin. The moment was one of the high points of Sievers's life, because
the way King drew from his faith the strength to carry on his own polit
ical struggle had inspired Sievers profoundly. In memory of that event,
Sievers had later hung a banner with sayings from King on the inner wall
of his church. Now, as evening fell on the night of October 9 in Leipzig,
with armed forces massing on the ring road outside his windows, Sievers
felt that his own moment of adulthood had arrived, and decided to let the
words of King guide him as he stepped forward into it.

King had stood on the steps of the Lincoln Memorial in 1963 and said,
"We must forever conduct our struggle on the high plane of dignity and
discipline. We must not allow our creative protests to degenerate into physical violence." Sievers exhorted the crowd to follow King's example. He
warned, "It will be a long process, it will be a long road . . . but on our road,
there will be no going back."[111]

Across town, the prayer session at the Nikolai Church was interrupted
when messengers delivered Kurt Masur's appeal for nonviolence, which
he had coauthored with three party secretaries and two others. It was
read aloud at the church and, later, broadcast over loudspeakers scattered
around the city. The fact that some, but not all, of the Leipzig party secretaries had signed the appeal with Masur and that its delivery to the Nikolai
had been permitted was a hint of a potential split within the party's district
leadership about how to proceed that night.[112]

The prayers came to an end in all four churches around 6:00 p.m. Despite the heavy police presence, participants then managed to make their
way to Karl Marx Square. This square had become the impromptu start for
ring marches because it was a natural staging area: a large open plaza, just
off the ring road on the eastern side of the city center, and only a couple
of minutes by foot from the Nikolai Church. There was, as a result, no
mystery about either when or where the demonstration would start, which
made it easier for security forces to ready themselves to block it.

On the night of the ninth, Schwabe remembered it as taking much
longer than a couple of minutes to get to the square, however. The sheer

press of the crowds heading there made him realize that the march that night was going to be like nothing he had ever seen in his life.[113] As they streamed eastward from the multiple churches and side streets of the city center and coalesced into one mass on the square, the marchers became conscious of their own enormous number for the first time. The previous Monday they had been in the thousands. Now they were closer to a hundred thousand, if not more.[114]

Before too long, the front of the massive group began to arc slowly around the ring to the northwest, in the direction of the main train station, even as the rear of the group was still in the process of swelling with other participants.[115] Hattenhauer, listening from solitary confinement in her cell on Harkort Street just off the southeastern section of the ring, began hearing a distant rumbling that sounded to her like thunder, or tank treads. She wondered what it meant for her. Her chief interrogator had made clear that once the shooting started outside the prison where she was being held, it would start inside as well, and the teenager would be put against a wall again, this time for a real execution.[116]

Among the marchers, her friend Schwabe found the lumbering movement of the crowd "simply overwhelming." For years, he thought, "we had tried to convince people to take their own destinies in their hands," and all of a sudden "our wish was coming true." He felt a deep sense "of pride that we had not let ourselves be intimidated by this state and by its security system."[117]

As the enormous mass of people moved slowly toward the main train station, it drew nearer to the so-called Eastern Knot, an area of the ring just before the station where the main road bent sharply to curve past a small pond and the station itself. Although Schwabe and the other marchers did not know it, this knot represented the most dangerous point on their route. There were security forces all over the city, but apparently that part of the ring, just before the train station, had been designated as the critical area to defend; according to a police officer on duty that night, security forces believed they had the best chance of stopping the march as it narrowed and slowed around the curve.[118] It was likely that the front line of the march would reach the Eastern Knot and the train station sometime after 6:30 p.m.

Hackenberg, the local party leader in charge of the deployed forces, tried to contact East Berlin as the marchers moved toward the knot. Technically, his attempt to call his superiors was unnecessary. He was the commander on-site and had received clear instructions from the man at the top, Honecker, to stop the demonstration. If all previous measures had failed to stop the march—and by that point they had—Hackenberg had full authority to use force to prevent the demonstrators from reaching the main train station.[119] No further consultation with East Berlin was required, but Hackenberg called anyway, specifically for the purpose of speaking to Krenz.

Why Hackenberg wanted to talk to Krenz at this critical moment is not entirely clear, but hints of the reasons survive in the remaining evidence. His main motivation seems to have been the news that a coup was coming. Word of Krenz's planned ouster of Honecker most likely came to Hackenberg's ears indirectly, from Krenz's friend Walter Friedrich, who had driven back to Leipzig after hearing about the potential putsch from Krenz himself. In Leipzig, Friedrich had informed Roland Wötzel, one of the party secretaries who signed the appeal with Masur, and Wötzel subsequently spent much of the evening with Hackenberg, so Wötzel probably passed on this sensational news.[120] Hackenberg's instructions to stop the demonstration with all means necessary came from Honecker—but there was now a chance that Honecker might not be in power much longer, so with his phone call the Leipzig commander most likely wanted to cover himself, in case the power hierarchy above him was about to crumble.

With the crowd approaching the Eastern Knot, Hackenberg managed, in Wötzel's presence, to get Krenz on the phone. In a later interview, Hackenberg recalled that he described the march to Krenz and estimated that there were "approximately one hundred thousand" protestors, a number that Krenz found shocking. Apparently the live video feed was not conveying the full size of the protest to East Berlin. Hackenberg added that he had spoken with Strassenburg, the head of police in Leipzig, and that it was apparent to both of them that any action by the security forces "would certainly not be bloodless." Hackenberg suggested letting the demonstration pass. Krenz was so stunned that he was unable to speak, Hackenberg recalled. When Krenz finally responded, he said that he was "unable to confirm" Hackenberg's suggestion. Instead, Krenz said that he needed to consult with someone—with whom was not clear—and that he would call back soon.[121] Hackenberg, Wötzel, and the other party secretaries in the room in Leipzig assumed Krenz meant he would confer with others quickly, most likely with Mielke, and call back within minutes, since time was running out.[122]

Krenz would later say that he did in fact call back immediately and that he ordered the troops in Leipzig to pull back.[123] There is no evidence of such an order from Krenz, however, or from any other leader of the SED in East Berlin. The evidence and testimonies that do survive tell a different story: for a long time, Krenz simply did not call. As Wötzel remembered, "A very, very long while passed, a very complicated time," until Krenz phoned again, at least half an hour later.[124] Hackenberg estimated that it was more like forty-five minutes until he heard again from Krenz, an eternity during the crisis.[125] During the interval, Police Chief Strassenburg called more units from outside Leipzig to the city in light of the size of the demonstration; the fresh police units began to move in.[126] Krenz still had not called back when the moment of decision arrived: the demonstrators were about to go through the Eastern Knot.

Hackenberg and the other party secretaries in the room with him hastily reviewed their options. While the surviving evidence is frustratingly thin and Hackenberg has died, it seems likely that at the critical moment he sought to balance a number of conflicting pressures. He had instructions to stop the progress of the march—but from Honecker, perhaps soon to be ousted by Krenz.[127] Hackenberg also knew that the East German regime was a centralized one and that all significant decisions had to come from East Berlin, not from second secretaries such as himself.[128] Even though, as acting first secretary, he notionally had the authority to start the attack, he would be unwise to do so without checking with party leaders—which he was trying to do, but without success. On top of his concerns about what was going on in East Berlin, he additionally had to deal with dissent in his own ranks in Leipzig. When some of Leipzig's secretaries had signed Masur's "Appeal of the Six" without seeking unanimity among all of the comrades, they had revealed to the public that the local party leadership was divided.[129] Hackenberg therefore knew that he did not have unanimous support for using force and must have worried that he could become a scapegoat, depending on who came out on top in the internal party struggles not only in Berlin but in Leipzig as well.

Finally, he knew that the odds that night were not in the SED's favor. He had around ten thousand men under his command. The highest internal prediction of the maximum size of the demonstration had been fifty thousand, but now he was facing double that number, if not more.[130] Of course, the marchers were unarmed, and a full-scale army deployment with parachutists and tanks would even out those odds. But for that kind of deployment he would need East Berlin's support, which at that moment was not forthcoming.[131] There was also no time to organize such a deployment before the march reached the train station, although Honecker

Marchers flood the ring road around the city center of Leipzig on the night of October 9. Aram Radomski took this photograph from the tower of the Reformed Church, which stands on the northwest arc of the ring. The video that he and Siegbert Schefke made of the same demonstration was subsequently smuggled across the Berlin Wall to a West Berlin television broadcaster. *(RHG Fo HAB 21002; photo by Aram Radomski)*

would in fact propose an airborne attack on the October 16 march.[132] The large number of marchers was thus of overwhelming significance. As one party leader later put it, "None of us was expecting to deal with masses" of that size.[133] And now, with the demonstrators closing in on the critical point, he and the other Leipzig secretaries were, as Wötzel later recalled, "left solely to our own devices."[134]

In the absence of a call from Krenz, and with the crowd closing in, Hackenberg found himself forced to make a decision on his own. At about 6:30 p.m. he issued an order to assume a defensive position. A written version of this order survives; it states that "all deployed forces" should "begin the switch to self-defense." They should attack only if either they or nearby buildings came under assault. If that happened, then they should "fight back with all means," but unless and until an attack by the crowd began, they should stand down.[135] In other words, contrary to their expectations and Honecker's still-existing instructions, Hackenberg instructed the security forces to let the demonstration pass.

Some members of those security forces had a hard time comprehending the sudden about-face. Apparently the use of fear, propaganda, and the threat of violence to make policemen do their duty had worked. A week after October 9, East German documentary makers managed to film interviews with police in Leipzig while memories were still fresh. These interviews revealed that the men under Hackenberg's command had been on a hair trigger. One police unit commander, Wolfgang Schröder, told the filmmakers that the arrival of the order to assume a self-defensive stance "was very close." The stand-down order arrived "just before our order to attack would have started." If it had not arrived when it did, he assured the filmmakers, he would have had his men "stop or break apart the demonstration" by force.[136] Another officer remembered hearing a sudden and unexpected command to "open the Eastern Knot, let the demonstrators go by, and step into the shadows." He was surprised, and knew then that there would be no bloodshed, but he also suspected that there would not be a GDR much longer.[137] One of the youngest members of the police, twenty-five-year-old Toralf Dörre, was also one of the last to get the order to pull back. "We had already received the order to start running in the direction of the demonstrators, and we had gotten to about thirty meters in front of them," he later recalled.[138] "There could not have been more adrenaline" surging through his system, "and then all of a sudden: Company halt! Turn around!"[139] Some members of the police were totally confused by what was going on and remained ready to charge. One complained that earlier that same morning their leaders had "made us hot like never before, and now absolutely nothing is happening?" He could not comprehend it: "I do not understand the world anymore."[140]

As the police stood down, the march began surging past the train station with Hackenberg still waiting for a call from Krenz or any other top party leader in East Berlin. According to Wötzel, Hackenberg finally exclaimed, "Now they don't need to call back anymore."[141] When Krenz finally did phone again, the Leipzig forces had long since taken up their defensive positions.[142] Krenz said that he approved of what Hackenberg had done. By then, there was little else that Krenz could do or say. Hackenberg had, in the end, made the decision to pull back in the presence of one hundred thousand protestors and in the absence of guidance from the center—a decision, Wötzel concluded, "for which one has to give him credit."[143]

Fʀoм ᴛʜᴇ oᴘᴇɴ-ᴀɪʀ tower of the Reformed Church, Radomski and Schefke scanned the distance for a sight of the demonstration. Finally the march curved around the Eastern Knot, flowed past the train station, and came into view. "Oh man, oh man, oh man," Radomski would remember thinking. As he described it later, the atmosphere "intensified."[144] The two young men in the church tower looked down on a "river of people." All at once, they became conscious of the "outrageousness" of it all, of the sheer power of protest.[145] The two East Berliners also became aware that irreversible events were under way, and felt grateful that they had found a way to film them. Radomski and Schefke agreed that if they could get the images out, "and if they run on Western television tomorrow, then that will change not only East Germany, not only all of Germany, but the world." They even speculated on whether or not their images might help to bring down the Berlin Wall.[146]

The march was so large, it took over two hours to pass by the tower of the Reformed Church. Within the body of the march itself, Schwabe was amazed that "there were so many people," yet he could feel "no aggression" at all. He soon broke off to go to a telephone and to call fellow dissidents in East Berlin, along with Solidarity colleagues in Poland and a host of other people.[147] He had good news to convey: the multiple appeals for non-violence—whether written on a yellow cloth, circulated by Masur and his coauthors, handed out by Wonneberger and his colleagues, spoken aloud by Sievers at the Reformed Church, or from other sources—had worked. Even members of the ruling regime had to acknowledge that the repeated calls for nonviolence by the leading figures of Leipzig and of the peaceful revolution had been decisive. Operational notes from the Stasi, made at 7:00 p.m. on the night of October 9, recorded that it was the "leaflets" that "were providing for the peaceful unfolding" of that night's march.[148] And in an interview years later, Hackenberg expressed praise for those people "who were in the demonstration and took pains to avoid any clashes, took pains to bring the demonstration to an end."[149]

If the calls for peaceful protest had failed and if the demonstrators had provoked the security forces, violence would have erupted in Leipzig, given Hackenberg's order to respond to any assault.[150] The self-discipline of the crowd ensured that such an outcome did not arise, however. Some of the security forces shared in the relief at the lack of bloodshed. As one deployed paramilitary trooper, Theo Kühirt, put it, it was almost unbelievable that a march of such size could stay as peaceful as it did. Earlier that night, upon taking his position, Kühirt had realized to his horror that no senior party officials had actually had the courage to come out on the street. As if that were not enough, a "sensible officer" gave him "a tip: disappear as soon as possible." Once the security forces had switched to a defensive posture, however, and the demonstrators started passing, Kühirt and company realized that while they had been expecting a "mob," they were instead confronted with "perfectly ordinary folks . . . shouting, 'We are the people.'"[151] Spontaneous and even friendly conversations broke out between members of the security forces and the demonstrators all along the ring, greatly improving the atmosphere.[152]

One demonstrator, Rainer Tetzner, recalled walking very close to the security forces. He could clearly see their clubs, helmets, shields, tear gas, and water cannon equipment, yet he and other protestors refused to be intimidated and shouted to them, "Not another China!" They also yelled to the security forces and to anyone else on the streets not yet in motion, "Join our ranks!" The shouts worked. People sitting in streetcars stalled by the march clambered out and joined the crowd. The ranks of onlookers became smaller and smaller as many decided to become marchers. As Tetzner recalled, by the time the demonstration got to the northwest arc of the ring "everyone was demonstrating with us, on the sidewalks, in the ten lanes of the ring road, on the tracks of the three streetcar lines." He could see "up to a hundred people, shoulder to shoulder, a river of people to which you could see no end, a river that nothing more could stop."[153]

The march's success showed that the growing wave of violence in the GDR had come to an end, that the regime had been forced into a defensive position, and that a peaceful revolution was now in full swing.[154] By about 8:30 p.m. the front line of the demonstration had swept around the full 360 degrees of the ring and returned to its starting point in Karl Marx Square. There the march began to dissolve as peacefully as it had formed, although some enthusiastic demonstrators reportedly started a second lap.[155] Meanwhile, Leipzig's main train station filled as thousands of out-of-town participants tried to make their way home.[156] Everyone involved knew that they had shared in a profound development. On the night of October 9, the activists from the Nikolai Church and the Monday marchers had won the fight for the ring road of Leipzig—and they had done so without resorting to violence.

Later that night, staff members from the West German television news show *Tagesthemen* were able to get through to Wonneberger and to broadcast a phone interview with him about the momentous events in Leipzig, despite the censorship of phone calls in the GDR. Wonneberger's relief and joy were manifest in his voice. He had, in the end, not even marched himself, because he had been too busy taking calls. In the interview, Wonneberger singled out for praise the party secretaries who had signed the appeal for nonviolence. He expressed hope that they would serve as an inspiration to their higher-ups, so that "perhaps a signal will come from the top as well."[157]

In a report later that night, Police Chief Strassenburg summarized what had happened from his point of view. A protest march of tens of thousands had come together and moved, slowly but as a well-defined group, through the city. At 6:35 p.m. he had received word that Hackenberg had decided "to undertake no active operations against these people if there were no activities hostile to the state and no attacks on security forces, buildings, and locations."[158] Unexpectedly meeting no resistance, the march had then continued along the ring road, where it had soon reached an odd bend in the road known as the "Round Corner." This corner was of particular interest to Strassenburg since the buildings looming over it housed not only his but also the Stasi's main Leipzig offices.[159] Once the protest reached that point, Strassenburg and Hummitzsch, the local Stasi leader, could follow the march with their own eyes.[160] Mielke even called Hummitzsch later to ensure that the Stasi offices had not been stormed by protestors as part of that night's protest. Mielke asked if "the house is still standing" and added that, in his opinion, the "working class had been attacked" on the night of October 9 in Leipzig.[161]

In his own report for Stasi headquarters, Hummitzsch wrote that from about 6:35 p.m. to 8:30 p.m. there had been an unapproved demonstration of "50,000 to 60,000, repeat 50,000 to 60,000, persons, including a substantial number who arrived by train or car from other districts." He added that "thousands of onlookers followed and accompanied" the demonstration. The chants that they shouted included "Gorbi, Gorbi," as a call for Gorbachev's help; "We are the people"; "Let the prisoners out"; and, perhaps most ominously for the regime, "We are staying here."[162]

Hummitzsch also spoke with Hackenberg at 9:01 p.m. to discuss, among other things, what the headline of the main Leipzig newspaper should be for the next day. In his notes of the conversation, Hummitzsch recorded that the top story should be praise for the security forces, whose actions were "characterized by level-headedness."[163] Unsurprisingly, the newspaper headline the next day was, in fact, "Characterized by Level-Headedness."[164]

Honecker's response to the march was unhinged. He wanted to try again to crush the demonstrations a week later, on Monday, October 16. Upon hearing that Leipzig party secretaries had signed Masur's appeal, Honecker reportedly sniped that "those who want to capitulate are already sitting in the district leadership."[165] The party leader called for the use of "all measures" on the following Monday, including an aerial assault by army parachutists and the deployment of Stasi "special forces," but he had lost too much ground.[166] For reasons that are not entirely clear, but which suggest that his control was already slipping, contradictory language appeared in his written orders of October 13 when they were circulated. These instructions said that security forces should use any means necessary to stop the October 16 march—but they should not use guns.[167] It seemed that even some party officials in East Berlin had finally noticed that the steadily increasing levels of violence had become self-defeating. And the entire issue became a moot point once Krenz began the process of ousting Honecker.

Dickel, the interior minister, would later lament that Krenz's coup ended any chance of a real crackdown in Leipzig. In a speech to his subordinates on October 21, Dickel complained about the legacy of the one hundred thousand marchers for the internal politics of the GDR. Dickel said that if it were up to him, he would love to go to Leipzig personally and beat the demonstrators into such misshapen pulps that "no jacket would fit them anymore," adding pointedly, "I was responsible in 1953 here in Berlin" during the crackdown on the uprising of that year. Under Krenz, however, Dickel had realized that he could not replay 1953. The party was going to have to become more tactical and clever about repressing dissent.[168]

A s MEMBERS OF the Leipzig security forces were drafting their official reports, Radomski and Schefke were trying to figure out how to get their own unofficial footage safely down from the tower of the Reformed Church. Throughout the peace prayers and the march they had stayed concealed, not least because the tower stood across the ring road from a large store and they could see men they assumed to be Stasi agents openly filming their own video from the store's roof. Radomski and Schefke knew that they were potentially in the Stasi's line of sight, and they did not want to attract attention.[169] Before, during, and after the demonstration, they stayed low and covered up the small red light on their Panasonic video camera.[170] And despite the pigeon dung, the damp, and the dark, Radomski and Schefke did not rush to get down from the church tower once the massive demonstration had finally passed by. Having gotten such important images on film, they did not want to have their lone videocassette confiscated at the last minute. They "sat around for an hour" after the march ended and came down only once they were absolutely certain that it was safe to do so.[171]

When it finally was, they went downstairs to Sievers. By coincidence, Sievers had recently acquired a VCR—a rare item in the GDR—with help from his in-laws in the West, and so he, Radomski, and Schefke decided to use it to view the tape. The minister found it impressive. He also knew that as soon as the images were shown, it would not be hard to guess from where they had been filmed.[172] Indeed, after the footage appeared on West German TV, members of his congregation asked if it had been filmed from the church's tower. Sievers thought it best to play dumb. He knew that his fellow minister in the church, Roland Schein, would not approve. Schein was deeply worried that helping protestors would lead to a visit from armed security forces. As Sievers put it, perhaps with some sympathy, Schein "was not in favor of anything that might get himself shot."[173]

As Sievers, Radomski, and Schefke watched the footage, one of Sievers's sons came in. Instead of trying to get him out of the room as he had done earlier that day, however, Sievers suddenly decided that he should watch too. His son was amazed to see on his family's television video footage of the event that had just occurred. He came to understand that it had been filmed by the two strangers in his home. When the video ended, still without exchanging any names, Radomski and Schefke packed up their equipment and left.[174] They met Cooper and Schwarz at the Hotel Merkur as planned. Schwarz remembered that the mood was curiously tense and relaxed at the same time. As he would later put it, "In that kind of situation, you do not spend a lot of time reflecting."[175]

After a quick bite to eat, the four packed into the borrowed East German car, which quickly started having mechanical difficulties. One of the engine's two cylinders had developed some kind of a problem. They pulled over at a garage, but when it became apparent that the cylinder could not be fixed quickly, they grew worried about lingering too long. The mechanic told them that they should keep their speed below sixty kilometers, or forty miles, per hour. Obeying, they slowly made their way to Schönefeld Airport, with the car emitting a foul smell the entire way.[176]

Cooper remembered feeling an enormous sense of relief when they pulled up to Schwarz's much nicer, Western car in the parking lot at the airport. Schwarz, taking the videocassette from Radomski and Schefke, departed with Cooper and dropped her off alone at the nearest suitable border crossing, so that she would not be associated with the transport of the video. He had asked neither her name nor the contents of the cassette. He did not want to know either, in case he was stopped.[177] Meanwhile, Radomski and Schefke continued back into downtown East Berlin. After reuniting vehicles with their owners, Schefke clambered back into his own apartment as he had left it: over the roof of a nearby building.[178]

With the cassette hidden in his underwear, Schwarz headed for a checkpoint in the early hours of October 10. Thanks to the CSCE, he usually had the privilege of being able to cross without a search, but in the tense days of October 1989 he was not certain whether the officials would respect that privilege. He was able to cross without incident, however, and delivered the cassette to Jahn, still not knowing what was on it.[179] Jahn took the cassette to his office at the West Berlin television station SFB.[180]

Looking at the raw video footage of the seemingly endless river of people in Leipzig, Jahn began crying. He recalled that when he had taken part in demonstrations in the early 1980s in his hometown, Jena, even thirty people had seemed like a lot. For the rest of October 10, he edited the video and ensured that it was broadcast as often as possible, not least because West Berlin and West German coverage could be received in much of East Germany. Foreign stations picked up the footage as well, spreading the images around the world. The footage was indeed seen as far away as America, just as Sievers had hoped that it would be.[181]

This video, along with some other clips that would trickle out of Leipzig later, had a dramatic and motivating effect on the peaceful revolution throughout the GDR. It also served to undermine the ruling regime. While the SED's violence was self-defeating, it became self-defeating more quickly because of the bright light that Western broadcasters could shine on it, thanks to Jahn's smuggling network. In other words, the efforts of activists such as Hattenhauer, Schwabe, Wonneberger, and their colleagues were sped along by the efforts of their chroniclers and witnesses, including Cooper, Jahn, Radomski, Schefke, and Schwarz. This symbiosis between the protestors and their publicizers was truly dangerous to the dictatorial regime.

For Radomski and Schefke, the triumph was bittersweet. They had achieved a major success and a measure of revenge, but the world did not know to whom it owed the images. Jahn had consistently kept Radomski's and Schefke's names secret, even though by 1989 their video footage was selling so well to television stations in the West that the two East Berliners actually owed taxes on the profits. As a result, when the major West German network ARD broadcast their hard-won October 9 footage from Leipzig on its evening news show, *Tagesthemen,* the show's anchorman indicated misleadingly that the video came from an Italian camera team.[182] Schefke was watching at home in East Berlin and felt frustrated. On one hand, he was already awash in Stasi surveillance and did not need more of it, or an arrest. On the other hand, he wanted recognition. "It wasn't exactly making us famous" to see their own work presented as the work of an Italian camera crew, Schefke thought. The thirty-year-old wanted to be able to brag once in a while, "to show off to women," to respond honestly when asked, "What do you do?" instead of mumbling something about being unemployed. "Telling a woman you were unemployed, it wasn't such a hit. It made us look like losers. We wanted to be able to tell women what great guys we were."

Jahn was worried about Radomski and Schefke getting worn down by working hard, enduring repeated interrogations, fearing prison, and failing to get any recognition. The grind was indeed getting to them. The two East Berliners were both worried enough that they had filmed short video clips of each other and sent them to Jahn to be played on Western television if they disappeared. Jahn was concerned that Radomski and Schefke might try to smuggle themselves out of East Germany, and so he told them to wait. After Leipzig, Jahn said, it could not be much longer before major change would come.[183]

The triumph was bittersweet for Wonneberger as well. For many years he had worked hard to promote change in his home country. He had endured not only constant surveillance by the Stasi but also ongoing tension with his church colleagues. October 9 was a night of success, but the strain of years of opposition work was about to take its toll on him. Three weeks later, he suffered a massive stroke that rendered him unable to talk. By 1991, he had been released from his ministry duties altogether due to his ongoing incapacitation. As his country finally gained the freedoms for which he had struggled, Wonneberger had to learn anew how to speak.[184]

Thanks to him and to the marchers of October 9, the regime was now facing a struggle of its own. On that night, there had been a yawning gap where orders from the center should have been. As one activist, Tobias Hollitzer, would later remark, the "only central decision . . . was the belated blessing of the facts on the ground that had already been created by the courage and peacefulness" of the protestors.[185] The SED had to recover from its defeat in Leipzig and to regain control somehow. Krenz decided that the best way to begin doing so was to commence his coup against Honecker. Then Krenz would try to suppress the widespread desire for travel and emigration as well as the rising power of the peaceful revolution, hoping to be more successful than Honecker had been. All of these challenges would come to a head at the same moment in November 1989, bringing the contest for control to the streets of East Berlin and to the Wall itself.

PART II

The Competition for Control in East Berlin

Chapter Four

The Revolution Advances, the Regime Plays for Time

I F PARTY LEADERS COULD HIDE from their subordinates on the night of October 9, they could not hide from the consequences afterward. Thanks to the inaction of the massed security forces in Leipzig, and the footage of that inaction broadcast on television channels that East Germans could receive, the feeling of fear on the part of potential protestors throughout the country diminished rapidly. Both the number and size of demonstrations throughout the GDR grew dramatically as a result.[1] A new spirit of cooperation among opposition leaders in various locations in the GDR also became evident. In the past there had often been friction between dissident groups in East Berlin and elsewhere in the country, such as in Dresden and Leipzig. There were, for example, disagreements over how much help to accept from the West and how much to involve Western media. The young American courier Belinda Cooper also remembered much acrimony between the East German opposition group that she was serving and people in West Berlin who were trying to support it.[2] For his part, Uwe Schwabe later recalled that East Berliners had, at times, accused him and his Leipzig colleagues of creating "action without content." In return, the Leipzig dissidents felt that Berliners were too ponderous and took themselves too seriously.[3] But, overall, the events of October 1989 fostered mutual sympathy, solidarity, and trust among dissidents throughout the country.

The Gethsemane Church in East Berlin, in particular, became a major venue for public events in solidarity with Leipzig opposition leaders.

Marianne Birthler, a youth liaison officer at the church, helped to organize such events. Born in 1948, Birthler had grown up in divided Berlin with a mother who had made her and her siblings pause and listen every Sunday at noon, when the ringing of the "Freedom Bell"—a gift from Great Britain and the United States for the tower of the Schöneberg Town Hall in West Berlin—was broadcast by radio. Even as a child, Birthler had been aware of the importance of Western broadcasters.[4]

Just as Leipzigers had used the Nikolai Church as an unofficial news agency, so too had the Gethsemane Church become an alternative clearinghouse for information by autumn 1989. Working together with leading activists from the Environmental Library, such as Tom Sello, dissidents in both the church and the library tried to draw attention to the crimes of the ruling regime. The goal was, as Sello put it, "not to let up," to keep up the pressure, to motivate others to get involved, and to shame the regime.[5] Both places had become a kind of refuge as a result. When East Germans had shouted "Gorbi, Gorbi" and other unapproved slogans at the Soviet leader during the fortieth-anniversary celebrations on October 7—Mikhail Gorbachev, reluctantly, had come to East Berlin for the event—and police had dispersed the crowds by force, those who had suffered personally or had witnessed the violence, such as seeing a police truck running over a protestor, felt the need to bear witness.[6] A number of such people ended up in Birthler's office in the church, where they would describe their experiences to her.[7]

Listening to so many tragic stories, she soon became overwhelmed and, to give herself a respite, started asking visitors to put their experiences on paper instead. Once she began reading the written versions, Birthler realized that she had unintentionally hit upon a very powerful idea. "As I read the first two or three," she recalled later, "I thought: 'My God! They all have to write.'"[8] By having all such visitors to her office produce written testimonies, and then compiling them into a catalog of cruelty, she realized that she could contradict misleading official announcements that the violent incidents had been rare or isolated. In total, Birthler and her coworkers assembled 160 detailed testimonies of police brutality, drawing the attention of the Stasi as they did so.[9] She distributed multiple copies of the catalog and even held a press conference about it with foreign journalists in attendance.[10]

Birthler spent the evening of October 9 at the Gethsemane Church. As the Monday march progressed in Leipzig, her church opened its doors to anyone who wanted to pray for the demonstration's success and to hear uncensored news from the Gethsemane's so-called contact telephone first-hand.[11] After Schwabe broke off from the Leipzig march, the Gethsemane Church was one of the first places that he called with an update. Birthler was on duty at the church's contact telephone and fully expected that Schwabe would be calling with a report of massive bloodshed. Decades later, she still remembered the joy she felt when the call came and she heard instead the words "The ring is free."[12]

She and her coworkers immediately told the assembled mass in the Gethsemane Church the amazing news, and "an unbelievable storm of applause" erupted. After they celebrated for a while, someone even got up the courage necessary to crack open the Gethsemane's front doors "to see what it looked like outside." Earlier, there had been barricades and lines of uniformed troops out front, but they had all disappeared. Now area residents were coming out of their apartments and putting candles on the streets where the police had been. A sea of tiny lights greeted Birthler and others as they pushed the doors of the Gethsemane Church fully open. Standing in the doorway and looking at the candlelight stretching off into the distance, she suddenly felt compelled to say, "This is how freedom feels."[13]

PARTY LEADERS HAD no such feelings of exhilaration as they assessed how they had reached this point and what needed to change. Erich Honecker's methods in Leipzig had been those of an older generation of Communists who had survived persecution under the Nazis through, in part, an uncompromising and rigid adherence to set policies.[14] The fact, obvious to all by October 9, was that this approach was no longer working. Even Erich Mielke, the leader of the Stasi, realized that Honecker had to go. On October 16, Mielke gave Egon Krenz a private warning about how dangerous matters were getting. The Stasi minister forwarded a report indicating that Honecker's hard-line handling of dissidents had not quashed their movement but instead generated sympathy among workers and even party members, a frightening development. Often such reports were circulated to all Politburo members, but Mielke sent this one only to Krenz.[15] This report also warned that "extremely critical attitudes were increasing both in number and intensity" and that the blame fell on "the party leadership." Mielke's cover note to Krenz emphasized that "the seriousness of the situation becomes . . . even more clear" when taking into account the fact that it "is now already a question of the workers" and their attitudes as well, not just a few dissidents.[16]

The subtext to Mielke's message was that there was always the potential for mass action to escalate to mass violence.[17] Although the large protests in Leipzig had been peaceful, in the eyes of the regime that could still change. An additional worry was emerging as well: members of the Stasi were being contacted by their colleagues in Moscow because of scattered but increasing incidences of confrontations in October 1989 between East German citizens and Soviet troops. Exact causes were difficult to determine—in one case, an East German said that Soviet troops were trying to pilfer his property—but to the SED leaders, the incidents raised a troubling new specter as well.[18]

Krenz decided that the time had come to proceed with the ouster. At the Politburo meeting of Tuesday, October 17, he and his co-conspirator Mielke arranged to have "reliable colleagues" near the meeting room in case Honecker tried to have his personal bodyguard restrain or arrest coup plotters.[19] When the meeting started, Honecker was startled by a motion to vote on his dismissal and that of two of his closest allies. At first he tried to act as if he had not heard the motion, proceeding to the top item on the scheduled agenda instead, but his comrades shouted him down. He found himself forced to listen as one member of the Politburo after another spoke in favor of his ouster.[20] Mielke stated that "we simply cannot start shooting with tanks." Speaking plainly, he said, "Erich," it is "the end." The vote to remove Honecker passed.[21] The next day, the party's central committee accepted Honecker's "resignation" and installed Krenz in his stead.[22]

Once the coup was publicized, however, it did not have the hoped-for effect. According to a Stasi report, Krenz's "election" was greeted "above all with skepticism, but also in many cases with rejection." Citizens of East Germany did "not trust Krenz to carry out the necessary new politics" that they regarded as essential.[23] Party members themselves were worried about the widespread popular resentment of Krenz's involvement in two notorious events: the egregious falsification of GDR election results from May 7, 1989, and the extensive praise of the Tiananmen Square massacre in June 1989. The people of the GDR viewed these as "heavy moral failings that Egon Krenz would not be able to make good." A British diplomat in East Berlin described popular attitudes toward Krenz as characterized by "intense antipathy."[24] Even after Krenz took over, a sense of "uncertainty, of being without direction, and of resignation" remained apparent within the party.[25] The regime received multiple reports on the worsening public opinion toward the regime despite Honecker's ouster.[26]

All the while, Leipzig activists kept up the pressure. Although Wonneberger's stroke would soon sideline him, the party's district office reported that the assertiveness of the Protestant ministers Führer and Sievers only continued to grow.[27] By Monday, October 30, seven churches in Leipzig were holding prayer sessions, and the march that night topped two hundred thousand participants. Some demonstrators reportedly carried West German flags with them.[28] Marchers had even lingered dramatically in front of the Stasi office in Leipzig that night. Officials inside wondered if the protectors were preparing to enter the building. They would eventually do so, although not until the end of the year. When they did, they would discover inside a mix of banality, bureaucracy, and even pornography. The walls and desks of the Stasi offices bore, among the expected paperwork, numerous explicit photographs of female body parts. There were also less than successful attempts at humor. One Stasi desk bore a paperweight reading, "Every third person who complains will be shot. Two people have been here already!"[29]

The reports of protestors lingering in front of the Leipzig Stasi headquarters on October 30 seem to have compelled Mielke to instruct his ministry to prepare to defend not only the Leipzig office but also other sites throughout the GDR. He called for the distribution of "fire extinguishers, blankets, water buckets," and chemical means of defense, although exactly what those were remains unclear.[30] Instructions were also issued to begin moving documents to secure locations or, in some cases, to start destroying them outright.[31] At the beginning of November, the Stasi agents of the so-called Department M, which censored mail in post offices, were told to dismantle their workstations and to remove all evidence of them.[32] Around this time, Mielke, a man of sharp political instincts, apparently realized it was time to abandon his own sinking ship. He sent an unusual letter to every single member of the Stasi at the start of November. Although not stating explicitly that he was resigning, it suggested that he had done so, or was about to do so, thus creating even more uncertainty and anxiety in the ranks about what was to come.[33]

IN RESPONSE TO the mounting pressure, Krenz, the new leader, employed rhetoric that sounded conciliatory. The Politburo's actions in late October and November 1989 under his leadership would reveal, however, that he ultimately suffered from the same intransigence as his predecessor. In contrast to later claims, no evidence has surfaced to show that once

Krenz and his supporters took over, they suddenly decided to open the Wall on November 9, 1989. Rather, they made reformist statements in public while maintaining as much control as possible behind the scenes. Even as Krenz discussed easing some travel restrictions publicly, his security and interior ministers advised him and the Politburo on October 30 that if they could not fight against "anti-socialist" organizations "with political means, then a possible declaration of martial law cannot be ruled out."[34]

Politburo members decided in late October to investigate ways to loosen travel restrictions slightly as a concession to popular pressure.[35] They aimed to produce an allegedly new travel law, but that law's bureaucratic fine print would still allow the party, through the state apparatus, to control the movement of its people. Passports and visas, both issued only with the approval of the relevant state offices, would remain required. In public, however, the measure was to be presented as a major change. Krenz signaled this new approach in a speech to the Volkskammer, the party-controlled GDR legislature. He told the parliament that it was necessary to think about "why so many people have turned their backs" on the GDR.[36]

Krenz hoped that such travel concessions might come with an additional benefit besides a cooling of the opposition's anger and momentum: crucial economic support from Bonn. Honecker's ouster had loosened the tongues of those in the know about the economic health of East Germany, which was poor. By 1989, the GDR was indebted beyond all hope to the West.[37] In the wake of Krenz's takeover, party leaders received an "unretouched" assessment of the economic health of the GDR. East Germany was approaching insolvency and was to the greatest possible extent dependent on Western credit.[38]

Even before Krenz took over, he corresponded about this dependency with Alexander Schalck-Golodkowski, one of the Politburo's savviest servants, a kind of in-the-shadows hustler who dealt with such issues. From his so-called Office of Commercial Coordination, Schalck had for years coordinated the subsidizing of East Germany by Bonn through various means.[39] He had also managed an enormous hard-currency slush fund under the personal control of Honecker, estimated to be worth 100 million DM, which had now passed to Krenz.[40] In October 1989, Schalck advised Krenz that it might be possible to solve the Politburo's travel and indebtedness problems at one stroke: loosen existing restrictions, and extract a reward from Bonn in return. The West German government was always pressing for more travel freedom, Schalck pointed out. But how could East Germans travel when their state had no hard currency to give them for the trip? Clearly, if the East was going to let its people go west, then West Germany would have to help. Schalck was reminding Krenz that East Germany could do what it had been doing for years—receive support from Bonn in exchange for easing restrictions on its people—but now on a massive scale. The Politburo could also renew its demands that the West Germans stop issuing passports to East Germans who made it to an FRG embassy in a third country, a practice that made emigration even easier for those who could escape the GDR.[41]

Put bluntly, the party would be selling its most precious asset, namely, the Berlin Wall, although no one discussed the concept in such terms at the time. Instead, in his description of it in Bonn, Schalck tried to phrase the idea as a general easing of travel restrictions. Implicitly, though, the Wall was on the trading block. The question now was whether, and what, the West would pay. Krenz agreed that the plan was worth investigating. Schalck began talks on October 24 with Rudolf Seiters, the head of the chancellery office, and Wolfgang Schäuble, the interior minister and confidant of the chancellor, to see what Bonn would give the SED in exchange for increased political liberties in the GDR and for "de facto unlimited travel between the two German states."[42]

Krenz personally followed up on the matter during a phone call with Helmut Kohl two days later. The East German leader pointedly referred to "the proposals that my emissary has made. The GDR is very interested in an answer," he added expectantly. Kohl would not be drawn into a detailed discussion, however. He countered by pointing out the need for a range of other reforms as well, including amnesty for political prisoners. Krenz replied that Kohl had clearly misunderstood what was on offer: the general secretary did not want to introduce reform in the GDR, turn to a new course, or bring about major change. There would be no big break with the past because "a socialist GDR remains in the interest of stability in Europe." Rather, Krenz's goals were more specific: a temporary loosening of travel restrictions before Christmas, as a gift to his people. The call between the leaders of the two German states ended inconclusively.[43]

In the hope that this strategy would eventually work, Krenz pressed on, despite the lackluster response from Bonn. An additional motivation for Krenz appears to have been memory of the opening of the Hungarian border and the chaotic scenes of tens of thousands fleeing; he did not want to risk a repetition of those events.[44] A working group began brainstorming in late October on what would eventually become a draft of a new travel law. The group operated under the premise that whatever regulation they produced should not result in "the depopulation of the GDR," should require applicants to get both "passport and visa"—that is, to ask for permission and receive approval—and should allow only 15 DM for travel purposes.[45] An internal note to the Politburo on October 26, 1989, suggested that if the idea was to be implemented, there would be a need to consider measures "for orderly processing at the border, especially to West Berlin."[46] At the same time, Krenz and his fellow Politburo members also started dropping hints to visiting politicians that travel restrictions might be loosened for Christmas.[47]

One such visitor was the Social Democratic mayor of West Berlin, Walter Momper, who in East Berlin on October 29 had his first official meeting with leaders of the opposition in the GDR. The organization New Forum had emerged as the single most important countrywide activist group, and in recognition of the group's growing popularity, Momper visited East Berlin to speak to Bärbel Bohley, one of its founders and leaders. As part of the trip, the mayor also spoke with Günter Schabowski, a Politburo member responsible for media affairs who, it was rumored, was now the number-two man in the party behind Krenz.[48] At the end of their long conversation, Schabowski mentioned casually to the mayor of West Berlin that there might be some easing of travel restrictions for Christmas. Momper later remembered that he felt "as if struck by an electric shock." He inquired about practical considerations, such as transport arrangements and the opening of additional border crossings between the two halves of Berlin—the very point that the internal Politburo note had raised. From Schabowski's surprised reaction to such seemingly self-evident questions, however, it became obvious to Momper that Schabowski had "not yet thought of any of the practical consequences." When the mayor pressed the matter, pointing out the need to plan for practicalities, Schabowski refused to consider such issues. He blithely assured Momper that since passports and visas would still be required, his regime would be able to limit the flow of travel to manageable levels very easily. The mayor finally gave up, deciding that Schabowski was making empty promises; in any case, Momper "was not there to give Schabowski lessons" in urban transport and event planning. The mayor did decide, just in case, to let the Western allies know of Schabowski's remarks, and Momper also formed a working group to speculate on the potential implications of those remarks. West Berlin, at least, would consider the practical consequences of a loosening of East German travel restrictions on some theoretical "Day X," as Momper called it, even if East Berlin would not.[49]

MAP 4.
DIVIDED BERLIN
IN 1989

Heiligensee/Stolpe

FRENCH
SECTOR

STASI PRISON,
HOHENSCHÖNHAUSEN ■

Bornholmer St.

Chaussee St.

Staaken

Invaliden St.   Friedrich St.
REICHSTAG ■   ■ ALEXANDERPLATZ
           ■ BRANDENBURG GATE   ■ STASI HEADQUARTERS,
                                    NORMANNEN ST.

BRITISH
SECTOR

Checkpoint
Charlie   Heinrich-
          Heine St.

US SECTOR

Sonnenallee

SOVIET
SECTOR

Dreilinden/
Drewitz

Waltersdorfer
Chaussee

▬▬▬ Course of the Berlin Wall
 O   Border Crossing Point
 ■   Point of Interest

0   5 mi
0   5 km

MEANWHILE, SINCE THE travel reform that Krenz had envisaged was taking shape in the form of a draft law, both Friedrich Dickel and Mielke, the interior and Stasi ministers, respectively, were becoming involved, since their agencies handled implementation of such laws.[50] Their ministries were, of course, notionally state offices but actually subordinate to the party organizations and to the Politburo (and Mielke was a Politburo member). Hence, when the Politburo wanted the security and interior ministers to do something, they did it.[51]

Dickel assigned his subordinate Gerhard Lauter the task of supervising the drafting of the law and other matters related to the potential practicalities of implementation.[52] Lauter, born in Dresden and educated in Leipzig, was a party loyalist in the extreme. He had risen rapidly through the ranks, first of the police and then of the Ministry of the Interior. Lauter had experience with both weapons and counterterrorism operations and had even taken part in a successful hunt for a deserter from the Soviet armed forces.[53] On top of all of this, he was also an "unofficial employee" of the Stasi, meaning that he served the Stasi in addition to the police and

Interior Ministry.[54] His loyalty and ambition earned him a swift ascent in the ministry hierarchy. In 1989, at the age of thirty-nine, he was already head of a department. His success was also due in part to his family name. His father, Hans Lauter, born in 1914, had joined a Communist youth organization as a teenager and at age nineteen was arrested by the Gestapo. After 1945, he resumed his party work and became an SED party secretary.[55] The elder Lauter was purged, rehabilitated, and then dismissed again over the course of a long career. The younger Lauter admired his father greatly and was proud to come from "the family of a party soldier," if a controversial one. Gerhard Lauter was, in essence, a party princeling.[56]

The younger Lauter and his colleagues produced the requested draft quickly and as instructed. Then, however, the process slowed down. To make sure that the members of the council of ministers could be held responsible for the draft, Lauter was told to secure signatures from each of them personally. The process took days. Often a minister would make Lauter wait for hours before providing a signature, which Lauter found extremely frustrating.[57] His draft was not ready until November 2.[58] Lauter was then instructed to defend the draft law on television. After he appeared on-screen in a police uniform, he realized that he had become "the villain" who would be blamed for the draft law, even though much of it had been ordered from on high.[59]

While Lauter sat in ministerial waiting rooms seeking signatures, new crises began to threaten the party's leaders. There were threats of massive strikes unless travel to Czechoslovakia under the old rules—with minimal paperwork, rather than with a passport and visa—resumed. The Politburo decided that it had to give in.[60] As a result, after travel to Czechoslovakia resumed under the old rules on Wednesday, November 1, the flood of refugees resumed as well. The West German embassy in Prague filled again. By Friday, November 3, more than four thousand East Germans had gathered at the Prague embassy, once more enduring miserable conditions. Even worse, Czech officials were livid at being forced to deal with such a situation yet again.[61] And, as if that were not enough, the West German equivalent of an ambassador to East Germany, Franz Bertele, informed Krenz on November 3 that his office, the permanent representation in East Berlin, which had allegedly been closed for renovations, would soon reopen. The real reason for its closure was that there had been 130 East German refugees sheltering in it as of August 7; Bonn had suddenly announced the closure as a way of preventing more people from entering.[62] Now Bertele was threatening Krenz with the information that the office would "reopen in the coming weeks," presumably to a new wave of refugees. Krenz asked Bertele if his office "might not perhaps need more time for the [renovation] work." Bertele did not respond.[63]

A S THESE DISCUSSIONS were taking place, the peaceful revolution in East Germany kept going from strength to strength. A kind of competition between the regime and the revolution for control over the streets of East Berlin was unfolding. Instead of using force, however, rock musicians used their voices and instruments to call for democracy, openness, and reform at a major concert, to the intense dismay of the Stasi.[64] Meanwhile, Bohley's organization, the New Forum, kept winning more and more adherents as it called for political reform. Bohley and her fellow organizers decided to take the symbolic step of applying to become an approved organization, although the group was growing rapidly even without official approval. On Krenz's personal instruction, she and her colleagues were denied that approval. The New Forum's popularity kept rising despite, or perhaps because of, the denial.[65] And a young pastor, Markus Meckel, together with friends and colleagues, similarly thumbed his nose at the ruling regime by founding a new and independent Social Democratic Party of East Germany, its predecessor having long since been subsumed by the SED.[66]

For Saturday, November 4, a theater group proposed a large public demonstration in East Berlin, meaning an event on the scale of the Leipzig Monday marches for the capital of the GDR. This move represented a new level of escalation in the struggle for the streets of East Berlin. Despite misgivings, the ruling regime decided to allow the event. It was not clear how the demonstration's organizers would react to a ban, and Krenz was trying to appear conciliatory in public. The party also scheduled Schabowski to represent the SED by speaking at the event.[67] And in an effort to assert his leadership, Krenz spoke, after just two hours' notice, on GDR television and radio stations the day before the demonstration. He told East Germans trying to leave the GDR to stay home: "Your place is here." Krenz then promised an announcement on travel and emigration policy in the near future, referring to the "soon-to-be published draft of a new travel law."[68]

Internally, the language used by Krenz and his comrades would have been less heartening had the public been aware of it. The Stasi worried that there might be attempts to storm the Wall by force during the November 4 demonstration. Also on that eventful Friday, Krenz issued an order that was forwarded by the Stasi to all of its district and other subordinate offices. The order instructed the secret police to prevent unauthorized attempts to cross the GDR's borders by "the use of bodily violence," if necessary. However, members of the Stasi were not supposed to use guns if there were "possible demonstrations."[69] Exactly what that meant for border officers was hard to discern. The Krenz regime seemed unable to deliver a straightforward message in any context. Krenz was, on one hand, promising reforms on television without really delivering them and, on the other, trying to maintain a repressive regime without giving the security forces the full license to use the weapons that they would need to do so.

As November 4 dawned, it became clear that the demonstration in East Berlin would be a truly huge event. An estimated half million participants flooded Alexanderplatz, in the heart of the city. Aerial photographs showed a city center completely darkened by the swarm of people. The event continued for much of the day with a long list of speakers, including Schabowski. Birthler was asked to be one of the speakers as well. Despite her anxiety about being in front of such a large crowd, she agreed to do so. She wore her boyfriend's coat to help her nerves, thinking that it would be as if he were hugging her while she stood onstage. Looking out at the sea of people, she found herself silently asking for forgiveness, realizing that she had been too pessimistic about her fellow East Germans. "I had not trusted the people to have so much self-confidence and courage," she recalled; she was amazed to see so much of both on display on November 4.[70] Aram Radomski, who also took part in that day's demonstration, found something else amazing in hindsight, namely, that neither he nor anyone else at the demonstration did what the regime feared most: charge the Wall. On November 4, that barrier, the regime's final circle of control, still held its power over the people of East Germany.

THE FOLLOWING MONDAY, November 6, all major GDR newspapers printed the text of Lauter's draft travel law.[71] Despite accompanying press articles praising it as a comprehensive change, the text that Lauter and his colleagues had produced was clearly no such thing.[72] For one, since it was a draft, not a law, it produced no actual change.[73] And even if it soon became law, under its rules would-be travelers still had to apply for permission, and through the exact same offices as before.[74] Although these offices were now supposed to make decisions "quickly," the actual processing time was thirty days to respond to applications for visits abroad (three days if urgent, but "urgent" remained undefined) and three to six months for those applying for emigration. Significantly, the draft still allowed the state to refuse applications for the familiar, nebulous reasons: in order to protect "national security, public order, the health or the morals or rights and freedom of others as necessary."[75] In addition, a paragraph noted that "approval of an application for travel does not mean that the citizen is entitled to any means of paying for the trip"—that is, any foreign currency.[76] Ernst Höfer, the East German minister of finance, aggravated the insult two days later when he was asked if there was any possibility that foreign currency might be made available. "We don't want to make promises we can't keep," he replied.[77] Finally, before the draft could become law, a thirty-day discussion period was supposed to take place, and a newly formed commission invited all East Germans to write letters with their opinions. Forty thousand letters resulted.[78] In short, the draft fulfilled the party's instructions. It would not depopulate the GDR, it still required travelers to seek approval and paperwork from the state, and it would not drain the country's coffers.

It would not satisfy the public, however. The draft provoked outrage both in East Berlin and in the rest of the country. Citizens complained to party offices about the "limiting of visa length to thirty days" and about "the length of time that it might take to process any resulting application," as well as about the fact that "the question of financial means is not resolved." Mayor Momper was visiting Prague when he got word that the draft had become public, and he had a version faxed to him in his Czech hotel. The wording confirmed Momper's worst suspicions about Schabowski's vague promises; the draft was, as he put it, "complete trash." The regime was offering travel freedom in name only. The fine print, allowing the state to choke off travel, had hardly changed from existing regulations. From Czechoslovakia, Momper issued a press release dismissing the draft entirely.[79]

In the meantime, Schalck kept trying to extract support from Bonn. The day the draft was published, Schalck met with the West German chancellery officials Schäuble and Seiters once more, and decided to be very specific about what he wanted. Schalck asked for a credit of about 10 billion DM in the next two years, and then 2 to 3 billion DM more per year, every year, starting in 1991. By way of exchange, Schalck made it clear that the credit would be "bound to a physical structure," implying the Berlin Wall. He also suggested that the Wall would open only if West Germany agreed to his proposal.[80]

The two West Germans, Schäuble and Seiters, would not take the bait.
Bonn knew that it was in a strong position. Kohl and his advisors were
savvy enough to realize that the overwhelmingly negative public response
to the draft law had put the East German ruling regime in a much worse
negotiating position.[81] Fueled in part by dismay at the draft, the Leipzig
protest the same day saw a half million people—equal to nearly the entire
population of the city—circle the ring road despite a cold, drenching rain.
The marchers demanded the abolition of travel and emigration restrictions
altogether.[82]

The impact of Lauter's draft even earned attention as far away as Washington. A senior staffer at the National Security Agency, Robert Blackwill,
assessed the draft for his boss, National Security Advisor Brent Scowcroft. As Blackwill put it, even though the draft had been a catastrophe, it
showed that "the future of divided Europe" was now up for grabs. "Nothing save the US-Soviet strategic relationship is more central to our national
security," Blackwill concluded. He felt that the best outcome would be
"gradual evolution toward internal liberalization in the GDR." However,
nightmarish outcomes were possible as well: "In the event of severe internal unrest in the GDR, our overriding objective should be to prevent a
Soviet military intervention, which could and probably would reverse the
positive course of East-West relations for many years to come." Even worse,
"it would raise the risk of direct US-Soviet military confrontation."[83]

Back in Bonn, Kohl and his team decided to respond by pressuring East
Berlin more than they had ever done before. They knew at this point that
the GDR had no hope of securing loans on the open market anymore and
that they were the country's only source of support.[84] Schäuble and Seiters
let Schalck know that if the Politburo wanted help, it would have to sacrifice its monopoly on power in exchange, and allow opposition parties to
contest free elections.[85] Kohl then upped the pressure on Krenz by making
these terms public. The chancellor announced them as part of a previously
scheduled address to the West German parliament on November 8. He
called for East Germany to institute "freedom of opinion, freedom of the
press, freedom of assembly, freedom for unions, party pluralism and, finally and self-evidently, free, immediate, and secret elections."[86] On top of
everything else, East Berlin would have to wait for a reply from Bonn to
its urgent requests for support. Further negotiations would be suspended
until after the end of Kohl's upcoming extended visit to Poland.

In short, more than any other single document, Lauter's draft, produced to the specifications ordered by the Politburo, showed the party

leadership's unwillingness to surrender control over the movement of its people—only three days before it supposedly made the radical decision to open the Wall.[87] Rather than win over protestors, the draft instead intensified awareness in the GDR and beyond that the party leadership was unwilling to implement real change. And the draft would soon have yet another consequence: it would exacerbate antagonism between the East German and Czech Politburos, two entities that had until recently been unified in their opposition to reform in the Soviet Union, Hungary, and Poland.

Czech party leaders were, by the start of November, unwilling to tolerate the renewal of chaos at the West German embassy in the heart of their capital. On Friday, November 3, Miloš Jakeš, the Czech party leader, gave the East German ambassador in Prague an ultimatum for Krenz, insisting that Krenz had to find some solution immediately, or else Czech authorities would consider closing the border to the GDR from their side.[88] The Czechs were worried that the refugees streaming across their country were inspiring local opposition movements. To emphasize the point, Jakeš apparently called Krenz personally as well, pressuring him into taking action.[89]

In response, the East German Politburo announced that, starting Saturday, November 4, East Germans in Czechoslovakia could emigrate to the West without having to return to the GDR in sealed trains. As a practical matter, this meant that any East German who could get to Czechoslovakia could now be more or less certain of proceeding directly to the West. That weekend alone, November 4–5, roughly twenty-three thousand East Germans emigrated through Czechoslovakia to West Germany, many heading for the town of Schirnding, which was close to the common border of the three states.[90] The East German Politburo hoped that the announcement of the draft law on November 6 would decrease this enormous exodus, but it did not.

Despite all the problems that it had failed to solve, Krenz and his Politburo colleagues refused to abandon Lauter's draft during a five-hour Politburo meeting that started on the morning of Tuesday, November 7.[91] This bizarre decision—a half million people had protested against the text in Leipzig, yet the party leaders thought they could cling to it—represented a major step down the path that would lead to the opening of the Wall. The Politburo decided to put a portion of the draft's wording on permanent emigration into effect immediately by fiat. The legal basis whereby this could happen was questionable, but that did not seem to bother the

Politburo. The idea also arose to create a new border crossing specifically for the resulting emigration, by opening a new checkpoint at a remote point on the German-German border near Schirnding. What did not arise was any provision for those who merely wanted to travel to the West temporarily; the Politburo's decision would affect only those willing to depart permanently. It represented a panicky and poorly thought-out response to pressure from Prague.[92]

The task of carrying out this idea fell once again to Dickel and Mielke, this time working closely with the foreign minister, Oskar Fischer, who was needed to deal with the Soviet ambassador, Vyacheslav Kochemasov.[93] Kochemasov had to be involved, because he was, of course, the essential conduit to Moscow. Krenz, as his predecessors had done for decades, was expected to communicate all matters of significance to the ambassador, who would then inform top party leaders in the Soviet Union, and finally pass Moscow's reply back to the East Germans. Because of this ongoing need for Soviet approval, Krenz had visited the Soviet embassy nearly every day since becoming the leader of his party.[94] As a result, Moscow's ambassador to East Berlin enjoyed, to a degree unthinkable to ambassadors from the West, enormous influence over the country in which he was nominally serving as an emissary from abroad, and that influence was still powerful in November 1989.

Kochemasov had been chosen for his post not because he had any particular linguistic or other skills related to the divided Germany but because he was someone Moscow could trust to execute party orders. Kochemasov had discovered that he would be going to East Berlin in a personal conversation with party leader Yuri Andropov—a former head of the KGB and one of the men most responsible for crushing the Hungarian uprising in 1956—rather than from the Soviet entity nominally in charge of ambassadors, the Foreign Ministry.[95] Andropov picked Kochemasov in full knowledge of the fact that Kochemasov was an admirer of the hard-liner Alexander Shelepin. Shelepin, a protégé of the Soviet leaders Joseph Stalin and Nikita Khrushchev, had been head of the KGB and a member of the Politburo and in 1959 had personally proposed the destruction of documents showing Soviet culpability in the execution of thousands of Poles at the Katyn massacre. The Soviet Politburo ordered the destruction to be carried out.[96]

Such were the leaders who had shaped Kochemasov's views. As a result of his background and personality, representatives of the other occupying powers in divided Berlin regarded him as an unreconstructed Stalinist.

They dreaded interacting with him. Once a British diplomat made the mistake of asking Kochemasov a contentious question just as British and Soviet delegation members were sitting down to lunch. The Brits had to stare hungrily at their smoked salmon for forty-five minutes as the Soviet ambassador held up lunch to lecture them in response.[97]

In 1989, Kochemasov was seventy-one. His younger deputy, fifty-seven-year-old Igor Maximychev, represented a stark contrast to his boss. A big man, well liked by representatives of the other occupying powers, Maximychev spoke fluent German after more than a decade of service in German cities on both sides of the Wall. Knowing that party issues fell to the ambassador, Maximychev tried to focus on more traditional diplomatic responsibilities. He had regular contact with his opposite numbers among the other Allied powers, such as his British colleague, Michael Burton, who particularly valued Maximychev's directness, intelligence, and wit. Jonathan Greenwald, an American diplomat at the US embassy in East Berlin, remembered Maximychev as "the guy who really knew what was going on."[98]

On November 7, Krenz instructed the GDR's foreign minister, Fischer, to speak with both Kochemasov and Maximychev as soon as possible. They met at 11:45 a.m. that same day. Fischer explained to the Soviets that the East German Politburo felt a sense of "duty" to ease the burden on its Czech counterpart, and also expressed his worry that if the party leadership in Prague carried out its threat to close the border from its side, the effect would be catastrophic. Fischer made explicitly clear to the Soviets, however, that "the border [between the] GDR/FRG will not be opened, because that would have an uncontrollable effect."[99] Rather, the plan was for the Politburo to open a new exit, or hole, on the border between the two states. East Germans could apply for permission to leave by this checkpoint rather than crossing through Czechoslovakia. Before enacting this plan, however, the East German Politburo members naturally wanted "the opinion" of their Soviet comrades.[100]

After Fischer left, Kochemasov instructed Maximychev and his staff to analyze the idea, which they nicknamed the "hole variant." They were to reassemble the next day for a "brain trust" briefing on how to respond. Maximychev and his colleagues concluded that the hole variant was a sign of Krenz's confusion and cowardice. Even though Fischer had explicitly said the GDR was not opening its border to West Germany, that would be the practical effect of the plan—but only at a remote location, and only for those willing to apply and to become exiles forever. Fischer's request for an "opinion" was only meant to implicate the Soviets in whatever would follow, which might be a disaster. As Maximychev put it, the East German Politburo was trying to spread blame around in advance.

Notably, at the time neither Maximychev nor anyone else at the embassy thought that a worst-case scenario—the opening of the Berlin Wall— could result, because the discussion was solely about a remote spot on the border, not about divided Berlin. For the Soviets, the legal status of the Berlin Wall was completely different from that of the German-German border. Since the four powers collectively still shared control in divided Berlin, all in the room assumed that the issue of the Wall was not even under discussion, given that the idea of convening those four powers was not part of Fischer's proposal. Instead, the question was only what to allow the East Germans to do near Schirnding.

Moscow should analyze carefully how to respond, Maximychev advised his boss, even though he knew this would be difficult given the timing of Fischer's request. Tuesday, November 7, and Wednesday, November 8, were business days in East Berlin but part of a major holiday in the Soviet Union, with parades and numerous receptions in honor of the success of the October Revolution. Many senior figures would remain unavailable through the end of the week. Second-tier officials and ones lower than that would be keeping desk chairs warm while waiting for the decision makers to return.[101] Kochemasov, with great effort, did manage to reach the Soviet foreign minister, Eduard Shevardnadze. According to Maximychev, Shevardnadze responded that "if our German friends think that such a solution is possible, then we will probably not register objections." Shevardnadze did, however, want the Foreign Ministry in Moscow to look closely at the idea before allowing Kochemasov to respond definitively to Krenz. In effect, Shevardnadze told his ambassador to wait out the holiday for a response.[102]

East German representatives appear to have broached the idea of the hole variant in Bonn as well, presumably still hoping for lucrative support. Just as there was a permanent representative, or pseudo-ambassador, from West Germany in East Berlin, so too was there a permanent representative from East Germany in Bonn, Horst Neubauer. One of Neubauer's subordinates apparently mentioned the hole variant to chancellery official Claus-Jürgen Duisberg, who asked for notice of when the plan might actually go into effect, but never received a reply.[103]

Having dealt, they believed, with the complaints from their Czech colleagues and alerted the Soviets, the top party leaders once again charged

Dickel with figuring out the details, and Dickel once again called on Lauter. Meanwhile, the SED's top leaders turned their focus inward, to party personnel issues. In the same way that Krenz was trying to create the appearance, without the reality, of travel freedom, so too did he decide to make it look as if the Politburo was accepting responsibility for the failings of its leadership without actually doing so. At the same marathon meeting on November 7 where Fischer received his instructions, Krenz had the entire Politburo agree to "resign" at the opening of the party's central committee meeting the next day. Immediately thereafter, however, there would be an "election" to repopulate the Politburo, at which time Krenz would have the central committee reelect most of the Politburo. As a result, most Politburo members would be able to measure their time in "retirement" in minutes. They could say that they had tried to accept responsibility and to step down, but the clamor for their return had simply been too great. The exercise would also serve as a means for Krenz to dismiss potential opponents and to create room for a few new supporters. After the Politburo meeting ended, for example, one of the names on the list of resignations, Werner Krolikowski, mysteriously disappeared from Krenz's list of names for reelection, thereby making Krolikowski's resignation real.[104]

As this plan went into effect, however, there would be some unexpected surprises. The central committee members, in contrast to their previous behavior as rubber stamps, would refuse to reelect three people on November 8, the first day of their three-day session. The vote counting would degenerate into a chaotic affair, since the central committee had little practice with voting not fully fixed in advance. Thus the party leaders became fixated on their own bureaucratic reshuffles, not realizing that they had set an irrevocable series of events in motion by approving the hole variant.[105] Given that the peaceful revolution had advanced to the point where it was producing events attracting half a million people, the resistance movement clearly had amassed a great deal of potential energy. Trying to open one little hole while holding back the bulk of that churning energy would turn out to be a deeply unwise decision.

Chapter Five

Failure to Communicate on November 9, 1989

ARLY ON NOVEMBER 9, Egon Krenz sought an update on the status of the hole variant. Of the men whom the Politburo had by now tasked with implementing it—the East German foreign minister, Oskar Fischer, charged with informing the Soviets and requesting their approval; the interior and Stasi ministers, charged with devising its wording; and the head of the council of ministers, charged with issuing it formally—only the first, Fischer, had made progress. Fischer had asked the Soviet ambassador for permission. Now all he could do was wait for a reply.

To find out where matters stood with everyone else, Krenz had his trusted comrade, Wolfgang Herger, start making calls about 8:00 a.m. on November 9 in an effort to prod everyone into producing results that same day. Herger made clear to the interior minister, Friedrich Dickel, that by the close of business he should complete his task to select some part of Gerhard Lauter's previous draft that could be enacted immediately by fiat in order to mollify the Czech leaders.[1]

It was clear to East Berlin party leaders that the patience of their Czech comrades was at an end. Huge numbers of GDR refugees were once again swarming through their country. More than thirty thousand East Germans made it to Bavaria in the beginning of November by way of Czechoslovakia. The Czechs kept repeating to the SED that these developments were unendurable, because they were inspiring the Czech opposition. If the comrades in East Berlin did not find some other solution soon, the Czechs would take independent action.[2] Hence there was an urgency to

Herger's phone calls on the morning of November 9. In reply, Dickel indicated that he had already assigned the thankless task to Lauter, the princeling, once again.[3]

Lauter and his colleagues thereby received an impossible challenge: mollify both the Czech Politburo and the wider East German population by opening the border a little bit, but only to those willing to leave forever, not to those wishing to take a short trip. And Lauter and company had to do so immediately, under the threat that Czechoslovakia might close the border from its side. Helping Lauter were three of his colleagues: Gotthard Hubrich of the Interior Ministry, and Hans-Joachim Krüger and Udo Lemme of the Ministry for State Security. Hubrich headed the Department of Internal Affairs at the Interior Ministry and therefore had the job of processing emigration applications.[4] Krüger was deputy leader of the Stasi department that enforced party discipline on the Interior Ministry, and Lemme served as head of the Stasi legal office. This group of four had collaborated previously on many occasions. As a result, the atmosphere in Lauter's office, where they met, was collegial, despite the stressfulness of the situation.[5] Although they were in the Interior Ministry building, the men all had strong Stasi affiliations: two were full-time staff members, and Lauter and Hubrich were or had been "unofficial co-workers" of Krüger's Stasi department.[6]

They commenced work at 9:00 a.m. on November 9 by checking that they had all received the same orders.[7] They agreed that they had. Lauter then boldly stated what he really thought of their orders: they were schizophrenic. They would increase, rather than decrease, emigration problems. As he put it to the group, "Everyone who wants to stay in the West is allowed to leave immediately? But the person who wants to come back to his work and his home is not allowed to go?" Lauter was certain that such a plan simply would not work. Even worse, he believed that it would achieve exactly what they were trying to avoid, namely, the depopulation of East Germany: "We will drive people out of the country."[8] Not everyone wanted to leave for good, after all. Reports were already coming in from border regions of East German citizens who had fled, seemingly permanently, but now wanted to return. On top of these considerations, Lauter also worried that issuing another unworkable regulation right after the fiasco of his November 6 draft would further inflame public hostility toward the ruling regime.[9]

These doubts had not just occurred to Lauter that very moment. It appears that he and Hubrich had discussed these worries between themselves and with their superiors before the start of the meeting, and that Lauter had come away feeling emboldened, although his instructions had not formally changed. His decision to risk criticizing his own orders in front of Stasi officers presumably arose from that previous conversation with his bosses. The Stasi officers do seem to have placed a call to their headquarters during the meeting, perhaps to check on the acceptability of what was being discussed, but they did not contradict Lauter, and their willingness to hear him out apparently emboldened him even more.[10]

Lauter then ventured into what was for him uncharted territory. He decided to exceed his orders, a step "that you got to take only once in your career," as he later put it. Lauter convinced the other three men that following the letter of their task would contradict its spirit, so they should go beyond their instructions. His motivation arose, he later claimed, not from clandestine opposition to his beleaguered socialist state but rather from his loyalty to it. As Lauter would explain afterward, "I did not want a coup." Rather, what he and his three colleagues did on November 9 "was in my view, and in the view of my three colleagues, meant to be stabilizing." At least, he conceded, that was what it was "supposed to be."[11]

The instructions given to this group were so specific that they even included a header for the document the four men were supposed to produce, namely, a text on "the permanent emigration of GDR citizens to the FRG via CSSR [Czechoslovak Socialist Republic]."[12] The four men kept the header, although it would not match the content of their text. Rather than simply take language concerning emigration out of the draft, as they were charged with doing, Lauter and the others decided instead to write a brand-new text that addressed both permanent emigration *and* temporary travel. Lauter and Hubrich had even apparently prepared some suggestions about wording.[13] By late morning, drawing on this wording and on some paperwork brought to the meeting by the Stasi comrades, the four produced the new text that would unexpectedly open the Wall that night.

The text stated that "the following temporary transitional rules for travel and emigration out of the GDR into foreign countries will be valid," pending a new law at some unknown date in the future. They also added that these temporary rules would be valid *"right away,"* a phrase that would have fateful consequences. With the stroke of a pen, the four midlevel bureaucrats thus declared the current rules to be suddenly null and void. The crises of the day demanded drastic measures, they concluded. According to these transitional rules, citizens could apply for permission to take "private trips to foreign countries" without needing to meet previously required conditions for those trips. Applications and approvals remained necessary, however.[14]

Remarkably, the group's text then included this statement: "Permanent emigration may take place over all border crossings between the GDR and FRG *and Berlin (West)*."[15] Their addition of divided Berlin to the text was the single most momentous component of their collective decision to exceed their own authority.[16] Lauter later explained it by saying that the four men did not worry about the approval of the four powers—who still held ultimate control in Berlin—because they assumed that such considerations were being handled by Fischer and others responsible for foreign policy. The diplomats at the Soviet embassy would be consumed with fury later that day when they heard that their authority in divided Berlin had simply been disregarded.[17]

That the four men were trying to shore up, rather than undermine, the state's control was apparent in their text's repeated insistence that applications remained necessary. The state, and by extension the party, still had to give permission for whatever border crossing was to take place. Regardless of whether an East German wanted to leave the country for good or just for a cup of coffee in the West, he or she would still need to apply and, as Lauter put it, "get at least some kind of stamp" before departing.[18] The group of four figured that by managing such applications, the regime could limit the flow of travel. Indeed, both the Stasi and the Interior Ministry would spend the rest of the afternoon working on guidelines for issuing such stamps.

The four men thought they had thereby succeeded at the impossible task given to them. Their text sounded as though it was promoting freedom of travel, but it contained enough caveats—it was only temporary, still required multiple forms of permission, and granted no foreign currency—to maintain control and to prevent the depopulation of East Germany. None of them would realize just how wrong they had been, and how far-reaching the unintended consequences of their actions would be, until it was too late.[19]

The group of four drafted a press release as well, and placed an embargo on the announcement of their text until the next morning, November 10, at 4:00 a.m. By midday they were done. They forwarded the paperwork to their superiors for approval and for transmission to the members of the Politburo in the central committee meeting.[20] Lauter kept waiting for a superior to berate him about what was, in essence, an unapproved effort by four second-tier bureaucrats to stabilize the GDR, but such a call never came. As far as he could tell, no superior noticed the discrepancy between the header of the text and its contents. Or if his bosses had noticed, they evidently agreed that the key element—control—was still provided for. One senior Stasi officer, General Gerhard Niebling, later recalled how he had scanned the result of their work and thought, "This is a significant easing of the rules," but "of course, naturally, permission still remains necessary." As he put it, the four men were clearly "not tearing down the Wall."[21]

Lauter also attributed the lack of a reaction to the intense pressure on party leaders on that day, November 9. He guessed that no one had time to read, let alone concentrate on, the fine print of a regulation, especially when everyone thought that they knew what it was: an excerpt from the already familiar draft. The only objection came from deputy officials at the Justice Ministry, who opposed the fact that the text simply declared the existing laws null and void, but Lauter was able to convince them of the necessity of doing so.[22]

At the end of the business day, Lauter felt comfortable leaving his office more or less on time. He and his wife had tickets to a theater performance that evening, and he wanted to keep his word to arrive on time for the start of the show. He had embargoed announcement of his text until 4:00 a.m. the next morning, and he planned to be back at work by then anyway. Once Lauter handled the objection from the Justice Ministry, he left the office, disappeared into a theater, and remained incommunicado for the rest of the evening. He would first hear of the scenes of chaos at the Wall upon returning home late that night from the theater with his wife. Their son would greet them at the door of their home, tell them that the interior minister had called repeatedly, and add, "Oh, and by the way, the Wall is open."[23]

A CROSS EAST BERLIN at the Soviet embassy, the deputy ambassador, Igor Maximychev, had a busy November 9 as well. He fielded repeated calls from East Berlin party leaders, who were anxious because there was still no reply from Moscow to Fischer's November 7 request for approval for the hole variant, and the Czechs were irate about the delay.[24] As far as anyone in the Soviet embassy knew, the plan remained the same as described to the Soviet ambassador and Maximychev two days earlier, namely, to open a hole for emigration at a distant point on the German-German border. Had anyone mentioned divided Berlin as well, Soviet alarm bells would have sounded loudly. But the Soviet embassy did not know that anything of the kind was under consideration. According to Maximychev, the question of "opening the borders" never came up.[25] Thanks to the embassy's ignorance of what Lauter and his colleagues had done, Moscow would eventually give approval to a plan that had long since been superseded.

In their ignorance, Ambassador Vyacheslav Kochemasov, Maximychev, and their subordinates tried time and time again to reach superiors in Moscow about the hole variant. The Soviet holiday was still making their job nearly impossible, however. Officially, the holiday was over—Thursday, November 9, was a business day in both East Berlin and Moscow—but since senior Soviet leaders had by that point endured a two-day marathon that included a parade on Red Square, an enormous reception at the Kremlin, and numerous smaller events, many of them were nowhere to be found. A Soviet Politburo meeting took place on November 9, but there was no sign that the attendees discussed any issues related to divided Germany at all, despite the outstanding urgent request from East Berlin.[26]

Since neither Kochemasov nor Soviet deputy foreign minister Ivan Aboimov had any luck in tracking down the foreign minister, Eduard Shevardnadze, despite repeated attempts, Aboimov finally advised Kochemasov to tell the East Berlin Politburo to go ahead with the hole variant.[27] Aboimov was exceeding his authority, but he had given up hope of reaching anyone more senior in time to respond before the Czechs did something rash. Kochemasov accordingly let the SED leadership know that Moscow had no objections, so the plan could proceed.[28] No one informed Kochemasov in response that the hole variant was obsolete and that an entirely different text now existed. It was a significant failure to communicate and to keep an ally up-to-date on developments. Years later, the former Soviet ambassador still could not understand the lapse: "In those days, I met Krenz almost daily, and he said nothing to me," which might have been a sign that Krenz himself did not know what was happening.[29]

Another failure to communicate then occurred, one involving the onward transmission of accurate information about the Soviet approval. It happened after couriers delivered copies of the group of four's text to the party's ongoing, contentious central committee meeting in the early afternoon of November 9. Emotions were running high on the second day of the three-day session. The central committee was officially an important decision-making body in the party, but due to its relatively rare meetings and large membership—more than 160 full members, plus another fifty candidates—it had always been the much smaller Politburo, with roughly two dozen members under the leadership of the general secretary, that actually ran the party and the country.[30] Now, however, the central committee was showing signs of independence, not least in its partial rejection of Krenz's Politburo resignation plan. It was a frightening development for those Politburo members now remaining.[31] As one observer later described the situation, "to call the top of the party chaotic, headless, and incapable of action" would be to flatter it too much.[32]

The group of four's text made it to Krenz's hands during what was supposed to be a break, but he decided to begin discussing the text immediately with the distracted and rattled members of the Politburo who were standing around him. Only about half of the members of the Politburo, most with cigarettes dangling from their lips or fingers, appear to have been standing near enough to Krenz to hear him; the rest were using the break to take a breather elsewhere. The Politburo member responsible for media who would end up announcing the text, Günter Schabowski, was not even present. Indeed, Schabowski had been absent for much of the formal central committee meeting altogether, for unclear reasons.

Krenz's words during the break seem to have provoked almost no reaction. Perhaps upon hearing the text's misleading title, the Politburo members tuned out, since they thought they already knew what it said, or perhaps they were simply too stressed to pay full attention during what was supposed to be a break. They may also have assumed that there would be a fuller discussion once the formal central committee session resumed after the break. In any event, no one seems to have pointed out the gap between the original Politburo instructions and the text Krenz held in his hands.

Someone did apparently ask Krenz the only truly significant question: whether what he was reading aloud had been cleared with the Soviets. The correct answer was no. Moscow, through its ambassador, Kochemasov, had approved only the hole variant. Krenz created a new misunderstanding, however, when he replied in the affirmative: yes, he said, he had heard from the Soviets, and the text had Moscow's approval.[33] Those words alone were probably good enough for many members of the Politburo to consider the matter closed. This failure of communication was a particularly significant one, since it implied top-level approval that did not in fact exist.

Yet another failure took place when Krenz decided to read the group of four's text to the full central committee meeting later that afternoon. In theory, he thereby created another window of opportunity for someone to question the wisdom of the text's wording. This window opened at 3:47 p.m., when Krenz interrupted the scheduled events, saying, "It is known to you that there is a problem that burdens us all: the issue of emigration." The "Czech comrades" were complaining bitterly, he went on, just as the Hungarian comrades had done earlier, about the baleful impact of the waves of East German émigrés flooding across their borders. Krenz added, "Whatever we do in this situation, we will be taking a wrong step." There were no good options. "If we close the borders to the CSSR, we thereby punish the decent citizens of the GDR, who then cannot travel and then . . . will try to influence us." Presumably he meant they would try to exert influence by protesting at home.

Krenz announced that, as a result of the Czech pressure, the council of ministers would be proposing a text. In effect, he was putting words in the mouths of the ministers sitting in front of him. That the general secretary of the SED could dictate to ministers of state what they were to say was standard practice, and even though the central committee had started to deviate from its scripted role, it had not yet gone so far as to challenge this practice, or Krenz directly. Krenz then indicated that the text he was about to read had been approved by the Politburo, without mentioning that the Politburo had "approved" it during the previous smoking break. This was another significant failure in communication, since Politburo approval signaled to the audience that the text was already a done deal. Krenz added that, since the matter was important, he would now read the precise wording aloud for "consultation" anyway, perhaps to mollify the newly tempestuous central committee, and proceeded to do so.[34]

Presented in this way by their political leader, and with many in the room apparently eager to get back to internal bloodletting and finger-pointing, the text elicited no serious challenges. No one used this window of opportunity to challenge the wisdom of its wording. The culture minister, Hans-Joachim Hoffman, did suggest a minor alteration: changing the phrase "the following temporary, transitional rules" to "the following rules," since he thought the implication that this latest concession was only temporary and could be revoked might inflame the opposition.[35] Krenz agreed, noting that since the text also stated elsewhere that it would be in effect only until a new law was passed, references to its temporary nature were redundant. Another central committee member asked how the text would be publicized. Krenz replied that a government spokesman named Wolfgang Meyer would issue it—as opposed to the politically much more significant Schabowski, who had started holding Western-style press conferences the day before to report on the results from the three-day central committee meeting.[36] But there were no criticisms or even attempts

This international press conference, held in East Berlin and televised live from 6:00 to 7:00 p.m. on November 9, 1989, became a crucial link in the unexpected chain of events that culminated in the opening of the Berlin Wall later that same night. Günter Schabowski (shown in bottom photo, and seated second from right on panel in top photo), a member of the East German Politburo, directed the conference, which took place before a large crowd of domestic and foreign journalists (shown in the fore-ground of the top photo). *(RHG Fo AnKae 485, 487; photo by Andreas Kämper)*

at sustained discussion. After calling, "All comrades agree?" and hearing no contradiction, Krenz was able to move on to another item only eight minutes later, at 3:55 p.m.[37]

No one in the room realized that they were approving a text that would open the Wall that night. No one mentioned, for example, the need to inform border guards.[38] Despite the devastating effects that emigration was having on the economy, no one questioned the idea of announcing this text on a business day.[39] The East German leaders in 1961, in contrast, had intentionally chosen a Saturday night for construction of the Wall in order to trap the maximum number of people of working age at home. Nor does anyone seem to have considered some of the tragic historical associations of November 9 in German history: it was the anniversary, among other things, of Hitler's Beer Hall Putsch and of a major Nazi attack on Jews, the so-called Kristallnacht. In short, there were no signs that party leaders realized that they were essentially approving their own political death warrant. It was a remarkable lapse of attention, one that opened a different window of opportunity—but for the peaceful revolution, not the ruling regime. Unlike the SED, the protestors would seize their opportunity later that night.[40]

Shortly after the central committee's brief discussion ended, party and Stasi offices began distributing the text, with the minor amendments from the central committee meeting inserted, to district and other subordinate offices.[41] When, at about 5:45 p.m., the office of the justice minister registered its objections with Lauter, they were too late to have any real consequences, even if Lauter had taken them seriously.[42] And as part of the notification process, the government press spokesman, Meyer, did in fact receive an assignment to announce the text at 4:00 a.m. the next morning, November 10.[43] Krenz, however, would soon forget his own statement that the government spokesman, not the party spokesman, should announce it, or perhaps he had a sudden change of heart. Either way, his last-minute change turned out to be a fateful switch, resulting in the final and most significant communication failure: Schabowski's press conference that night.

SCHABOWSKI PUT IN a brief appearance at the central committee about 5:00 p.m. Exactly where he had been for most of the day, instead of at the meeting where he was about to summarize for the world media live on television at his 6:00 p.m. press conference, was not clear; he would later say that he had been advising journalists.[44] Schabowski had not spent much time learning how to conduct a Western-style live broadcast. His primary experience was with East German–style journalism, in which party leaders simply dictated to media outlets what to report after events were already over, so familiarity with actual events as they unfolded was not a high priority.[45] Given this background, it was not surprising that he thought he could handle the world press without actually attending the central committee meeting.

When Schabowski stopped by, asking what he should tell reporters, Krenz suddenly pressed the group of four's text into his hand, seemingly forgetting that the government spokesman, Meyer, had already been charged with announcing it. Krenz would later say that in handing over the text, he told Schabowski it would be "world news." This seems un-likely, as Schabowski did not bother to look at the text until he was live on air.[46] As he remarked afterward, why should he have done so? Even though Schabowski had not been present either for the smoking-break reading of the text or for the brief discussion in the full meeting, he felt comfortable accepting the paper from Krenz.[47] As he later put it, "I can speak German and I can read a text out loud without mistakes," so no preparation was necessary.[48] Although he still had a short drive over to the International Press Center on Mohren Street ahead of him and could have looked at the text in the car, he did not.[49] His cavalier attitude meant that his live press conference would become the emblematic moment of the ruling regime's collapsing ability to govern.

Indeed, Schabowski almost forgot to announce the text on air at all. He instead opened his press conference by reading long-winded lists of names of speakers at the day's meeting. It was a disappointment for the journalists from around the country and the world who had traveled to East Berlin to hear him speak. Peter Brinkmann, a Hamburg-based writer for the West German *Bild* newspaper, had arrived hours early to drape a jacket protec-tively over a seat in the front row. No one moved it, despite an enormous crush of observers that forced late arrivals to perch on the edge of the stage where Schabowski and his aides sat, so Brinkmann kept his spot. As soon as the press conference started, however, Brinkmann wondered why he had bothered to arrive so early, or even to attend at all. Schabowski, ac-companied on the stage at the front of the auditorium by the largely silent minister of trade, Gerhard Beil, and central committee members Helga Labs and Manfred Banaschak, provided only vacuous summaries of recent party debates, not news. It was all "blah blah blah," Brinkmann remem-bered. "It was deadly boring."[50]

Tom Brokaw, the US anchor who had traveled much farther than Brinkmann to be present at the press conference, recalled having a similar reaction. A couple of days earlier, he, Jerry Lamprecht, the network's head of foreign news coverage, and Bill Wheatley, the executive producer of *NBC Nightly News,* had agreed that the recent events in East Germany seemed potentially interesting enough to merit a live broadcast. NBC had already covered a number of developments in Europe closely, most notably the successes of Solidarity, and a focus on East Germany after the recent large demonstrations in Leipzig and East Berlin seemed to be an obvious next step. Brokaw and his producers decided that the anchor would head for divided Germany but that they would reserve the final decision on whether to broadcast live until they saw what Brokaw could uncover.[51]

None of the reporting that he had been able to do since arriving, however, had turned out to be interesting enough for a live broadcast on NBC back in the United States. Brokaw could tell that Schabowski's remarks were not worthy of a live broadcast either, in part because the anchorman could hear a translation through an earpiece, and in part because he could see other journalists in the overheated room, including the Associated Press correspondent next to him, falling asleep.[52] It was because of his producer Michele Neubert, a German-speaking British citizen and an employee of NBC's Frankfurt bureau, that Brokaw and his team were even at the interminable press conference. She had the job of organizing interviews for Brokaw when he was on the road in Europe and had booked one with Schabowski because the East German could speak broken English. It had taken some effort. She had spent days tracking down Schabowski, and it had seemed like a success when he agreed to give NBC an exclusive interview immediately following his November 9 press conference. Thus the reason that she, Brokaw, Brokaw's right-hand man Marc Kusnetz, and NBC's audio and video technicians were there was not so much to listen to the press conference itself as to be ready to talk to Schabowski immediately afterward. She already had another crew of camera and audio technicians set up in a side room, ready to begin taping the interview. But now that they were enduring the boring press conference as a prelude to the one-on-one conversation, Neubert began to wonder whether they would get anything usable out of Schabowski.[53]

Suddenly Neubert went on high alert. An Italian journalist, Riccardo Ehrman, had asked Schabowski a question about travel possibilities for East Germans. Schabowski's long-winded, German-language answer was not what Neubert had expected. Schabowski had started by replying in the same vague way in which he had answered all of the questions until then, with frequent pauses and abundant use of the German-language equivalent of "uh": "We know about this tendency in the population, about this need of the population, to travel or to leave. . . . And . . . uh . . . we have the intent . . . to implement a complex renewal of society . . . uh . . . in that way to achieve, through many of these elements . . . uh . . . that people do not see themselves obliged to master their personal problems in this way." Vague elaborations on the theme of societal renewal and many, many more "uhs" followed. Then, however, Schabowski added, "Anyway, today, as far as I know . . . a decision has been made." He glanced sideways at the subordinates sitting with him on the stage as if looking for confirmation, but nothing was forthcoming.

Schabowski pressed ahead, saying, in between pauses and "uhs," that the party had decided "to issue a regulation that will make it possible for every citizen . . . to emigrate." He would now read a text of the new rules, he said, as soon as he could find it. He began digging through his thick stack of papers.[54] Now not just Neubert but also the German-speaking NBC sound technician, Heinrich Walling, seemed visibly shocked. Brokaw looked at Walling questioningly. Walling whispered to Brokaw in English, "It's the end of the Cold War." In an op-ed in the *New York Times* ten days later, Brokaw would recount his amazement at that moment. It was as surprising as if "an alien force" from outer space had just invaded the room, he wrote.[55]

A frenzy of questions erupted in German. "Without a passport, without a passport?" shouted one reporter. "When does that go into force?" shouted another. The chaotic outburst visibly irritated and disoriented Schabowski. Trying to regain control, he distractedly started saying, "So, comrades!" to the crowd, but "comrades" was a term of address only for fellow party members, not the world media. Stalling while he kept searching through his papers for the text, he stated, wrongly, that the journalists had already received copies.[56]

Schabowski became even more visibly rattled as he continued to fumble with his papers, and it was only with help from an aide that he finally found the group of four's text. As if to make up for the time lost, he began reading the text aloud very quickly. Startled journalists heard him say the following words so rapidly as to be nearly incomprehensible: "Private trips to foreign countries may, without presenting justifications—reasons for trip, connections to relatives—be applied for. Approvals will be distributed in a short time frame." In other words, the text, contrary to his introduction of it, concerned not just emigration but private travel and short trips as well. Some of the reporters in the room interrupted Schabowski, unable to restrain themselves. One asked once more if a passport was needed. Schabowski, once more, did not answer. Other queries followed insistently. Brinkmann shouted the truly crucial question: "When does that go into force?" Schabowski scanned the unfamiliar text in his hands again and picked out some of the words that he saw printed on it: "*right away*."[57]

Brokaw, his crew, and everyone else in the room were now paying full attention. The wire journalists in particular, such as the Associated Press correspondent next to Brokaw, were under pressure to be the first to report any big news, and this seemed to be very big news indeed. Some wire reporters even left the room while Schabowski was still speaking. Journalists without early prototypes of cell phones or nearby offices wanted to be the first to get into the East Berlin press center's phone booths. These were scarce commodities guarded by an overseer who, everyone knew, had to signal the Stasi before letting correspondents use the phone lines. The wait for the Stasi to prepare to monitor a call could be of indeterminate length and could cost crucial time.[58] Brokaw and his crew, however, had the luxury of a vehicle waiting outside with a car phone that, unlike a lot of the handheld prototypes, actually worked. The NBC team had suddenly switched from dreading their pre-booked interview with Schabowski to eagerly anticipating it. It was now the exclusive that everyone wanted. Neubert began mentally planning an exit strategy for getting out of the auditorium and ready for the interview as quickly as possible.[59]

There were more shouted questions, such as "Is that also valid for West Berlin?" Schabowski did not answer. The query came again. Reluctantly he looked at the text once more and, to his own surprise, saw that it included the words "*Berlin (West)*." Flustered and surprised, he confirmed that the announcement applied to West Berlin. This confirmation generated yet more questions, all shouted on top of each other.

Finally, Daniel Johnson, a foreign correspondent for Britain's *Daily Telegraph*, stood up and asked loudly, "What will happen with the Berlin Wall now?"[60] The room suddenly became quiet as everyone waited expectantly for the answer, but only a long, fraught silence followed. It seemed as though Schabowski had suddenly lost the power of speech. Finally the East German Politburo member ended the excruciating pause with the following words: "It has been drawn to my attention that it is 7:00 p.m. This is the last question, yes, please understand!" Then Schabowski suddenly tried to link the status of the Wall to the painfully slow process of disarmament, saying that the questions about the border "would definitely be positively influenced if the FRG and if NATO would commit themselves to and carry out disarmament, just as the GDR and other socialist states have already completed certain preliminary steps." With that confusing statement hanging in the air, and with Johnson and everyone else still waiting for a response to the question of what would happen to the Wall, Schabowski abruptly said, "Thank you very much!" and ended the press conference. It was 7:00:54 p.m. He had intentionally closed the conference without determining the fate of the Wall.[61] That task would, as a result, he left to the participants in the peaceful revolution later that night.

A T THAT VERY same moment, the mayor of West Berlin, Walter Momper, found himself on his Berlin's side of the Wall. He was on the eighteenth floor of the Springer Building, a tall structure built by anti-Communist publisher Axel Springer to loom over the Wall. Momper was there to attend the Golden Steering Wheel Award ceremony for automotive design, which was hosted by the Springer publishing group. Earlier that day, he had heard a rumor that something about travel was being discussed at the central committee meeting in East Berlin. However, there had been a number of such rumors recently and all of them had been false, so the mayor would later recall that he doubted this new rumor as well. In fact, he was so skeptical that, after mentioning the new rumor briefly to the transport senator for West Berlin, he forgot about it entirely. It suddenly came back to him when both his driver and Bruno Waltert, the editor of the Springer group's *Berliner Morgenpost* newspaper, simultaneously burst into the awards ceremony and ran up to him. The driver told Momper that his car phone was ringing constantly; the editor, who had skipped the ceremony to watch Schabowski's press conference live on a television in his office downstairs, told the mayor what he thought he had heard.[62]

Momper decided to go first to Waltert's office to watch a video replay of the press conference. Afterward, the mayor could not help walking over to the window of the Springer Building and staring down at the Wall. The evening mist reflected its harsh lighting. It was about 7:15 p.m. on November 9, and it was clear to Momper that "everything looked the same as ever." He later remembered thinking about "this cold strip, the source of our German unhappiness," and how it showed no sign of change whatsoever. Momper felt fairly certain that at that very moment, "an attempt to flee" across the Wall "would still be suicidal."

Considering his options, the mayor soon decided on a course of action. It was still not entirely clear to him what Schabowski's press conference had meant, but he told himself that his motto for the rest of the night would be "as if." Act as if the Wall were open. Act as if it would be the most natural thing in the world for Berliners to celebrate a reunion. Act as if the main concerns, such as the form of transport that East Berliners would use once they arrived in the West, were now all mundane. The mayor also realized just how useful it was that he and his colleagues had started thinking about exactly such practicalities as part of their speculation on what Schabowski's stray remarks of October 29 had meant, and whether a "Day X" was coming. Now, such preliminary speculation would help inform, and lend credence to, what he intended to say to the mass media. In short, Momper's plan was to act as if he were certain that the border was open and only questions about practicalities remained, thus making it as difficult as possible for the East German ruling regime to revoke Schabowski's statements.[63]

To put his plan into effect, Momper headed directly for the studio of SFB, the West Berlin television broadcaster where Jahn worked. The mayor had a police car accompany him with sirens and lights blaring. Once Momper got to the studio and on air, he announced, with a calm he did not actually feel, that the night divided Berlin had desired for twenty-eight years had arrived. Without mentioning any particulars, since he did not know them himself, he spoke in dry terms about public transport options. He encouraged East Germans to leave their cars at home and instead take the buses and trains. Momper figured that his comments would reach an unusually large audience in both the East and the West that night because, thanks to a major soccer match, television viewership would be exceptionally high. He kept talking in this manner for a while, thinking, "Just keep acting 'as if,' and it will build pressure" on the East German regime.[64]

Meanwhile, on the other side of the Wall, listening to Schabowski speak on a television in the Soviet embassy, Maximychev felt as if the East Germans had stabbed him and his colleagues in the back. He had his own "as if." As if the East Berliners had the authority to decide on the Berlin Wall, he thought indignantly; they most certainly did not. "Earlier, no one said a single word about West Berlin," Maximychev would later complain.[65] He began to feel a sense of fury.[66] How could Schabowski dare to say that his text applied to the borders of West Berlin without Soviet permission? What was his embassy going to do? What would the Western allies think?

The other three occupying powers in divided Germany—the British, the French, and the United States—were as surprised as the Soviets. The news reached Robert Corbett, the British commandant, at an extravagant fiftieth-birthday party for the head of a West Berlin radio station.[67] The prime minister, Margaret Thatcher, would not be pleased. She had reportedly confided her concern about developments in divided Germany to Wojciech Jaruzelski, the Polish president, in the autumn of 1989, adding that "reunification would be absolutely unacceptable. One could not allow an Anschluss, otherwise the FRG would swallow Austria too."[68]

In Washington, James Baker, the secretary of state, was lunching with the Philippine president, Corazon Aquino, at the State Department when an aide handed him a slip of paper with surprising news on it: "The East German Government has just announced that it is fully opening its borders to the West. The implication from the announcement is full freedom of travel via current East German/West German links between borders."[69] Baker offered a spontaneous toast and, as soon as he could politely extract himself from the lunch, went to the White House to discuss the situation with President George H. W. Bush.

The president, busy preparing for the state dinner with Aquino that evening and a departure to Texas to commemorate the upcoming Veterans Day holiday there, made time to speak with journalists.[70] He issued a prepared statement saying that he welcomed "the decision by the East German leadership to open its borders" but stressed that it was important to keep a cool head.[71] As Lesley Stahl of the *CBS Evening News* reported afterward, "President Bush walked a delicate line today between his own policy of prudence toward Eastern Europe" and triumphalism. "The last thing he wants is to ignite an explosion of change and declaring victory." Bush made clear that "there will be no gloating from the White House over the developments in East Germany. Mr. Bush went so far as to suggest that East Germans not leave their country." The network broadcast Stahl saying to Bush, "You don't seem elated and I'm wondering if you're thinking of the problems." Bush agreed: "I'm not an emotional kind of guy." By coincidence, that day the president had received advance word from journalist Tim Russert that NBC would shortly be airing the results of a poll on presidential popularity. This poll showed that, as of November 1989, Bush was enjoying higher approval ratings than his predecessor, Ronald Reagan. It must have seemed to Bush like validation for his more cautious approach to foreign policy.[72]

Perhaps the world leader put in the most awkward position by Schabowski's surprising announcement, however, was Helmut Kohl. Had anyone in Bonn known the significance of what was happening in East Berlin, Kohl and the bulk of chancellery officials would not have departed for Poland on November 9 for a major, extended visit to mark the fiftieth anniversary of the opening months of the Second World War. But they did not know, so the West German chancellor and his enormous entourage arrived in Poland as planned at 3:00 p.m. for the start of a visit scheduled to last until November 14. The top tier of West German correspondents had accompanied the chancellor as well, meaning that they were also badly located to cover the unexpected story back in divided Berlin.[73]

Kohl's schedule for this trip included not only a state dinner and multiple events in Warsaw but also trips to a number of other locations in the country in the upcoming days.[74] Kohl wanted to show by the length of his visit that Germans and Poles had moved beyond their tragic past and that Bonn would support Warsaw as it moved forward into a new, more democratic future. As Kohl had explained to French president François Mitterrand three days before his departure, he planned to give Poland a "significant economic and financial program of help."[75]

Upon arriving, the chancellor spoke with Tadeusz Mazowiecki, the former Solidarity activist and new prime minister. Kohl also had a meeting with the Solidarity leader and Nobel laureate Lech Wałęsa at 6:05 p.m.[76] Since Poland and both East and West Germany shared a time zone, Kohl and Wałęsa met as Schabowski's press conference was unfolding in East Berlin. Wałęsa surprised Kohl by asking what it might mean for Poland if the Wall opened. It was a purely speculative question, as they did not receive news about the press conference during their meeting. Kohl dismissed the idea that the Wall might open, but remarked that the East German ruling regime was clearly on its way out, and added that Honecker's violent, hard-line course had been self-defeating. If Honecker had allowed free elections two years previously, Kohl speculated, his party might have survived; now it was too late. Still, Wałęsa would not be deterred. The Nobel laureate expressed concern over both the potential for "revolutionary chaos" in East Germany and the chance that it would push Polish concerns to the back burner. Kohl remained unperturbed. He responded by praising the peaceful nature of the protest in East Germany, saying that even though recent demonstrations in the GDR were topping half a million participants, "not a single window pane had been broken. That was indeed worthy of note."[77] But Wałęsa was prescient in his questions and concerns. By the time the two men ended their conversation and Kohl left to prepare for the state dinner at 8:30 p.m., reports about Schabowski's remarks had started circulating in Poland as well as in divided Germany.

Kohl and most of his advisors were attending meetings in Warsaw, not watching Schabowski on television. Eduard Ackermann, the chancellor's media advisor, and Joachim Bitterlich, an advisor on Western Europe, were two of the few who had remained in Bonn. Unlike Kohl and his aides in Warsaw, Ackermann and Bitterlich were able to watch television coverage of Schabowski.[78] Ackermann called Warsaw and said that he needed to speak to the chancellor himself as soon as the state dinner would allow.[79]

At the dinner, Mazowiecki gave a speech in which he uttered the oddly appropriate words "We live in a time of breakthroughs."[80] Once the meal was over, Kohl finally had a chance to speak to Bonn. "Mr. Chancellor, as we speak the Wall is falling!" Ackermann announced as Bitterlich listened. Kohl reacted with skepticism: "Are you sure?" The aide responded that yes, he was sure, because he had already heard reports of East Berliners getting out. Kohl was still uncertain, asking who else was there with Ackermann and whether they were taking advantage of the empty office to enjoy drinks on the job. His aides assured him that they were not, and agreed to keep Kohl updated.[81] It was not possible to get Western television channels in Warsaw, even in the West German embassy, so the chancellor would have to rely on their phone calls from Bonn for his information that night, but even that source of information would be problematic. The fixed phone lines in the guesthouse where they were staying were presumably under surveillance. Kohl's foreign policy advisor, Horst Teltschik, who was in Warsaw as well, remembered that other than the landline, they had only an old-fashioned field telephone of the type used by the military, but that it was antiquated and barely usable.[82]

What they did have, however, was a bottle of Crimean sparkling wine, the Soviet version of champagne. It had been a welcoming gift from the Poles, placed in the guesthouse upon their arrival. Teltschik and Kohl's assistant Juliane Weber decided to treat themselves to glasses in honor of the news, but Kohl refrained. Teltschik recalled that the chancellor felt very out of the loop. Kohl soon decided to take the dramatic step of interrupting the state visit for a brief return trip to the West. He initially intended to go only to his office in Bonn, where he would have access to secure means of communication, but it soon became apparent that he would have to stop in West Berlin as well, because the city's politicians were organizing a public event for November 10, and it would look as if Kohl were not in charge if it went ahead without him.[83]

Teltschik was hardly the only one to reach for a bottle in celebration. Back in divided Berlin, a little before 8:00 p.m., Albrecht Rau, the owner of a West Berlin café directly opposite the Checkpoint Charlie border crossing, carried a tray with a bottle of sparkling wine, glasses, and steaming cups of coffee over to the East German guards at Checkpoint Charlie. They had long been his unapproachable neighbors. Now, escorted by customers from his café, Rau figured it was time to get to know them. The guards were amazed and nervous. Saying they could not drink on duty, they refused Rau's offer. The café owner and his companions then said "bottoms up" to each other anyway, but the guards insisted that they should finish their drinks back at the café, not at the checkpoint. As the group turned around and exited Checkpoint Charlie, still carrying drinks, flashbulbs suddenly blinded them. Journalists who had only just arrived on the western side of the checkpoint mistook the glasses of bubbly in the hands of the café owner and his Western customers as signs that they were in fact East Germans, celebrating their newfound ability to cross to the West. One photographer, working for the wire service DPA, sent a picture of the "East Germans" out on the wire service not long after 8:00 p.m., giving the false impression that East Berliners were already leaving, perhaps the source of Ackermann's misinformation.[84]

In fact, for hours after Schabowski's press conference ended, there would be no unapproved exits from East Berlin. It was not at all clear what would happen next. The regime still had its final barricade, the Berlin Wall, with all of its fortifications and manpower. It would take more than just a bungled press conference to open it. For that, the certainty of journalists who thought they knew what they had heard, the courage of dissidents willing to believe them, and the confusion of border guards would all be necessary. It would be as the culmination of decisions made on the spot, by individuals in a tense and dramatic situation, that the final act of November 9 would unfold.

PART III

The Contest of Wills at the Wall

Chapter Six

The Revolution, Televised

WHEN GÜNTER SCHABOWSKI's press conference ended, the journalists in the room asked themselves what had just happened.[1] Because they had not received a copy of the group of four's text, despite Schabowski wrongly asserting on camera that they had, the reporters—especially wire correspondents, under pressure to send news immediately—had to rely solely on Schabowski's confusing statements in the closing minutes of the press conference in deciding what to report.

Unsurprisingly, their initial accounts varied. The first wire report came from Reuters at 7:02 p.m., even as journalists still inside the press conference room were mobbing the stage in the hope of getting clarification from Schabowski. "Leaving via all GDR checkpoints immediately possible," Reuters reported, and then followed up with a longer notice saying that "East German citizens wanting to depart can, starting immediately, use all border crossings . . . those who want to depart no longer need to take a detour via Czechoslovakia. The responsible police offices are instructed to issue visas for emigration immediately." At 7:04 p.m., a West German wire service announced that "starting immediately," GDR residents could exit "directly through all checkpoints between the GDR and the FRG." At the same moment, ADN, the East German news agency, released the group of four's text. The staff at ADN apparently felt that if Schabowski could ignore the embargo until 4:00 a.m. on November 10, they could as well. Next, the Associated Press chimed in at 7:05 p.m. with "GDR opens borders."

Television coverage appears to have started as late as 7:17 p.m. The first major evening news show to air after the press conference, broadcast by the West German network ZDF, decided to cover Schabowski only as its sixth item of news. Once it had dispensed with the previous five, ZDF reported that "starting immediately, East German citizens are allowed to exit directly over all border crossings between the GDR and the Federal Republic of Germany. With this decision today, a temporary rule until the passage of a new travel law has been created."[2] Its competitor news broadcast at the other major West German network, ARD, airing at 8:00 p.m., informed viewers that the "detour" through Czechoslovakia had become unnecessary and that the Wall "should become permeable." Its coverage then turned to a long report on Chancellor Helmut Kohl's visit to Poland, which had clearly been intended as the main story for the evening.[3]

Despite their reports, journalists remained unsure about what was actually unfolding. Since the Stasi conducted surveillance on foreign journalists, their confusion that night is manifest in the ministry's files. At 7:17 p.m., for example, one television reporter called his office in Cologne to say that Schabowski "probably had not even known himself what he was announcing." This journalist and his conversation partner agreed that the new rules applied solely to émigrés, not to anyone just wanting to travel. Cologne advised the reporter in West Berlin to "keep your camera team ready" just in case.[4]

Back at the International Press Center, Tom Brokaw, Marc Kusnetz, and Michele Neubert hurried into the side room already prepared for Brokaw's one-on-one conversation with Schabowski. They hoped that, despite the chaos erupting in the main auditorium of the press center, the East German would keep his word to give them an exclusive interview. Fortunately for them, Schabowski wanted to get out of the auditorium as quickly as possible too. An English-speaking reporter had pushed his way up to the front of the room and was trying to convince the East German to translate the wording of the new regulation into English. Dismayed, Schabowski refused to do so, saying, "It is too difficult for me to express it in English." After exchanging a few more words with the crowd of journalists jostling each other, Schabowski put up his hands and said that he needed to get back to the central committee meeting, so "please permit me to leave." In fact, he intended to exit the auditorium, to give Brokaw the promised interview, and to go home, but presumably he thought it would sound better to plead that he had to get back to work.[5]

Elbowing his way out, Schabowski finally managed to make his way into the side room where Brokaw, Kusnetz, Neubert, and the NBC camera crew were waiting for him.[6] After he entered, Neubert used her own back to barricade the door against entry by other reporters, who kept trying to push their way in during the roughly ten-minute interview. Brokaw immediately started asking the Politburo member the questions every journalist wanted to ask: "Mr. Schabowski: Do I understand it correctly? Citizens of the GDR can leave through any checkpoint that they choose for personal reasons? They no longer have to go through a third country?" In broken English, Schabowski responded, "Uh . . . they are not further forced to leave GDR by . . . uh, uh . . . transit, uh, through another country." Brokaw tried again: "It is possible for them to go through the Wall at some point?" "It is possible for them to go through the border," was Schabowski's response. Brokaw followed up by saying, "Freedom of travel?" Schabowski replied, "Yes of course," and then added, "It is no question of tourism. It is a permission of leaving GDR."

Schabowski's English skills were not equal to the challenge of discussing the provisions of the regulation, as he himself had just admitted moments earlier in the main auditorium. Brokaw and the producers in the room with him, Kusnetz and Neubert, had to make a very quick judgment call as a result: how should they interpret Schabowski's answers? Schabowski had just, on camera, replied "Yes of course" when asked if his words meant freedom of travel for East Germans. He had also confirmed that East Germans could "go through the border." In addition, Schabowski had confirmed earlier during the press conference itself—also on camera—that the border under discussion included the one around West Berlin. The assembled journalists had no way of knowing, of course, about Schabowski's unfamiliarity with the group of four's text. Taken at face value, his comments implied that freedom of travel had come to both the GDR and to East Berlin, and that was what Brokaw and his team decided to report. Still, in his initial broadcast, Brokaw would state—correctly and more accurately than some of the German-language coverage—that the new border-crossing options required visas beforehand.[7]

After the brief interview ended, and despite his remarks that he needed to return to the central committee, Schabowski tiredly made his way to his chauffeured car and asked the driver to take him home. Home was East Berlin's gated Wandlitz compound, where the party's elite resided, securely sealed off from the rest of the population. Schabowski and his family were in house number nineteen, down the street from Mielke. He could still remember decades later how, when his car pulled up on the evening of November 9, he saw almost no lighted windows in the houses in the compound. The leaders of the party, he guessed, had not even watched his press conference.[8]

In contrast, Brokaw, Kusnetz, and Neubert left the room in a state of excitement as they headed for their own car and driver. Other journalists, watching them exit the room where they had been speaking to Schabowski, shouted at them, "Is it true?" As he and his producers rushed out, Brokaw hurriedly replied over his shoulder, "It's true, the Wall is coming down." Brokaw's comments carried a special weight with the members of the world media who heard them, since he was the only one who had had the chance to get clarification from Schabowski one-on-one that night. These comments increased the degree of certainty that other journalists displayed when they communicated with their own editors and networks.[9]

Brokaw and his producers soon found their driver and, using their car phone, called New York. The network decided that Brokaw would provide an immediate voice update from that car phone, since the full *Nightly News* television show was still about five hours away. Kusnetz stood outside the vehicle to ensure that there was no disruption while Brokaw spoke live on NBC from the car phone and provided a quick summary of the press conference. The technology of the day did not allow the network to show a live shot of Brokaw as well, however. Live images required a "satellite window," or pre-booked time for satellite use, but such periods had to be scheduled well in advance. NBC did have a satellite window reserved for the potential *Nightly News* broadcast from West Berlin, but only starting at the beginning of the show, which would not be until 12:30 a.m. Berlin time, or 6:30 p.m. Eastern Time.[10]

The network had also secured the necessary city permits for a potential broadcast from a location in West Berlin near where the Wall ran in front of the Brandenburg Gate. NBC's head of foreign news coverage, Jerry Lamprecht, had instructed *Nightly News* crew members to secure those permits and to make extensive preparations at the site. Overseen by Maralyn Gelefsky, by the evening of November 9 they had already built a twenty-by-twenty-foot platform. They had also installed powerful floodlights known as HMIs, anticipating a broadcast in the middle of the night, Berlin time. Lamprecht and Gelefsky even arranged for a cherry picker to be brought in, so that camera operators could get overhead shots of the Wall behind Brokaw if needed. There were also small trailers available for editing tape on-site.[11]

The setup was so perfect that conspiracy theorists would later suggest that NBC must have received some secret advance word of the opening of the Wall, but all NBC staff present that historic night deny it. The whole *Nightly News* installation was simply on standby; the final decision to broadcast the show live from West Berlin had not yet been made when Schabowski started his press conference. Indeed, Brokaw had even apologized to Gelefsky earlier that day, saying that all her hard work was probably for naught, since there was nothing to merit airing *Nightly News* from the Berlin Wall after all. He had also told Cheryl Gould, a senior producer coordinating the show from the NBC control room in New York, that "we came all this way and there is no real story."[12]

After his interview with Schabowski, however, it was clear to Brokaw and his team that both the satellite window and the setup had suddenly become invaluable. They were the only such preparations by any network from any country at the visually stunning site. Now the live broadcast of *Nightly News* was obviously a go.[13] Brokaw and his producers made their way back from East Berlin through Checkpoint Charlie to their location at the Wall near Brandenburg Gate. Observing the network's team from the eastern side of the Wall, Stasi agents noted when the NBC floodlights snapped on at 7:50 p.m., as preparations for the show began.[14]

There was, however, one enormous problem: there were not yet any images of East Germans actually crossing through, or over, the Wall. Kusnetz remembered it as a "stomach-churning situation." Brokaw had already announced on NBC that the Wall was going to open, and the network had made the decision to broadcast from West Berlin. For that broadcast, starting at 12:30 a.m. local time, they clearly needed images of people crossing the Wall—and it was the responsibility of Kusnetz and the camera operators working for him to find and to feed such images to New York. The clock was ticking, and Wheatley, the show's executive producer, kept asking, "When are we going to get that feed?" Answering, "It'll be there," Kusnetz tried to figure out what to do.[15]

H E WAS HARDLY the only one wondering what to do. A similar question occurred to those East Germans on duty along the Berlin Wall that night, especially at the biggest inner-city border crossing, the one on Bornholmer Street. The "control territory," as the Stasi called it, of this checkpoint in the north of the divided city covered about seven hundred by four hundred feet, or roughly six and a half acres, and contained a dense complex of buildings, gates, security fortifications, and lanes for both pedestrians and cars.[16]

Bornholmer managed a number of different kinds of traffic. Residents of both West Berlin and West Germany used the crossing to move from

The Stasi took this aerial photo of the Bornholmer Street border crossing, with West Berlin at the top on the far side of the bridge, in about 1985. The checkpoint itself is the large, walled-off complex in the center of the photo. It includes a number of barriers, lights, service buildings, and, at left, numbered lanes for processing vehicles. *(MfS, from file HA XXII 5724/2, 34, on display at Bornholmer Street in 2013; photo by the author)*

West to East and back again, while travelers with diplomatic credentials took advantage of special reserve lanes to shorten their wait times. These lanes also allowed, at least for a time, the cook for the Swiss embassy in East Berlin to run his own personal love ferry. He would regularly carry his girlfriend through Bornholmer in his car trunk for shared nights out in West Berlin. The authorities at Bornholmer began to suspect something but did not know if the cook enjoyed diplomatic immunity, meaning they were not sure whether they had the right to search his trunk. The bureaucrats got busy. An internal investigation came to the conclusion that the cook was not covered by immunity, and both he and his trunk-riding girlfriend were hauled over (and out) the next time they tried to head to the West.[17]

Schabowski's press conference on November 9 put Bornholmer in a particularly difficult position because while the crossing was big and well fortified, it was in a tricky location—at least from the point of view of the East German regime. The site was highly accessible. It was near Schön-hauser Allee, a major access road to downtown. It could easily be reached with public transport. Bornholmer also stood near the Prenzlauer Berg residential district of East Berlin, where large numbers of "hostile-negative forces"—such as Aram Radomski and Siggi Schefke—lived.[18]

On the evening of November 9, those two "hostile negatives" were indeed heading to the border crossing. Radomski had watched Schabowski's press conference live at his girlfriend's place on Metzer Street in Prenzlauer Berg. After the opening minutes, she had found it so tedious that she had wandered away. Radomski, however, had kept watching. "Aram, turn that TV off, that's all just shit," she had called out to him from another room. Radomski had refused, saying, "Hold on, something seems new to me . . . I don't know what exactly."[19] Over the protests of his girlfriend, Radomski watched and listened as Schabowski mumbled his way through his confusing text about emigration. As the press conference abruptly ended, Radomski decided that he wanted to find out what Schabowski's statement of "*right away*" meant. After a futile attempt to persuade his girlfriend to come with him, he left her apartment and went to the nearby Metzer Eck pub, a regular hangout for Radomski, Schefke, and their friends.

Sure enough, Schefke was already drinking at the bar, along with a few others. Radomski shouted, "Good thing you're here. We need to go to the Bornholmer Street border crossing immediately!" The rest of the men at the bar thought Radomski was crazy, but Schefke trusted Radomski's intuition, even though he himself had not heard the press conference. The two hurried off with the parting words "If we are not back in two hours, then we are in the West." Their friends laughed at their self-delusion.[20] The two men stopped briefly at Schefke's place on nearby Gotland Street, on the way to Bornholmer, in order to grab some of his stash of West German currency, just in case. They then drove the short remaining distance to Bornholmer and parked the car on a nearby street, not suspecting how long it would be before either of them would see it again.[21]

Bornholmer had become a giant magnet, just as the Nikolai Church had one month to the day earlier—and it was not just Berliners who were showing up. Katrin Hattenhauer was headed to Bornholmer as well. On

October 9, she had been in solitary confinement in Leipzig, wondering if the noise she could hear in her cell came from tank treads and if she was about to be executed.[22] Word of what was actually happening outside that day, however, had spread through the prison by messages tapped on walls and heard through toothbrush cups used as earpieces. The sound of laughter, specifically banned, had begun echoing in the prison corridors.[23] Then, a few days later, Hattenhauer had mysteriously been released from solitary confinement in Leipzig but told that she had a restriction on her movement, so she should not leave the city limits.[24] Ignoring the restriction, in November Hattenhauer had gotten on a train to see friends in East Berlin. She intended to celebrate with them through the night until the dawn of her twenty-first birthday, November 10, 1989. On the evening of the ninth, she and her friends chose a bar near the Bornholmer Street border crossing for the start of her birthday celebration. Their evening took an unexpected turn, however, once they heard about Schabowski's press conference secondhand. Although they learned the news later than Radomski and Schefke, when they did hear it, Hattenhauer and her Berlin friends had the same idea: go to Bornholmer, the nearest border crossing, and see what might be possible.[25]

Neither Radomski, Schefke, nor Hattenhauer had a detailed plan, only an intuitive sense that now was the moment to show up and to speak up. Radomski was guessing that the new rules applied only to those who were prepared to emigrate for good, which neither he nor Schefke was. He wondered, however, how a border official could enforce such rules. How would checkpoint authorities make sure that someone who was leaving was leaving forever? Would they really refuse reentry? He figured that he and Schefke could say that they wanted to emigrate, just to see what would happen. Radomski also had a camera with him and hoped for some interesting photos, although in the chaos of the evening it would be smashed.[26]

Radomski and Schefke remembered being among the first dozen or so "early adopters" of the new regulations to arrive at Bornholmer. The two immediately started asking the border officials posted at the eastern entry to the checkpoint whether they could exit, but they were turned back. Radomski next demanded to speak to a senior officer, and someone came out to talk with him, but the answer was no different. He and Schefke decided to keep complaining and probing nonetheless.[27]

Inside the Bornholmer border-crossing complex itself, the senior officer on duty that night was Harald Jäger. Jäger, born in 1943, had long been a loyal servant of the regime: by 1989, he was a veteran with twenty-five

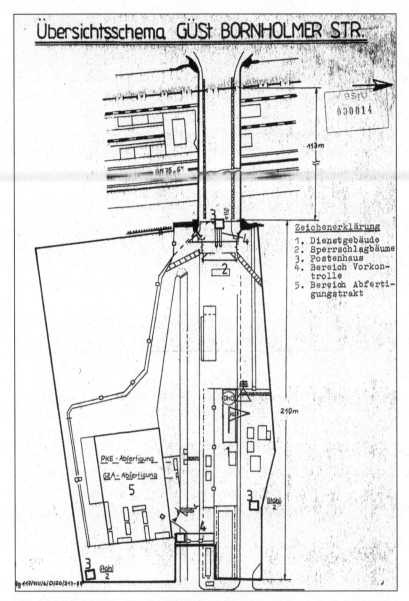

This Stasi map of the Bornholmer Street border crossing complex, with the eastern entry at the bottom and West Berlin at the top above the dashed line, indicates its east-west length as being 210 meters (roughly 700 feet) with an additional bridge span to the west of 113 meters (roughly 400 feet). The typed map key at right reads roughly: "Explanation of Symbols: 1. Service Buildings; 2. Barrier Gates; 3. Guard Posts; 4. Pre-Control Area; 5. Customs and Passport Clearance Area." The area to the bottom left, marked with the number 5, contains the vehicle processing lanes.

(MfS, from file BStU, MfS HA I, Nr. 3510, 14)

years of service at Bornholmer. At the age of eighteen, he had started working as a border policeman, following in the footsteps of his father, and had signed up just in time to contribute to the construction of the Berlin Wall. Both father and son felt that the overriding goal of their state should be to avoid another war on top of the two brutal conflicts that had already occurred that century. The younger Jäger was convinced for that reason that the Berlin Wall had been tragic but necessary. In his eyes, it had been preferable to what he saw as the alternative: war between the Warsaw Pact and NATO.[28]

In 1964, three years after the Wall went up, Harald Jäger secured a position in passport control at Bornholmer Street. Over the following twenty-five years, he worked his way up to the rank of lieutenant colonel and deputy head of the passport control unit.[29] Despite the military-sounding title and the fact that he worked at the border, his post was in many ways a desk job. A normal workday for Jäger consisted of inspecting the papers of travelers crossing at Bornholmer. He or his colleagues would take photos of an individual's papers by placing them on a table with a camera underneath. A live feed would transmit the photos to backroom operatives. The operatives would go through a massive card catalog to see if their colleagues needed to take action of some kind. By 1989, the card catalog at Bornholmer Street contained about sixty thousand names, twenty to a card.[30] The names were mostly those of West Berliners and West Germans (many of whom were former East Berliners and East Germans) along with a few other foreigners who crossed regularly. Numbers on the cards corresponded to the control measures the Stasi would undertake against that individual. A number in the eight hundreds meant that the secret police would maintain surveillance on the traveler during the visit to the East. A number in the two hundreds usually meant "do not let this person into the GDR at all." The backroom operatives would activate a light signal based on the cards: green light, no operational measures necessary, traveler can cross; red light, measures necessary. In addition, Jäger, his colleagues, and the customs officers might initiate a conversation to figure out the purpose of a traveler's trip, or might inspect vehicles and bags.[31] While he carried a pistol, Jäger had never killed an attempted border crosser.[32] He was essentially a record keeper, one of the deputies to the senior figure who kept tabs on the identities of those individuals crossing at Bornholmer.

Authority at this checkpoint, and at all border crossings, was actually split among three groups: border guards, customs officers, and passport control officers such as Jäger. This division of labor meant they were all

Stasi file photo of Harald Jäger, the senior officer on duty at Bornholmer Street on the night of November 9, 1989. The photo is undated but, judging by Jäger's age, shows his appearance roughly as it would have been in 1989. *(MfS, from file BStU HA KuSCH AKG KA HM Jäger, Harald)*

keeping an eye on one another. The first group, the border guards, bore responsibility for physically protecting the Wall and its checkpoints. There were seven border guard regiments for the roughly hundred-mile-long Wall overall, each with one thousand to fourteen hundred troops; on an average night, about half a dozen of them were on duty in the Bornholmer checkpoint itself.[33] The second group, the customs officials, carried out basic searches of people attempting to cross the border. There were a little under twenty of them on duty at Bornholmer that night. But the most important group at any border crossing was always the passport control unit, because it represented a kind of Stasi branch office at the checkpoint. Jäger, his boss, and all of his colleagues worked for the Ministry for State Security and reported directly to superiors at that ministry.[34] To conceal their identities, they wore uniforms identical to those of the border guards, and so to travelers they were indistinguishable from those guards. Everyone who worked at the border crossing, however, knew that the official in charge of the passport control unit on any given day was the senior Stasi officer on duty, and therefore the man in charge. The head of the Bornholmer passport control unit in 1989 was Werner Bachmann, not Jäger, but during the key hours of November 9 Bachmann would be absent, having been called away to a night meeting.[35]

As a result, the night of the ninth unfolded on Jäger's watch as he supervised about a dozen passport control staff members. He had reported for duty at eight o'clock that morning for an uninterrupted twenty-four-hour shift.[36] Eating dinner in one of the Bornholmer control buildings, he watched Schabowski's press conference live, together with some of his men. Unable to restrain himself, he yelled "Bullshit!" at the television screen, then immediately called Colonel Rudi Ziegenhorn, the superior officer on duty at the Stasi's Operational Command Headquarters on Schneller Street that night to find out what had happened. Ziegenhorn surprised Jäger by replying that everything remained the same as always.[37] Manfred Sens, the officer in charge of the border guards at Bornholmer on the evening of November 9, also tried to get instructions by calling his regiment command, but Sens's superior officer knew nothing out of the ordinary either.[38] Next, Jäger called the sentries on watch at the border crossing's eastern entry, near where Radomski and Schefke were causing trouble. They reported that within minutes of the end of the press conference at 7:00 p.m., about ten to twenty people had gathered and were demanding to be allowed to pass.

In Jäger's decades on the job, he had dealt now and again with such unapproved attempts to cross. Especially at night and under the influence of alcohol, would-be border crossers would show up, and border officials would admonish, detain, or otherwise deter them. Jäger and his men even had a nickname for such characters: "wild pigs." What was new on the night of November 9, however, was not only the rapidly increasing number of "wild pigs" but also their determination. They simply would not leave.

Jäger called Colonel Ziegenhorn again. The colonel said that the troublemakers should be made to wait around for a while and then "sent back." Jäger communicated these instructions to the staff at the eastern entry at about 7:30 p.m. In return, they informed him that the number of "wild pigs" had jumped from ten or twenty to fifty or one hundred. Some were even approaching in vehicles. Jäger directed his men to tell the crowd that there were no instructions to let them out.[39] However, people were appearing not only at Bornholmer Street but also at other crossing points. Stasi officers in the passport control unit at the Sonnenallee checkpoint, for example, reported similar developments. By 7:45 p.m., a crowd of East Germans were pressuring the border officials there to let them pass, citing as justification "the reports appearing in the mass media."[40]

People had also begun to call various regime offices. As early as 7:14 p.m., one East German called a council of ministers office to complain that the travel application offices all seemed to be closed despite Schabowski's announcement. At 7:20 p.m. came another call, asking whether the newly approved travel could take place by train.[41] And one East Berlin resident named Peter Leonhardt dialed a local police station that evening, requesting to speak to the senior officer on duty. When put through, he explained that he had just heard Schabowski say that applications for travel were being accepted immediately, so he wanted to deliver his application that very minute on the phone. The officer on the other end of the line had no idea how to respond and replied that he knew nothing about it. Leonhardt persisted. The police officer said that he would call Leonhardt back and, amazingly, actually did, saying that while "usually" Schabowski was right, in this case the rules were valid only the next day. Leonhardt's query led to orders to all major Berlin police stations, telling police to respond in a similar manner to other callers.[42]

B ACK AT BORNHOLMER, by 8:30 p.m. Radomski and Schefke had a lot of company. Jäger's men estimated that the crowd was now well into the hundreds, possibly more. A police car turned up, and the officer inside tried using a loudspeaker to announce that crowd members should go to a nearby station to receive a visa and to return only after they had one. This announcement made matters worse. People either ignored it, thus placing the authority of the police in question, or did in fact go to the nearest station, only a few minutes away on foot. The officers on duty there had no idea what the people were talking about and no authority to distribute such instant visas, and so sent them away. In some cases the round-trip from Bornholmer to the police station and back took as little as ten minutes, with the result that the "wild pigs" came back enraged at having been sent on a fool's errand.[43]

Whether at Bornholmer, Sonnenallee, or elsewhere, officials were soon outnumbered as the number of determined border crossers rose into the thousands. But, if they were smaller in number, the officials were still powerful, because they had access to weapons. A number of them were carrying pistols, including Jäger, and they also had larger machine guns on-site. As a result of both Karin Gueffroy's successful efforts to publicize the death of her son Chris in February and the incident in which a Stasi officer had shot at escapees in full view of Western cameras in April, Jäger and his men had received the instructions issued reluctantly by Honecker to refrain from using those firearms. But the border officials still had the weapons in their possession. Moreover, there had long been ambiguity surrounding the orders to shoot. The excuse of using deadly force to defend one's own life could serve as a justification for gunfire under nearly any circumstances. Since they thought their checkpoint to be under siege, it was not out of the question in their minds that their lives might in fact be in danger.[44] Jäger was particularly worried that members of the crowd might try to grab weapons from checkpoint staff.[45]

Jäger called Ziegenhorn repeatedly, trying to get some kind of instructions on how to deal with the chaotic situation, but Ziegenhorn replied every time that it was business as usual. Jäger kept calling in hope of getting a more useful response. Later, Jäger would estimate that he placed about thirty phone calls in the course of the night, all in a mostly fruitless attempt to get new instructions in light of the dramatic developments unfolding in front of him. There was only one time when Ziegenhorn told Jäger to vary from normal procedure, and what Ziegenhorn instructed would end up making matters worse.

Ziegenhorn said that he would secretly add Jäger to a conference call with Ziegenhorn's own Stasi superiors, including Gerhard Neiber, a deputy of Mielke's. Ziegenhorn told Jäger that he should "be quiet" and not let anyone know he was on the line. Jäger was patched into the call as Ziegenhorn summarized Jäger's reports from Bornholmer. Not knowing that Jäger was listening in, Neiber asked brusquely, "Is this Jäger capable of assessing the situation realistically or is he simply a coward?"[46]

At that, Jäger's connection suddenly cut off. Holding the dead phone in his hand, Jäger felt a wave of anger wash over him. For close to two hours he had been dealing with an unprecedented and threatening situation. He had received no substantive replies to his urgent, repeated requests for guidance. He had been on duty for over a dozen hours and would be there, at a minimum, all night. And, as if the chaos at his place of work were not enough, the next day he had to face a personal issue as well: he had undergone tests to diagnose whether or not he had cancer, and was scheduled to get the results.[47]

Jäger felt himself reaching his limit. He had provided twenty-five years of loyal service at Bornholmer. He had served three years before that, too, including the period during the construction of the Wall. In all that time, he had received a number of awards for his service and gotten only one minor black mark on his record. He knew about the mass flight from his state, and he also knew that the GDR was in trouble, yet he remained willing on a dark November morning to put on his uniform and to report for a twenty-four-hour shift. Now his superiors were questioning his ability to provide an accurate situation report and suggesting that he was a coward. Looking back, Jäger would see that his choices from then on were affected by that moment. A man who had not disobeyed an order in nearly three decades had, with that insult, been pushed too far.[48]

The crowds at Bornholmer continued to grow. Standing in the front ranks of the assembled crowd, Radomski and Schefke demanded loudly, again and again, that the border guards let them pass. Hattenhauer and her friends were by now on their way to Bornholmer as well, along with many others. Inside the control barracks, before Jäger could translate his anger into action, Ziegenhorn called back. The colonel told Jäger that there were new instructions: to prevent the situation from getting worse, all passport control units should institute what they soon started calling the "let-off-steam solution." This solution would, in theory, work as follows: Jäger was to instruct his men to identify a handful of the most aggressive members of the crowd—people like Radomski and Schefke—and to pull them out. Then Jäger's subordinates should tell the troublemakers individually that they could exit. Before actually letting them out, however, Jäger's staff should first record their personal information and then place a stamp in their personal identity paperwork right next to the ID photo or even on it. The stamp in that unusual location would serve to invalidate the ID and to end the GDR citizenship of its bearer—although no one should tell the unwitting expellees that, because it might cause more problems. The idea was that the most aggressive troublemakers would then trickle out in a controlled way to the West and disappear for good. Ziegenhorn and his superiors apparently hoped that, with the worst irritants out of the picture, the crowds at the checkpoints would disperse. Only if the troublemakers tried to reenter the GDR later were they to be informed that they had no right of return. Ziegenhorn issued these instructions not only to Bornholmer but to other border crossings as well.[49] Later that same night, Ziegenhorn's superior, the head of Stasi Main Department VI himself, General Heinz Fiedler, confirmed in writing that the stamp near or on the photo invalidated the ID and left the recipient without any right of return.[50]

Jäger, still angry, was skeptical about this plan, but he began to implement it around 9:00 p.m. He had his men begin the process of fishing the most worrisome people out of the crowd and opened three control windows for the purpose of processing these troublemakers.[51] Since Radomski and Schefke had been doing their best to complain and to make noise for hours—as Radomski later claimed, "We were the loudest!"—they were among the first taken aside.[52] The two dissidents, along with others, were then taken into the checkpoint facility proper. Officials recorded all of their personal information and stamped their IDs. Perhaps to drive the point home, the official who stamped Schefke's ID did so directly on his photo. The two activists had thereby just been expelled from East Germany and did not even know it.[53]

As if in a dream, they suddenly found themselves walking across the bridge just beyond the border crossing and into the West. Schefke was sure that at any moment they would be grabbed by Stasi agents and thrown into the back of a truck, but it did not happen. The western side of Bornholmer, they soon discovered, was a sleepy and run-down district of West Berlin named Wedding. Late on a Thursday in November, Wedding was not exactly glamorous. Schefke later recalled that his first thought upon seeing West Berlin was "Wow, is this really the West? We must be in the middle of nowhere!" They decided to go downtown by taxi. Only when they had successfully gotten into a cab did Schefke decide that they really must be in the West, because the taxi was a Mercedes.

In the cab, they then had to reply to the driver's question, "Where to?" Because of their hesitation and appearance, the driver sensed that there was something unusual about his passengers. Upon hearing that they were from East Berlin, the driver tried to throw them out, concerned that they would only have Eastern currency, which would have been of little value in West Berlin. Radomski and Schefke showed the driver their Western cash. Not knowing that it would cost them most of it, they asked to be taken to an apartment in the Schöneberg district where a couple of Schefke's acquaintances lived. Schefke had met one of them during a biking trip in Hungary before he had been banned from traveling. As the East Germans got out of the taxi in Schöneberg, they told the driver, despite his earlier rudeness, "Go back to that bridge, you'll earn a lot of money tonight."[54]

Schefke's acquaintances were suitably shocked to see the East Berliners. After the initial greetings, Radomski and Schefke borrowed their phone to call Jahn.[55] Jahn had his hands full. He was on the job at the Berlin TV station SFB, where Momper was broadcasting his "as if" commentary. Jahn was simultaneously appearing in and coordinating his station's news coverage that night—all as he tried to take in the news on a personal level. He had been forcibly thrown out of East Germany in 1983, and now it seemed that the Wall, which stood between him and his hometown, Jena, was coming down.[56]

Still, when Radomski and Schefke reached him to say that they were in the West, Jahn did not believe them. To prove that they were not joking, the two East Berliners described the unusual winding staircase in the penthouse where their West Berlin friends lived. Jahn knew the same West Berliners and was familiar with the staircase. He suddenly realized that Radomski and Schefke were telling the truth. They had made it to the West. The Wall had opened.

Jahn immediately said to the East Berliners that they should get right back into a cab and come to SFB. Jahn would put them in front of cameras and have the two of them announce to the world that the Wall was open. They would reveal themselves as smugglers of information in the most spectacular possible way; they would find the recognition that they had been craving. The unreal aspect of the evening and the fear of the repercussions from the Stasi were still too strong, however. Neither Radomski nor Schefke had fully processed the collapse of control on the part of the East German regime. They worried about the consequences when they tried to return to East Berlin and so declined Jahn's request. Schefke replied to Jahn regretfully with words along the lines of *No, I cannot go on television tonight, because I would like to be able to go back.*

Disappointed, Jahn said that he understood. The three decided to meet later, once Jahn felt that he could leave the television studio. They would rendezvous at a bar called the Cuckoo's Egg, where another former East Berliner and dissident worked. After celebrating with their West Berlin friends in their penthouse for a while, Radomski and Schefke headed back to the border. There they blended in with the expectant West Berlin crowds while waiting for more East Germans to cross.[57]

Radomski and Schefke were at that moment rare exceptions, however. Most of the potential border crossers, such as Hattenhauer and her friends, were still in East Berlin, where the Stasi's plan to let only the biggest troublemakers through was backfiring spectacularly. Rather than reducing pressure, word of people actually getting out spread like wildfire. People suddenly thought, "Here we go," and expectations rose with frightening swiftness, Jäger recalled. The remaining crowds quickly figured out the system: if they yelled loudly enough, they could get out, and so they acted accordingly. Jäger called Ziegenhorn yet again to report on the problematic nature of their tactics, but Ziegenhorn responded, "There is nothing else," so they pressed on. Jäger also activated an alarm system that called up extra troops to join him, bringing the number of men on duty at the checkpoint to about sixty.[58]

Then Jäger learned of yet another problem: the let-off-steam plan was creating a crisis at the western entry to Bornholmer as well as on the eastern side. Among the first people let out had been young parents. Unlike Radomski and Schefke, the parents had only wanted to take a quick look in the immediate area just to the west of Bornholmer and then rejoin their young children, who were at home in bed and asleep. Flush with the heady experience of a swift visit to the West, they had returned quickly to the western entry of the checkpoint and had happily presented their IDs, saying in merry tones, "Here we are again! We are coming back!" And in response, they heard that they could not go home. No one had told them that the stamps on the ID photos in their outstretched hands represented their permanent expulsion from East Germany.[59]

At first they did not understand, but then they realized that the officers were serious. The construction of the Wall had, as all Berliners knew, split families without warning. Affected relatives had been forced to wait years to be reunited, if at all, and often were only able to do so with help from Bonn.[60] Now the East German ruling regime threatened to shatter families once again, just as it had done in 1961. Overwhelmed, the parents gave full vent to a powerful mixture of emotions.

The border officials posted at the western entry, cowed by the intensity of their reaction, called for Jäger to come deal with the anguished parents. When Jäger got to the western outpost of his checkpoint, he gave in to his own personal anger as well. He had been skeptical of the plan to allow the troublemakers through, and now found that he was unwilling to argue with grieving parents on behalf of superior officers who had insulted him. Jäger snapped.

Despite having personally received instructions from Ziegenhorn to prevent anyone with a stamp on or near their photo from reentering East Germany, he told the young parents that he would make an exception for them. Hearing that, other East Germans standing near the western outpost who also wanted to return asked to be allowed back in as well. Jäger felt that, having already taken one step on the path toward disobedience, he might as well take a few more. He instructed the officials at the western entry to let several others return as well. Jäger then returned to the heart of the checkpoint. The thought crossed his mind that he ought to at least tell Ziegenhorn what he had just done, but then he thought, why bother?[61]

A s THE CROWDS at the border crossings swelled, an East German television channel—in other words, an organ of the ruling regime—interrupted the broadcast of a movie and cut to an announcer, who stridently declared, "Trips have to be applied for!" The East German news show *AK Zwo* repeated this admonition at 10:28 p.m.[62] Such statements contrasted with the steadily more exuberant media coverage issuing from Western radio and television stations. Still, the anchorman of the Western news show *Tagesthemen*, broadcast on the national German network ARD, had to go on air that night a bit later than his usual 10:30 p.m. start time because of his producers' decision to wait for the end of the soccer match before starting the news. Nothing took precedence over the big game in the soccer-mad country, not even the end of the Cold War.

At about twenty minutes before eleven, Hanns-Joachim Friedrichs, the ARD anchorman, could finally open his show with the following words: "In using superlatives, it is necessary to be cautious, but tonight one is allowed to risk using one." He then forgot to use a superlative at all, saying instead, "This ninth of November is a historic day. The GDR has announced that its borders are, starting immediately, open for everyone." Friedrichs announced that his news show would turn live to a journalist at the Berlin Wall. Once Robin Lautenbach, the correspondent in West Berlin, appeared on camera standing at the Invaliden Street border crossing, however, Lautenbach could only show what looked from the West very much like an average night at that location. As a result, ARD was forced to air a prerecorded report on the history of the Wall instead of dramatic live shots. Closer to 11:00 p.m., the network wanted again to cut to an exciting sight, but Lautenbach could only say again, in apologetic tones, "Perhaps the big rush has possibly not happened yet."[63]

By about a quarter past eleven, the crowd on the eastern side of Bornholmer had grown into the tens of thousands, filling all of the approach streets. It was impossible for latecomers to get close to the border now, either on foot or in a vehicle. Loud chants of "Open the gate" erupted regularly. Jäger had by this point made dozens of phone calls since 7:00 p.m. in an attempt to get orders that were capable of ratcheting down the tensions. Instead of receiving such instructions, however, he had heard himself called a coward and received instructions that had made matters worse, and now was facing a situation that had become uncontrollable: a sea of thousands of agitated, chanting people. He worried that he and his men might soon be in danger.

Adding to Jäger's worries was the fact that Western camera crews were showing up on the eastern side of checkpoints. A camera team led by Georg Mascolo for the show *Spiegel-TV* was particularly irritating the guards at Bornholmer. Mascolo's crew members ignored prohibitions against filming inside a border-crossing complex, audaciously climbing on its fences to secure better camera angles, despite repeated instructions from Bornholmer officials to stop. In their search for the best possible sightlines for filming, the camera team even used their Western IDs to pass through the checkpoint, then turned around while still in the crossing area and filmed looking backward from the West at the East Germans stuck behind the barriers. At that point, such behavior became too much for Bornholmer officials. They herded Mascolo and his crew into a control building in the center of the checkpoint, close to the final barrier gate, and began questioning them.[64]

Surveying the scene, Jäger sensed that the time had come to make a fateful decision. He looked at the colleagues standing nearby and said words to the effect of *Should we shoot all these people or should we open up?* Jäger was in charge and did not need their assent, but given the enormity of the choice facing him, he wanted a sense of the mood of his men. They all knew their instructions from April 1989 not to use their guns, but they were also not about to let themselves be attacked. The crowd of tens of thousands had stayed peaceful so far but could turn violent at any moment, they thought.

Jäger realized that he was "done" with Ziegenhorn.[65] A little before 11:30 p.m., Jäger went to the phone and called his commanding officer to inform him of a decision he had made: "I am going to end all controls and let the people out." Ziegenhorn disagreed, but Jäger no longer cared, and ended the call. His steps down the road of disobedience had taken him to the point where he was willing to ignore his superior entirely.[66] He began implementing his decision. Jäger's subordinates Helmut Stöss and Lutz Wasnick were the ones who received the order to open the main gate, a task that had to be completed by hand.[67] Obeying, Stöss and Wasnick grabbed the handles on the barrier and began to pull. Before they could open the gate all the way, however, an enormous crowd started pushing through it from the eastern side. Mascolo and his crew could not believe their luck: from the control building where they had been herded, they had a perfect line of sight on the event. Mascolo's camera operator, ignoring the guards around him, threw his video camera on his shoulder and started filming. His footage captured the precise moment when the crowd pushed the gate wide open, with Stöss and Wasnick stumbling backward to get out of the way.[68] Cheers, jubilation, kisses, and tears followed as tens of thousands of people began sweeping through. The massive, unstoppable, joyous crowd poured through the gate and toward the bridge beyond, where even more camera operators caught the flood of people on film as it surged into West Berlin.

The Berlin Wall had opened—but not by force of arms. The breakthrough was nonviolent. While the enormous crowd of protestors had loudly and insistently demanded to pass, they had remained peaceful and had not smashed their way through with force, even though Jäger and his men had feared that they might. Thanks to the presence of so many camera crews, the simultaneous collapse of the regime's control of the Wall and the ultimate moment of peaceful success for the revolution were both caught on film and, soon thereafter, televised.

The moment was an overwhelming emotional experience for everyone present, including Jäger and his men. Stöss later said that he could not stop asking himself one question over and over: "Why have I been standing here for the last twenty years?"[69] Jäger was on the verge of tears. To prevent his men from seeing their acting commander cry, he ducked into a nearby control building. There he found one of his subordinates, already hunched over and weeping. Jäger pulled himself together and comforted the man.[70]

The East Germans who passed through the gate also shed tears, but theirs were of joy, not confusion or sorrow. Before too long, Hattenhauer and her friends were in the West. She had gone from solitary confinement and fear of execution to a birthday in West Berlin, all in less than a month. As she later put it, it was "the best birthday present" she could imagine.[71] Another young woman, an employee of the Central Institute for Physical Chemistry, was on her way home from a visit to a sauna when the news of the night inspired her to head for Bornholmer. Her name was Angela Merkel. She had chosen a career in chemistry, not in politics, but that night would change her life. Merkel had been born in Hamburg in 1954, and even though she and her immediate family had moved to East Germany in 1957, she still maintained contact with an aunt in her hometown. On the night of November 9, once she made it to West Berlin, Merkel would call that aunt to say that she had crossed the border. It would be the first of many nights of crossing the East-West divide for Merkel, in both literal and figurative terms.[72] She would soon become active in the new East German party Democratic Awakening, which would enter into an election alliance with the CDU, eventually bringing Merkel into the latter

Following Harald Jäger's decision to open the gates at the Bornholmer Street border crossing on the night of November 9, massive crowds flow through the final barrier gate of the checkpoint and over the bridge (top rear of photo) into West Berlin.

(RHG Fo AnKae 541; photo by Andreas Kämper)

party's ranks. As a member of the CDU, Merkel would start her phenomenal rise to the chancellorship of united Germany.[73]

Not even Schabowski could resist seeing for himself what was going on. After getting late-night reports in Wandlitz, he had his driver take him back downtown on a brief tour of some of the border crossings, including Bornholmer. Schabowski then returned home to Wandlitz for the second time that night without having tried to interfere or indeed to do anything at the checkpoints. Schabowski later said that, after returning home, he spoke to Krenz on the phone and found Krenz was consoling himself with the belief that "the ones who are leaving today, they will come back."[74]

Krenz would later say that he had spent that evening, after the late conclusion to the day's central committee session around 9:00 p.m., issuing orders to open all of the border crossings.[75] Evidence supporting this claim has not been found. Instead, the evidence that survives shows individual checkpoint officials making uncoordinated decisions. Bornholmer was the first location where the senior figure on-site opened the barriers, and after images of the massive crowd running across the bridge there started appearing on TV, it became harder and harder for the other border crossings to hold out.[76] The anxious officials at Checkpoint Charlie had, after turning down the drinks offered to them by the café owner across the street, actually sealed off the border entirely with large rolling barriers. Before too long, however, they gave up trying to keep the barriers in place and let people cross. The staff at the Sonnenallee checkpoint had been using the let-off-steam protocol as well. The officials there had been keeping a detailed list of people expelled, but by midnight they ceased trying to keep track of people's identities. Sonnenallee informed Stasi headquarters that, as of 12:17 a.m. on November 10, they were "opening everything."[77] One by one, border officials elsewhere along the Wall similarly let the crowds pass—although some guards viewed the concession as only a temporary retreat.

THERE WAS NO crossing point at the Brandenburg Gate. Yet both Easterners and Westerners were drawn to it that night. For a while, the Wall in front of it remained as forbidding as ever. Gradually, however, a few individuals started braving its heights. According to Stasi reports, people began climbing on the Wall near the Brandenburg Gate at about 9:00 p.m. but initially were willing to obey orders to come down. The secret police noted that by 11:57 p.m., however, climbers were no longer listening.[78] An unplanned collaboration was unfolding: the NBC floodlights made it much easier for climbers to scramble up to the top of the Wall, and in turn, NBC's cameras filmed the striking sight. Then, minutes before the 12:30 a.m. start of the broadcast, a camera operator hand-delivered footage from the opening of Bornholmer to Kusnetz. By the time the cameraman got to Kusnetz, he was gasping for breath from the effort of running across much of Berlin. The footage was just what Kusnetz needed to feed to Wheatley, the show's executive producer, back in New York: a video clip from Bornholmer would be the perfect start to the *Nightly News* broadcast.[79]

There was still one big potential problem with the live broadcast, however. Shortly before Brokaw was to go on air, security officials on the eastern side of the Brandenburg Gate had started using water cannons to force people off the Wall. The spray was not as powerful as it could have been because the hoses seemed to be leaky, but its impact was still strong enough to cause most climbers to get down. One young man, determined to stay on the Wall nonetheless, was handed an umbrella by the crowd to use as a shield. The spray bounced off the umbrella and shimmered in the bright floodlights as he held the flimsy shield between himself and the stream from the water cannons.[80]

Viewing images of these developments at NBC headquarters in New York, Wheatley and Gould wondered what they would do if the water cannons also managed to hit Brokaw while the show was on the air. Wheatley decided to have a backup anchorman, Garrick Utley, ready to take over from New York on a moment's notice if Brokaw was knocked down.[81] Meanwhile, Gould made her final preparations in the control room and communicated directly with Brokaw, half a world away, through his earpiece. By that point, Gould, the first woman to hold such a job at a major network, had been producing for years, but the night of November 9 would be a singular broadcast for her. The veteran producer remembered that, moments before the show went on air, she heard her heart pounding in her chest. She knew that she was orchestrating the coverage of one of the most momentous events of her lifetime. Brokaw also had some last-minute worries. Telling himself, "This is a big deal, don't screw it up," he calmed his nerves and turned to the camera to begin.

"A historic moment tonight," he intoned over the opening video clip of the throngs at Bornholmer, now accompanied by soaring music. "The Berlin Wall can no longer contain the East German people. Thousands, pouring across at the Bornholmer Bridge!" After the clip ended, NBC cut to its first live shot of Brokaw. Viewers in the United States suddenly saw the astonishing image of Brokaw, the Wall, the Brandenburg Gate, the hoses, the spraying water glinting in the floodlights, and, as if that were not enough, right in the center of the screen, one soaking-wet celebrant now standing defiantly on the top of the Wall and waving his arms in victory. One of Brokaw's producers, Lamprecht, later remarked that the scene looked as if it had been staged by a Las Vegas promoter.[82]

Despite the deafening commotion around him, Brokaw calmly proceeded to summarize the events of the day, pulling in prepared and live segments. Behind the scenes, NBC officials scrambled to bargain for a larger satellite window on short notice so that they could continue broadcasting beyond the time slot that they had already booked. They were able to talk other broadcasters into giving NBC their satellite time. In the end, Brokaw was able to introduce *Nightly News* afresh every time the show began airing in another US time zone.[83] When the run of airings finished, he led an hour-long special for the network. It was well into November 10 before he got a break.

Ironically, given his millions of viewers, one person who did not hear or see the NBC coverage that night was Brokaw's wife. Her husband had spent much of 1989 on airplanes, broadcasting everywhere from China to Eastern Europe to the Philippines, so the fact that he was abroad again was nothing unusual. She had not even turned on the television that evening, and Brokaw had not found a spare minute to go to a phone and to call her. Only when she was walking their Labrador through New York the next morning and ran into friends who spontaneously said, "Tom has never been better," did she hear the news.[84]

CROWDS KEPT FLOODING across the border through the early hours of November 10. Word of Jahn, Radomski, and Schefke's plan to celebrate at the Cuckoo's Egg somehow spread among their friends, and throughout the night one East German after another walked through the door of the West Berlin pub. Radomski was proud of his fellow East Berliners. Even in the midst of chaos and in an unfamiliar city, they knew how to find the party.

After years of working with Jahn without ever having met him, Radomski and Schefke finally saw him in person for the first time that night at the Cuckoo's Egg. They had learned to trust and to like each other by courier and by phone. Now they could actually share a drink. As they settled in for a celebration that would seemingly never end—it would be five days before Schefke finally picked up his car, still parked near Born-holmer Street border crossing—Radomski remembered thinking, "Now the story is at an end, and the party begins." There would of course be new adventures, challenges, disappointments, and hurdles in the years to come. Many of their dissident friends would in fact be displeased by the open-ing of the Wall, feeling that they had been on the verge of democratizing East Germany themselves, and now they were facing a takeover by West Germany instead.[85] That night, however, Jahn, Radomski, and Schefke felt that the risks that they had taken, the interrogations, and the time in prison had all been worth it. The story of their personal struggles had come to a breathtakingly swift and resoundingly happy conclusion.

Chapter Seven

Damage Control?

A S THE RAUCOUS CELEBRATIONS inside the Cuckoo's Egg continued, outside "the largest block party in history" was taking place,
in the words of NBC correspondent Martin Fletcher. To Fletcher,
the party was "made even more inspiring because it was a double block
party—East and West."[1] People were literally dancing in the streets—
not a few of them to the words of David Hasselhoff's song "Looking for
Freedom," which had spent eight weeks as the number-one hit in West
Germany in 1989. It would not be long before a promoter would bring
Hasselhoff to Berlin, put him in a suit rigged with lights, and have him
perform the song standing near the remains of the Wall.

On November 10, beyond the loud music and lights, however, another
story was unfolding. In places, the East German security forces tolerated
the partying, drinking, and climbing on the Wall, but in other places they
intervened to end the celebrations. The NBC cameras on the cherry picker
at the Brandenburg Gate began capturing images of East German security
officials violently removing people on the eastern side of the Wall, in stark
contrast to the scenes of happiness that predominated in the West. It made
for an odd juxtaposition with the scenes of joy and was difficult to explain
on the fly. At some point on November 10, Brokaw found that he had to
provide narration for the footage of celebrants being hauled off forcibly
by East German security forces. Guessing that maybe they had become
drunk and disorderly, he admitted, "We don't know what happened to
these people."[2]

Neither he nor any other journalist knew that reservists had been sent
to reseal the area around the Brandenburg Gate. By about 3:20 a.m., as

Brokaw was getting ready to introduce *Nightly News* for the West Coast of the United States, the reservists and other security forces retook control of the area around the gate. Around 4:30 a.m., the Stasi received a report that the area was completely clear.[3] Similarly, officials at various other border crossings tried to reclaim control, and some even managed to do so. By 2:40 a.m., Oberbaum Bridge checkpoint officials reported that they had "succeeded in restoring a normal situation."[4] One Stasi officer at Invaliden Street later reported calling up armed reinforcements—saying, "we could have just set the weapons to fire fully automatically" and sprayed bullets "with our eyes closed"—but Stasi files record that, as of about 3:30 a.m. border officials had reinstated order without recourse to such measures.[5] In addition, a Stasi-wide order went out on November 10, instructing all staff to remain on duty until further notice.[6] At an internal Stasi assessment that day, General Rudi Mittig deemed the events of the previous night the consequence of "increased activity on the part of imperialist intelligence agencies and their agents," who, he claimed, had been planning to "storm the Wall" since October 7.[7]

Over at the Interior Ministry, the main author of the text that had unexpectedly opened the Wall, Gerhard Lauter, was working through the night as well. He and his wife had seen the theater production and returned home, only to be greeted by their son's astonishing announcement that the Wall was open. Without even taking off his coat, Lauter had headed right back to his office, certain "that a catastrophe had taken place."[8] When he got there, he looked at the board of lights signaling incoming phone calls and saw that every light was on. At first by himself, then with support after he roused colleagues, he tried to answer the phone calls, whether from high-level party members or even from the US ambassador, who somehow got through to Lauter on that chaotic night. Lauter estimated that he fielded hundreds of phone calls. At one point his boss decided that, on top of everything else, Lauter should also go on news broadcasts on the morning of November 10 in a retroactive attempt to explain that applications were still necessary.[9]

L AUTER WAS HARDLY the only middle-tier official working through the night in East Berlin. The Soviet embassy, which contained both the offices and residences of embassy staff, sat prominently on Unter den Linden near the Brandenburg Gate. Even decades later, Igor Maximychev, the deputy ambassador, could still recall the noise of the massive shuffling of feet going by his windows in the direction of the gate through the night. His boss, the ambassador, had gone to sleep before the rush to the gate had started, so Maximychev was the senior official awake at the embassy, the most important Soviet political institution in East Germany, when the Wall opened. It was, in the first instance, up to him to respond.[10]

He and the other embassy staff—most notably Vladimir Grinin, the future Russian ambassador to united Germany—debated their options. Maximychev later explained that they were conscious of a number of pressing concerns, although minute-by-minute reporting on events to Moscow was not one of them. Such reporting was the responsibility of the massive East German outpost of the Soviet secret police, the KGB, in East Berlin. Ivan Kuzmin, a senior KGB agent in East Germany, later confirmed that his outpost did send reports on the events of the evening from the GDR to Moscow during the night, but they do not seem to have reached senior political figures.[11]

Rather, the embassy staff had the more significant and delicate responsibility of communicating with top party leaders back in Moscow about the political impact of the events and what the next steps should be. Such communication would clearly be difficult, not only because it would involve awakening the ambassador but also because of the time difference involved. Events had broken late on November 9 in divided Germany, which meant that they had broken in the early hours of November 10, Moscow time.

Maximychev worried about the unintended consequences of middle-of-the-night efforts to wake important people in Moscow. "We all had an ill-defined fear of what might happen if, in the middle of the night, we disrupted everyone with our news. It would have been hard to avoid the impression that we were sending a call for help." Maximychev was also concerned that the people whom he could readily get on the phone in Moscow in the early hours of the morning—as he put it, "the junior people, those who were unavoidably the only ones reachable on duty in the night hours"—might exceed their authority and introduce "measures that we would all bitterly regret later." Anyone he contacted in Moscow, Maximychev assumed, would then immediately call East German Politburo members as well. The deputy ambassador felt certain that some East German leaders remained "active supporters of a 'Chinese' variant" and might use the crisis to say that the moment had come to crack down. Maximychev was also conscious of the fact that leaders of East Germany often pretended to speak Russian better than they in fact did, since there was political pressure on them to possess perfect command of the language. As a result, they would act as if they could field phone calls in Russian without translation, even if they were not up to the task. Late at night and in a crisis situation, their language skills might not be sufficient to allow them to understand critical information, and that could cause additional problems all on its own.

In short, as Maximychev later explained, he was convinced that it would not take much for an attempt at damage control by the Soviet embassy to turn into a crisis. The deputy ambassador believed that even "a single shot on this night would have been the same as a worldwide catastrophe."[12] His fears mirrored those of both Kuzmin, the senior KGB agent, and Chancellor Kohl. Kuzmin later remarked that on November 9–10, there was not only "a real danger of bloodshed" but also the possibility of "involvement of the Soviet fighting forces."[13] And Kohl wrote in his memoirs, though without revealing his sources, that he had learned that opponents of Gorbachev's reform in both the KGB and the Stasi wanted to use the chaos in divided Berlin that night as a pretext for deploying Soviet troops in East Germany to reseal the border.[14]

Maximychev, after weighing all of these concerns, decided to do nothing. Neither he nor any other member of the embassy staff awakened their boss, the ambassador. They did not attempt to contact Moscow. Maximychev figured they would hear soon enough from party leaders in the morning, and he was right.

Once the day began in Moscow, the phone in the Soviet embassy in East Berlin started ringing continuously. After the long night without communication and all of the previous days of fruitless attempts to track down someone in authority about the hole variant, it suddenly felt to Maximychev as if, in the course of November 10, "half of official Moscow personally called the embassy" in East Berlin. All Soviet callers had the same question: "Was all of that agreed with us?" Maximychev would accurately respond, "Not with the embassy, maybe directly with Moscow?"[15] The embassy had dealt only with the approval of the hole variant, nothing more.[16] Ambassador Vyacheslav Kochemasov, looking back years later, still felt a great deal of "bitterness" about these events. In his memoirs, Kochemasov speculated not only on "what the leadership of the GDR should have done" but also on what he and his comrades might have done differently.[17] The former ambassador was vague on what, exactly, could have been done differently, but presumably it involved a more aggressive response.

MAXIMYCHEV'S SUSPICIONS that the East Berlin Politburo might in fact still be willing to respond aggressively, or perhaps to use force, were not unfounded. On November 10, Krenz raised the alert status of the army. The People's Army had been absent from the events of the night before, largely due to timing. Senior defense officials had scheduled a high-level meeting of commanders at a base in Strausberg, on the outskirts of East Berlin, for the night of the ninth. This meeting had been originally scheduled to start at 7:00 p.m., after the return of senior military officials from that day's central committee meeting in the center of town. Their subordinates, who were not politically significant enough to have attended the downtown meeting, assembled as scheduled shortly before 7:00 p.m., in order to be present at the very moment their senior officers arrived, so not one of them was able to view the crucial final minutes of the Schabowski press conference. Senior officers, in the central committee meeting that was running hours late, also did not see the press conference. Manfred Grätz, a deputy defense minister waiting that night in Strausberg, sat in the conference room for hours with his colleagues until the minister for defense and other senior leaders finally arrived around 10:00 p.m. As Grätz would later put it, "We sat around a lot, we talked a lot, we talked uselessly, and time ran out."

Once their superiors did arrive, the first order of business was not the situation on the streets, of which they were still unaware, but internal infighting. Grätz and a number of his colleagues, after sitting there for hours, found that the first item on the agenda was criticism of themselves. Reports of disturbances at border crossings trickled in around midnight, but as the checkpoints were in the first instance the responsibility of the Stasi, no one broke off the assembly, or even added a discussion of the events to the agenda. As Grätz would later conclude, "This was shameful."[18] As the magnitude of what had happened became clear, however, Krenz convened a special command group of the National Defense Council early on November 10, and had troops trained in military operations in urban terrain begin preparations for deployment.[19]

Party leaders convened as well: the three-day central committee meeting resumed for its final session on November 10. Although this meeting would seem to be an ideal opportunity for strategizing, the session opened at 9:00 a.m. without a word from anyone, including Krenz, about the night before. It was an impressive act of denial. In the course of that morning, however, Kochemasov had begun calling Krenz and kept calling

After day dawned on November 10, the scene at the Wall in front of the Brandenburg Gate differed greatly from all other days since the Wall's construction on August 13, 1961. Throughout Berlin, celebrants rejoiced in the opening of the barrier; here, thanks to the flat top at this location, they were able to stand on the Wall. *(SBM, Photo 0022-09214; photo by Margret Nissen)*

repeatedly, insisting that the leader of the SED provide not only the embassy but also Moscow with some immediate explanation about what had happened. By 10:00 a.m., perhaps because of this pressure from the Soviets, Krenz made a few references to the members of the central committee about the events at the border. However, the meeting broke up early, at 1:10 p.m. instead of 6:00 p.m., without having dealt in any serious way with the opening of the Wall. The power and relevance of the party were buckling and collapsing under the strain of events, caused by a combination of the party's own incompetence and the peaceful revolutionaries' willingness to seize the opening that the incompetence had provided.

Krenz tried to mollify Moscow by sending a telegram directly to Gorbachev, in which he made the inaccurate statement that "as of 6:00 a.m. this morning" the situation at the border had been brought under control, and that only East Germans who had applied for and received a visa were being let out.[20] In fact, individual checkpoints were still acting more or less on their own. One factor making a more coordinated response difficult was the rise of finger-pointing and anger about the night before. Some border guards could not suppress their rage at party leaders over what they had been forced to endure. On November 10, the Stasi compiled a long list of complaints. There were expressions of anguish, lamenting that "this short-notice regulation" had come as a "total surprise." As one guard put it, "You cannot just give out information like that on the margins of a press conference." There was concern that what had happened would lead to "an increasing loss of motivation" for the border authorities. A member of one of the border guard regiments spoke for many when he said, "I am asking myself whether the party is still able to lead the state." Another said simply, "I do not understand the world anymore." There were some positive comments: one man pointed out that he and his colleagues had received "more flowers and wine" the previous night than in all the years before. Complaints were much more numerous, however.

Perhaps the clearest statement of the fury felt by border guards was addressed to Krenz personally. A group of party members in Border Regiment 36 wrote directly to him, saying that "we regard the events of November 9–10, 1989," as "pure and simple betrayal and scorn for the performance of the protective and security forces." They had, "without being informed," found themselves "forced to abandon all military and party principles." The signers of the letter demanded "that the responsible comrades be held accountable" for this betrayal.[21]

A S THE EAST GERMAN regime and their Soviet allies failed to find some effective way to respond to the accidental opening of the Wall, observers on the other side of the Iron Curtain tried to understand the events of November 9–10 and how they had missed predicting them. The West Berlin police were baffled. The Stasi, still spying on them even after the Wall opened, found that West Berlin police were skeptical that there had been a "decision" to open the Wall at all. In their view, East Germans had been attempting "to maintain the possibility of total control over GDR citizens under somewhat different circumstances."[22]

At the elite political level in West Germany, Kohl's senior foreign policy advisor, Horst Teltschik, and another chancellery official, Dieter Kastrup, recalled that their "intelligence services completely missed everything." Had Kohl's senior advisors heard from their intelligence operatives, or from those of any of the Western countries who were their partners, that the Wall might possibly open, the chancellor and nearly his entire staff would not have headed to Warsaw that day.[23] Later, intelligence chiefs would face criticism for not providing advance word on the "order" to open the Wall.

The intelligence services of the Western occupying powers, along with their leaders, were also surprised by events and assumed that they were intentional. Due to the time difference, that very same day President George H. W. Bush was able, in his own words, to "welcome the decision by the East German leadership to open the borders to those wishing to emigrate or travel."[24] Other world leaders did the same in the following days. The British prime minister, Margaret Thatcher, issued a press release welcoming the regime's "decision to lift travel restrictions."[25] Meanwhile, in West Berlin, members of the British Military Government provided blankets, tents, and space for emergency housing. They also sent food trucks to the border to provide for the masses of visitors.[26] Privately, Thatcher expressed worry about what was happening—not because it seemed unplanned, but because it might inspire a resurgence of German nationalism. As one of her aides put it, "The Prime Minister was frankly horrified by the sight of the Bundestag [the West German parliament] rising to sing *Deutschland über alles* when the news of the developments on the Berlin Wall came in." She apparently did not know that West Germany had substituted the words from the third, less objectionable verse of the anthem for those of the first in 1952, although the music, by Joseph Haydn, had remained the same.[27]

Thatcher's Foreign Office guessed correctly that Gorbachev had been surprised by events. On Saturday, November 11, the British ambassador to Moscow wrote his superiors that "Gorbachev's policy in Eastern Europe is being overrun by events. . . . Gorbachev's problem now is to control the forces that he has unleashed. I do not think the Russians know how to do this. Hence their public silence."[28] The West German ambassador to Moscow also noted in a telegram to Bonn that there was "no official or media reaction" to November 9.[29]

The Soviet silence did, in fact, conceal the confusion that Gorbachev and his most significant foreign policy advisors, such as Anatoly Chernyaev, were experiencing. They were certain of one aspect of the story: If there had been a decision to open the Wall, they and their embassy in East Berlin had not been part of it. Now they were unsure about how to respond in public. Chernyaev confided his initial reactions to his diary. He was rueful overall, but generous toward Gorbachev. When "the Berlin Wall fell," it meant that "a whole era of the socialist system ended." As a result, "now only our 'best friends' Castro, Ceausescu, Kim Il-Sung are left. They hate us passionately."

But, Chernyaev concluded, "the Berlin Wall, that is the main thing," because its passing represented "the end of Yalta, the finale for the Stalinist legacy," and the "overcoming of Hitler's Germany." In the Wall's surprising opening, Chernyaev saw a kind of unexpected victory for Gorbachev: "He has proven himself to be truly great, because he sensed the path of history and helped it to follow its natural path."[30]

Gorbachev was worried enough about the path of history to have a spoken message passed to Helmut Kohl on November 10, once the chancellor arrived in West Berlin. Earlier that day, Kohl had informed Tadeusz Mazowiecki, the unhappy Polish prime minister, that he needed to interrupt his visit to Poland in order to return briefly to divided Germany.[31] Kohl and his entourage then flew to Hamburg, where, as occupation air travel rules still required, they switched to a US aircraft to fly to West Berlin. The chancellor had wanted to go directly to Bonn, but the announcement of a large public event in front of the Schöneberg Town Hall prompted him to make a stop in West Berlin first.[32]

The Soviet ambassador to West Germany, Yuli Kvitsinsky, tracked down Kohl and Teltschik by phone after they arrived in West Berlin. Teltschik received the call in a local government office, and the Stasi managed to conduct surveillance of it. Such problems were part of the reason Kohl wanted to hurry back to Bonn, where he had more secure means of communication. Teltschik asked Kvitsinsky, "Mr. Ambassador, how is it going?" The ambassador replied, "Ach, okay. A little hectic." Teltschik agreed: "You can say that again." Then the ambassador got right to the reason for his call: "Do you have a pencil?" Teltschik said yes, and Kvitsinsky read the message from Gorbachev for Kohl, which expressed Gorbachev's worry about the unexpected events in divided Berlin and asked for Kohl's help in ensuring that developments "not be allowed to get out of hand."[33]

When he had the full message, Teltschik said goodbye to the Soviet ambassador and returned to Kohl's side, repeating the message to Kohl just as the chancellor was preparing to speak at the Schöneberg rally. It was clear that dealing with Gorbachev and his anxieties would be a high priority, but that could be done only from Bonn. Kohl and Teltschik would make it back to their capital city that night, but not until they had put in an appearance at a second rally in West Berlin aimed at CDU supporters and paid a brief visit to Checkpoint Charlie to see the ongoing celebrations with their own eyes.[34] The intense time pressure meant that they could not linger, however. They had promised to return to Poland as soon as possible but had to get to Bonn first to make a number of pressing calls, not least to Gorbachev, from the chancellery's secure phone lines. Copies of Gorbachev's message had also gone out to the three Western powers in Berlin, so the chancellor urgently needed to coordinate a response with them as well.[35] When Kohl finally made it back to Bonn late that night, he would spend much of the night on the phone.[36]

The next day Kohl also spoke with Krenz and congratulated him on "the important decision on the opening," but soon after, a report arrived in Kohl's office detailing the utter chaos of that opening. The chancellor learned of the total confusion of East German border officials: that they had had no clear orders, that their responses to the press conference had varied widely, that even as Bornholmer Street officials had opened their main barrier gate, Invaliden Street had refused to let people through. The confidential analysis came to the conclusion that the freedom at the borders "might not be lasting."[37]

Although this report to the chancellor did not note it, West Berlin's mayor had unknowingly escaped a risky situation at Invaliden Street. Momper had spent most of the night on television but left the studio to open an emergency meeting of the Berlin senate at 10:00 p.m., which, like his on-air remarks, focused on practical issues such as transport. He also made contact with the Western occupying powers. Fortunately for Momper, most of them were all at the same fiftieth-birthday party as the British commander, so he could talk to them, one after another, on the same phone call.[38]

Momper ended up back in a television studio and was on air when he received a note saying that there was a large exodus of people leaving Bornholmer Street. He decided that he had to go to the Wall, and headed for the crossing that he himself used most frequently, Invaliden Street, because he thought he might recognize some of the guards there.[39] After trying and failing to find someone on the East German side who could tell him what was going on, Momper decided to address the crowd personally. At 1:35 a.m., Momper used a megaphone to urge the crowds at the checkpoint to remain calm and to allow passage through the border crossing.[40]

According to the Stasi, there were more than twenty thousand people in the area at the time, many of them drinking. Apparently seeing the mayor of West Berlin speaking at their border crossing so incensed some of the checkpoint officials at Invaliden Street that they considered forcibly wrestling him into one of the on-site detention units. Hearing this later, Momper thought it fortunate that cooler heads had prevailed, because

Crowds took advantage of a new path across the former death strip to cross from one side of Berlin to the other after the opening of the Wall. *(SBM, Photo 0008-12158; photo by Lothar Scholz)*

there was a chance that the West Berliners would have tried to intervene, and violence could have ensued.[41]

The French ambassador to East Berlin, in a telegram to Paris, questioned whether the term "'opening' of the Wall" was accurate and reported that the East German regime was still trying to enforce the requirement for applications. GDR media were also making pointed announcements that the relevant offices would open for passport and visa applications at 8:00 a.m. on November 10.[42] And at 2:00 a.m. on November 10, a radio announcement by an East German broadcaster said that border controls would, in fact, be fully reinstated six hours later, at 8:00 a.m.[43]

Decades of arbitrary repression left many East Germans willing to believe that this reinstatement would happen. Tom Sello, the Environmental Library activist who had worked together with the Gethsemane Church to publicize the crimes of the regime, had not gone to the Wall at all by the morning of November 10. Instead, he had been in the library most of the night, using the time between his day-job shifts to print copies of an underground newspaper with a mimeograph machine. He felt that he could not stop. The newspaper was relatively new and an important source of uncensored updates for East Germans, so Sello wanted to ensure that it would be ready to distribute on time.[44]

When his wife heard at 7:15 a.m. that there would be a border reclosure in forty-five minutes, however, she told him, and they both believed it. They dropped everything and took their children to the nearby Invaliden Street border crossing. The Sello family made it there on foot at ten minutes before eight, only to find the pedestrian approach overwhelmed with a massive crowd. It was clear that they would not reach the front of the line by 8:00 a.m.

Sello noticed, however, that cars were moving through the crossing. Such was the mood of the day, and so great his belief that the border would, in fact, be resealed, that Sello intentionally leapt in front of a moving vehicle, waving his arms. The car stopped, and Sello begged the driver for a ride, explaining that he "wanted his children to see where their grandmother lived" in the West. Sello's mother would come to them, but the children had never been able to visit her, and Sello wanted it to happen "at least once in their lives." Indicating the mob of people waiting at the pedestrian exit, Sello convinced the driver that the only way his family could get out before the reclosure of the border would be in the stranger's vehicle. The driver agreed, and took them through the checkpoint to a pay phone in the West so that they could call Sello's mother and have her come find them.[45]

Sello need not have thrown himself in front of a moving car. The idea of reinstating border controls by 8:00 a.m. proved to be impossible. The tide of people was simply too large and the collapse of the regime's authority too complete.

As Sello was standing at a West Berlin pay phone and dialing his mother, across town Tom Brokaw's right-hand man, Marc Kusnetz, was heading back to his hotel room. He had helped to conduct hours of interviews through the night, mostly near the base of the Wall. Above his head, people had begun to use chisels, hammers, and even their bare hands to chip away souvenir pieces of the Wall, generating clouds of grayish dust. When he got into his hotel bathroom, he could see in the mirror that his face was completely covered in a thick layer of chalky powder. He hunched over the sink, splashing water on his face and replaying the unbelievable events of the night in his mind. As he watched the "gray, gritty stuff" come off his face and swirl downward, he suddenly realized that he was watching the Berlin Wall go down the drain.[46]

WITHIN THE NEXT three days, it is possible that as many as three million GDR citizens visited West Berlin and West Germany.[47] Of all the checkpoints, Bornholmer not only opened first but also saw the most people leave. Officially, Jäger and his subordinates reported to Stasi headquarters that on the night of November 9–10, about twenty thousand pedestrians and a thousand drivers had left for the West via their checkpoint. The actual numbers were almost certainly higher. Optimistically, someone at Bornholmer also recorded that every single one of those twenty thousand pedestrians had returned and that about six hundred of the vehicles had as well.[48]

The numbers reported for the next day were higher: an estimated 120,000 pedestrians and nearly five thousand cars headed for West Berlin via Bornholmer Street alone, out of an estimated total of over five hundred thousand exits by foot and more than twenty-six thousand by vehicle.[49] Other border crossings reported thousands of pedestrians and drivers exiting as well.[50] An internal Stasi report estimated that many of those exiting failed to return, resulting in a net population loss.[51]

Still trying to the last to maintain control over the movement of its people, the regime kept insisting for days that travelers needed to apply for visas. Over five million were reportedly granted by November 15, although it is hard to know whether East German officials put out an inflated number in order to make compliance seem more widespread than it actually was.[52] The West Berlin newspaper *Tagesspiegel* reported that the GDR offices responsible for visa distribution were "overrun" and could not distribute visas fast enough, however, so clearly many East Germans believed that their regime still held power over them.[53]

Military units stayed on alert status until November 11, at which point the regime finally had them stand down, and ended the requirement for all Stasi employees to remain on duty.[54] Only on November 14 did the GDR finally and definitively bring all ambiguity about gunfire at the border to an end by halting the practice. The dog runs survived until December 1989, when state authorities finally began to break them down as well. What happened to the miserable animals thereafter is unclear, but if it was consistent with their previous treatment by border soldiers, it was as depraved and inhumane as the Wall itself had been.[55]

Epilogue

Violence and Victory, Trust and Triumphalism

He was not one of those
who turn around one more time
after everything has been decided.

—DURS GRÜNBEIN[1]

THE OPENING OF THE Berlin Wall, itself a consequence of a highly unlikely series of events, set in motion subsequent events of enormous reach and import. Although an end to the division of Germany had not been on Gorbachev's agenda, the developments of November 9 suddenly put it there. Other leaders also had to reassess their priorities and to decide swiftly on their next steps. It was as if a starter's gun had suddenly signaled the beginning of a race that no world leader had been expecting to run: the race to define the political structure of post–Cold War Europe.

George H. W. Bush moved quickly and decisively in cooperation with Helmut Kohl to ensure that Washington and Bonn won that race and dominated the shaping of post-Wall Europe and transatlantic relations. Their main goal, which they accomplished skillfully, was to maintain a strong US presence in post–Cold War Europe and to extend existing Western institutions eastward—and, as Robert Gates, the deputy national security advisor and later defense secretary, put it, "to bribe the Soviets out."[2] Even though Bush used the phrase "new world order" in public, in private the language that he used while strategizing was more suitable to old-fashioned hardball politics. When he and Kohl met at Camp David in February 1990 and the question of compromising with Moscow arose, Bush responded, "To hell with that! We prevailed and they didn't. We can't let the Soviets clutch victory from the jaws of defeat."[3] Bush and Kohl made certain, above all, that it would be possible for NATO not only to endure beyond the end of the contest with the Soviet Union in Europe but also to expand eastward beyond its 1989 border in the middle of divided Germany. Meanwhile, Kohl also worked with Mitterrand and other West European leaders—and in agreement with the newly elected heads of East European states and governments—to find ways to allow the European Community or EC, the immediate predecessor to the European Union, to expand eastward as well. The two most significant Cold War institutions of the West, NATO and the EC, thus retained their dominant roles in the post–Cold War world, the rhetoric about a "new world order" notwithstanding.[4]

A similar process unfolded inside Germany itself. A statewide election in the GDR on March 18, 1990, saw the CDU's Lothar de Maizière become prime minister. The real victor of that election, however, was Kohl. The West German chancellor had personally run large campaign rallies for the CDU in East Germany, even though he was not on the ballot and the GDR was still a separate state. The main thrust of Kohl's rallies was a promise to reunify the country on West German terms as rapidly as possible. Kohl's personal efforts proved controversial but also influential: the CDU won an unexpected and resounding victory.

Since the voters had rewarded him and his party handsomely, he was able to make good on his promise. Kohl and his advisors devised a plan for adding the territory of East Germany to the FRG, thereby extending West German laws and institutions to the East, and secured the agreement of both the GDR government and the occupying powers to follow this plan—although Soviet approval came only as a result of large financial incentives from Bonn. By doing this Kohl avoided the process of drafting a new constitution, the idea originally envisaged in Article 146 of the FRG's Basic Law. The authors of the Basic Law had inserted this article to make clear that the document was a kind of "placeholder" for West Germany, in force only until Germans could unite in free self-determination and produce a constitution, presumably by holding a formal convention. Over the intervening four decades, however, the Basic Law had proven too successful to risk discarding it, and in 1990 the prospect of holding a new constitutional convention had come to seem too daunting to risk trying it. Kohl chose instead to rely on the Basic Law's Article 23, which allowed new states to join the Federal Republic. This article had enabled a region on the Franco-German border called the Saarland to become a West

German state in 1957, following a vote by its residents to do so.[5] Using that precedent, East Germany could divide itself into a collection of states, and those states could then join West Germany as a group. This plan worried the Poles, however. They were concerned that the FRG might also wish to make parts of Poland that had previously belonged to Germany into new states as well. Kohl, de Maizière, and their respective governments moved forward with Article 23 proceedings despite the Polish worries, and the resulting five new states were able to join West Germany on October 3, 1990, less than a year after the Wall opened.[6]

Throughout the course of this unification process in 1990, the chancellor emphasized the need to move as quickly as possible. In private, he explained his haste as a way of gathering his harvest before the storm. What kind of storm was left vague, but he apparently feared a change of heart, or change of leader, in Moscow before unification could be formally completed.[7] His fears were not unfounded: Gorbachev was proving unable to manage the forces that his reforms had unleashed in the USSR. Soviet hard-liners wanted to oust him and to undo his changes, while avid reformers and nationalist leaders wanted to go even further than Gorbachev himself was willing to do. The hard-liners would launch a coup against Gorbachev in 1991, but by that point it was too late to turn back the clock. Instead, the Soviet Union collapsed into its components, a process speeded along by ambitious Gorbachev opponents such as Boris Yeltsin. A host of new states emerged, redrawing borders from Europe to Asia. The Cold War contest between the Soviets and the West was no more.[8]

The decisions made by Bush, Kohl, Mitterrand, and other Western leaders in the wake of the opening of the Berlin Wall defined European politics for the next era.[9] Some former dissidents celebrated the arrival of this new era, but other activists from Warsaw Pact countries responded to it with dismay. Rather than witnessing the dawn of a "new world order," they saw a world still dominated by the Western institutions of the Cold War. They had hoped instead for the creation of more (or at least the expansion of existing) pan-European organizations such as the CSCE, the series of conferences originating in Helsinki that had pressured the members of the Soviet bloc to respect human rights. In addition, following their opposition to the missiles of not only the Warsaw Pact but also NATO, they hoped that Central and Eastern Europe would withdraw from both military blocs and demilitarize. The lack of an effective pan-European security organization became particularly painful to them after violent confrontations broke out in Yugoslavia in the 1990s and no European institution proved capable of ending the conflict on its own.[10] But the former dissidents in East Germany were largely powerless; the political parties affiliated with them had performed poorly in the March 1990 election in the GDR, and the United States remained hostile toward demilitarization and neutrality in Central Europe.[11] There was another reason why leading East German activists had a hard time advocating for their causes. The pattern of dissident leaders gaining power after 1989 by transitioning to top political posts—along the lines of Václav Havel in Czechoslovakia, or Lech Wałęsa in Poland—was not replicated in united Germany.[12] As Hattenhauer put it, the GDR's dissidents had to compete with a "perfect second version" of their own country, complete with established political leaders, and they did not fare well in that competition.[13]

A FTER THE opening of the Wall, the SED and the Stasi had tried to keep functioning as they had always done. The SED renamed itself the Party of Democratic Socialism, but was unable to hold on to its dominant role in the GDR after the election of March 1990. And the Stasi faced new challenges from peaceful revolutionaries. Upon entering secret police buildings in Leipzig and elsewhere in the GDR, they had discovered Stasi employees assiduously following Mielke's instructions to destroy the organization's files. To curb these efforts, activists occupied Stasi offices and called for the ministry to be dismantled altogether; their intervention ultimately succeeded. An enormous debate over whether to allow public access to the files that had been saved by the activists followed. The solution came in the form of the Stasi Archive Law of united Germany, which granted access to the files under strict guidelines.[14] Similarly, East German border officials saw their former authority disappear rapidly. Their employment officially ended on September 30, 1990, three days before German unification. A reminder of the extent of the border guards' ability to use force emerged from the dismantling process: dismissed guards returned more than fifty-four thousand guns and over three thousand tons of ammunition. Presumably they kept some for themselves or sold such items on the black market as well.[15]

The Wall itself started to disappear quickly. Soon after November 9, 1989, workers began using heavy construction equipment to tear down both the Wall and the border fortifications between the two Germanys. The Bornholmer Street checkpoint was razed to the ground; the only remaining traces, other than some wiring, were faded lines and white numbers that had marked the pavement where, for so many years, cars had waited to cross. Twenty years later, even these final traces disappeared when a developer built a grocery store at the site.[16]

Meanwhile, the individuals most directly involved in the Wall's demise returned to the mundane concerns of everyday life, albeit under vastly different conditions than before. Harald Jäger, by opening the Wall, had put himself out of work. Since his cancer tests turned out to be negative, he still had decades of working life left, but he never found steady employment again. He held a series of odd jobs instead, including one as a taxi driver in united Berlin. His last position was as a security guard. After retiring, he moved to a small garden cottage in a rural area outside Berlin. Under the provisions of the complicated regulations governing post-unification pensions, he was allocated a small monthly amount by way of retirement support, enough to get by.[17]

Jäger's willingness, at times, to talk to journalists and to scholars about his decision on the night of November 9, 1989, did create a certain amount of awareness of his role. The fact that he had been a long-serving Stasi officer meant that he would never receive any awards or medals, however. Film and television producers would occasionally create docudramas including a character based on Jäger, although such portrayals were not always flattering—a problem that Katrin Hattenhauer, the Leipzig activist who had been in solitary confinement in October 1989, faced as well. After unification, she had moved on with her life by relocating to Berlin and becoming an artist. She never bothered to read her own Stasi files, but had to revisit her past in an unwelcome way, and even threaten legal action, when a group of television producers who had seen her files announced that they wanted to make a movie based on her life. In their proposed script, they wrongly implied that she had betrayed her friends while in prison and that the main motive for her actions had been love for a Western man. With the help of the Stasi Archive and lawyers, she was able to convince them to cancel their intended project.[18]

In the view of other former activists, post-unification public recognition could be problematic in another way as well: it did not, in their opinion, always fall on the most deserving recipients. Christian Führer and Hans-Jürgen Sievers, the ministers of the Nikolai and the Reformed Churches of Leipzig, respectively, both continued their work, with the difference that Führer became a celebrity and had to make room in his calendar for one award ceremony after another. He received, among other recognitions, the Theodor Heuss Medal in 1991, the Augsburg Peace Prize together with Gorbachev in 2005, and the Hans Böckler Medal in 2008. Former activists repeatedly asserted that—though many church members such as Führer had contributed to the success of the Monday marches—if there was any one minister who should be singled out, it should be Christoph Wonneberger. However, Wonneberger's devastating stroke of October 1989, which rendered him mute for years as he struggled to learn how to speak again, had taken him out of both the public scene and popular memory. The activists' efforts eventually bore some fruit. When Führer, along with Schwabe and Gesine Oltmanns, learned that they would be receiving awards from the president of united Germany in 1994, the three agreed to request as a group that Wonneberger receive one as well. And Wonneberger got more belated recognition in 2014 when the selection committee for the German National Prize similarly decided to grant an award not only to Führer but also to Schwabe and Wonneberger.[19]

Another kind of memory lapse was intentional. An investigative committee in Saxony charged with uncovering the abuses of former regime leaders began work after unification, but its task proved to be difficult. Documents mysteriously disappeared from archives when investigators came searching for them, and interviews yielded repeated cases of amnesia and statements such as "I cannot remember" or "That was beyond my knowledge."[20] These difficulties in Saxony matched those of similar investigations elsewhere in the five new states.

Legal efforts to bring the crimes of the former East German regime to light were also subjected to the criticism that they were nothing more than "victors' justice."[21] Courts in the united Germany did, nonetheless, hold a number of trials of former border guards and SED officials. One of the prime movers behind these trials was the tireless Karin Gueffroy, whose son Chris had been killed while trying to escape to West Berlin in February 1989. She collected as much evidence from her son's killing as possible, and her efforts resulted in the very first legal proceedings arising from the shootings at the Berlin Wall. Starting on September 2, 1991, the four border guards involved in her son's death went on trial. Karin was soon shocked by the amount of hostility directed at her. She received repeated death threats and her home was burglarized; she assumed these were the actions of former Stasi agents and their sympathizers.[22]

The proceedings at court were hardly more auspicious. The lawyers for the defense were allowed to accept payments from a media group. Perhaps not surprisingly, evidence from the unfolding trial found its way into various broadcasts and publications. At one point a magazine even printed a photograph of Chris's corpse on an autopsy table. Representatives of the magazine distributed copies at the courthouse—including one to Karin, who had never seen the gruesome image before, and who began to weep. She later declared the moment of seeing that photo as "the worst thing that had happened to me since Chris's death."[23]

In 1994, after a lengthy trial and appeal, all of Karin Gueffroy's efforts yielded only one conviction, of the marksman with the "shooter's cord" who had fired the fatal bullet into her son's heart. His sentence was light.[24] Karin could at least share the burden of keeping Chris's memory alive with her son's former friends, such as Dirk Regel, who, like Chris, had dreamed of seeing America. After the Wall fell, Regel did not just visit the United States, he moved to San Francisco permanently. He earned an MBA and became a US citizen in 2013. Despite living so far from Berlin, Regel remained in regular contact with the mother of his deceased friend. He told her that, at least in his own mind, Chris had come to California with him.[25]

In all, about 250 people were charged for their actions at the former border, resulting in roughly 130 convictions. By and large these convictions were of former lower-level officials and guards, but ten former SED leaders, including both Egon Krenz and Günter Schabowski, were among them.[26] Because of his advanced liver cancer, which his physicians had initially diagnosed and concealed in 1989, Honecker was released from legal proceedings in 1993. The disease killed him roughly a year later.[27]

Yet another way former East Germans sought justice was in the court of public opinion. This was the route that Roland Jahn chose. On November 10, after helping to broadcast the news of the opening of the Wall and celebrating in the Cuckoo's Egg, he traveled to his East German hometown, Jena. He wanted, for the first time since having been expelled forcibly from the GDR in 1983, to walk through the door of his parents' house, which he soon did. He had more serious business in mind, too. On another trip he took a camera team with him to the nearby city of Gera, where he had been imprisoned. He and his colleagues came across one of his former Stasi interrogators, who asked, "What, now you want revenge?" Jahn replied simply, "No, justice."[28] Jahn filmed and produced countless news reports and documentaries, uncovering the banality, corruption, and venality of the former East German ruling regime. He and Marianne Birthler, the Gethsemane Church activist who had cataloged police brutality, served as the second and third directors, respectively, of the Stasi Archive in united Germany. The first person to run the archive was another former dissident, Joachim Gauck, who went on to become president of Germany in 2012.

Jahn's former partners, Aram Radomski and Siggi Schefke, both thrived in unified Germany. At long last, they enjoyed the opportunity to receive both recognition and material rewards for their labors. Radomski converted his talent as a clandestine photojournalist into a profitable career in business, founding a successful company that produced large-format prints of photographs as wallpaper.[29] Schefke also drew on his background as a kind of undercover correspondent to build his post-Wall career. He moved from Berlin to Leipzig to accept a job at a regional broadcaster, and about twenty years after the Wall opened, together with his wife and children, he embarked on his own American dream as well. The Schefke family bought a second home in Miami, Florida, after falling in love with the city on a vacation. Schefke also treated himself to a sleek black Mercedes. When former dissident friends teased him about the luxuries, he responded that he had not helped to cause a revolution so that he could stay home and keep driving a car with a two-cylinder engine.[30]

Among those who prospered after the fall of the Wall were Tom Brokaw and his *Nightly News* producers. They continued their already successful careers in broadcast news—although, surprisingly, they did not win a single Emmy Award for their exclusive coverage of November 9–10, 1989. Perhaps the seeming inevitability of the Wall's opening made NBC's decision to broadcast from divided Berlin look obvious, rather than farsighted, to those charged with dispensing the awards.

Former servants of the East German and Soviet ruling regimes met with difficulties of their own after the Wall. Helmut Hackenberg, the Leipzig party secretary who ordered his forces to assume a defensive position on October 9, appears to have suffered a nervous breakdown shortly afterward.[31] Gerhard Lauter, the prime author of the text that opened the Wall, moved from Berlin to Leipzig after his employer, the Ministry of the Interior, and his state, the GDR, both ceased to exist, although he remained a believer in the ideals of Communism. He practiced law in Leipzig for a time before retiring to live in a modest apartment outside the city center. Igor Maximychev, the deputy Soviet ambassador, moved back to Moscow and wrote books about European politics. His younger colleague, Vladimir Grinin, continued his career as a diplomat and returned to the former Soviet embassy on Unter den Linden in Berlin in 2010 as the Russian ambassador. And Vladimir Putin, the KGB officer in Dresden, returned home full of regret at how "the Soviet Union had lost its position in Europe."[32] He began a career in politics fuelled by a desire to restore Russia, at least, to what he viewed as its rightful position.

Putin's later political prominence was the exception: on the whole, the individuals most directly involved in the dramatic events of November 9 faded from public view and led prosaic lives after the dust had (literally) settled. For at least some former East Germans, the everyday realities of capitalist life proved to be disappointing. An unexpected wave of public nostalgia for the certainties of life in the GDR, even if they had been constraining, began to emerge. But as Durs Grünbein, one of the most successful writers to emerge from the former East Germany, suggested in an essay about Bornholmer Street nineteen years after the fall of the Wall, the legacy of the events there on November 9 meant that there was no turning around.[33] The opening of the Wall was the point of no return in the collapse of the Cold War.

IT WAS NOT only contemporaries who largely forgot the individuals directly involved in that opening. Later scholars accepted at face value Krenz's claim that he had been responsible for it.[34] In this narrative, East Germans are passive recipients of a gift handed to them from their leaders on high. A variant of this is the idea that, in some practical way, a detailed road map for the Wall's opening emerged after President Ronald Reagan's 1987 speech in Berlin, in which he demanded that Mikhail Gorbachev "tear down this wall."[35] And academics who do acknowledge the chaotic nature of the border-opening process have nevertheless started to discount it and the peaceful revolution of 1989. According to scholars in this camp, if the Leipzig ring road had not opened on October 9 or the Wall had not fallen on November 9, these events would have happened the next day, or the next day, or soon after that. How those events actually happened is thus not of great importance.[36]

The evidence presented in this book shows just how wrong such views are. The Wall's opening was not a gift from political elites, East German or otherwise, and was in no way predetermined. It resulted from a remarkable constellation of actors and contingent events—and not a little courage on the part of some of the individuals directly involved—that came together in a precise but entirely unplanned sequence. And the larger, successful peaceful revolution surrounding the opening was a truly rare event, one to be considered carefully, not discounted. The history of 1989 shows just how many things have to go right for such a revolution to succeed.

Rather than rely on false assumptions that matters were inevitable and preordained, we should remember Bloch's warning about the bias of hindsight. The paradox of unexpected events, such as the opening of the Wall on November 9, 1989, is that they are improbable outcomes—but after they occur, they seem inevitable.[37] In 1989, on both sides of the border between the two Germanys, hundreds of thousands of troops along with thermonuclear weapons stood at the ready. Gorbachev had certainly been trying to reduce tensions, but he could have been felled by a single bullet, and the capability of the Soviet Union to start a nuclear war remained. Local actors were capable of using force as well. If a member of what Karin Gueffroy had called the brutal quarter had been on duty at Bornholmer Street on the night of November 9, the outcome of the events of that night could have been very different.

Looking back twenty-five years later, Krenz, who had initially claimed authorship of the peaceful outcome in late 1989, conceded that "we were closer to a civil-war-like situation than many people want to believe today." On the day that the Wall opened, there existed "the real danger of a military escalation in which the superpowers could have become involved."[38] Krenz's latter-day remarks suggest that violence remained an option well into 1989; it had certainly been Erich Honecker's preferred method of proceeding. As Kohl repeatedly pointed out, if Honecker had instituted reforms, he might have been able to save himself and his party, but he preferred the use of force instead. While such violence might have been a sensible response early on (from the point of view of the regime) when protests were small and could be crushed in secrecy, such violence became a much riskier strategy once the ranks of protestors swelled and the possibilities for information leaking out multiplied. Once that happened, the use of violence carried added costs that ultimately served to undermine the regime.[39]

A comparison with the People's Republic of China is useful in illuminating this point, the numerous differences between China and East Germany notwithstanding. Unlike Honecker, Deng Xiaoping, the de facto leader in Beijing in 1989, appears to have understood this dynamic—that violence cannot easily be scaled up, that bloodshed on a large scale carries added costs—and adjusted his course accordingly. Deng authorized the bloody crackdown in Tiananmen Square in June 1989 in order to keep the party's control over the country intact in the short term, but he realized that he needed a different strategy to succeed in the long term. When the time came to hand out jobs in the political reshuffle after the bloodshed, he snubbed the hard-liners in Beijing who had overseen the crackdown.[40] Instead, he summoned Jiang Zemin, the Shanghai party chief, to become the new general secretary. Deng also intensified the drive to liberalize China's economy. He thereby managed to keep political control for his ruling party. Honecker, a vastly less skilled leader than Deng, had no such insight. His unwavering use of violence in response to the events of the autumn of 1989, unaccompanied by reforms, contributed greatly to his own ouster, the collapse of his regime, and the collapse of Soviet control of Eastern Europe.[41] Given the East German ruling regime's violent inclinations, the opening of the Wall on November 9, 1989, was not inevitably peaceful.

In short, how the Wall opened is a story of highly contingent events. Many of the causes would even be historical trivialities, if not for what followed. These causes—such as the presence of the words "Berlin (West)" and "right away" in Lauter's draft, the myriad failures of communication on November 9, the confusion of Schabowski's press conference that evening, the insults paid to Jäger by his superiors that night—show that significant events do not always happen for significant reasons.

Moreover, even if it were somehow possible to guarantee a constellation of causes that would ensure a peaceful opening of the Wall on any given day, how that opening actually occurred November 9 was extremely for tuitous in foreign policy terms. If the Wall had fallen later, Gorbachev would have been under far more pressure from the hard-liners who would eventually stage a coup against him.[42] Inside the Soviet military and other institutions were a number of leaders who, unlike Gorbachev, were still very much willing to enforce with violence what they believed to be their legitimate rights in East Germany.[43] The timing was also fortuitous with regard to the United States. Kohl often remarked on how lucky it was that the Wall opened before Saddam Hussein invaded Kuwait in the summer of 1990 and Iraq became the highest priority of the Bush administration.[44]

UNDERSTANDING HOW the Wall opened also helps us to understand why it did. The opening resulted from a dramatic interaction between long-term causes, such as the global superpower contest and the economic decay of the Soviet Union, and shorter-term developments, such as the growing inability of the East German ruling regime to govern and the rise of a peaceful revolution. A dramatic interaction between these two sets of causes was catalyzed by local actors in 1989. Since the longer-term causes have received the attention they deserve, but the shorter-term causes and catalysts have not, it has been the purpose of this book to tell the story of the latter.[45] To summarize them briefly, by the autumn of 1989, weakened by Gorbachev's reforms and its own ineptitude, the SED's authority was slipping, but the party still retained its capability for violence. A series of mistakes by the regime, however, such as sealing the GDR's borders, using violence on its own anniversary, and above all botching the process of rewriting travel regulations, created an opening for the newly emboldened opposition movement. Encouraged not only by its own successes earlier that autumn but also by the ongoing sense that the Soviets would not intervene, the civil resistance movement turned the potential for change inherent in the regime's mistakes into actual change. It brought down the Wall on November 9, 1989.

By contrasting the behavior of revolutionaries during this sequence of events with that of party leaders, we can better appreciate the proximate causes of the opening of the Wall. One of them was the resistance movement's adherence to nonviolence, since the regime's use of brutality had only served to inspire more converts to that movement. As Jahn put it, the state created its own enemies with its use of force. There was, of course, always the temptation for protestors to give in to rage as well, and that temptation became a reality in Dresden as the "last trains to freedom" passed through the city. And any crowd numbering in the thousands or tens of thousands of course carries within itself an implicit potential for violence, a potential not lost on the rulers. But the protestors in Saxony successfully returned to nonviolence, as shown by their actions in Leipzig on October 9. Ultimately their peaceful conduct allowed them to garner followers and to swell their own ranks in a way that they had never previously been able to accomplish, and to capitalize on mistakes by dictators.[46]

Another cause was the willingness of peaceful revolutionaries to trust one another.[47] Again and again, the story recounted in these pages shows that members of the ruling regime did not have confidence in each other or in their subordinates, such as Jäger, and that their lack of trust hindered effective action. This lack is surprising, given the fact that most party leaders had known each other or worked together for years or even decades. In contrast, among members of the opposition, there was a willingness to trust complete strangers in potentially life-threatening situations. The Leipzig interrogators at one point demanded to know of Hattenhauer how she and her friends held together, despite the Stasi's actions against them. She replied that shared suffering welded people together more strongly than shared success. As she put it, "Where the hammer has come down, whatever is underneath is going to hold together."[48] So they held together and, despite betrayals, remained willing to trust outsiders. Hattenhauer and other dissidents understood this as a conscious choice. They were small in number and could not have functioned without taking on new converts and the skills and energy that they had to offer, in part to compensate for those who had been imprisoned or who had headed west. As Wonneberger later put it, "We consciously chose to be naive."[49] Their example suggests that movements, like states, prosper when their leaders have the skills necessary to maintain confidence among themselves.[50]

The story told here also shows the significance of even small steps—whether taken by international organizations, outside broadcasters, or video-smuggling operations—aimed at promoting human rights inside dictatorial regimes. Even though churches in the GDR were subject to heavy Stasi surveillance and some church leaders betrayed the trust of their parishioners by serving as Stasi agents, the shelter that many religious establishments managed to provide to dissenters proved crucial. Similarly, the small measures implemented by the CSCE Final Act and its follow-up agreements, most notably the one emerging from Vienna, had a crucial cumulative impact. It was, to cite just one example, largely thanks to the relaxed border crossing restrictions provided by CSCE to Western journalists in Eastern Europe that Schefke's most reliable courier, Ulrich Schwarz, could reliably cross the border without being searched and thereby deliver videocassettes to Jahn.[51] Again, such small measures mattered.

Yet another short-term reason the Wall opened was the power of the applied combination of protest and publicity. In other words, both the local activists and their immediate chroniclers—in this case, video camera operators working together with major Western media outlets—were essential in bringing down a dictatorial regime. Peaceful revolutions face steep odds and limited chances of success, but the more publicity they can generate, the better their chances. The dictators in this case were right to fear not only dissidents but also camera crews, who covered the regime's retreat, thereby emboldening protestors and unsettling armed border staff. By the night of November 9, when the people appeared at the Berlin Wall and demanded to know of the border officials, *Will you let us pass?*, those people had become so certain of themselves, and the officials so unsure of themselves, that the answer was *We will.*

Finally, this examination of the proximate reasons why the Wall opened suggests that outsiders should exercise caution when estimating the impact of their own contributions. The evidence presented in these pages shows that outsiders mattered more in the longer term than in the shorter, and that the agency of local actors was decisive in the final instance. The attractiveness of the freedoms of the West, both political and commercial, served as motivation for large numbers of East Germans, judging by their

These photos from 2010 show the final traces of the Bornholmer Street checkpoint shortly before the construction of a grocery store eradicated them completely. The white lane lines of the former vehicle control area and the faded lane numbers were still visible on the pavement more than two decades after the collapse of the Wall. *(Photos by the author)*

vote for rapid unification on West German terms in March 1990. But while the superpowers and their allies played significant roles in shaping the context in which the Wall could open, they did not open it themselves. The Wall fell because of the decisions, both intentional and unintentional, made by people in the GDR, both dissidents and loyalists. In the years since, many US policy makers have undervalued, or failed to understand, this dynamic. Washington has instead seen itself as the primary author of developments that rapidly and at little risk tore down a wall and overthrew dictators. Such self perceptions have, among other things, made relations with a still-resentful Russia difficult, and contributed to misguided attempts to "repeat" the performance.[52]

A physical expression of this belief is the fact that memorials dedicated to the opening of the Berlin Wall in the United States are more elaborate than anything in Germany. Among many other locations in the United States, the town of Fulton, Missouri—where Winston Churchill, the former British prime minister, gave his "Iron Curtain" speech—boasts an enormous installation of sections of the Wall. Multiple presidential libraries also have pieces of the Wall presented in a dramatic fashion, most notably the Ronald Reagan and George H. W. Bush Presidential Libraries. Even the statue of Reagan in the US Capitol Rotunda contains a band of concrete chunks from the Berlin Wall beneath the former president's feet.[53]

These memorials have no direct parallel in Germany—other than an exact duplicate, or "sister casting," of the Bush Library statue, given to the city of Berlin by American donors as a gift for a location in the south of the city where US troops used to reside.[54] In contrast, while the location of the Wall's first opening at Bornholmer Street was renamed November 9, 1989 Square, the dominant structure at that site remains a grocery store. Some information panels advise passersby of what once happened there, but they are already falling prey to vandals and weather, and do not match the massive US memorials.[55]

This present lack of a major single monument to the opening of the Wall actually speaks well of the attitudes of today's Germans. Fragile information panels at Bornholmer are much less likely to incite feelings of nationalism and triumphalism than mighty statues.[56] There are also smaller memorials scattered at sites along the former path of the Wall, now a bike path, particularly at locations where deaths occurred. And at its Bernauer Street location, the Berlin Wall Foundation focuses its energies on keeping alive an awareness of the Wall's inhumanities, not on celebrating its demise in a triumphalist manner. The foundation does so by maintaining, among other memorials, a still-standing stretch of the former Wall and an installation dedicated to those who died at it.[57]

When the German parliament in 2007 set aside 10 million euros for a central, celebratory sculpture or other structure in Berlin, the international design competition that took place afterward ended in 2009 with a hung jury and no winner, despite receiving more than five hundred submissions.[58] A potential Leipzig memorial has also run into difficulties.[59] Given the tragic history of the twentieth century, Germans are wise to proceed cautiously in celebrating their own victories. Whether or not it was a wise decision to resume the Berlin design competition in 2010—and, this time, to choose a model for a "Freedom and Unity Memorial" for construction—remains to be seen.[60]

We end as we began: with Tocqueville, because he understood how evils once patiently borne can suddenly become intolerable once their removal seems within reach. By the night of November 9, 1989, East Germans had indeed reached the point where the Wall had become intolerable, once the Schabowski press conference presented them with an opportunity to remove it. The failures of the ruling regime and the success of the revolutionary movement of fall 1989 combined to give both activists and average East Germans the confidence needed to seize that opportunity, and to turn a bungled press announcement into the end of the regime's control over their lives. In seizing that opportunity, however, East Germans behaved in a way that ran counter to another of Tocqueville's predictions: they did not resort to the violence that Tocqueville theorized would follow. The way that later observers still underestimate the significance of this accomplishment amazes Birthler and other former East German revolutionaries. In her view, outsiders seem to think that "it was the opening of the Wall that brought us our freedom." She views this as a fundamental misreading of the situation, and she is right. Rather, "it was the other way around. First we fought for our freedom; and then, because of that, the Wall fell."[61]

Acknowledgments

This book has been a particular pleasure to write, not least because it has allowed me to combine my research of recent years with my earlier interest in, and work on, this topic. Parts of this research even date back to my time as a graduate student at Yale University, where I received support not only from Yale's International Security Studies Program but also from both the German Academic Exchange Service (or DAAD in its German initials) and the Alexander von Humboldt Foundation. I remain grateful, all these years later, to these institutions and to the people in charge while I had the good fortune to be affiliated with them. Later, while serving as an untenured, then tenured, member of the faculty of the University of Cambridge in England, I received support from the Humboldt Foundation once again, the London School of Economics, St. John's College, and the Mershon Center of The Ohio State University, for which I am thankful. After my return to the United States to become a professor at the University of Southern California (USC), the American Academy in Berlin, the Institute for Advanced Study in Princeton, the Mudd Library of Princeton University, and the National Endowment for the Humanities all provided funds and often office space to help me to continue my research on the collapse of the Cold War.

In the closing years of my work on this project, USC provided both generous research funding and support for a workshop that gave me a chance to bring together colleagues from around the world. I am grateful to the workshop participants and particularly to Erin Barber, Mai'a Davis Cross, Rob English, Travis Glynn, Pat James, John Odell, Indira Persad, Marisela Schaffer, Karen Tang, Marc Trachtenberg, and Albert Shaumyan for their help in securing the funding for, and with the running of, this workshop. I am additionally thankful to the administration of USC for providing an extended leave to allow me to accept a visiting professorship in both the Government and History Departments of Harvard University. Because of these departments and the Center for European Studies, I was able to draw on Harvard's wonderful libraries as I completed the writing of this book. I am deeply grateful to the administrators, deans, department chairs, and staff members who helped to make my stay at Harvard both possible and enjoyable, including David Armitage, Filomena Cabral, Timothy

Colton, Trisha Craig, Paul Dzus, Grzegorz Ekiert, Laura Falloon, Laura Fisher, Janet Hatch, Elizabeth Johnson, Peter Marsden, Mary McConnell, Elaine Papoulias, Anna Popiel, Mike Smith, and Diana Sorensen.

When it came time to turn the manuscript into a book, Andrew Wylie and his staff, particularly Devin Kennedy and Kristina Moore, provided expert advice on the process. They connected me for the first time with the New York publishing world and with Basic Books. My editor at Basic, Lara Heimert, has repeatedly shown the depth of her experience with her wise advice on how to edit and to shape the final text. I am also grateful to Dan Gerstle, Chris Granville, Mike Morgenfeld, Leah Stecher, Michelle Welsh-Horst, and Sue Warga for their help in the final production of the book.

This volume would not have been possible without the cooperation of former participants in the events themselves. More than fifty of them made time to answer my many questions. They are named individually in the list of interviews, but I would like to express my thanks to them collectively here, as well as mention a few who went out of their way to help me even more. In particular, I am grateful to both Katrin Hattenhauer and Siegbert "Siggi" Schefke for giving me the necessary legal authority to view and to copy the full contents of their Stasi files. I would also like to acknowledge Christopher Ochs and Tom Sello at the Robert Havemann Foundation in Berlin, and Rainer Eckert and Uwe Schwabe at the Forum for Contemporary History in Leipzig, for assisting me both with their own memories and in finding interview partners, photographs, and readings. Similarly, Peter Brinkmann and Georg Mascolo generously provided not only their own personal recollections but also video recordings from the night of November 9, and Brinkmann and Rainer Eckert shared forthcoming manuscripts as well. Hans-Jürgen and Wilma Sievers walked me through some of the key locations of the Leipzig Monday marches and shared extensively from their own memories as they did.

Archivists and institutional historians are essential to a project such as this, and I was fortunate to work with truly excellent ones. In particular, I would like to thank Karin Göpel, Sylvia Gräfe, Robert Holzweiss, Dan Linke, Diana Manipud, Knud Piening, Zachary Roberts, Patrick Salmon, Lianne Smith, and Claudia Zenker-Oertel. Two librarians at the University of Wisconsin, Wayne Gathright and Andrea Rohlich, went above and beyond the call of duty to provide me with copies of important materials from Saxony in their holdings. The fact that the University of Wisconsin has, as far as I can tell, the only copies of these significant sources in the United States is a sign that someone very smart is in charge of collecting materials in Madison. I must also express my deep gratitude to Roberto Welzel at the Stasi Archive for responding with unflagging good humor and patience to a stream of detailed questions and document requests over many years, and for thereby helping me to understand how the Ministry for State Security worked.

A number of colleagues and friends also gave willingly of their time through-out the course of this project, whether by answering questions about how to find relevant articles, books, or interview partners, commenting on panel papers, inviting me to speak about my work, offering guest room space, proofreading, or simply providing good humor, support, or chocolate, whichever was most needed. I am grateful to Colleen Anderson, James Cacciola, Bill Cameron, Peter Chapman and Christopher Fowler, the Choi-Undheim family, Linda Cole, Alice Conklin, Greg Domber, Mateusz Fałkowski, Philipp Gassert, the Hadshiew-Tetu family, Hillary Hahm, Hope Harrison, the Lynn family, Michael Mayer, Geof-frey Parker, the Raskob family, Marie Pierre Rey, Ernst Georg Richter and Dor-othea Scherließ-Richter, Andreas Rödder, Teresa Shibuya, Ray and Eileen Silva, Amy Simonds and Tom Taylor, the Spaner family, Teresa Walsh, and, of course, my longtime (but hopefully not long-suffering) friend Jenni Siegel. Ambassador Philip Murphy of the US embassy in Berlin and his staff member Russell Singer were kind enough not only to invite me to the ambassadorial residence for a dinner but also to enable me to attend a speech in Berlin by President Barack Obama in June 2013. Arthur Goldhammer, the world's finest French translator, generously provided the English versions of the Tocqueville and Bloch quotations that open the book. Walter Süß gave freely of his time and of his wisdom from his decades of work at the Stasi Archive, and I am thankful to him. The director of the Berlin Wall Foundation, Axel Klausmeier, and its curator of collections, Manfred Wichmann, helped me enormously with their insights and their recom-mendations on books, photographs, and sources. I am also particularly grateful to my friend Hans-Hermann Hertle, the author of the best German-language books on the Wall and the moving spirit behind a number of seminal documen-tary films on the subject. Whether through his help in arranging a number of my initial interviews—even joining me for my first conversation with Harald Jäger—or through our years of conversations on the inner workings of a dicta-torship, he has generously helped me to understand the history of the city that he and his wife, Hilde Kroll, call home.

To those colleagues and friends on whom I imposed to read most or all of the manuscript, sometimes more than once, I do not believe that I can adequately express how important their help was. I will simply say thank you to Frédéric Bozo, Catherine Epstein, Jacques Hymans, Serhii Plokhy, and Odd Arne Westad for taking time away from their own work as professors, respectively, of history and international relations at the Sorbonne, of modern European history at Am-herst College, of international relations at USC, of Ukrainian and East European history at Harvard University, and of international history at the London School of Economics. Kathy Conley and Chris Miller improved the entire manuscript greatly with their strategic insights, thereby making it clear that they could take my job as a historian any day, although the US Air Force officer corps would have suffered badly if I had ever stood in for either of them. Jan Otakar Fischer, the director of Northeastern University's Berlin Architecture Program, made time not only to read the entire manuscript twice but also to visit numerous historical sites, including Stasi headquarters, and to bike the path of the former Wall with me, sharing generously of his knowledge all the while. In the final months of writing, my old friend John Logan Nichols, director of admissions at the United Nations International School, was kind enough to read the final text carefully and to save me from a number of grammatical errors.

For my beloved husband, Mark Schiefsky, there was truly no escape from the unending series of draft chapters dropped in the middle of his own work as the chair of the Department of the Classics at Harvard University. Fortunately for me, his learning and wisdom are so great that they easily span the time from antiquity to 1989. He has earned so many spousal points by editing this manuscript that it is seriously in doubt as to whether I will ever catch up. I hope that I have many remaining years to try.

It is, of course, ultimately one's family that makes all accomplishments possible and worthwhile. The furry members of my family, Juno and Toby, our rescue kitties, never failed in their job of keeping me company at the keyboard during the years of writing and editing. I must also express my appreciation for the support of my husband's relatives: Joan Oosterhuis, Tanya Oosterhuis, Donald Schiefsky, and the late and much-missed Mary Ann Schiefsky. The entire Michigan branch of the Sarottes, Claus and Rita Wulf, and the Scheffler family all provided support and good humor. Dianne and Albert Minicucci, my godparents, have been unparalleled family-by-choice for decades. Steven Sarotte, my brother, helpfully reminded me that David Hasselhoff opened the Berlin Wall whenever I was on the verge of forgetting it.

Finally, the memory of my parents, Frank and Gail Sarotte, remains sustaining even though they are gone. When I lost them both in 2009, I do not know what I would have done without Dianne and Al, my brother, and my husband. They kept me going during the dark time. For that—and for all the memories that we share of the love of my wonderful parents, and for all of the love over the years, and for all of the love over the years still to come—I dedicate this book to them.

Brief Timeline of Major Events
Highlighted in the Text

Spring/Summer 1989: Hungary dismantles the fortifications on its border with Austria, but Hungarian security forces still prevent East Germans from crossing, in accordance with treaty obligations with East Germany.

Sept. 11, 1989: Hungary begins allowing East Germans to leave for the West; in response, East Germany soon takes steps to prevent its citizens from traveling to Hungary in the first place, with the result that many instead seek refuge in the West German embassies in Prague and Warsaw.

Late Sept. 1989: Erich Honecker, the party leader and de facto head of East Germany, returns to his post after an extended sick leave.

Sept. 25, 1989: The first major attempt by Leipzig Monday marchers to circle the city's ring road.

Sept. 30, 1989: West German foreign minister Hans-Dietrich Genscher and chancellery official Rudolf Seiters travel to Prague to inform the East Germans on the embassy grounds that, per a one-off agreement with the ruling regime in East Berlin, they may exit for the West, but only if they travel in sealed trains through GDR territory. A similar agreement is reached for the East Germans at the Warsaw embassy.

Oct. 1, 1989: The first set of sealed trains begins travel through the GDR to West Germany, but soon after more East Germans seek refuge in the embassy in Prague.

Oct. 3, 1989: East Germany effectively seals its own citizens in by requiring multiple forms of state permission for exit to any neighboring country, including to fellow Warsaw Pact states, which had previously been accessible with minimal paperwork.

Approximately Oct. 3–8, 1989: Violent encounters between protestors and security forces rock the region of Saxony and the city of Dresden in particular as another set of sealed trains makes its way through the GDR; protests continue even after some of the trains have passed and others are rerouted away from Dresden.

Oct. 7, 1989: The fortieth anniversary of the founding of the GDR; celebrations are marked by violence between security forces and protestors throughout the country.

Oct. 9, 1989: At least 70,000 people participate in the Monday march in Leipzig; party leaders estimate the number to be 100,000. The march successfully circumnavigates the ring road.

Oct. 17, 1989: At a Politburo meeting, Egon Krenz overthrows Honecker to become the leader of the party. The change is announced publicly the next day as Honecker's "resignation."

Nov. 1, 1989: Under threat of strikes, the East German regime allows travel to Czechoslovakia to resume, resulting in a new wave of East Germans seeking refuge in the West German embassy in Prague.

Nov. 4, 1989: An estimated half million people attend a massive demonstration in the heart of East Berlin.

Nov. 6, 1989: The East German regime publishes a draft of a new travel law; the draft is widely condemned, including by roughly half a million marchers in Leipzig that night.

Nov. 9, 1989: The Berlin Wall opens.

Mar. 18, 1990: Free elections take place in the GDR.

Oct. 3, 1990: Germany reunifies when the territory of the GDR is converted into five new FRG states; as part of the FRG, these states immediately come under the jurisdiction of both the EC and NATO, thereby extending those organizations eastward beyond their 1989 borders for the first time in the post-Wall era.

Additional Information About, and Abbreviations in, the Notes and Bibliography

The spellings of some names may vary between the text and the notes. For example, the usual English-language versions of the names Kochemasov and Maximychev change to German-language renditions, which are sometimes inconsistent, in the notes if the source cited is in German (i.e., usually to Kotchemassow or Maximytschew). Similarly, the German double s, or ß, does not appear in the text, but does appear in notes citing older sources where it was still used.

Locations of primary sources (archives, collections of published documents, collections of documents distributed at scholarly conferences) are abbreviated as indicated below, and their full citations appear in the bibliography (to aid in the finding of the correct reference in the bibliography, the lead editor's last name is given below where relevant). The bibliography contains primary sources, memoirs, and autobiographical accounts; these are cited where appropriate in the notes as well. Because of space constraints, however, secondary sources appear in full citation only on first reference in the notes, and in short reference for all subsequent citations.

Any emphasis is present in the original unless otherwise indicated in the note. Citations from Stasi documents use the post-1990 Stasi Archive's page numbering if inserted, otherwise the original page numbers are given. Finally, the archival abbreviations below are for overall collections and major subcollections. Some minor abbreviations, used internally in archives, are not included, since they are available on the archival website and/or at the archive itself.

BArch	Bundesarchiv (West German, then German, Federal Archive)
BArchK	Bundesarchiv, Koblenz (site of former West German archive)
BDE	Bestand Deutscher Einheit (German Unity Collection), part of German Foreign Ministry Political Archive collection
BEL	Bezirkseinsatzleitung (District Deployment Leadership, East German term)
BP	James A. Baker III Papers, Princeton University

BPB   Bundeszentrale für politische Bildung (Federal Center for Politi-
            cal Education, Germany)
BRD   Bundesrepublik Deutschland (Federal Republic of Germany)
BStU   Bundesbeauftragter für die Unterlagen des Staatssicherheitsdienstes
            der ehemaligen Deutschen Demokratischen Republik (Commis-
            sioner for the Files of the State Security Service of the former Ger-
            man Democratic Republic, German name for the Stasi Archive)
CWIHPPC   Cold War International History Project Paris Conference
DA   Demokratischer Aufbruch (German name for Democratic Awak-
            ening, new East German political party in 1989)
DBPO   *Documents on British Policy Overseas*, published collection of Brit-
            ish documents, Salmon, ed.
DDR   Deutsche Demokratische Republik (German Democratic Republic)
DESE   *Deutsche Einheit Sonderedition (German Unity Special Edition),*
            published collection of West German documents, Küsters, ed.
DFUA   *La diplomatie française face à l'unification allemande (French Di-
            plomacy and German Unification),* published collection of French
            documents, Vaïsse, ed.
FRL   *Die friedliche Revolution in Leipzig (The Peaceful Revolution in
            Leipzig),* published collection of East German documents, Hol-
            litzer, ed.
FUF   *Freunde und Feinde (Friends and Enemies),* published collection of
            East German documents, Dietrich, ed.
GC   Georgia Conference proceedings, National Security Archive
GHWBPL   George H. W. Bush Presidential Library
GÜST   Grenzübergangsstelle (East German term for a border crossing)
KCLMA   King's College Liddell Hart Military Archive
memcon   Memorandum of conversation
MG   Михаил Горбачев и германский вопрос *(Mikhail Gorbachev
            and the German Question),* published collection of Russian docu-
            ments, Gorbachev, ed.
NSA   National Security Archive
PA-AA   Politisches Archiv, Auswärtiges Amt (Political Archive, Foreign
            Ministry, Germany)
PC   Prague Conference proceedings, National Security Archive
RRPL   Ronald Reagan Presidential Library
SAPMO   Stiftung/Archiv der Parteien und Massenorganisationen der
            DDR (Foundation /Archive of GDR Parties and Mass Organiza-
            tions, now part of BArch)

SPD	Sozialdemokratische Partei Deutschlands (Social-Democratic Party of Germany)
SS	*Schlußbericht des Sonderausschusses (Final Report of the Special Committee)*, report on the investigation of the state of Saxony into regime crimes in the GDR
ZRT-WD	*Der Zentrale Runde Tisch der DDR (Central Round Table of the GDR)*, published collection of East German documents, Thaysen, ed.

Interviews

Most interviews took place either in person or on the phone. If so, either the city and date, or "phone" and date, are listed below. If the interview took place via email, then the month or months of correspondence are given, as there were in all cases a series of emails over multiple dates.

Barkley, Richard; email, November 2013
Baum, Karl-Heinz; phone, August 13, 2013
Bindenagel, J. D.; phone, June 28, 2008
Birthler, Marianne; Berlin, June 25, 2013
Bitterlich, Joachim; Berlin, June 1, 2012, and June 17, 2013
Brinkmann, Peter; Berlin, June 24 and December 13, 2013
Brokaw, Tom; phone, July 26, 2013, and New York, May 14, 2014
Burton, Sir Michael; phone, August 8, 2013
Cooper, Belinda; phone, August 13, 2013
Eckert, Rainer; Leipzig, December 12, 2013
Elbe, Frank; phone, June 10 and 11, 2009
Fletcher, Martin; phone, August 19, 2013
Frick, Helmut; emails, October–November 2013
Gelefsky, Maralyn; phone, August 19, 2013
Genscher, Hans-Dietrich; Wachtberg-Pech, June 2, 2009
Gerz, Wolfgang; emails, October 2013
Gould, Cheryl; phone, August 16, 2013
Greenwald, Jonathan; phone, November 13, 2013
Grinin, Vladimir; Berlin, December 19, 2013
Gueffroy, Karin; Berlin, December 20, 2013
Hattenhauer, Katrin; Berlin, December 17, 2013
Horváth, István; emails, August–September 2013
Jäger, Harald; Werneuchen, June 8, 2012, with Hans-Hermann Hertle; phone, July 2, 2013
Jahn, Roland; Berlin, June 24, 2013
Johnson, Daniel; emails, October 2013
Kastrup, Dieter; emails, August 2013
Kiessler, Richard; Brussels, March 20, 2009
Krenz, Egon; emails, September–October 2013

Kusnetz, Marc; phone, August 28, 2013, and New York, March 3, 2014
Lamprecht, Jerry; emails, August–September 2013
Lauter, Gerhard; Leipzig, June 21, 2013
Leary, Mike; phone, September 19, 2013
Lipping, Imre; emails, November 2013
Mascolo, Georg; Cambridge, Massachusetts, November 4 and 25, 2013
Maximychev, Igor; emails, July–September 2013
Meckel, Markus; Berlin, June 1, 2012, and June 17, 2013
Momper, Walter; Berlin, June 17, 2013
Munro, Colin; emails, August–September 2013
Neubert, Michele; phone, August 28, 2013, and London, December 10, 2013
Poppe, Ulrike; Berlin, June 25, 2013
Radomski, Aram; Berlin, June 20, 2013
Regel, Dirk; phone, January 12, 2014
Schefke, Siegbert (Siggi); Leipzig, June 21 and December 12, 2013; Cambridge,
      Massachusetts, April 1, 2014
Schwabe, Uwe; Leipzig, December 12 and 13, 2013
Schwarz, Ulrich; Berlin, June 25, 2013
Sedlmaier, Benedikt; Berlin, June 18, 2013
Sello, Tom; Berlin, August 30, 2006, and June 20, 2013
Sievers, Hans-Jürgen; phone, August 19, 2013, and Leipzig, December 13, 2013
Teltschik, Horst; phone, June 12, 2008, and Berlin, June 25, 2013
Von Studnitz, Ernst-Jörg; emails, October 2013
Walling, Heinrich; phone, September 4, 2013
Wheatley, Bill; phone, March 5, 2014
Wonnberger, Christoph; Leipzig, December 12, 2013
(A phone interview with Kurt Masur could unfortunately not take place due
to Prof. Masur's unexpected hospitalization and subsequent illness. Christian
Führer and Günter Schabowski did not respond to requests for interviews; other
interview partners said that they were both in ill health.)

Notes

Note to Epigraph

1. Alexis de Tocqueville, *L'ancien régime et la révolution* (Paris: Michel Lévy Frères, 1856), 269–270; Jon Elster, ed., *The Ancien Régime and the French Revolution,* trans. Arthur Goldhammer (Cambridge: Cambridge University Press, 2011), 157. The original quotation in French is as follows: "Ce n'est pas toujours en allant de mal en pis que l'on tombe en révolution. Il arrive le plus souvent qu'un peuple qui avait supporté sans se plaindre, et comme s'il ne les sentait pas, les lois les plus accablantes, les rejette violemment dès que le poids s'en allège. . . . Le mal qu'on souffrait patiemment comme inévitable semble insupportable dès qu'on conçoit l'idée de s'y soustraire." To provide clarity for this excerpt, minor changes to the translation as originally published were undertaken in consultation with the translator.

Introduction: Discovering the Causes of the Collapse

1. These sentences are the concluding lines to Marc Bloch, *Apologie pour l'histoire* (Paris: Armand Colin, 1974), 160. The original quotation in French is as follows: "Pour tout dire d'un mot, les causes, en histoire pas plus qu'ailleurs, ne se postulent pas. Elles se cherchent. . . ." The translation of this quotation is from Arthur Goldhammer and I am grateful to him for it. For a full English translation of this book, see Marc Bloch, *The Historian's Craft: Reflections on the Nature and Uses of History and the Techniques and Methods of the Men Who Write It,* trans. Peter Putnam (New York: Vintage, 1964); Putnam's translation of this quotation is at 197.

2. It seems that the unusual shape of the Wall at this location was the result of an earlier face-off between US and Soviet tanks over Checkpoint Charlie. The regime appears to have feared that the West might move tanks to the Brandenburg Gate as well, and so constructed the Wall at this site to serve as a particularly effective barrier to tanks. Hence its squat, thick nature. For more on this point, see Johannes Cramer et al., *Die Baugeschichte der Berliner Mauer* (Petersberg: Imhof Verlag, 2011), 236–238, 305, particularly the photos at 236 and 305.

3. A video clip of this broadcast is available at www.nbcnews.com/id/33590933/#.UnEBuFGRP0c.

4. Hans-Hermann Hertle, *Die Berliner Mauer: Biografie eines Bauwerks* (Berlin: Links, 2011), 178–181; and Ilko-Sascha Kowalczuk, *Endspiel: Die Revolution von 1989 in der DDR* (Munich: Beck, 2009), 303–305.

5. Historian and theorist William Sewell has written convincingly of the need to investigate both *how* and *why* when looking at historical events. He laments that, too often, historians have "generally disdained the study of mere events and sought to instead discover general causal patterns underlying historical change." Rather, he sees a need to look both at events and structures and at their interaction: "I argue that events should be conceived of as sequences of occurrences that result in transformations of structures." Sewell provides a useful definition of a historical event as "(1) a ramified sequence of occurrences that (2) is recognized as notable by contemporaries, and that (3) results in a durable transformation of structures." He also argues that "changes tend to be clustered into relatively intense bursts. . . . Lumpiness, rather than smoothness, is the normal texture of historical temporality." See William H. Sewell Jr., "Historical Events as Transformations of Structures: Inventing Revolution at the Bastille," *Theory and Society* 25 (1996): 841–881, quotations at 841–844; I am grateful to Mary Lewis for drawing my attention to this article.

6. Christopher Clark expressed a similar thought in his own study of a brief but critical time period, namely the summer of 1914, in a way that applies to this book as well: "Questions of why and how are logically inseparable, but they lead us in different directions. The question of *how* invites us to look closely at the sequences of interactions that produced certain outcomes. By contrast, the question of *why* invites us to go in search of remote and categorical causes. . . . The why approach brings a certain analytical clarity, but it also has a distorting effect, because it creates the illusion of a steadily building causal pressure; the factors pile up on top of each other pushing down on the events; political actors become mere executors of forces long established and beyond their control. The story this book tells is, by contrast, saturated with agency." See Christopher Clark, *The Sleepwalkers: How Europe Went to War in 1914* (New York: Harper, 2013), xxix.

7. One such inaccurate claim—that the East German regime purposely authored the opening of the Wall—has found its way, despite a lack of evidence, into not only popular accounts but also otherwise carefully researched peer-reviewed academic histories in the intervening decades. To cite just two recent examples, see George Herring, *From Colony to Superpower: U.S. Foreign Relations Since 1776* (Oxford: Oxford University Press, 2008), 905, and Jonathan Haslam, *Russia's Cold War: From the October Revolution to the Fall of the Wall* (New Haven, CT: Yale University Press, 2011), 390–391; both of these sources are discussed further in the epilogue. Many eyewitnesses later claimed that they saw it all coming; see, for example, John Kornblum, "November 9, 1989," *Berlin Journal* 18 (Fall 2009): 10, where he remarks that "Most surprising to me about the events of November 9, 1989 was that so many people were surprised by them [*sic*]" since he was not. In contrast, the former US ambassador to East Germany in 1989, Richard Barkley, remarked in an interview with the author that neither he nor "anyone else in the US government" foresaw the opening of the

Wall, but "it is amazing how wise some of them have become in the intervening twenty-five years."

8. On such dramatic moments of rupture, see Sewell, "Historical Events," and Charles Maier, "Civil Resistance and Civil Society," in Adam Roberts and Timothy Garton Ash, eds., *Civil Resistance and Power Politics: The Experience of Non-Violent Action from Gandhi to the Present* (Oxford: Oxford University Press, 2009), 272–276, especially 276: "The historian should not abandon the search for the long-term or structural vulnerability, but neither should he or she forget that the *journée*, at least the repeated *journée, and* the *place* are the decisive theatres for radical upheaval. In physics and in the social sciences, sudden changes of state, discontinuities, bursts of self orga nization are fundamental challenges to explanation. Every smooth curve or continuous function potentially decomposes into jagged fragments at potentially any point."

9. Revolutions are rapid transformations of a state, its structures, and its dominant political principles through the mobilization of large numbers of its residents. This definition draws on the work of Mark Beissinger, who has combined aspects of two commonly used versions, that of Charles Tilly and that of Theda Skocpol. Beissinger sees Tilly's definition of revolution (as "a situation of dual sovereignty in which non-ruling contenders mobilise large numbers of citizens for the purpose of gaining control over the state") as narrower than Skocpol's, which emphasizes "the rapid transformation of a country's state and class structures and its dominant ideology." See Mark R. Beissinger, "Nationalism and the Collapse of Soviet Communism," *Contemporary European History* 18, no. 3 (2009): 343; Charles Tilly, *Contention and Democracy in Europe, 1650–2000* (Cambridge: Cambridge University Press, 2004); and Theda Skocpol, *States and Social Revolutions: A Comparative Analysis of France, Russia and China* (Cambridge: Cambridge University Press, 1979). As for "civil resistance" and "peaceful revolution," which I am using interchangeably in this book, I rely on the definition provided by Adam Roberts: "Civil resistance is a type of political action that relies on the use of non-violent methods. It is largely synonymous with certain other terms, including 'non-violent action,' 'non-violent resistance,' and 'people power.' It involves a range of widespread and sustained activities that challenge a particular power, force, policy, or regime—hence the term 'resistance.'" Adam Roberts, "Introduction," in Roberts and Garton Ash, eds., *Civil Resistance*, 2. For more on the nuances in various terms used to describe civil resistance in the East German context, see Ilko-Sascha Kowalczuk, "Artikulationsformen und Zielsetzungen von widerständigem Verhalten in verschiedenen Bereichen der Gesellschaft," in Deutscher Bundestag, 12. Wahlperiode, Enquete-Kommission, ed., *Materialien der Enquete-Kommission "Aufarbeitung von Geschichte und Folgen der SED-Diktatur in Deutschland"* (Bonn: Bundestag Drucksache 1994), vol. 7, pt. 2:1203–1284.

10. Broadly speaking, writers have generally focused on one or the other, namely, on the character and collapse of the ruling regime and other political elites, or on the experience of the broader population and of the protest movement. Authors focusing on elites tend to emphasize the East German ruling regime's "dissolution" or even "self-dissolution" when explaining the story of the fall of the Wall. See, for example,

Klaus-Dietmar Henke, "Zu Nutzung und Auswertung der Unterlagen des Staats-sicherheitsdiensts," *Vierteljahreshefte für Zeitgeschichte* 41, no. 4 (1993): 575–587; Hans-Hermann Hertle, *Der Fall der Mauer: Die unbeabsichtigte Selbstauflösung des SED-Staates* (Opladen: Westdeutscher Verlag, 1996) (the title in English is "The Fall of the Wall: The Unintentional Self-Dissolution of the SED State"); Charles S. Maier, *Dissolution: The Crisis of Communism and the End of East Germany* (Princeton, NJ: Princeton University Press, 1997); and Armin Mitter and Stefan Wolle, *Untergang auf Raten* (Munich: Bertelsmann, 1993). Other scholars, in contrast, focus on the wider population, the question of how GDR citizens could conduct "perfectly ordinary" lives in spite of various institutions of control, and the ways that popular movements eventually rejected dictatorial leaders. See, for example, Mary Fulbrook, *The People's State: East German Society from Hitler to Honecker* (New Haven, CT: Yale University Press, 2005), 11–23, which proposes the concept of a "participatory dictatorship" as a way of reconciling these two approaches, and Kowalczuk, *Endspiel*. For a comparison of these two approaches, see Gary Bruce, *The Firm: The Inside Story of the Stasi* (Oxford: Oxford University Press, 2010), 1–19.

11. Odd Arne Westad, *The Global Cold War: Third World Interventions and the Making of Our Times* (Cambridge: Cambridge University Press, 2005), 401–403.

12. For more on the conflicts within the Soviet Union and the rise of Solidarity, see Gregory Domber, *Empowering Revolution: America, Poland, and the End of the Cold War* (Chapel Hill: University of North Carolina Press, 2014); Serhii Plokhy, *The Last Empire: The Final Days of the Soviet Union* (New York: Basic Books, 2014); and Vladislav Zubok, *A Failed Empire: The Soviet Union in the Cold War from Stalin to Gorbachev* (Chapel Hill: University of North Carolina Press, 2007).

13. Archie Brown, *The Rise and Fall of Communism* (London: Vintage Books, 2010), 527. For more on the argument that Gorbachev intended to wage the Cold War in a different way, not to end it, see Sergey Radchenko, *Unwanted Visionaries: The Soviet Failure in Asia at the End of the Cold War* (Oxford: Oxford University Press, 2014).

14. For more on Stalin's death and its consequences in 1953, see Christian Ostermann, ed., *Uprising in East Germany 1953: The Cold War, the German Question, and the First Major Upheaval Behind the Iron Curtain* (New York: Central European University Press, 2001), and Klaus Larres and Kenneth Osgood, eds., *The Cold War After Stalin's Death: A Missed Opportunity for Peace?* (Lanham, MD: Rowman and Littlefield, 2006).

15. It is possible to research this speech in the original sources at the Reagan Library; see in particular RRPL, White House Staff Member and Office Files, Files of Peter M. Robinson, Files 1983–1988, Series I, Drafts, Box 9, Subject File, Notes from Berlin Pre-Advance. Also useful are the speechwriter's own comments; see Peter Robinson, *It's My Party: A Republican's Messy Love Affair with the GOP* (New York: Warner Books, 2000), and Peter M. Robinson, "Four Words That Moved the World: 'Tear Down This Wall,'" *Wall Street Journal*, June 9, 2012. See also Romesh Ratnesar, *Tear Down This Wall: A City, a President, and the Speech That Ended the Cold War* (New

York: Simon and Schuster, 2009), which includes the text of the speech; the quotation from Reagan's speech is at 210.

16. On Gorbachev-Reagan summits and Soviet-US relations, see Melvyn Leffler, *For the Soul of Mankind: The United States, the Soviet Union, and the Cold War* (New York: Hill and Wang, 2007); Jack F. Matlock Jr., *Reagan and Gorbachev: How the Cold War Ended* (New York: Random House, 2004); and James Graham Wilson, *The Triumph of Improvisation: Gorbachev's Adaptability, Reagan's Engagement, and the End of the Cold War* (Ithaca, NY: Cornell University Press, 2014). For differing views on the significance of US foreign policy in the 1980s, see John Lewis Gaddis, *The Cold War* (New York: Penguin, 2006); Tony Judt, "A Story Still to Be Told," *New York Review of Books,* Mar. 23, 2006; and James Mann, *The Rebellion of Ronald Reagan: A History of the End of the Cold War* (New York: Viking, 2009). On the superpower arms race in particular, see David E. Hoffman, *The Dead Hand: The Untold Story of the Cold War Arms Race and Its Dangerous Legacy* (New York: Anchor, 2010).

17. For analysis of one or both of the superpowers over the course of the entire Cold War, see, to name just a few, Brown, *Rise and Fall;* Gaddis, *Cold War;* John Lamberton Harper, *The Cold War* (Oxford: Oxford University Press, 2011); Tony Judt, *Postwar: A History of Europe Since 1945* (New York: Penguin, 2005); Leffler, *For the Soul of Mankind;* Westad, *Global Cold War;* and Zubok, *Failed Empire.*

18. Bloch, *Apologie,* 160. On Bloch's life and tragic death, see Carole Fink, *Marc Bloch: A Life in History* (Cambridge: Cambridge University Press, 1989), 86, 318–322.

19. On hindsight bias and on Tocqueville, see Timothy Garton Ash, "1989!" *New York Review of Books,* Nov. 5, 2009; Timothy Garton Ash, *The Magic Lantern: The Revolution of '89 Witnessed in Warsaw,* updated ed. (New York: Vintage Books, 1999), 142; Maier, "Civil Resistance," 275–276; and Maier, *Dissolution,* epigraph. On the significance of agency, see Clark, *Sleepwalkers,* xxix.

20. In these notes, I have listed when possible multiple pieces of evidence to support any given citation, in order of significance for that particular citation: audio, video, or written materials from the original time period; later interviews and other autobiographical narratives; and the relevant secondary literature and/or journalism. In cases where there was a single source, I have indicated that in the note, and, if that source was an interview, often signaled that in the text as well, by saying, "as person X later remembered," or "later recalled," or similar formulations.

21. Stasi Archive staff members are, for example, required to black out certain private details about the people discussed in the sources but, given the sheer mass of material involved, there is still more than enough information on display. More information about the rules governing use of the Stasi Archive is available on its website, in English as well as in German, at www.bstu.bund.de/EN/Home/home_node.html.

22. It is worth noting that the party was in all cases superior to the state in the countries of the Warsaw Pact. For more on the pact, see Vojtech Mastny and Malcolm Byrne, eds., *A Cardboard Castle? An Inside History of the Warsaw Pact* (New York: CEU Press, 2005).

23. A full list of the primary sources consulted and interviews conducted appears in the bibliography. The analysis here also builds upon some of my related works, such as *1989: The Struggle to Create Post–Cold War Europe* (Princeton, NJ: Princeton University Press, 2009); "Perpetuating U.S. Preeminence: The 1990 Deals to 'Bribe the Soviets Out' and Move NATO In," *International Security* 35 (July 2010): 110–137; and "China's Fear of Contagion," *International Security* 37 (Fall 2012): 156–182.

24. A catalyst is defined here as an agent that provokes or speeds a significant change or action. As Richard Ned Lebow has rightly argued, in our quest to discover deeper patterns in history we all too often underestimate the significance of short-term catalysts. We do so at our peril; "underlying causes, no matter how numerous or deep-seated, do not make an event inevitable." Rather, moments of dramatic change result not just from deeper trends but also from triggering agents and events. Moreover, catalysts are not like buses; they are not insignificant or interchangeable, and do not appear with regularity. Rather, they are worthy of study in their own right. See Richard Ned Lebow, "Contingency, Catalysts, and International System Change," *Political Science Quarterly* 115, no. 4 (Winter 2000–2001): 591–616, quotation at 591. The author is grateful to Jacques Hymans for pointing out this article. As the political scientist Robert Jervis has suggested, there is also need to question at what level we look for causation. In other words, as summarized by Lebow, Jervis argues that "structural change may be the product, not the cause, of behavior—the opposite of what most realist theories contend." Robert Jervis, *System Effects: Complexity in Political and Social Life* (Princeton, NJ: Princeton University Press, 1997), summarized by Lebow in "Contingency, Catalysts," 616.

25. These individuals shared little and mostly did not even know each other. The dissidents and the loyalists in particular were diametrically opposed to each other in their actions toward the ruling regime. They had crucial characteristics in common, however: they were neither members of the top political elite nor simply part of a broader mass of spectators to events; they were not in charge in 1989, but they were in the middle of the action. The contingencies of that autumn unexpectedly elevated their importance suddenly and dramatically. As a result, to understand how and why the Wall opened, it is essential to understand what can be called their "history from the middle" as well as the larger context. On this concept of history from the middle, see Paul Kennedy, "History from the Middle: The Case of the Second World War," *Journal of Military History* 74 (Jan. 2010): 35–51; and Paul Kennedy, *Engineers of Victory: The Problem Solvers Who Turned the Tide in the Second World War* (New York: Random House, 2013), xvii. On the need to ask where the main actors are to be found and who they were, see Michael Richter, *Die friedliche Revolution: Aufbruch zur Demokratie in Sachsen, 1989/90* (Göttingen: Vandenhoeck and Ruprecht, 2009), 21.

26. For more on the history of Berlin, Prussia, and Germany, not only in the bloody twentieth century but also in preceding centuries, see David Blackbourn, *History of Germany 1780–1918: The Long Nineteenth Century* (Oxford: Wiley-Blackwell, 2003); Christopher M. Clark, *Iron Kingdom: The Rise and Downfall of Prussia, 1600–1947* (Cambridge, MA: Harvard University Press, 2006); Gordon Craig, *Germany*

1866–1945 (Oxford: Oxford University Press, 1978); Mary Fulbrook, *A Concise History of Germany,* 2nd ed. (Cambridge: Cambridge University Press, 1991); Harold James, *A German Identity* (London: Phoenix, 1994); and Brendan Simms, *Europe: The Struggle for Supremacy, from 1453 to the Present* (New York: Basic Books, 2013).

27. Again, for similar (and, for this book, very apt) thinking, see Clark, *Sleepwalkers,* xxix: "a single, symbolic event—however deeply it may be enmeshed in larger historical processes—can change politics irrevocably, rendering old options obsolete and endowing new ones with an unforeseen urgency."

28. For more on the challenges facing nonviolent protest, see Roberts and Garton Ash, eds., *Civil Resistance;* see also Peter Ackerman and Jack DuVall, *A Force More Powerful: A Century of Non-Violent Conflict* (New York: Palgrave, 2000); Gene Sharp, *From Dictatorship to Democracy: A Conceptual Framework for Liberation* (New York: New Press, 2012); Sidney Tarrow, *The Language of Contention: Revolutions in Words, 1688–2012* (Cambridge: Cambridge University Press, 2013); and Sidney Tarrow, *Strangers at the Gates: Movements and States in Contentious Politics* (Cambridge: Cambridge University Press, 2012).

29. For more on this phenomenon, see Hal Brands, *From Berlin to Baghdad: America's Search for Purpose in the Post–Cold War World* (Lexington: University of Kentucky Press, 2008); Barbara J. Falk, "From Berlin to Baghdad: Learning the 'Wrong' Lessons from the Collapse of Communism," in George Lawson, Chris Armbruster, and Michael Cox, eds., *The Global 1989: Continuity and Change in World Politics* (Cambridge: Cambridge University Press, 2010), 243–270; and Ellen Schrecker, ed., *Cold War Triumphalism: The Misuse of History After the Fall of Communism* (New York: New Press, 2004). On US hubris more generally, see Peter Beinart, *The Icarus Syndrome: A History of American Hubris* (New York: Harper, 2010), and Fredrik Logevall and Campbell Craig, *America's Cold War: The Politics of Insecurity* (Cambridge, MA: Harvard University Press, 2009), 350. On the larger historical significance of the phrase "Berlin to Baghdad," see, among other sources, Sean McMeekin, *The Berlin-Baghdad Express: The Ottoman Empire and Germany's Bid for World Power* (Cambridge, MA: Harvard University Press, 2010).

30. My comments here—on the general applicability of specific cases of historical extremity—draw on the pathbreaking analysis by John Dower of the Japanese experience after World War II: ". . . it is such moments of extremity that often best reveal the essence of things. I myself find the concrete details and textures of this extraordinary experience of a whole country [Japan] starting over absorbing, but they do not strike me as alien, exotic, or even mainly instructive as an episode in the history of Japan or of US-Japanese relations. On the contrary, what is most compelling from my own perspective is that defeat and occupation forced Japanese in every walk of life to struggle, in exceptionally naked ways, with the most fundamental of life's issues—and that they responded in recognizably human, fallible, and often contradictory ways that can tell us a great deal about ourselves and our world in general." John Dower, *Embracing Defeat: Japan in the Wake of World War II* (New York: Norton, 1999), 29. I am grateful as well to Axel Klausmeier, the director of the Stiftung Berliner Mauer,

for a discussion on this point in June 2013. See also Rainer Eckert, *SED-Diktatur und Erinnerungsarbeit im vereinten Deutschland* (Berlin: Metropol Verlag, 2011), 12, and Henke, "Zu Nutzung und Auswertung," 575–587.

31. In his own article on the French Revolution, Sewell also emphasizes the key role of violence in a revolution. In Sewell's view, the central importance of the French Revolution was that it created a modern definition of revolution, namely, an event where popular violence combines with popular sovereignty to enhance the power of the people. See Sewell, "Historical Events," 860–861.

32. To assemble this story, and the abundant evidence on which it is based, into some kind of comprehensible format, this book presents its history as a series of ever smaller circles. The largest outer circle is the broader context of global history in the twentieth century. Set within that, the next concentric circle is the Cold War contest in Europe, and, within that, competition for control of the Saxon region of the GDR. The story then narrows to the streets of East Berlin and, finally, to the gates of the Berlin Wall itself.

Chapter 1: A Brutal Status Quo

1. Author's interview with Gueffroy.

2. For an insightful analysis of the varying responses to life under dictatorial control and the range of behaviors used to signal refusal of that control, see Fulbrook, *People's State*, 11–23, and Kowalczuk, "Artikulationsformen und Zielsetzungen." See also Ulrike Poppe, Rainer Eckert, and Ilko-Sascha Kowalczuk, eds., *Zwischen Selbstbehauptung und Anpassung: Formen des Widerstandes und der Opposition in der DDR* (Berlin: Links, 1995).

3. Author's interview with Gueffroy.

4. For an overview of the Cold War division of Europe, see Harper, *Cold War*; for more on the division of Germany specifically, see Edith Sheffer, *Burned Bridge: How East and West Germans Made the Iron Curtain* (Oxford: Oxford University Press, 2011).

5. On the Soviet empire, see Plokhy, *The Last Empire*, and Zubok, *A Failed Empire*. On the division of Europe, see James Cronin, *The World the Cold War Made: Order, Chaos, and the Return of History* (New York: Routledge, 1996), which rightly points out on p. 2 that "internal and external relations reinforced each other"; Judt, *Postwar*; Mark Mazower, *Dark Continent: Europe's Twentieth Century* (New York: Vintage, 2000); and Westad, *Global Cold War*, 397. See also John Mueller, "What Was the Cold War About?" *Political Science Quarterly* 119, no. 4 (2004–2005): 609–631.

6. For more on conditions in defeated Europe after World War II, see William I. Hitchcock, *The Bitter Road to Freedom: A New History of the Liberation of Europe* (New York: Free Press, 2008).

7. For a first-person account of the experience of such rapes, see Anonymous, *A Woman in Berlin*, trans. Philip Boehm (New York: Metropolitan Books, 2005). On the Soviet occupation of Germany generally, see Norman Naimark, *The Russians in*

Germany: A History of the Soviet Zone of Occupation, 1945–1949 (Cambridge, MA: Harvard University Press, 1995).

8. For more on the creation and history of the FRG, see Carolyn Woods Eisenberg, *Drawing the Line: The American Decision to Divide Germany: 1944–1949* (Cambridge: Cambridge University Press, 1996); Klaus-Dietmar Henke, *Die amerikanische Besetzung Deutschlands* (Munich: Oldenbourg, 1995); and Andreas Wirsching, *Abschied vom Provisorium 1982–1990: Geschichte der Bundesrepublik Deutschland* (Stuttgart: DVA, 2006).

9. Harold James, *A German Identity* (London: Phoenix, 1994), 240. On the broader theme of provisionality, see Wirsching, *Abschied vom Provisorium*.

10. For a brief history of the division of Germany, see Henry Ashby Turner, *Germany from Partition to Unification*, 2nd ed. (New Haven, CT: Yale University Press, 1992). For more on transatlantic relations during the Cold War, see Jussi M. Hanhimäki, Benedikt Schoenborn, and Barbara Zanchetta, *Transatlantic Relations Since 1945: An Introduction* (New York: Routledge, 2012), and Mary Nolan, *The Transatlantic Century: Europe and America, 1890–2010* (Cambridge: Cambridge University Press, 2012).

11. For more on the 1940s and the division of Europe, see William Hitchcock, *The Struggle for Europe: The Turbulent History of a Divided Continent 1945 to the Present* (New York: Doubleday, 2003), and, by the same author, *Bitter Road;* see also Mazower, *Dark Continent.* By way of comparison, on the later process of overcoming the division of Europe, see Jan Svejnar, "Transition Economies: Performance and Challenges," *Journal of Economic Perspectives* 16, no. 1 (Winter 2002): 3–28, and Jan Svejnar et al., "The Effects of Privatization and Ownership in Transition Economies," *Journal of Economic Literature* 47, no. 3 (Sept. 2009): 699–728.

12. On the FRG becoming a NATO member in 1955, see Helga Haftendorn, "[West] Germany's Accession to NATO: 50 Years On," *NATO Review,* June 1, 2005.

13. "Gespräch des Bundeskanzlers Kohl mit Präsident Bush in ertweitertem Kreise, Bonn," May 30, 1989, doc. 1, DESE 272–273. Also, a note in BDE, PA-AA, ZA 140.711E, indicates that in June 1989, the Soviet forces in divided Germany changed their name from "Gruppe der sowjetischen Streitkräfte in Deutschland" to "Westgruppe der sowjetischen Streitkräfte." On nuclear weapons and transatlantic politics during the Cold War, see Francis J. Gavin, *Nuclear Statecraft* (Ithaca, NY: Cornell University Press, 2012), and Marc Trachtenberg, *A Constructed Peace: The Making of the European Settlement 1945–1963* (Princeton, NJ: Princeton University Press, 1999); see also James Sheehan, *Where Have All the Soldiers Gone? The Transformation of Modern Europe* (Boston: Mariner Books, 2008).

14. On the history of the Berlin Wall, see Pertti Ahonen, *Death at the Berlin Wall* (Oxford: Oxford University Press, 2011); Hope Harrison, *Driving the Soviets Up the Wall* (Princeton, NJ: Princeton University Press, 2004); and Gerhard Sälter and Manfred Wilke, *Ultima Ratio* (Berlin: Konrad Adenauer Stiftung, 2011).

15. Speech by Honecker, Jan. 19, 1989, BArch, SAPMO, DY 30/2333, 16, 21–22.

16. Walter Süß, *Staatssicherheit am Ende: Warum es den Mächtigen nicht gelang, 1989 eine Revolution zu verhindern* (Berlin: Links, 1999), 93 n. 97.

17. For more on these issues, see Fulbrook, *People's State,* 4; Hans-Hermann Hertle and Stefan Wolle, *Damals in der DDR: Der Alltag im Arbeiter- und Bauernstaat* (Munich: Bertelsmann, 2004), 239–240; Maier, "Civil Resistance," 266–267; Bernd Schäfer, *Staat und katholische Kirche in der DDR* (Cologne: Böhlau, 1999); and Clemens Vollnhals, ed., *Die Kirchenpolitik von SED und Staatssicherheit* (Berlin: Links, 1996).

18. Author's interviews with Hattenhauer, Schwabe, and Wonneberger.

19. Interview with Bärbel Bohley in Alexander Kluge and Cassian von Salomon, prod., *Der letzte Sommer der DDR,* Spiegel-TV documentary, 2009. See also Bärbel Bohley, Gerald Praschl, and Rüdiger Rosenthal, eds., *Mut: Frauen in der DDR* (Munich: Herbig, 2005); Maier, "Civil Resistance," 268; and Jens Reich, *Abschied von Lebenslügen: Die Intelligenz und die Macht* (Berlin: Rowohlt, 1992).

20. Bruce, *The Firm,* 2, 10, 183–184; see also Kristie Macrakis, *Seduced by Secrets: Inside the Stasi's Spy-Tech World* (Cambridge: Cambridge University Press, 2008). For photos of some of the disguises used by Stasi agents, see Simon Menner, *Top Secret: Images from the Stasi Archives* (Berlin: Hatje Cantz, 2013).

21. Bruce, *The Firm,* 10, says there were "precisely 91,015 full-time Stasi employees and 173,000 informants," the latter usually known as "IMs"(from the German *inoffizieller Mitarbeiter*). For years, experts generally accepted that there had been, as Bruce stated, close to 200,000 IMs. That number became an issue of controversy in 2013 with the publication of Ilko-Sascha Kowalczuk, *Stasi Konkret: Überwachung und Repression in der DDR* (Munich: Beck, 2013). On 217–232, Kowalczuk claimed that the number was lower than previously thought and was actually closer to 100,000.

22. A series of guides on the Stasi Archive website describes the functions of the various branches of the Stasi; see www.bstu.bund.de/DE/Wissen/Publikationen/Reihen /Handbuch/handbuch_node.html. See also Hertle, *Berliner Mauer,* 116; Kowalczuk, *Stasi Konkret,* 16; and, on the Stasi reporting to the SED, Daniela Münkel and Jens Gieseke, eds., *Die DDR im Blick der Stasi* (Göttingen: Vandenhoeck, 2010).

23. On the Soviets in the GDR, see Wjatscheslaw Kotschemassow, *Meine letzte Mission* (Berlin: Dietz, 1994); specifically on the KGB in the GDR, see Christopher Andrew and Oleg Gordievsky, *KGB: The Inside Story of Its Foreign Operations from Lenin to Gorbachev* (New York: HarperCollins, 1990), 512–514; on the KGB's Karlshorst outpost in particular, see the thread "KGB Residentur Karlshorst" in the Forum section of the Geschichtsspuren.de website, www.geschichtsspuren.de/forum /kgb-residentur-karlshorst-t7614.html.

24. See, for example, BStU Zentralarchiv, MfS-HA KuSch Nr. 186, 195–197; and "Dresden, 22. Dezember 1988," BStU, BV Dresden Abt. II, 10448.

25. Hertle, *Berliner Mauer,* 22–23, 106–116. For an overview of the history of the Wall, see Frederick Taylor, *The Berlin Wall: A World Divided, 1961–1989* (New York: Harper, 2008); specifically on its construction, see Frederick Kempe, *Berlin 1961: Kennedy, Khrushchev, and the Most Dangerous Place on Earth* (New York: Putnam, 2011).

26. Walter Momper, *Grenzfall: Berlin im Brennpunkt deutscher* (Munich: Bertelsmann, 1991), 135.

27. Hertle, *Berliner Mauer,* 23.

28. Ibid., 136–137; and Hans-Hermann Hertle, *Chronik des Mauerfalls: Die dramatischen Ereignisse um den 9. November 1989,* 12th ed. (Berlin: Links, 2009), 29–35.

29. Dietmar Schultke, *"Keiner Kommt Durch": Die Geschichte der innerdeutschen Grenze und der Berliner Mauer* (Berlin: Links, 2011), 192–198.

30. Hertle, *Berliner Mauer,* 23.

31. Ahonen, *Death,* 40–42, 219–220; and Hertle, *Berliner Mauer,* 23, 106–121.

32. Interview with Schabowski in Hans-Hermann Hertle, Theo Pirker, and Rainer Weinert, "Der Honecker muß weg!" Berliner Arbeitshefte und Berichte zur sozialwissenschaftlichen Forschung, Freie Universität, Berlin, 1990.

33. Hertle, *Berliner Mauer,* 136–137, and Hertle, *Chronik,* 29–35.

34. Stiftung Friedliche Revolution, ed., *Vor 25 Jahren: Die friedliche Revolution 1989, ein Wochenrückblick* (Berlin: Medialis Offsetdruck, 2013), 4. Kalenderwoche.

35. Heinz Keßler, Marlies Menge, and Theo Sommer, "'Karten auf den Tisch und anfangen!'" *Die Zeit,* Sept. 30, 1988; and Süß, *Staatssicherheit am Ende,* 149–150.

36. Author's interview with Regel.

37. Author's interview with Gueffroy; and Ahonen, *Death,* 242–246.

38. Author's interview with Gueffroy; and Ahonen, *Death,* 244; Sven Goldman, "Er wollte zur Golden Gate Bridge," *Tagesspiegel,* Feb. 5, 2014. See also information about Chris Gueffroy on the Stiftung Berliner Mauer website, www.berliner-mauer-gedenkstaette.de/de/1989-0-332,454,2.html.

39. Ahonen, *Death,* 246.

40. Author's interview with Gueffroy. See also the documentary film produced by the Bundesstiftung zur Aufarbeitung der SED-Diktatur, *Das kurze Leben des Chris Gueffroy.*

41. Through this and other means, Karin Gueffroy, along with her other son and friends of Chris, such as Dirk Regel, succeeded in producing widespread international condemnation of her son's death. Author's interviews with Gueffroy and Regel; and Bundesstiftung zur Aufarbeitung, *Das kurze Leben;* Süß, *Staatssicherheit am Ende,* 149–150.

42. She was particularly amazed that all of this could be happening despite Gorbachev's reforms. For more on those reforms, see Archie Brown, *The Gorbachev Factor* (New York: Oxford University Press, 1997), and Anatoly Chernyaev, *My Six Years with Gorbachev,* trans. and ed. Robert English and Elizabeth Tucker (Philadelphia: University of Pennsylvania Press, 2000).

43. Author's interview with Gueffroy.

44. Hertle, *Berliner Mauer,* 181; and Hans-Hermann Hertle and Maria Nooke, eds., *Die Todesopfer an der Berliner Mauer 1961–1989* (Links: Berlin, 2009), 429–437.

45. Kowalczuk, *Endspiel,* 304.

46. Internal report cited in Süß, *Staatssicherheit am Ende,* 151 nn. 397, 398; see also 148–154 for more on the order to shoot at the border and the impact of the April incident.

47. "Niederschrift über die Rücksprache beim Minister für Nationale Verteidigung, i.V. Generaloberst Streletz," Apr. 3, 1989, BStU, MfS, ZA, HA I 5753, 2–5, available online.

48. "HA I beim Kommando Grenztruppen, Niederschrift," Pätz, Apr. 12, 1989, BStU, MfS, ZA, HA VI 1308, 27, available online; and Hans-Hermann Hertle, "Prämien für Todesschützen," *Berliner Illustrierte Zeitung,* Mar. 28, 1999.

49. "Ausführungen des Gen. Ministers," Apr. 28, 1989, BStU, MfS, ZA, ZAIG 8677, 171–172, available online; see also Süß, *Staatssicherheit am Ende,* 153.

50. Carl Duisberg to Chef BK, "Regelung in humanitären Fragen," in BArchK, B 136, Grüner Ordner 11, doc. 563, B136/21859; and Hertle, *Berliner Mauer,* 142. On the larger history of the practice, see Claus J. Duisberg, *Das deutsche Jahr: Einblicke in die Wiedervereinigung* (Berlin: Siedler, 2005), and Ludwig A. Rehlinger, *Freikauf: Die Geschäfte der DDR mit politisch Verfolgten 1963–1989* (Frankfurt: Ullstein, 1991).

51. Manfred Görtemaker, *Der Weg zur Einheit* (Bonn: BZPB, 2009), 12, has a useful overview of such accords; see also Hertle, *Berliner Mauer,* 136–137, and, for more on the 1970s, M. E. Sarotte, *Dealing with the Devil* (Chapel Hill: University of North Carolina Press, 2001).

52. On the history of the CSCE generally, see Daniel Thomas, *The Helsinki Effect: International Norms, Human Rights, and the Demise of Communism* (Princeton, NJ: Princeton University Press, 2001). See also BStU, MfS, HA I 15215, 3–9, and Walter Süß, "Der 9. November 1989," in Klaus-Dietmar Henke, ed., *Die Mauer* (Munich: dtv, 2011), 228.

53. "ZK Hausmitteilung," Krenz to Honecker, Mar. 13, 1989, BArch, SAPMO, DY 30/IV 2/2.039/307, 88–90, available at www.bstu.bund.de/DE/Wissen/DDR Geschichte/Revolutionskalender/Maerz-1989/Dokumentenseiten/13-Maerz/13_mar _text.html?nn=1932236.

54. See the discussion of this issue in FRL 76.

55. For the original 1975 Final Act, see "Helsinki Final Act Signed by 35 Participating States," OSCE website, www.osce.org/mc/58376; for the 1989 Vienna CSCE Concluding Document, see "Concluding Document of the Third Follow-up Meeting, Vienna," OSCE website, www.osce.org/mc/40881. On the significance of Vienna in particular, see William Korey, *The Promises We Keep: Human Rights, the Helsinki Process, and American Foreign Policy* (New York: St. Martin's, 1993), 257–259. On the CSCE, the GDR, and the USSR, see Anja Hanisch, *Die DDR im KSZE-Prozess 1972–1985: Zwischen Ostabhängigkeit, Westabgrenzung, und Ausreisebewegung* (Munich: Oldenbourg, 2012), and Yuliya von Saal, *KSZE-Prozess und Perestroika in der Sowjetunion: Demokratisierung, Werteumbruch und Auflösung 1985–1991* (Munich: Oldenbourg, 2013). On CSCE and international relations, see Oliver Bange and Gottfried Niedhart, eds., *Helsinki 1975 and the Transformation of Europe* (New York: Berghahn, 2008); Sarah Snyder, *Human Rights Activism and the End of the Cold War* (Cambridge: Cambridge University Press, 2011); and Thomas, *The Helsinki Effect.*

56. On the challenge of acting as the equivalent to the United States, see Westad, *Global Cold War,* 401–403.

57. Brown, *Rise and Fall,* 482–521; Mikhail Gorbachev, *Memoirs* (New York: Doubleday, 1995), 501–527; and Marie-Pierre Rey, "'Europe Is Our Common Home': A Study of Gorbachev's Diplomatic Concept," *Cold War History* 2 (Jan. 2004): 33–65. See also Michail Gorbatschow, *Alles zu seiner Zeit* (Hamburg: Hoffmann und Campe, 2013).

58. The new rules were, in many cases, more restrictive than the ones they replaced (only appearing on the surface to be an improvement) and sparked widespread negative reactions. See "Hinweise zur Reaktion der Bevölkerung," Jan. 27, 1989, BStU, MfS, ZA, ZAIG 4246, 1–11; and "Information," n.d. but from context after Jan. 27, 1989, BArch, SAPMO, DY 30/IV 2/2.039/307, 20–25, both available online; see also BStU, MfS, Rechtstelle 101, 100, and Hans-Hermann Lochen and Christian Meyer-Seitz, eds., *Die geheimen Anweisungen zur Diskriminierung Ausreisewilliger* (Cologne: Bundesanzeiger Verlag, 1992), 7–17, 251–254.

59. "Der Minister, Diensteinheiten, Leiter," Jan. 23, 1989, BStU, MfS, ZA, HA IX 687, 134–136, available online; see also the BStU online history at www.BStU.bund .de/DE/Wissen/DDRGeschichte/Revolutionskalender/August-1989/august89_node .html.

60. "Information für die Mitglieder und Kandidaten des Politbüros," Apr. 14, 1989, BArch, SAPMO, DY 30/332, 2–4. See also "Schreiben Mielkes an die Leiter der Diensteinheiten zur Veröffentlichung des KSZE-Dokuments," BStU, MfS, ZA, HA IX 687, 134–136, and "Ausführungen des Gen. Ministers," Feb. 1, 1989, BStU, MfS, ZAIG 5342, 1–70, both available online.

61. "Referat für die Arbeitsberatung der SED-Kreisleitung im MfS in Üdersee," Jan. 31–Feb. 2, 1989, BStU, MfS, SED-KL 4575, 496–552, available online.

62. See the discussion to this effect in "Fernschreiben des Staatssekretärs Bertele an den Chef des Bundeskanzleramtes, Berlin (Ost)," Sept. 22, 1989, doc. 45, DESE 415–416; on the impact of the CSCE on transnational human rights issues generally, see Snyder, *Human Rights Activism.*

63. In the end, her other adult son received permission to emigrate as well but chose to stay in the GDR because he did not want to leave his girlfriend; author's interview with Gueffroy.

64. Author's interview with Gueffroy.

Chapter 2: Marginal to Massive

1. A copy of this 1969 agreement is in BStU, MfS, Rechtsstelle 101, starting at 70.

2. "Memorandum of the International Committee of the Central Committee of the CPSU to Alexander Yakovlev," Feb. 1989, in GC.

3. "Ergebnisse der Bearbeitung von Schreiben, die von Angehörigen des MfS im Zusammenhang mit der Nichtauslieferung der Zeitschrift 'Sputnik' 10/89 an das ZK der SED gerichtet wurden," Jan. 19, 1989, BStU, MfS, ZA SED-KL 4581, available online.

4. "Notiz über die Besprechung des Genossen Ministers mit dem Stellv. des Vors. des KfS der UdSSR . . . Genossen Generalmajor Schebarschin," Apr. 7, 1989, BStU, MfS, ZAIG 5198, 128–129, available online.

5. "Notiz zur Absprache," May 5, 1989, BStU, MfS, HA VI 4748, 141–143, discusses the "Konzeption zur militärischen Besetzung von Berlin-West, bestätigt durch den NVR," and explains how, after the "Einmarsch in Berlin-WEst [*sic*]" of "Kontingente der NVA," next "[es] folgen ihnen Kräfte des MfS zur Lösung spezifischer Aufgaben." This document then details which specific buildings in West Berlin will be occupied, including the Reichstag.

6. "From the Conversation Between Gorbachev and Kohl, One-on-One," June 12, 1989, MG, 161.

7. For a summary of Soviet worries about this process, despite Gorbachev's overall trend toward reform, see "Memorandum to Alexander Yakovlev from the Bogomolov Commission," *Cold War International History Project Bulletin* 12–13 (Fall/Winter 2001): 52–61. On Solidarity and its legacy more generally, see Domber, *Empowering Revolution,* and Grzegorz Ekiert, *The State Against Society: Political Crises and Their Aftermath in East Central Europe* (Princeton, NJ: Princeton University Press, 1996).

8. Chris Gueffroy died during the night of Feb. 5–6, 1989. For more on the Polish roundtable, see Marjorie Castle, *Triggering Communism's Collapse: Perceptions and Power in Poland's Transition* (Lanham, MD: Rowman and Littlefield, 2003), and Timothy Garton Ash, *The Polish Revolution* (New Haven, CT: Yale University Press, 2002); for more on Gueffroy, see Stiftung Friedliche Revolution, ed., *Vor 25 Jahren.*

9. On the Polish roundtable talks and the election in summer 1989, see "Minutes No. 64 from an Expanded Meeting of the PZPR CC Secretariat," June 5, 1989, NSA, www2.gwu.edu/~nsarchiv/news/19991105/Doc-57.htm; Castle, *Triggering Communism's Collapse,* 146–195; Gregory Domber, "Reevaluating US Policy," *Journal of Cold War Studies* 13, no. 3 (2011): 52–82; Domber, *Empowering Revolution;* and Garton Ash, *The Polish Revolution,* 363.

10. On the roundtable, see "Opening Full Session of the National Roundtable Negotiations," June 13, 1989, Cold War International History Project, http://legacy .wilsoncenter.org/coldwarfiles/index-54563.html; András Bozóki, ed., *The Roundtable Talks of 1989: The Genesis of Hungarian Democracy* (Budapest: CEU Press, 2002); John Prados, *How the Cold War Ended: Debating and Doing History* (Washington, DC: Potomac Books, 2011), 228–231; and Németh-Gorbachev memcon in Csaba Békés and Melinda Kalmár, "The Political Transition in Hungary, 1989–90," *Cold War International History Project Bulletin* 12–13 (Fall/Winter 2001): 76–77. On differences between the Hungarian and Polish roundtables, see Garton Ash, *Magic Lantern,* 55–57.

11. See the documents on these negotiations in Békés and Kalmár, "Political Transition in Hungary," 83–84; see also PA-AA, BDE, ZA139.937E, Aug. 18, 1989.

12. On the reburial specifically, see Garton Ash, *Magic Lantern,* 47–51, and Rudolf L. Tökés, *Hungary's Negotiated Revolution* (Cambridge: Cambridge University Press, 1996), 306–308; see also Michael Meyer, *The Year That Changed the World: The Untold Story Behind the Fall of the Berlin Wall* (New York: Scribner, 2009). In East Germany,

the Stasi paid close attention to the reburial; see "Monatsübersicht Nr. 6/89," BStU, MfS, ZA 5337, 97–98, available online. On the process of reform in Hungary in the late 1980s generally, see M-KS-288-5/1050, reprinted in CWIHPPC; "Memorandum of the International Committee of the Central Committee of the CPSU to Alexander Yakovlev"; Charles Gati, *Failed Illusions: Moscow, Washington, Budapest and the 1956 Hungarian Revolt* (Stanford, CA: Stanford University Press, 2006), 3–6; and István Horváth, *Die Sonne ging in Ungarn auf* (Munich: Universitas, 2000), 298–358.

13. Excerpt from Gorbachev-Németh conversation, Mar. 3, 1989, in GC; on the Stasi, see Süß, *Staatssicherheit am Ende*, 154–157; see also Constantine Pleshakov, *There Is No Freedom Without Bread! 1989 and the Civil War That Brought Down Communism* (New York: Farrar, Straus and Giroux, 2009), 101.

14. Similarly, West German diplomats also wondered what the potential classification as refugees could mean for the East Germans in Hungary. See Staatssekretär Dr. Sudhoff, Bonn, "Mein Gespräch mit dem ungarischen AM Horn [Aug. 14, 1989]," Aug. 18, 1989, PA-AA, BDE, ZA178.925E; see also Horváth, *Die Sonne*, 290–294.

15. "Hinweise auf wesentliche motivbildende Faktoren," Sept. 9, 1989, BStU, MfS, Sekr. Mittig 27, 122–129. On the question of motivations for emigration, see also Robert Darnton, *Berlin Journal* (New York: Norton, 1991), 15–16.

16. "Hinweis zum verstärkten Mißbrauch des Territoriums des UVRs durch Bürger der DDR," July 14, 1989, BStU, MfS, ZA, ZAIG 5352, 124–134, available online; see also the online annotation, www.bstu.bund.de/DE/Wissen/DDR Geschichte/Revolutionskalender/August-1989/Dokumentenseiten/14-Juli/14_jul _text.html?nn=1930872.

17. Mielke complained about these developments in a speech on June 29, 1989, BStU, MfS, ZA, ZAIG 4021, 79–89, available online, and by August they had grown worse, according to "Monatsübersicht 8/89," BStU, MfS, ZA ZAIG 5338, 1–34, available online, and Süß, *Staatssicherheit am Ende*, 154–158. On the broader significant of emigration for the GDR, see Gareth Dale, *The East German Revolution of 1989* (Manchester: Manchester University Press, 2005), 223–230.

18. See the records related to the embassy refugees in PA-AA, BDE, such as B85-2340, B85-2346, ZA139.918E; for more on Hungary generally, see Andreas Oplatka, *Der erste Riß in der Mauer* (Vienna: Paul Zsolnay Verlag, 2009).

19. The "two-track" nature of the West German policy response to the refugee crisis, run partly by Kohl and partly by Genscher, required some explanation to Washington; the US ambassador to Bonn, Vernon Walters, sent the National Security Council staffer Robert Hutchings a detailed memo explaining the division. Walters, memo to Hutchings, Aug. 12, 1989, CF 01413-012, in Hutchings Files, FRG Cables, GHWBPL.

20. "Schreiben des Bundeskanzlers Kohl an den Generalsekretär und Staatsratsvorsitzenden Honecker," Aug. 14, 1989, doc. 22, DESE 355–356; see also docs. 24–25, DESE, 358–372, and the various documents in BArchK, B136-37241 from Aug. 1989.

21. See "Vermerk, Betr.: Konsultationsgespräche mit Ungarn am 27.07.1989, Dg21/HA Leiter Alföldy (A1)," July 28, 1989, PA-AA, BDE, B85-2.339; "Betr.:

UNHCR, Hier: Einrichtung eines Büros in Budapest," August 9, 1989, PA-AA, BDE, ZA140.734E; and also letter from Genscher to Horn, n.d. but from context written Aug. 9–14, 1989, PA-AA, BDE, ZA140.734E.

22. See the correspondence on the closure in BArchK, B136-37241, Aug. 1989, and BArchK, B136, Grüner Ordner 11, Aug. 10, 1989; in PA-AA, BDE, ZA140.733E, Aug. 10, 1989; and "Vorlage des Ministerialdirigenten Stern an den Chef des Bundeskanzleramtes Seiters, Bonn," Aug. 8, 1989, doc. 20, DESE 351–353. See also doc. 37 in Detlef Nakath and Gerd-Rüdiger Stephan, eds., *Countdown zur Deutschen Einheit: Eine dokumentierte Geschichte der deutsch-deutschen Beziehungen 1987–1990* (Berlin: Dietz, 1996), 197.

23. "Asshole" comment in entry for Oct. 11, 1989, diary of Anatoly Chernyaev, available on the National Security Archive website, which translates the insult as "scumbag," www2.gwu.edu/~nsarchiv/NSAEBB/NSAEBB275/1989%20for%20posting.pdf; for the translation given above, see doc. 57, GC.

24. Honecker would only find out about the illness that would eventually kill him accidentally, from a television news report months later. After his downfall, he faced the prospect of legal proceedings due to misuse of state funds for personal purposes. Honecker's sympathizers, in response, combed through his medical records to find a reason that he might be unfit to stand trial and, in so doing, found the evidence of cancer. The diagnosis leaked out to the media before the patient himself heard the news privately. As a result, a televised news broadcast would stun him with the revelation. See "Außerhalb der Tagesordnung," Aug. 22, 1989, BArch, SAPMO, DY 30/IV 2/2.039/76; Michael Funken, *Das Jahr der Deutschen* (Munich: Piper, 2008), 72; and Norbert Pötzl, *Erich Honecker* (Stuttgart: Deutsche Verlagsanstalt, 2003), 336–337.

25. On the laming of the Politburo, and Krenz in particular, in summer 1989 and its far-reaching consequences, see "Interview mit Generalsekretär Egon Krenz 19.11.1989," BArch, SAPMO, DY 30/IV 2/2.039/342, 181–182; Ekkehard Kuhn, *Der Tag der Entscheidung: Leipzig, 9. Oktober 1989* (Berlin: Ullstein, 1992), 78; Helmut Müller-Enbergs et al., eds., *Wer war wer in der DDR?* (Berlin: Links, 2010), 890–891; Colin Munro, "Britain, Berlin, German Unification, and the Fall of the Soviet Empire," *German Historical Institute Bulletin* 31, no. 2 (Nov. 2009): 61–62; and Walter Süß, "Selbstblockierung der Macht," in Konrad Jarausch and Martin Sabrow, eds., *Weg in den Untergang: Der innere Zerfall der DDR* (Göttingen: Vandenhoeck, 1999), 243–248. For more on Mittag, see his autobiography, Günter Mittag, *Um jeden Preis* (Berlin: Aufbau-Verlag, 1991).

26. Staatssekretär Dr. Sudhoff, Bonn, "Mein Gespräch mit dem ungarischen AM Horn [Aug. 14, 1989]," Aug. 18, 1989, PA AA, BDE, ZA178.925F, 7.

27. Ibid. For more on Gyula Horn's worldview, see his memoir, *Freiheit die ich meine: Erinnerungen des ungarischen Außenministers, der den Eisernen Vorhang öffnete*, trans. Angelika and Péter Máté (Hamburg: Hoffmann, 1991).

28. On the appeal to Hungary of US most-favored-nation trading status and emigration, see Hutchings Files, Oct. 18, 1989, CF 01410 Hungary, GHWBPL; on the transition in Eastern Europe generally, see György Dalos, *Der Vorhang geht auf: Das Ende der Diktaturen in Osteuropa* (Munich: Beck, 2009).

29. See "Vermerk des Bundesministers Genscher über das Gespräch des Bundeskanzlers Kohl mit Ministerpräsident Németh und Außenminister Horn, Schloß Gymnich," Aug. 25, 1989, doc. 28, DESE 377–380, and "Gespräch des Bundeskanzlers Kohl und des Bundesministers Genscher mit Ministerpräsident Németh und Außenminister Horn während des Mittagessens, Schloß Gymnich," Aug. 25, 1989, doc. 29, DESE 380–382; see also, in the Foreign Ministry archive, "Vermerk über das Gespräch am 25. August 1989," PA-AA, BDE, ZA178.925E, 1–5. Kohl provided more information on the Schloß Gymnich meeting in his memoir: Helmut Kohl, Kai Diekmann, and Ralf Georg Reuth, *Ich wollte Deutschlands Einheit* (Berlin: Ullstein, 1996), 71–74.

30. Notes from the East Berlin Politburo discussion of advance word of this decision, Aug. 29, 1989, DY 30/IV 2/2.039/76, 45–55, and "Vermerk," Mittag-Horn conversation, Aug. 31, 1989, DY 30/J IV 2/2A/342, both in BArch, SAPMO; see also "Vermerk," Fischer-Horn conversation, Aug. 31, 1989, PA-AA, BDE, ZR467-09. The French ambassador to Moscow reported that Moscow had not been consulted, only informed; see doc. 3, Sept. 21, 1989, DFUA, 67, and Horváth, *Die Sonne,* 324. Oplatka, *Der erste Riß,* 216, suggests that Moscow had previously indicated to Budapest that it had a free hand in this matter.

31. Günter Buchstab and Hans-Otto Kleinmann, eds., *Helmut Kohl Berichte zur Lage, 1989–1998* (Düsseldorf: Droste, 2012), xvii; Oplatka, *Der erste Riß,* 212; and Hans-Peter Schwarz, *Helmut Kohl: Eine politische Biografie* (Munich: Deutsche Verlags-Anstalt, 2012), 491–517.

32. Letter from Eduard Shevardnadze to Oskar Fischer, Sept. 1, 1989; "Vermerk über das Gespräch des Ministers für auswärtige Angelegenheiten der DDR, Genossen Oskar Fischer, mit dem außerordentlichen und bevollmächtigten Botschafter der UdSSR in der DDR, Genossen W.I. Kotschemassow," Sept. 7, 1989; and "Übersetzung aus dem Russischen," Sept. 7, 1989, all in PA-AA, BDE, ZR469-09.

33. "Telegramm des Bundeskanzlers Kohl an Ministerpräsident Németh," Sept. 12, 1989, doc. 40, DESE 404.

34. Horváth, *Die Sonne,* 333.

35. Author's interview with Schwabe; and Susanne Lohmann, "The Dynamics of Information Cascades: The Monday Demonstrations in Leipzig, East Germany, 1989–91," *World Politics,* 47, no. 1 (Oct. 1994): 64.

36. "Vermerk," Seiters-Horváth memcon, Sept. 19, 1989, BArchK, B136-37241; and author's interview with Horváth.

37. See *DDR Journal zur November Revolution* (a compilation of news reports from 1989, collected and reprinted by the West Berlin newspaper *taz* in 1990), 15.

38. Fischer conveyed Shevardnadze's words to Honecker in telegram, Oct. 2, 1989, BArch, SAPMO, DY 30/IV 2/2.039/342, 49–51; this topic was also discussed in the author's interview with Kastrup.

39. "Protokoll der Sitzung des Politbüros," Sept. 29, 1989, BArch, SAPMO, DY 30/J IV/2/2A/3243. On the confiscation of property, see various documents in BArch, SAPMO, DY 30/J IV 2/2A/3245.

40. "Vermerk, Betr.: Gespräch BM mit AM Schewardnadse am 27.09. in New York (Kleiner Kreis)," Sept. 27, 1989, ZA178.931E, and note from Genscher to Shevardnadze, Sept. 29, 1989, ZA178.924E, both in PA-AA, BDE.

41. See the extensive West German chancellery paperwork on making these arrangements in docs. 51–57, DESE 429–442; for memoir accounts, see Hans-Dietrich Genscher, *Erinnerungen* (Berlin: Siedler, 1995), 15–25, and Richard Kiessler and Frank Elbe, *Ein runder Tisch mit scharfen Ecken: Der diplomatische Weg zur deutschen Einheit* (Baden-Baden: Nomos, 1993), 33–38.

42. Author's interviews with Elbe, Genscher, Kastrup, Kiessler, and Seiters; see also Sarotte, *1989*, 31–33, 234 nn. 86–89.

43. "Fernschreiben des Staatssekretärs Bertele an den Chef des Bundeskanzleramtes, Berlin (Ost)," Oct. 2, 1989, doc. 52, DESE 430–432; and Süß, *Staatssicherheit am Ende*, 252.

44. "Vermerk, Betr.: Gespräch von BM Seiters mit dem Leiter der ständigen Vertretung der DDR, Neubauer, am 02. Oktober 1989, 14.00 Uhr," BArchK, B136-37241; "Fernschreiben," Oct. 2, 1989, DESE 430–432; and author's interviews with Elbe and Kastrup, who were on the trains.

45. The number of East Germans transported comes from a speech by Rudolf Seiters; the author is grateful to him for a copy of it.

46. Telegram from Dickel, Oct. 3, 1989, 3:40 p.m., in SS, Anlage VIII, 1632–1633; see also "Hinweise zu den unterbreiteten Varianten," BStU, MfS, ZAIG 7438, 12–17; and Süß, *Staatssicherheit am Ende*, 252.

47. BStU, MfS, Rechtsstelle 100, HA Konsularische Angelegenheiten, "Reiseverkehr DDR-CSSR," n.d. but from context on or about Oct. 3, 1989, 9–15.

48. Paula Butturini, "East Germany Closes Its Border After 10,000 More Flee to West," *Chicago Tribune*, Oct. 4, 1989; see also Florian Huber, *Schabowskis Irrtum: Das Drama des 9. November* (Berlin: Rowholt, 2009), 17.

49. Tobias Hollitzer, "Der friedliche Verlauf des 9. Oktober 1989 in Leipzig," in Günther Heydemann, Gunther Mai, and Werner Müller, eds., *Revolution und Transformation in der DDR* (Berlin: Duncker and Humblot, 1999), 251; and Uwe Schwabe, "'Symbol der Befreiung': Die Friedensgebete in Leipzig," *Horch und Guck* 23 (1998). The author is grateful to Schwabe for a digital version of this article, which indicates that from Aug. 1989 to Apr. 1990 there were a total of 3,115 demonstrations in East Germany, of which 963 were in Saxony, the highest single total. For more on Saxony, see Alexander Fischer and Günther Heydemann, eds., *Die politische "Wende" 1989/90 in Sachsen: Rückblick und Zwischenbilanz* (Weimar: Böhlau Verlag, 1995), and Eckhard Jesse, ed., *Friedliche Revolution und deutsche Einheit: Sächsische Bürgerrechtler ziehen Bilanz* (Berlin: Links, 2006).

50. Albert O. Hirschmann, "Exit, Voice and the Fate of the German Democratic Republic," *World Politics* 45 (Jan. 1993): 173–202.

51. On organizing the next round of trains, see East German documents from on or about Oct. 4, 1989, in BArch, SAPMO, DY 30/IV 2/2.039/342; BArch, SAPMO, DY 30/J IV/2/2A/3245; BStU, MfS, SdM 664, 59–60; and SS, Anlage VIII, 1634.

See West German documents on the same subject in BArchK, B136-37241, Oct. 4–6, 1989, and docs. 55–56 from Oct. 3–5, 1989, DESE 437–441. There were originally supposed to be fifteen trains, but in the end only eight actually made the trip; see Funken, *Das Jahr,* 237 n. 105, and Süß, *Staatssicherheit am Ende,* 259 n. 114.

52. On the situation in Dresden and the violent proclivities of the local Stasi leader, Horst Böhm, see information provided by the Stasi Archive at www.BStU.bund.de /DE/Wissen/DDRGeschichte/Revolutionskalender/Oktober-1989/oktober89_node .html.

53. "Auszug aus Lagefilm v. 04.10.1989," SS, Anlage I, 82–86; "Telegram, BV Dresden," Oct. 4, 1989, in SS, Anlage I, 101–105; "Telegramm," Oct. 5, 1989, SS, Anlage I, 125–129. No evidence of Putin's personal participation in these specific events has yet surfaced, but Putin has described the angry crowds of 1989 in Dresden in general terms in Vladimir Putin with Nataliya Gevorkyan, Natalya Timakova, and Andrei Kolesnikov, *First Person: An Astonishingly Frank Self-Portrait by Russia's President Putin,* trans. Catherine A. Fitzpatrick (New York: PublicAffairs, 2000), 69–80. See also Funken, *Das Jahr,* 82–94, and Süß, *Staatssicherheit am Ende,* 252–259, 259 n. 114.

54. "Telegramm," Oct. 5, 1989, SS, Anlage I, 128; and interview with Rolf Sickert, Fall of the Wall Collection, KCLMA.

55. Entry for Oct. 5, 1989, diary of Anatoly Chernyaev, available on the National Security Archive website, www2.gwu.edu/~nsarchiv/NSAEBB/NSAEBB275/1989%20 for%20posting.pdf.

56. "Auszug aus Lagefilm vom 5.10.89," SS, Anlage I, 115–117; "Aktenvermerk," Oct. 5, 1989, SS, Anlage I, 130; and Süß, *Staatssicherheit am Ende,* 257.

57. See the interviews with Dresden detainees in the KCLMA Fall of the Wall collection, most notably the interview with Andreas Gönsch. See also Funken, *Das Jahr,* 84, and Süß, *Staatssicherheit am Ende,* 262.

58. On the impact of the exodus on the GDR population, see Lohmann, "Dynamics," 64; the documentary *Der letzte Sommer der DDR;* and author's interview with Schwabe.

59. Author's interviews with Schwabe and Wonneberger. On the work of the Rev. Matthias Berger for the Stasi under the code name "Carl," see "Institutionen, Organisationsstrukturen und Ereignisse," FUF 465; for an example of regime pressure on the churches of Leipzig, see "Auszug aus einer Information," doc. 63, FUF 176–178; see also the evidence of regime pressure on Leipzig church leaders in FRL 250. On the church-state relationship in East Germany generally, see Vollnhals, ed., *Die Kirchenpolitik.*

60. "Fernschreiben des Staatssekr. Bertele an den Chef des Bundeskanzleramtes, Berlin (Ost)," Sept. 20, 1989, doc. 43, DESE 410; on the plans of the Stasi to keep control in Sept. 1989, as Bertele expected it would, see "Hinweis auf ein weiteres 'Montagsgebet' in der Nikolaikirche in Leipzig," Sept. 19, 1989, FRL 353.

61. "Fernschreiben des Staatssekr. Bertele an den Chef des Bundeskanzleramtes, Berlin (Ost)," Sept. 22, 1989, doc. 45 in DESE 415–416. Skepticism toward these

groups came not just from contemporaries; Maier, "Civil Resistance," 269, retroactively (in 2009) classified them as unimportant as well, seeing instead a healthy ruling regime: "The bottom line was that, as of the summer of 1989, these circles of dissenters, and other small groups officially unregistered, could hardly trouble the regime, which in any case had infiltrated most of them with Stasi collaborators. Pre-existing oppositional groups had hardly achieved a troubling profile. The German Democratic Republic remained a state and society with a highly organized group life. Teams, factory associations, musical and hobby groups thrived." The regime still had "remaining inner sources of stability," and "the Stasi's role of subverting social protest remained significant."

62. For more on those activists, see Bohley, Praschl, and Rosenthal, eds., *Mut*, 10–11; Ilko-Sascha Kowalczuk and Tom Sello, eds., *Für ein freies Land mit freien Menschen: Opposition und Widerstand in Biographien und Fotos* (Berlin: Robert-Havemann-Gesellschaft, 2006), 208–211; and Müller-Enbergs et al., eds., *Wer war wer*, 494–495, 1206. See also Torsten Moritz, *Gruppen der DDR-Opposition in Ost-Berlin gestern und heute* (Berlin: Verlag für Wissenschaft und Forschung, 2000).

63. On the history of the theological department, or faculty, see Andreas Gößner and Alexander Wieckowski, eds., *Die theologische Fakultät der Universität Leipzig: Personen, Profile und Perspektiven aus sechs Jahrhunderten Fakultätsgeschichte* (Leipzig: Evangelische Verlagsanstalt, 2005). I am grateful to Hans-Jürgen and Wilma Sievers for a copy of part of this book.

64. See the report on environmental damage in the region of Leipzig by the regional news agency MDR, "Die misshandelte Umwelt der DDR," n.d., www.ndr.de /geschichte/grenzenlos/glossar/ddrumwelt100.html.

65. See, for example, interview with Helmut Hackenberg, Fall of the Wall Collection, KCLMA.

66. Schwabe, "'Symbol der Befreiung.'"

67. For more on the musical significance of Leipzig and some of the musicians who lived and worked there, see John Eliot Gardiner, *Bach: Music in the Castle of Heaven* (New York: Knopf, 2013), and www.kurtmasur.com/bio.html. On Leipzig more generally, see Elizabeth Pond, *Beyond the Wall* (Washington, DC: Brookings, 1993), 111, and Hans-Jürgen Sievers, ed., *Stundenbuch einer deutschen Revolution: Die leipziger Kirche im Oktober 1989* (Göttingen: Vandenhoeck, 1990), 25–26.

68. For materials from the illicit June 10, 1989, music festival and crackdown, see FRL 208–215.

69. Jesse, ed., *Friedliche Revolution*, 286–287; Kuhn, *Der Tag*, 22–23; and Lohmann, "Dynamics," 67. The significance of Leipzig as a place for protest was also discussed in author's interview with Birthler.

70. "Information 150/89," n.d. but from accompanying cover note May 23, 1989, BStU, MfS, ZA, BdL/Dok. 008932, 2.

71. Christian Führer, Anne Ascher, and Patricia Holland-Moritz, *Und wir sind dabei gewesen: Die Revolution, die aus der Kirche kam* (Berlin: Ullstein, 2008), 113–118; and

"Führer contra Weißgerber," *Leipziger Volkszeitung,* June 8, 2009. The author thanks Schwabe for a copy of the latter.

72. On the interaction between the missiles and the peace prayers, see Maier, "Civil Resistance," 266–267, and Uwe Schwabe, "Die Entwicklung der Leipziger Opposition in den achtziger Jahren am Beispiel der Friedensgebete," in Heydemann, Mai, and Müller, eds., *Revolution und Transformation,* 171. On the politics of superpower missiles in Europe more generally, or "Euromissiles," see Jeffrey Herf, *War by Other Means: Soviet Power, West German Resistance, and the Battle of the Euromissiles* (New York: Free Press, 1991); Leopoldo Nuti, ed., *The Crisis of Détente in Europe: From Helsinki to Gorbachev, 1975–1985* (New York: Routledge, 2009); Kiran Klaus Patel and Kenneth Weisbrode, eds., *European Integration and the Atlantic Community in the 1980s* (New York: Cambridge University Press, 2013); and the Wilson Center's online document collection about Euromissiles at www.wilsoncenter.org/publication /the-euromissiles-crisis-reader.

73. I am grateful to Kathy Conley for her remarks on this point.

74. On antinuclear protests and peace activism, see Lawrence S. Wittner, *Toward Nuclear Abolition: A History of the World Disarmament Movement: 1971 to the Present* (Stanford, CA: Stanford University Press, 2003), 31–144, 147, and Matthew Evangelista, *Unarmed Forces: The Transnational Movement to End the Cold War* (Ithaca, NY: Cornell University Press, 1999). See also Jonathan Haslam, *The Soviet Union and the Politics of Nuclear Weapons in Europe 1969–1987: The Problem of the SS-20* (London: Macmillan, 1989).

75. Maier, "Civil Resistance," 267, talks about ministers in the tradition of "Karl Barth or Bishop Dibelius who sought to preserve the apolitical autonomy of an independent Church amidst totalitarian pressures." For more on what took place at the peace prayers themselves, see the documentary collection FUF, and Hermann Geyer, *Nikolaikirche, Montags um fünf: Die politischen Gottesdienste der Wendezeit in Leipzig* (Darmstadt: WBG, 2007).

76. On Christoph Wonneberger's early years and brief stint with the Stasi, see Thomas Mayer, *Der nicht aufgibt: Christoph Wonneberger, eine Biographie* (Leipzig: Evangelische Verlagsanstalt, 2014), 9–58, esp. 28 (a reprinted document from the Stasi) and 49–50 (on alternatives to military service); see also Andreas Peter Pausch, *Widerstehen: Pfarrer Christoph Wonneberger* (Berlin: Metropol, 2014). For more on contacts between East German and Polish dissidents, see Basil Kerski, *Die Dynamik der Annäherung in deutsch-polnischen Beziehungen* (Düsseldorf: Düsseldorf University Press, 2011).

77. Author's interview with Wonneberger.

78. Author's interviews with Hattenhauer and Schwabe; Funken, *Das Jahr,* 122–125; Kowalczuk and Sello, eds., *Für ein freies Land,* 208–211; and Uwe Schwabe, "Die Entwicklung der Leipziger Opposition," 171.

79. The Stasi Archive contains, unsurprisingly, extensive files on Hattenhauer, her arrests, and her interrogations. The author is grateful for Katrin Hattenhauer for

providing the legal permission *(Einwilligung)* necessary to view the transcripts of her interrogations, as well as the rest of the files, and also for Hattenhauer's own description of her arrests and incarceration. For the "provocative questions" quotation, see "Einleitungsbericht zur OPK 'Meise,'" Aug. 10, 1989, BStU Lpz. AOPK 3993/92, 10.

80. Bohley, Praschl, and Rosenthal, eds., *Mut,* 10–11; Katrin Hattenhauer biography on her website, www.katrin-hattenhauer.de/biografie_en.html; Müller-Enbergs et al., eds., *Wer war wer,* 494–495; and Doug Saunders, "Half a Life Ago, Katrin Blew the Wall Down," *Globe and Mail,* Nov. 6, 2009.

81. For biographical information on Schwabe, see www.runde-ecke-leipzig.de /sammlung/Zusatz.php?w=w00195.

82. For a copy of the list with Schwabe at position one, see BV für Staatssicherheit Leipzig, "Im Rahmen des Vorbeugungskomplexes zuzuführende Personen," Oct. 9, 1989, FRL 413; see also Schwabe, "'Symbol der Befreiung.'"

83. Author's interview with Schwabe.

84. See ZAIG-Information 25/89, Jan. 16, 1989, in BStU, ZA, ZAIG 3734, 1–7, also available online. For more details on activists in Leipzig, see Wayne C. Bartee, *A Time to Speak Out: The Leipzig Citizen Protests and the Fall of East Germany* (Westport, CT: Praeger, 2000), and Thomas Mayer, *Helden der Friedlichen: 18 Porträts von Wegbereitern aus Leipzig Revolution* (Leipzig: Evangelische Verlagsanstalt, 2009). See also Kerry Kathleen Riley, *Everyday Subversion: From Joking to Revolting in the German Democratic Republic* (East Lansing: Michigan State University Press, 2008).

85. Bohley, Praschl, and Rosenthal, eds., *Mut,* 201–207; and Schwabe, "'Symbol der Befreiung.'"

86. "Absprache zwischen Referatsleiter der Abt. XX und Eppisch," Mar. 23, 1989, FUF 277 n. 406. A video interview with Wonneberger can be seen at www.youtube .com/watch?v=_6lwz-bSe5I.

87. Foreword by Fischer in Sievers, ed., *Stundenbuch,* 15.

88. Bohley, Praschl, and Rosenthal, eds., *Mut,* 203; Tobias Hollitzer and Reinhard Bohse, eds., *Heute vor 10 Jahren: Leipzig auf dem Weg zur friedlichen Revolution* (Fribourg: InnoVation Verlag, 2000), 364; and FRL 76; see also Lochen and Meyer-Seitz, eds., *Die geheimen Anweisungen.*

89. Transcript of remarks by Führer on Sept. 4, 1999, in Hollitzer and Bohse, eds., *Heute vor 10 Jahren,* 356.

90. There would be countless books, events, and memorials bearing these words after the revolution succeeded. A book by Gerhard Ritter would even use both phrases: *Wir sind das Volk! Wir sind ein Volk!* (Munich: Beck, 2009). At the time, however, there were those in the West who, in response to hearing *Wir sind ein Volk,* "We are one people," from their much poorer Eastern neighbors, would respond with *Wir auch,* "We are too."

91. Führer, Ascher, and Holland-Moritz, *Und wir sind dabei,* 190.

92. Ibid., 119; and Schwabe, "Die Entwicklung der Leipziger Opposition," 160–164.

93. Führer, Ascher, and Holland-Moritz, *Und wir sind dabei,* 188–189.

94. Schwabe, "Die Entwicklung der Leipziger Opposition," 164–166; and Hollitzer and Bohse, eds., *Heute vor 10 Jahren,* 68.

95. "Brief des Vorsitzenden des KV St. Nikolai, Pf. Führer, an Pf. Berger, Pf. Wonneberger und Sup. Magirius," June 9, 1988, doc. 61, FUF 175; see also doc. 64, FUF 178–179.

96. Letter from Magirius to Wonneberger, Aug. 25, 1988, FRL 24, see also 25–27; Bohley, Praschl, and Rosenthal, eds., *Mut,* 204; Führer, Ascher, and Holland-Moritz, *Und wir sind dabei,* 192–193; Günter Hanisch et al., eds., *Dona nobis pacem: Fürbitten und Friedensgebete Herbst '89 in Leipzig* (Berlin: Evangelische Verlagsanstalt, 1990), 11–13, and Kowalczuk, *Endspiel,* 311. See also Martin Jankowski, *Der Tag, der Deutschland veränderte: 9. Oktober 1989* (Leipzig: Evangelische Verlagsanstalt, 2007), and Reiner Tetzner, *Leipziger Ring: Aufzeichnungen eines Montagsdemonstranten* (Frankfurt: Luchterhand, 1990).

97. "Mitschrift der Erklärung von Sup. Magirius," Aug. 29, 1988, Doc. 69, FUF, 183.

98. Summarized in FUF, 184 n. 234; see also Hollitzer and Bohse, eds., *Heute vor 10 Jahren,* 68–72, and Schwabe, "'Symbol der Befreiung.'"

99. "Treffbericht eines Führungsoffiziers des MfS," Sept. 13, 1988, Doc. 87, FUF, 209.

100. "Mitschrift einer Intervention von Pf. Führer," Aug. 29, 1988, Doc. 70, FUF, 184–185.

101. The protest letter is summarized in FUF, 184, n. 234.

102. Führer, Ascher, and Holland-Moritz, *Und wir sind dabei,* 193–195; Hollitzer and Bohse, eds., *Heute vor 10 Jahren,* 70; and Schwabe, "'Symbol der Befreiung.'"

103. "Leipziger Friedensgebet abgewürgt," article from underground newspaper *Umweltblätter,* Oct. 1988, reprinted as Doc. 89, FUF, 214–215.

104. Remarks by Ernst Demele, in Hollitzer and Bohse, eds., *Heute vor 10 Jahren,* 366.

105. Author's interview with Schwabe.

106. Ibid.

107. Ibid.

108. Both Hollitzer and Bohse, eds., *Heute vor 10 Jahren,* 64, and Schwabe, "'Symbol der Befreiung,'" point out that there had previously been events outside of the Nikolai Church in the past, such as after a peace prayer in Nov. 1983, when participants took lighted candles out of the church, but they were sporadic. After the 1988 expulsion, however, the regularity of the outdoor events, combined with the other developments of the late 1980s, helped to turn the outdoor events into massive marches.

109. Bohley, Praschl, and Rosenthal, eds., *Mut,* 205. On the importance and theatricality of protest in public, see Maier, "Civil Resistance," 264.

110. See the analysis of these events in FRL 27 and in Hollitzer and Bohse, eds., *Heute vor 10 Jahren,* 72.

111. Mike Leary, "100,000 Protest in E. Germany," *Philadelphia Inquirer,* Oct. 10, 1989; and author's interview with Leary.

112. "Chiffriertes Fernschreiben," Sept. 12, 1989, Helmut Hackenberg to Horst Dohlus, in SS, Anlage II, 556–558, refers to Stasi attempts to achieve "eine zeitliche und örtliche Verlegung der Montagsgebete."

113. Transcript of remarks by Führer on Sept. 4, 1999, in Hollitzer and Bohse, eds., *Heute vor 10 Jahren,* 359.

114. Führer, Ascher, and Holland-Moritz, *Und wir sind dabei,* 194–198; Hollitzer and Bohse, eds., *Heute vor 10 Jahren,* 359; and Schwabe, "'Symbol der Befreiung.'"

115. See the analysis of these events in FRL 102; Hanisch et al., eds., *Dona nobis pacem,* 12; Kowalczuk, *Endspiel,* 311; and Schwabe, "Die Entwicklung der Leipziger Opposition," 167. Hard feelings still remained over a decade later; at a 1999 event, an activist speaking on a panel with Führer called the latter's description of 1988–1989 a lie. See the transcript of this event in Hollitzer and Bohse, eds., *Heute vor 10 Jahren,* 360–364. See also an essay by Hans-Friedrich Fischer, the Catholic priest who served as moderator between Führer and the activists, in Sievers, ed., *Stundenbuch,* 15–20.

116. Rat des Bezirkes Leipzig, Stellvertreter des Vorsitzenden des Rates für Inneres, "Information," Mar. 16, 1989, FRL 98.

117. See the analysis of the May Day march, FRL 102.

118. "Kopie des Briefes des OBM der Stadt Leipzig, Seidel," Aug. 25, 1989, Doc. 191, FUF 376–377.

119. "Auszug aus dem handschriftlichen Protokoll der 50. Sitzung des KV St. Nikolai," May 8, 1989, Doc. 156, FUF 318–319.

120. "Xerokopie [*sic*] des Briefs von Landesbischof Hempel," May 31, 1989, Doc. 173, FUF 352–353.

121. "Dienstbesprechung," Aug. 31, 1989, MfS, ZAIG B/215, reprinted in Arnim Mitter and Stefan Wolle, eds., *Ich liebe euch doch alle! Befehle und Lageberichte des MfS Januar-November 1989* (Berlin: BasisDruck, 1990), 125.

122. "Auszug aus Mitschrift des Oberstleutnant [*sic*] Seidel zur Dienstversammlung," Sept. 2, 1989, Doc. 195, FUF 379; see also Doc. 196, FUF 380–382, and Hollitzer and Bohse, eds., *Heute vor 10 Jahren,* 329.

123. Bohley, Praschl, and Rosenthal, eds., *Mut,* 10, 216; see also photos, 222–223.

124. The Stasi's records from Hattenhauer's September incarceration survive in BStU, Lpz AU 1793–89, Strafakte I, Hattenhauer (see especially 7–9); BStU, BV Lpz AGL 2793, Sept. 12, 1989, 20–22; BStU, Lpz AU 1793–89 Handakte Hattenhauer; and BStU, Lpz AOPK 3993-92. The author is also grateful to Hattenhauer for discussing the experience with her in detail. For more on the nature of Stasi detention practices generally, see Katrin Passens, *MfS-Untersuchungshaft: Funktionen und Entwicklung von 1971 bis 1989* (Berlin: Lukas Verlag, 2012).

125. A transcript of this particular interrogation survives in "Abschrift," June 10, 1989, Leipzig, Hattenhauer, BStU, Leipzig AOPK 3993/92, 43–46. See also Müller-Enbergs et al., *Wer war wer,* 494–495, 1206–1207; Saunders, "Half a Life Ago"; and Hattenhauer's biography on her website at www.katrin-hattenhauer.de/biografie_en.html.

126. "Aktennotiz von Pf. Führer," Sept. 18, 1989, doc. 208, FUF 399–400; and "Brief der Superintendentur Leipzig-Ost (Briefkopf) und des KV St. Nikolai (Führer)," Sept. 20, 1989, doc. 212, FUF 404.

127. "Chiffriertes Fernschreiben," Sept. 26, 1989, Helmut Hackenberg to Erich Honecker, in SS, Anlage II, 568–569.

128. "Brief vom Vorsitzenden des KV St. Nikolai (Pf. Führer) an den KV St. Thomas (Pf. Ebeling)," Oct. 3, 1989, Doc. 234, FUF, 444–445 (the Thomas Church's leaders changed their minds on Oct. 6); "Immer loyal," *Spiegel* 11 (1990): 22–23; and Sievers, ed., *Stundenbuch*, 68–70.

129. "Erklärung der Volkskammer zu den aktuellen Ereignissen in der VR China," June 8, 1989, doc. 190, in Werner Meißner and Anja Feege, eds., *Die DDR und China 1949 bis 1990* (Berlin: Akademie Verlag, 1995), 397–398. For more on the events in Tiananmen Square and their impact, see Jean-Philippe Béja, ed., *The Impact of China's 1989 Tiananmen Massacre* (New York: Routledge, 2010); Andrew J. Nathan, Perry Link, and Zhang Liang [pseud.], eds., *The Tiananmen Papers: The Chinese Leadership's Decision to Use Force Against Their Own People—In Their Own Words* (New York: PublicAffairs, 2001); David Shambaugh, *China's Communist Party: Atrophy and Adaptation* (Berkeley: University of California Press, 2008); and Jeffrey N. Wasserstrom and Elizabeth J. Perry, eds., *Popular Protest and Political Culture in Modern China,* 2nd ed. (Boulder: Westview Press, 1994). See also Karrie J. Koesel and Valerie J. Bunce, "Diffusion-Proofing: Russian and Chinese Responses to Waves of Popular Motivations Against Authoritarian Rulers," *Perspectives on Politics* 11, no. 3 (Sept. 2013): 753–768.

130. On the support of the SED Politburo for the Chinese leadership, see "Protokoll Nr. 22," June 6, 1989, BArch, SAPMO, DY30/J IV 2/2/2331; see also the letters collected by the Stasi in BStU, MfS, HA II 26624. On the protestors, see "Personenfeststellungen zum Sicherungsbereich 'Botschaft der VR China,'" June 7, 1989, www.BStU.bund.de/DE/Wissen/DDRGeschichte/Revolutionskalender/Juni-1989 /juni89_node.html.

131. Records from Krenz's visit to China (from Sept. 25 to Oct. 2, 1989) are available in PA-AA, BDE, ZR 2496-90; excerpts also available in Meißner and Feege, eds., *DDR und China,* 412–414. See also Hollitzer and Bohse, eds., *Heute vor 10 Jahren,* 415–416 n. 583, and Sarotte, "China's Fear of Contagion."

132. Telegram from Honecker to first secretaries in all party districts, Sept. 22, 1989, BStU, SdM664, 61.

133. Führer, Ascher, and Holland-Moritz, *Und wir sind dabei,* 207; Hollitzer, "Der friedliche Verlauf," 253; and Hollitzer and Bohse, eds., *Heute vor 10 Jahren,* 371.

134. Mario Niemann, *Die Sekretäre der SED-Bezirksleitungen* 1952–1989 (Paderborn: Ferdinand Schöningh, 2007), 121–122, 355, 361; and Pötzl, *Erich Honecker,* 17.

135. Kotschemassow, *Meine letzte Mission,* 168. On the phenomenon of the opposition, not the regime, shaping events in Leipzig, see Eckert, *SED-Diktatur,* 12.

136. Interview with Günter Schabowski, CNN Cold War Collection, KCLMA.

137. "Information," 428/89, Sept. 26, 1989, in BStU, ZAIG 3748; "ZK Hausmitteilung," Oct. 3, 1989, BStU SdM 664, 62–63; "ZK Hausmitteilung," Oct. 3, 1989, DY 30/IV 2/2.039/317, BArch; and "Information," Oct. 3, 1989, MfS, ZAIG, Nr. 435/89, reprinted in Mitter and Wolle, eds., *Ich liebe euch doch alle,* 190–191. See also Mielke, Sept. 13, 1989, BStU, ZA, Neiber 364, 242–246, available online; Hollitzer, "Der friedliche Verlauf," 256–261; Kuhn, *Tag der Entscheidung,* 52; and Neues Forum, ed., *Jetzt oder nie—Demokratie! Leipziger Herbst '89* (Leipzig: Forum Verlag, 1989), 305.

138. Statement of unit member Gerald Pilz, Oct. 2, 1989, reprinted in Sievers, ed., *Stundenbuch,* 55–56; and Walter Süß, "Der friedliche Ausgang des 9. Oktober in Leipzig," in Martin Sabrow, ed., *1989 und die Rolle der Gewalt* (Göttingen: Wallstein Verlag, 2012), 178–180.

139. Kommandeur Günter Lutz, im Auftrag der Kampfgruppenhundertschaft "Hans Geiffert," "Staatsfeindlichkeit nicht länger dulden," *Leipziger Volkszeitung,* Oct. 6, 1989, reprinted in Hollitzer, "'Heute entscheidet es sich,'" *Horch und Guck* 23 (Feb. 1998): 25.

140. "Plan der Maßnahmen zur Gewährleistung der Sicherheit während des 40. Jahrestages der Gründung der Deutschen Demokratischen Republik — 6. bis 8. Oktober 1989," Sept. 27, 1989, BStU, MfS, ZAIG 7314, 1–30, quotation at 4, also available online; this document was issued by Mielke and confirmed by Honecker personally. See also "Hinweise für Kollegiumssitzung," Oct. 3, 1989, BStU, MfS, ZAIG 8680, 1, 15–21, also available online.

141. *DDR Journal zur November Revolution,* 41–42.

142. Volkspolizei-Kreisamt Leipzig, Der Leiter, "Zusätzliche Maßnahmen," Sept. 27, 1989, FRL 404; see also Mielke to the leaders of duty units, Oct. 5, 1989, reprinted in Mitter and Wolle, eds., *Ich liebe euch doch alle,* 195–198.

143. Portion of police document reprinted in Hollitzer and Bohse, eds., *Heute vor 10 Jahren,* 413.

144. See the file on the visit, Oct. 2–9, 1989, ZR 2495–90, BDE, MfAA, PA-AA; and "Einige Fragen und Probleme," Oct. 25, 1989, BArch, SAPMO, IV 2/2.039/317. See also Hollitzer, "Der friedliche Verlauf," 255; Sarotte, "China's Fear of Contagion"; and Bernd Schäfer, "Die DDR und die 'chinesische Lösung,'" in Sabrow, ed., *1989,* 153–172.

145. Neues Forum, ed., *Jetzt oder nie,* 83–84; the name of the housewife was Susanne Rummel.

146. Neues Forum, ed., *Jetzt oder nie,* 84; the name of the woman was Gudrun Fischer. See also Pond, *Beyond the Wall,* 93. For a description of, and photos from, the violence on the anniversary day, Oct. 7, see FRL 390–391.

147. Author's interviews with Greenwald and Lipping.

Chapter 3: The Fight for the Ring

1. On the disappearance of relevant documents, see Hollitzer, "Der friedliche Verlauf des 9. Oktober 1989 in Leipzig," 250, 268–269; see also Süß, "Der friedliche Verlauf," 188 n. 54.

2. "Information," 452/89, n.d. but from context Oct. 9, 1989, BStU, ZAIG 3748, 16; Führer, Ascher, and Holland-Moritz, *Und wir sind dabei,* 217; and Sievers, ed., *Stundenbuch,* 73.

3. Neues Forum Leipzig, *Jetzt oder nie,* 305.

4. "Mitschrift des Leiters der Abt. XXII der BVfS Leipzig von der Dienstversammlung beim Leiter der BVfS Leipzig, Manfred Hummitzsch, am 30.9.1989, BStU Leipzig, Abt. XXII, Arbeitsbuch 4255," 7–8, quoted in Hollitzer, "Der friedliche Verlauf," 255.

5. Hollitzer, "Der friedliche Verlauf," 260; and Süß, "Der friedliche Ausgang," 183–184.

6. ARD, *Tagesschau,* Oct. 8, 1989; and author's interview with Leary.

7. The estimate of 50,000 appears in "Entschluß des Chefs der BDVP Leipzig zum Ordnungseinsatz am 9. Oktober 1989," SS Anlage II, 663. A note typed on this document indicates that it was confirmed personally by Interior Minister Dickel. See also Süß, "Selbstblockierung der Macht," 239; and Jens Gieseke, "Der entkräftete Tschekismus," in Sabrow, ed., *1989,* 57–66.

8. Erich Honecker regarded his country's newspapers in particular almost as his own personal hobby and put a lot of effort into the details of coverage. The results were obvious: reporting on the Leipzig trade fair, one newspaper published over forty pictures of Honecker in a single issue; see Hannes Bahrmann and Christoph Links, *Chronik der Wende: Die DDR zwischen 7. Oktober und 18. Dezember 1989* (Berlin: Links, 1994), 18–19, and interview with Schabowski in Hertle, Pirker, and Weinert, "Der Honecker muß weg!," 8–11.

9. Author's interviews with Baum and Leary. The former was intimidated into not going to Leipzig; the latter went but was escorted out to the city limits. In an interview, Hackenberg confirmed that there had been a "Drehverbot"; see interview with Hackenberg, Fall of the Wall Collection, KCLMA. See also Hartmut Zwahr, "Die Revolution in der DDR 1989/90," in Fischer and Heydemann, eds., *Die politische "Wende,"* 205–215.

10. For discussion of the actions of the army, or NVA, in Dresden, see Hollitzer, "Der friedliche Verlauf," 259.

11. Albrecht Hinze, "Eine Legende zerbröckelt," *Süddeutsche Zeitung,* Nov. 21, 1989; see also Victor Sebestyen, *Revolution 1989: The Fall of the Soviet Empire* (New York: Vintage, 2009), 337–338.

12. Interview with Gerhard Straßenburg, Fall of the Wall Collection, KCLMA; and interviews with Straßenburg and Wötzel in Kuhn, *Der Tag,* 52–53.

13. See the analysis of the Oct. 8 meeting in FRL 410.

14. Erich Mielke to "Diensteinheiten, Leiter," Oct. 8, 1989, BStU, MfS, BdL, Doc. 006920, also available online; a copy of this telegram, with a different title and the addition of a handwritten transmission time of 5:58 p.m. and receipt time of 6:20 p.m., is in FRL 411. For more on the structure of the Stasi and its official and unofficial staff, see David Childs and Richard Popplewell, *The Stasi: The East German Intelligence and Security Service* (London: Macmillan, 1996); Jens Gieseke, *Die hauptamtlichen*

Mitarbeiter der Staatssicherheit: Personalstruktur und Lebenswelt, 1950–1989/90 (Berlin: Links, 2000); Jens Gieseke, *Die Stasi 1945–1990* (Munich: Pantheon, 2011); and Helmut Müller-Enbergs, ed., *Inoffizielle Mitarbeiter des Ministeriums für Staatssicherheit: Richtlinien und Durchführungsbestimmungen* (Berlin: Links, 1996).

15. BV für Staatssicherheit Leipzig, Kreisdienststelle Leipzig-Stadt, "Im Rahmen des Vorbeugungskomplexes zuzuführende Personen," Oct. 9, 1989, FRL 413.

16. Hollitzer, "Der friedliche Verlauf," 271; Mielke, "Diensteinheiten, Leiter," Oct. 8, 1989; ARD *Tagesthemen* broadcast, Oct. 9, 1989. For more on the preparations for Oct. 9, 1989, in Leipzig, see the various documents in FRL 410–413. For an earlier instance of monitoring of journalists in Leipzig, see "Information," 435/89, BStU, ZAIG 3748, 12–14. For an earlier instance of preventing undesirable persons from travel, see Mielke's instructions of Oct. 5, 1989, when he instructed the Stasi to prevent undesirables from traveling to Berlin during the fortieth-anniversary celebration period surrounding Oct. 7; the goal, as he put it, was "keine Überraschungen zulassen!" Ministerium für Staatssicherheit, der Minister, Diensteinheiten, Leiter, Oct. 5, 1989, FRL 406.

17. Hollitzer and Bohse, eds., *Heute vor 10 Jahren,* 466–467; FRL 425, has a picture of one of the cameras set up in Leipzig for the feed to Berlin and a copy of some of the technical orders for safeguarding its operation.

18. On the control of the party over nearly all organizations in East Germany, see Kowalczuk, *Stasi Konkret,* 16.

19. For assessments of the paramilitaries from later in October, see "Einschätzung der Kampfkraft und Einsatzbereitschaft der Kampfgruppen," Oct. 23, 1989, BStU, MfS, HA VII 68, 248–260, also available online; and "Information," Oct. 15, 1989, ZAIG Nr. 457/89, reprinted in Mitter and Wolle, eds., *Ich liebe,* 221–222. See also "Kampfgruppen," FUF 470, and Süß, "Der friedliche Ausgang," 190.

20. On the coup against Gorbachev, see Plokhy, *The Last Empire.*

21. Kotschemassow, *Meine letzte Mission,* 169; and Angela Stent, *Russia and Germany Reborn: Unification, the Soviet Collapse, and the New Europe* (Princeton, NJ: Princeton University Press, 1999), 90–91. In a separate account, Valentin Falin, a Soviet official and Germany expert, said in an interview that, starting in Aug. 1989, Soviet troops had an order not to intervene in events such as those in Leipzig, but did not say who issued it; Krenz challenged the idea that there was such an order, saying that if there had been one, he would have known about it. See Kuhn, *Der Tag,* 29–31.

22. Süß, *Staatssicherheit am Ende,* 417. On the Soviet Union in divided Germany generally, see Brown, *Rise and Fall*; Jacques Lévesque, *The Enigma of 1989: The USSR and the Liberation of Eastern Europe* (Berkeley: University of California Press, 1997); Naimark, *The Russians in Germany*; and Odd Arne Westad et al., eds., *The Soviet Union in Eastern Europe 1945–89* (New York: St. Martin's Press, 1994). For a theoretical assessment of the GDR-USSR relationship, see Alexander Wendt and Daniel Friedheim, "Hierarchy Under Anarchy: Informal Empire and the East German State," *International Organization* 49 (Autumn 1995): 689–722.

23. "Fernschreiben an alle 1. Sekretäre der Bezirksleitungen der SED," Oct. 8, 1989, 11:00 a.m., in BArch DY 30/IV 2/2.039/314.

24. Records from this meeting are lacking, unfortunately, but its content can be surmised from paperwork and instructions issued later; see Hollitzer, "Der friedliche Verlauf," 261.

25. Kotschemassow, *Meine letzte Mission,* 168–169.

26. Hollitzer, "Der friedliche Verlauf," 261.

27. Ibid., 248–249; Süß, "Der friedliche Ausgang," 187–195. See also telegram, Hackenberg to Krenz, Oct. 5, 1989, doc. 235, FUF 445–447. The original German for "district deployment command" is "Bezirkseinsatzleitung," often abbreviated in the documents as BEL.

28. Telegram, Hackenberg to Krenz, Oct. 5, 1989, doc. 235, FUF 445–447; and Kuhn, *Der Tag,* 47–50.

29. For more on Tiananmen Square, see Sarotte, "China's Fear of Contagion."

30. Martin Jankowski, "Sieg ohne Helden," *Deutschland Archiv* 41 (2008): 821; Martin Jankowski, *Der Tag, der Deutschland veränderte: 9. Oktober 1989* (Leipzig: Evangelische Verlagsanstalt, 2007); Hollitzer, "Der friedliche Verlauf," 270; and Süß, "Der friedliche Ausgang," 183–184.

31. See the photos of armored vehicles, dogs, water cannons, and other equipment in Leipzig in Oct. 1989 in Wolfgang Schneider, *Leipziger Demontagebuch* (Leipzig: Kiepenhauer, 1990); the police and Stasi documents with details of preparations for Oct. 9 in Leipzig, such as Volkspolizei-Kreisamt Leipzig, "Entschluß des Leiters des VPKA Leipzig, Fritzsche, Oberst der VP, Bestätigt: Chef der BDVP Straßenburg Generalmajor," Oct. 8, 1989, FRL 407; the various handwritten notes on preparations, in FRL 408; and "Vorschlag zu Aufgabenstellung," n.d. but from context, part of Oct. 9 preparations, and handwritten documents, FRL 412. See also the overview of security preparations provided in Hollitzer, "Der friedliche Verlauf," 262–279, and Süß, "Der friedliche Ausgang," 183–184.

32. Hinze, "Eine Legende zerbröckelt"; and Kuhn, *Der Tag,* 74–75.

33. See the photo of one of the horse stalls used for this purpose, FRL 412; see also Hollitzer, "Der friedliche Verlauf," 265; and Kuhn, *Der Tag,* 63–64.

34. In the video documentary by Andreas Voigt and Gerd Kroske, *Leipzig im Herbst: Aufbruch '89, ein DEFA-Dokument,* 1989, filmed between Oct. 16 and Nov. 7, 1989, demonstrators from Oct. 7 describe being locked inside horse stalls with multiple other prisoners for extended periods with no provision for water, food, or toilets.

35. Interview with Straßenburg in Kuhn, *Der Tag,* 46.

36. According to Volkspolizei-Kreisamt Leipzig, "Entschluß des Leiters des VPKA Leipzig," Oct. 8, 1989, FRL 407, the security forces were assembled near the Ostknoten, or "Eastern Knot," on the ring, a tactically advantageous spot just shy of the main train station, and were to prevent "eine weitere Bewegung in Richtung Hauptbahnhof" (see "Sicherungsbereich 2—Georgiring/Ostknoten" section of Entschluß, reproduced as sections 4 and 5 in FRL 407).

37. Telegram from Straßenburg, Oct. 9, 1989, to Ltr. VPKÄ, Ltr. StVE, Kdr., FRL 406; see also the related documents, FRL 407–412.

38. "Entschluß des Chefs der BDVP Leipzig zum Ordnungseinsatz am 9. Oktober 1989," SS Anlage II, 665–667; as mentioned in n. 7, a written note on this document indicates that Dickel confirmed it.

39. Hollitzer, "Der friedliche Verlauf," 273.

40. Interview with Silvio Rösler, Fall of the Wall Collection, KCLMA.

41. Interview with Uwe Chemnitz, Fall of the Wall Collection, KCLMA.

42. Interview with Gisela and Wolfgang Rähder, Fall of the Wall Collection, KCLMA.

43. Interview with Jens Illing, Fall of the Wall Collection, KCLMA.

44. Remarks by Toralf Dörre, formerly of the Volkspolizei-Bereitschaft Essenerstr. Leipzig, on Oct. 7, 1999, reprinted in Hollitzer and Bohse, eds., *Heute vor 10 Jahren*, 486–487.

45. Interview with Illing, Fall of the Wall Collection, KCLMA.

46. Page from diary of Superintendent Dr. Johannes Richter, Oct. 9, 1989, reprinted in FRL 409.

47. Führer quoted in Kuhn, *Der Tag*, 74.

48. Photographs of the pages of Friedrich's letter are reprinted in Kuhn, *Der Tag*, 91–111; the suggestion that it was time for Honecker to go is at 109. Krenz confirms that Friedrich came to see him on that day and for that purpose; see Egon Krenz, *Herbst '89* (Berlin: Neues Leben, 1999), 89–92. The Stasi got wind of this event somehow: see BStU, BV Lpz Abt. XX 1722, Oct. 10, 1989, "Meinungen zur aktuellen Lage im Rat des Bezirks," 2–3.

49. Kuhn, *Der Tag*, 84–90.

50. Interview with Krenz and letter from Friedrich to Krenz, both in Kuhn, *Der Tag*, 87–111.

51. "Lagefilm zum Einsatz/der Absicherung des 'Friedensgebetes' am 09.10.1989," SS, Anlage II, 628. The original wording in German on the cloth was "Leute keine sinnlose Gewalt, reißt euch zusammen, laßt die Steine liegen."

52. On Zimmermann's outing of himself as a Stasi agent, see "Startrampe für Spione," *Spiegel* 5 (1991): 50–52. See also FUF 566, which discloses his Stasi cover name as "Karl Erb." Zimmermann is often misidentified as a pastor but was an employee of the theological faculty of the University of Leipzig. See Gößner and Wieckowski, eds., *Die theologische Fakultät*, for a history of the faculty.

53. "Aufruf der Sechs," reprinted in Kuhn, *Der Tag*, 122–123. See also Hackenberg's version of how the appeal came to be, saying that local party leaders had in fact come up with a similar idea for such cooperative measures themselves earlier that morning, in interview with Hackenberg, Fall of the Wall Collection, KCLMA.

54. Author's interviews with Schwabe and Wonneberger.

55. Author's interview with Wonneberger; the leaflet itself, or "Appell," is reprinted in FRL 418. On the experience of distributing the leaflet and nearly being arrested for it, see interview with Gisela Kallenbach, CNN Cold War Collection, KCLMA.

56. Jahn worked with a number of other "information smugglers" in East Germany as well, but by 1989 Radomski and Schefke were his main sources of visual images. Author's interviews with Jahn, Radomski, and Schefke.

57. Author's interview with Jahn; Gerald Praschl, *Roland Jahn: Ein Rebell als Behördenchef* (Berlin: Links, 2011), 118–141; and, on the CSCE's effects, Korey, *Promises,* chapter 3.

58. Siegbert "Siggi" Schefke, *Leipzig—Städteverfall in der DDR,* initial broadcast Sept. 12, 1989, *Kontraste,* SFB/ARD; see also remarks by Schefke reprinted in Hollitzer and Bohse, eds., *Heute vor 10 Jahren,* 477–478.

59. Author's interviews with Radomski and Schefke.

60. Author's interviews with Jahn, Radomski, and Schefke; see also Hollitzer and Bohse, eds., *Heute vor 10 Jahren,* 478.

61. "Beabsichtigtes Treffen feindlicher Kräfte in Prag," BStU, MfS, HA XX/9 1772, 9.

62. Photographs of both the video camera and the concealing carrier bag used by Radomski and Schefke are in FRL 432–433.

63. Jahn quoted in Praschl, *Roland Jahn,* 220.

64. Author's interview with Jahn; and Funken, *Das Jahr,* 20.

65. For biographical information about Radomski, see Kowalczuk and Sello, eds., *Für ein freies Land,* 380–383; see also the online biographical information at www.chronik-der-wende.de.

66. Author's interview with Radomski; and Kowalczuk and Sello, eds., *Für ein freies Land,* 380–381.

67. Author's interviews with Radomski and Schefke. On the East German band Feeling B, some of whose members then formed Rammstein, and the importance of rock music to the GDR opposition, see Kowalczuk, *Endspiel,* 158–162.

68. See the internal Stasi documentation summarizing the reasons for taking Schefke under surveillance in BStU, BV Berlin, AOP 5761-91, Schefke, especially 12. For a summary of Schefke's biography, see Hollitzer and Bohse, eds., *Heute vor 10 Jahren,* 474–475.

69. No less than a Stasi crown prince, Sven Schwanitz, was in charge of the operation of watching over "Satan." Sven was the son of Wolfgang Schwanitz, the senior Stasi officer in line to take over the entire ministry once its eighty-one-year-old leader, Mielke, finally relinquished the reins that he had held for over three decades. As a result, Sven's last name entitled him both to authority beyond his age and to the highest-profile operations, such as those against Schefke. On Schwanitz and Schefke, see Frank Junghänel, "In der Zeitschleife," *Berliner Zeitung,* Oct. 9, 2009; for more information on Mielke and Schwanitz, see the relevant entries in Enbergs et al., eds., *Wer war wer,* and Süß, *Staatssicherheit am Ende,* 81–82.

70. For instructions from the Stasi to have his employer make leaving work for his dissident activities difficult, see "Eröffnungsbericht," Berlin, Mar. 1, 1988, Abteilung XX/2, BStU, 29. For Schefke's response to the subsequent actions by his employer,

see "Sachstandbericht zum OV 'Satan,'" Sept. 18, 1988, Berlin, Bezirksverwaltung für Staatssicherheit Berlin, Abteilung XX, BStU, AOP 5761-91, 95. The author is grateful to Schefke for providing the legal permission *(Einwilligung)* necessary to view his complete Stasi files.

71. "Sachstandbericht zum OV 'Satan,'" 92–96; see also Kowalczuk, *Endspiel,* 216, and Vollnhals, ed., *Die Kirchenpolitik.*

72. See the collection of Stasi documents about the East Berlin Protestant church that sheltered the library, the Zionskirche, on the Stasi Archive website, www.bstu .bund.de/DE/Wissen/DDRGeschichte/Vorabend-der-Revolution/1987_Buerger echtler-Umweltbibliothek/_node.html.

73. Author's interview with Jahn; Lina's quotation in Praschl, *Roland Jahn,* 77. Further autobiographical information in Roland Jahn, "'Du bist wie Gift,'" *Spiegel* 25 (1983): 78–84; see also Ralf Huisinga, *Roland Jahn und die Friedensgemeinschaft in Jena* (Munich: Grin Verlag, 2006); and Kowalczuk and Sello, eds., *Für ein freies Land,* 321–324.

74. "9. Juni 1983, Bericht," Bezirksverwaltung für Staatssicherheit, Stellvertreter Operativ, Gera, 67–70, in BStU, "Aktion 'Gegenschlag,'" BStU-Außenstelle Gera; quotation at 69.

75. Author's interview with Jahn.

76. "9. Juni 1983, Bericht," 69. For good measure, the Stasi noted the name, birthdate, and home address of the sleeping-car conductor, in case later follow-up with the conductor might be needed, were he tempted to talk.

77. Author's interview with Jahn.

78. Author's interviews with Jahn and Poppe; Kowalczuk, *Endspiel,* 235–253; Kowalczuk and Sello, eds., *Für ein freies Land,* 306–311; and Praschl, *Roland Jahn,* 80–178. On East German dissent generally, see John C. Torpey, *Intellectuals, Socialism and Dissent: The East German Opposition and Its Legacy* (Minneapolis: University of Minnesota Press, 1995).

79. Ilko-Sascha Kowalczuk, ed., *Freiheit und Öffentlichkeit: Politischer Samisdat in der DDR 1985–1989* (Berlin: Robert-Havemann-Gesellschaft, 2002), 216 n. 1. For more on Jahn's network, see Praschl, *Roland Jahn,* 118–141.

80. Author's interview with Jahn; and Funken, *Das Jahr,* 25–31.

81. "Eröffnungsbericht," Mar. 1, 1988, BStU, MfS Archiv der Zentralstelle, BVfS Berlin, AOP 5761/91, 21–32.

82. "Vermerk über den Rapport zum OV 'Satan,'" Aug. 21, 1989, BStU, AOP 5761-91, Abteilung XX/9, 56; and author's interview with Schefke.

83. Extensive Stasi files are available on one of Schefke's "friends," a man named Falk Zimmermann, who was in fact an undercover Stasi operative, reporting on Schefke for years in exchange for payment. Zimmermann's Stasi code name was "Reinhard Schumann." See the multiple volumes of his Stasi files in BStU, Reg.-Nr. BV Berlin/ XV/1619/79, "Reinhard Schumann." Tina Rosenberg, *The Haunted Land: Facing Europe's Ghosts After Communism* (New York: Random House, 1995), 358–372, also describes Zimmermann's work, although on the basis of interviews rather than the actual Stasi files.

84. Author's interviews with Radomski and Schefke.

85. Author's interview with Radomski.

86. Author's interviews with Radomski and Schefke; and remarks by Schefke in Hollitzer and Bohse, eds., *Heute vor 10 Jahren,* 478–482.

87. Author's interview with Schefke; and remarks by Bickhardt in Hollitzer and Bohse, eds., *Heute vor 10 Jahren,* 442–443.

88. Author's interviews with Radomski and Schefke.

89. Author's interviews with Radomski and Schefke; and Funken, *Das Jahr,* 31.

90. Author's interview with Sievers; interview with Sievers in Hollitzer and Bohse, eds., *Heute vor 10 Jahren,* 432–434; and Hans-Jürgen Sievers, ed., *In der Mitte der Stadt: Die Evangelisch-Reformierte Kirche zu Leipzig von der Einwanderung der Hugenotten bis zur friedlichen Revolution* (Leipzig: Evangelische Verlagsanstalt, 2000), 141.

91. Author's interviews with Radomski and Sievers.

92. Author's interviews with Radomski, Schefke, and Sievers; and Praschl, *Roland Jahn,* 171–172.

93. Author's interview with Sievers; see also interview with Sievers in Hollitzer and Bohse, eds., *Heute vor 10 Jahren,* 432–434.

94. Author's interviews with Radomski, Schefke, and Schwarz.

95. In the wake of the Helsinki Final Act of 1975, the GDR let the West German newsweekly *Spiegel,* along with others, open bureaus in East Berlin. On Helsinki and its legacy, see Korey, *Promises,* and Snyder, *Human Rights Activism.*

96. Schwarz's predecessor, Jörg Mettke, was also thrown out, for an article about forced adoptions; author's interview with Schwarz. See also Jochen Bölsche, "Das Geheimnis der Tarantel," *Spiegel* 33 (2000): 56–70.

97. One of the many Stasi files on Schwarz is available at BStU, MfS HA II/13, Nr. 1228, OV "Tarantel."

98. The group was called "Arche." On Cooper's role, see Carlo Jordan and Hans Michael Kloth, eds., *Arche Nova* (Berlin: BasisDruck, 1995), 99–111.

99. Author's interviews, with Cooper, Schefke, and Schwarz; see also Funken, *Das Jahr,* 31.

100. Author's interviews with Schefke and Sievers.

101. Führer, Ascher, and Holland-Moritz, *Und wir sind dabei,* 214.

102. Ibid., 213–216.

103. Hollitzer and Bohse, eds., *Heute vor 10 Jahren,* 464.

104. Hackenberg quoted in Hollitzer, "Der friedliche Verlauf," 272.

105. For speculation on how many of the party members due to pack the church actually showed up, see Süß, "Der friedliche Ausgang," 190–192.

106. Führer, Ascher, and Holland-Moritz, *Und wir sind dabei,* 216–218; and interview with Führer in Kuhn, *Der Tag,* 120.

107. "Bericht des Sekretärs der SED-Stadtleitung Leipzig," Oct. 10, 1989, doc. 244, FUF 458–460.

108. Interview with Führer in Kuhn, *Der Tag,* 120–122; and Süß, "Der friedliche Ausgang," 191–192.

109. Author's interview with Sievers; and "Auszug aus dem Fernschreiben des Chefs der BDVP Leipzig [Straßenburg] an den Minister des Inneren," Oct. 10, 1989, 1:45 a.m., FRL 430.

110. Author's interview with Sievers.

111. Author's interview with Sievers; and "Manuskript der Predigt von Pfarrer Hans-Jürgen Sievers in der Reformierten Kirche," Oct. 9, 1989, FRL 422. For the text of the 1963 "I Have a Dream" speech, see, among other places, www.archives.gov/press/exhibits/dream-speech.pdf; on King in divided Berlin, see the German Historical Institute website, www.aacvr-germany.org/index.php/images-7/dr-martin-luther-kings-visit-to-cold-war-berlin.

112. In a later interview, Hackenberg claimed that he had allowed delivery and reading of the appeal because he agreed with it in principle, but had not signed it himself because the fact that only some, not all, of the party secretaries in Leipzig had signed it revealed a split in the party. See interview with Hackenberg, Fall of the Wall Collection, KCLMA. See also "Chronik der Wende: Oktober 9, 1989," video series, RBB Media, 1994, and Süß, *Staatssicherheit am Ende,* 310–312.

113. Author's interview with Schwabe.

114. Karl-Dieter Opp, Peter Voss, and Christiane Gern, *Die volkseigene Revolution* (Stuttgart: Klett-Cotta, 1993), 47. Opp and his co-authors analyzed the Oct. 9 protest and estimated that the number of participants may have been as high as 166,000; they concluded that the commonly used estimate of 70,000 is almost certainly too low.

115. "Lagefilm zum Einsatz/der Absicherung des 'Friedensgebetes' am 09.10.1989," SS, Anlage II, 634.

116. Author's interview with Hattenhauer; see also Bohley, Praschl, and Rosenthal, eds., *Mut,* 10–11; Hattenhauer's biography on her website, www.katrin-hattenhauer.de/biografie_en.html; and Saunders, "Half a Life Ago."

117. Author's interview with Schwabe.

118. Interview with police Oberstleutnant Wolfgang Schröder in Kuhn, *Der Tag,* 80; and Martin Jankowski, "Sieg ohne Helden," 821–823.

119. On Hackenberg's operational authority as district deployment leader, see Hollitzer, "Der friedliche Verlauf," 248.

120. Süß, "Der friedliche Ausgang," 188–190.

121. Interview with Hackenberg, Fall of the Wall Collection, KCLMA; and interview with Krenz in Kuhn, *Der Tag,* 133.

122. Interview with Wötzel in Kuhn, *Der Tag,* 130–133.

123. Krenz would also say that there had never been any order to shoot in Leipzig, which may have been accurate since Hackenberg did not issue it, but that does not explain why large numbers of the deployed forces stated that they had received an order to shoot (as described in this chapter). See Hinze, "Eine Legende zerbröckelt," and interview with Egon Krenz, Fall of the Wall Collection, KCLMA.

124. Interview with Wötzel in Kuhn, *Der Tag,* 130, 134.

125. Interview with Hackenberg, Fall of the Wall Collection, KCLMA.

126. Hinze, "Eine Legende zerbröckelt"; Hollitzer, "Der friedliche Verlauf," 278; and Süß, *Staatssicherheit am Ende*, 307.

127. Süß, "Der friedliche Ausgang," 195.

128. Nieman, *Sekretäre*, 337.

129. Süß, *Staatssicherheit am Ende*, 310–312.

130. As mentioned above in note 7 to this chapter, the estimate of 50,000 appears in "Entschluß des Chefs der BDVP Leipzig zum Ordnungseinsatz am 9. Oktober 1989," SS Anlage II, 663.

131. Süß, "Der friedliche Ausgang," 195–202.

132. "Aktennotiz zur Einweisung am 14.10.1989, 08.00 Uhr, beim Chef des Hauptstabes des MVR," SS Anlage II, 690, this document also appears in FRL 442.

133. "Protokoll, 22. Sitzung der Bezirksleitung," Nov. 21, 1989, FRL 432.

134. Interview with Wötzel in Kuhn, *Der Tag*, 135. Straßenburg has provided a different history of this evening. He claimed that his orders on Oct. 9 were to avoid the use of violence, and that in pursuit of that goal he was the one who instructed the forces to take up a self-defensive post; see interview with Straßenburg, Fall of the Wall Collection, KCLMA. A minor point of interest in this interview is that the questioner had to request that Straßenburg stop ogling a female member of the crew recording it. In contrast with Straßenburg's account, the surviving written documentation cited here, plus the fact that Hackenberg was the highest de facto authority on-site, suggests that Hackenberg's account is more credible. Hackenberg does indicate that he consulted with Straßenburg a number of times in the course of the evening, and the written record makes clear that he did, so it is possible that the idea of reverting to self-defense arose in a mutual conversation. Ultimately Hackenberg had to implement it, however.

135. The full original in German is as follows: "09.10.89, 18.35 Uhr, Vorsitzender BEL und Chef [Hackenberg]: Nach Bestätigung wird befohlen, keine aktiven Handlungen gegenüber den Demonstranten zu unternehmen. Befehl Chef: An alle Einsatzkräfte ist der Befehl zu erteilen, daß der Übergang zur Eigensicherung einzuleiten ist! Einsatz Kräfte nur bei Angriffen auf Sicherungskräfte, Objekte und Einrichtungen. Bei Angriff-Abwehr mit allen Mitteln. Verkehrsorganisatorische Maßnahmen einleiten." In SS Anlage II, 679. See also interview with Wötzel in Kuhn, *Der Tag*, 130–133, and Niemann, *Die Sekretäre*, 345.

136. On-camera testimony of Oberstleutnant Schröder, Kommandeur der 5. VP-Bereitschaft, in Andreas Voigt and Gerd Kroske, producers, *Leipzig im Herbst: Aufbruch '89, ein DEFA-Dokument*, video documentary filmed Oct. 16–Nov. 7, 1989; see also interviews with Wötzel and Straßenburg in Kuhn, *Der Tag*, 131–133, and Süß, "Der friedliche Ausgang," 196–197.

137. Volkspolizeihauptmann Dieter Zarges, quoted in Jankowski, "Sieg ohne Helden," 823.

138. Remarks by Dörre in Hollitzer and Bohse, eds., *Heute vor 10 Jahren*, 485–487.

139. Quotation from interview with Dörre in Funken, *Das Jahr*, 134–135; see also Hollitzer and Bohse, eds., *Heute vor 10 Jahren*, 485–487.

140. "Information zum Stimmungs- und Meinungsbild nach dem Einsatz am 09.10.1989 in Leipzig," BStU, BV Lpz Abt. VII 907, 184.

141. Interview with Wötzel in Kuhn, *Der Tag,* 134.

142. Hollitzer, "Der friedliche Verlauf," 278 n. 139; Hollitzer and Bohse, eds., *Heute vor 10 Jahren,* 466–467; and Doris Mundus, *Leipzig 1989: A Chronicle* (Leipzig: Lehmstedt Verlag, 2009), 24–25.

143. Interview with Hackenberg, Fall of the Wall Collection, KCLMA; and interview with Wötzel in Kuhn, *Der Tag,* 135. See also the analysis of these events in FRL 424. On the number of participants at the Oct. 9 march, still in dispute, note that, like Hackenberg, the GDR Ministry of the Interior also estimated that the crowd had been "ca. 100.000 Mann" in "Auszug aus dem Lagefilm der Führungsgruppe des MdI," Oct. 9, 1989, FRL 429. See also Opp, Voss, and Gern, *Die volkseigene Revolution,* 47; "Information über eine nicht-genehmigte Demonstration im Stadtzentrum von Leipzig am 9.10.1989," BStU, MfS, Neiber 617, 100–106, and BStU, "Oktober 1989: Offene Krise und Machtwechsel," available online at www.BStU.bund.de/DE/Wissen/DDRGeschichte/Revolutionskalender/Oktober-1989/oktober89_node.html.

144. Author's interview with Radomski.

145. Ibid. On the massive size of the march, see FRL 429.

146. Author's interviews with Radomski and Schefke.

147. Author's interview with Schwabe.

148. "Notizen des Referatsleiters des Referats XX/7 zur Referatsleitersitzung der Abteilung XX der BV Leipzig des MfS am 09.10.1989, 19.00 Uhr," doc. 243, FUF 458.

149. Interview with Hackenberg, Fall of the Wall Collection, KCLMA.

150. Maier, "Civil Resistance," 262, discusses what might have happened if violence had broken out.

151. Interview with Theo Kührt, "Angehöriger der Kampfgruppen," in Neues Forum, ed., *Jetzt oder nie,* 90–92.

152. Interview with Schröder, in Kuhn, *Der Tag,* 137–138.

153. Tetzner, *Leipziger Ring,* 18–19; and Reiner Tetzner, *Kerzen-Montage verändern die Welt: Warum die Waffen wirklich schwiegen* (Leipzig: Haus des Buches, 2009). See also the pictures of the demonstrators in Schneider, *Leipziger Demontagebuch,* 44–45, which show marchers filling the breadth of the wide ring road.

154. For more on the phenomenon of the revolution gaining power in the GDR, see Eckert, *SED-Diktatur,* 12, and Süß, *Staatssicherheit am Ende,* 313–314.

155. Author's interview with Schwabe.

156. The Ministry of the Interior estimated that 5,500 people used the train station to depart afterward; see "Auszug aus dem Lagefilm der Führungsgruppe des MdI," Oct. 9, 1989, FRL 429.

157. *Tagesthemen* broadcast, night of Oct. 9, 1989, ARD archive.

158. Report of BDVP Leipzig, Chef, Straßenburg, Oct. 10, 1989, 1:45 a.m.; see also Kuhn, *Der Tag*, 11.

159. For Stasi photos of the round corner, see BStU, BV Leipzig, Abt. RD 762, 114–117. I am grateful to Hans-Jürgen and Wilma Sievers for visiting it with me.

160. Interview with Straßenburg in Kuhn, *Der Tag*, 132–133.

161. Manfred Hummitzsch, "Montagseinsätze, handschriftliche Aufzeichnungen," BStU Außenstelle Leipzig, BVfS Leipzig, Leitung 00591, 48.

162. "Information über eine nicht-genehmigte Demonstration im Stadtzentrum von Leipzig am 9.10.1989," BStU, MfS, Neiber 617, 100–106, also available online.

163. Hummitzsch, "Montagseinsätze," 41; also reprinted in FRL 431.

164. "Gepragt von Besonnenheit," *Leipziger Volkszeitung*, Oct. 10, 1989, reprinted in FRL 431.

165. Honecker quoted in Krenz, *Herbst '89*, 96.

166. "Aktennotiz zur Einweisung am 14.10.1989, 08.00 Uhr, beim Chef des Hauptstabes des NVR," SS Anlage II, 698; and FRL 442; see also Hertle, *Fall der Mauer*, 130; Hollitzer and Bohse, eds., *Heute vor 10 Jahren*, 469; and Kuhn, *Der Tag*, 11.

167. "Über Maßnahmen zur Gewährleistung der Sicherheit und Ordnung in LEIPZIG," Befehl Nr. 9/89, Oct. 13, 1989, SS, Anlage VIII, 1655–1657.

168. "Auszug aus einer Rede von Innenminister Friedrich Dickel," Oct. 21, 1989, FRL 454. Dickel appears to have agreed with Hackenberg that the marchers numbered 100,000 (see section 4 of speech). For more information on 1953, see Ostermann, ed., *Uprising in East Germany 1953*.

169. Author's interviews with Radomski and Schefke; Führer, Ascher, and Holland-Moritz, *Und wir sind dabei*, 221; and remarks by Schefke in Hollitzer and Bohse, eds., *Heute vor 10 Jahren*, 478.

170. Author's interview with Radomski.

171. Author's interviews with Radomski and Schefke; and remarks by Schefke in Hollitzer and Bohse, eds., *Heute vor 10 Jahren*, 478.

172. Author's interviews with Radomski, Schefke, and Sievers.

173. Author's interview with Sievers.

174. Author's interviews with Radomski, Schefke, and Sievers; interview with both Sievers and his son Ulf Sievers in Hollitzer and Bohse, eds., *Heute vor 10 Jahren*, 432–434, 444. Note that there are differing versions of the story of the filming on Oct. 9 in circulation. For example, the Hollitzer and Bohse edited volume includes remarks to the effect that other people had filmed from the tower that night as well. Since the accounts of Cooper, Jahn, Radomski, Schefke, Schwarz, and Sievers in separate interviews were all consistent with each other, were consistent with the surviving video footage, and yielded a common recollection of the involvement of only those three men plus a church custodian, their version is included in the text above. The only minor disagreement in these six accounts is over how long the church custodial worker, who had the key necessary to open the locked door to the tower, spent with

Radomski and Schefke. For the alternative version, see the remarks of Thomas Ru-dolph, and Sievers's refutation of them, in Hollitzer and Bohse, eds., *Heute vor 10 Jahren,* 445–446. Sievers recollects that other people did come to his church to make photographs and film, but not on Oct. 9; author's interview with Sievers. Similarly, Mayer, *Der nicht aufgibt,* 107, suggests that a Leizpig activist named Katrin Walther made a prior agreement with Sievers to allow Radomski and Schefke to use the tower on Oct. 9, but none of the six participants in events interviewed by the author recalled such an agreement.

175. Author's interview with Schwarz.

176. Author's interviews with Cooper and Schefke; and Praschl, *Roland Jahn,* 171–173.

177. Author's interviews with Cooper and Schwarz.

178. Author's interviews with Radomski and Schefke.

179. Author's interviews with Jahn and Schwarz.

180. For more on Jahn's work with SFB, see Praschl, *Roland Jahn,* 162.

181. Author's interview with Jahn and Neubert; and Funken, *Das Jahr,* 31.

182. *Tagesschau* and *Tagesthemen,* Oct. 10, 1989, in ARD-NDR archive; and Funken, *Das Jahr,* 31.

183. Author's interviews with Jahn and Schefke.

184. Author's interview with Wonneberger; Funken, *Das Jahr,* 126; Kowalczuk and Sello, eds., *Für ein freies Land,* 211; and Mayer, *Der nicht aufgibt,* 122–144.

185. Hollitzer and Bohse, eds., *Heute vor 10 Jahren,* 467; and Kuhn, *Der Tag,* 10.

Chapter 4: The Revolution Advances, the Regime Plays for Time

1. Hanns Jürgen Küsters, "Entscheidung für die deutsche Einheit," DESE 61; see also the graphic in Richter, *Die friedliche Revolution,* book endpapers.

2. Author's interview with Cooper.

3. Schwabe, "Symbol der Befreiung," n. 11. On the Berlin-Dresden relationship, see Jesse, ed., *Friedliche Revolution*; on opposition movements generally, see Erhard Neubert, *Geschichte der Opposition in der DDR 1949–1989* (Bonn: BPB, 1997).

4. Author's interview with Birthler.

5. Author's interview with Sello; original German, "nicht nachlassen."

6. On Gorbachev's visit to East Berlin, see telegram, "Amembassy Moscow to Sec-state Washdc," Oct. 6, 1989, CWIHPPC; records from Gorbachev's visit in BArch, SAPMO, DY 30/J IV 2/2A/3239; "Stenografische Niederschrift des Treffens der Genossen des Politbüros des ZK der SED mit . . . Gorbatschow, am Sonnabend, den 7. Oktober 1989 in Berlin-Niederschönhausen," doc. 21, in Daniel Küchen-meister and Gerd-Rüdiger Stephan, eds., *Honecker Gorbatschow Vieraugengespräche* (Berlin: Dietz Verlag, 1993), 252–266; analysis of Gorbachev's visit in BDE, ZA 140.711E, PA-AA; and entry for Oct. 8, 1989, diary of Anatoly Chernyaev, avail-able on the National Security Archive website, www2.gwu.edu/~nsarchiv/NSAEBB /NSAEBB275/1989%20for%20posting.pdf. On violence near the Gethsemane

Church, see Momper, *Grenzfall,* 106. For the story of Klaus Laabs, the protestor who was run over and nearly killed by a police vehicle, see *taz DDR-Journal,* 41–42.

7. On the violent reaction of the security forces to the anniversary overall, see Süß, *Staatssicherheit am Ende,* 239–293.

8. Author's interview with Birthler.

9. Author's interview with Birthler. See one of the Stasi reports on Birthler in BStU, MfS, ZAIG 4599, 155–158, also available online.

10. Author's interview with Birthler; see the reports on her in BStU, MfS, HA IX 2638; and, on the BStU website, see "Gedächtnisprotokolle, Tage und Nächte nach dem 7. Oktober 1989, Berlin," www.BStU.bund.de/DE/Wissen/DDRGeschichte /Revolutionskalender/Oktober-1989/Bilder/Gedaechtnisprotokolle_pdf.pdf.

11. See photos of such events in the Gethsemane Church in Oct. 1989 in FRL 347; coverage of the Gethsemane Church on *Tagesthemen,* ARD, Oct. 7, 1989; and a Politburo assessment of events at the church in "Information über die aktuelle Lage in der DDR," Oct. 17, 1989, BArch, SAPMO, DY 30/IV 2/2.039/342, 88–98.

12. Author's interviews with Birthler and Schwabe; and Marianne Birthler, "Oppositionelle Gruppen in der DDR der 80er Jahre und ihre Rolle in der friedlichen Revolution," in Horst Möller and Aleksandr Tschubarjan, eds., *Mitteilungen der Gemeinsamen Kommission für die Erforschung der jüngeren Geschichte der deutsch-russischen Beziehungen* (Munich: Oldenbourg, 2008), 281.

13. Author's interview with Birthler.

14. For more on older Communists and their experiences, see Catherine Epstein, *The Last Revolutionaries: German Communists and Their Century* (Cambridge, MA: Harvard University Press, 2003), 262–263.

15. Süß, *Staatssicherheit am Ende,* 339.

16. "Weitere Hinweise auf Reaktionen der Bevölkerung," and cover note from Mielke to Krenz, Oct. 16, 1989, BStU, MfS, ZAIG 4259, 10–14, also available online.

17. On the potential for violence, see Detlef Pollack, "Die Friedlichkeit der Herbstakteure 1989," in Sabrow, ed., *1989,* 124.

18. See incident reports in BStU, MfS, ZAIG 14169.

19. Hans-Hermann Hertle and Gerd-Rüdiger Stephan, eds., *Das Ende der SED: Die letzten Tage des Zentralkomitees* (Berlin: Links, 1997), 52.

20. Interview with Günter Schabowski, Fall of the Wall Collection, KCLMA.

21. Vote recorded in "Protokoll Nr. 43," from Politburo meeting of Oct. 17, 1989, BArch, SAPMO, DY 30/J IV/2/2A/3247, 9. See also Schabowski interview, Fall of the Wall Collection, KCLMA; Mielke comments in "Gerhard Schürer, Persönliche Aufzeichnung über die Sitzung des Politbüros," Oct. 17, 1989, reprinted in Hertle, *Fall der Mauer,* 434; Funken, *Das Jahr,* 58–80, and Süß, *Staatssicherheit am Ende,* 339–341.

22. "Protokoll der Aktivtagung der Parteiorganisation im MfS am 18.10.1989," Oct. 20, 1989, BStU, MfS, SED-Kreisleitung 19, 2, also available online, reports on these events. Honecker's wife, the education minister, Margot Honecker, resigned as well; see "Protokoll Nr. 46," BArch, SAPMO, DY 30/J IV/2/2A/3251, 7. See also

remarks in the interview with Schabowski, Fall of the Wall Collection, KCLMA. Schabowski suggests that there was supposed to be a real vote at the central committee meeting on Honecker's successor, but Krenz maneuvered it so that he was the only person considered and then appointed.

23. "Information über Meinungen von Bürgern," Oct. 19, 1989, BStU, MfS, Berlin XV Nr. 49, reprinted in Jens Schöne, *Die friedliche Revolution* (Berlin: Berlin Story Verlag, 2008), 80.

24. "Einige Fragen und Probleme," Oct. 25, 1989. See also the letters received by Krenz's office in BArch, SAPMO, IV 2/2.039/323; Munro, "Britain, Berlin," 62; and Süß, *Staatssicherheit am Ende*, 348.

25. Mielke Referat, Oct. 21, 1989, BStU, MfS, ZAIG 4885, also available online.

26. "Einige Fragen und Probleme," Oct. 25, 1989; see also "Hinweise über Reaktionen progressive Kräfte," Oct. 8, 1989, BStU, MfS, ZAIG 5351, 55–62, also available online.

27. "Chiffriertes Fernschreiben der Bezirksleitung Leipzig an . . . Egon Krenz," n.d., from context Oct. 30, 1989, BStU, MfS, SdM 664, 1–3.

28. Telegram from BL Leipzig, Oct. 31, 1989, BArch, SAPMO, IV 2/2.039/317. See also the information delivered to Helmut Kohl about the Oct. 30 march in "Vorlage des Ministerialdirigenten Jung an Bundeskanzler Kohl, Bonn," Nov. 3, 1989, doc. 72, DESE 478–479.

29. See photos of the interior of the Leipzig Stasi headquarters in Bürgerkomitee Leipzig, ed., *Stasi intern* (Leipzig: Forum Verlag, 1991).

30. "Aufgabenstellungen," Oct. 31, 1989, BStU, MfS, BdL/Dok 005033, also available online.

31. "Reduzierung des Bestandes an dienstlichen Bestimmungen und Weisungen in den Kreisdienststellen/Objektdienststellen," Nov. 6, 1989, BStU, MfS, BdL/Dok. 005592, 1–6, also available online; see also BStU, MfS, HA I 16938, 129, n.d., but from context on or about Nov. 11, 1989.

32. "Thesen für Dienstkonferenz des Leiters der Abt. M des MfS Berlin," Nov. 9, 1989, BStU, ZA, Abt. M 1025, 59–63, also available online.

33. Letter from Mielke, Nov. 2, 1989, BStU, MfS, BdL/Dok. 004400, also available online.

34. "Vorlage für das Politbüro des ZK der SED," Oct. 30, 1989, BArch, SAPMO, DY 30/J IV 2/2A/3252, available online on BStU website. See also Martin Sabrow, "'1989' und die Rolle der Gewalt in Ostdeutschland," in Sabrow, ed., *1989*, 22–30.

35. See the online commentary to "Entwurf des Gesetzes," Nov. 6, 1989, www .bstu.bund.de/DE/Wissen/DDRGeschichte/Revolutionskalender/November-1989 /Dokumentenseiten/06-November_b/06_nov__b_text.html?nn=1930806.

36. "Erklärung von Egon Krenz vor der Volkskammer der DDR," Oct. 24, 1989, draft in BArch, SAPMO, J IV 2/2A/3249, 9–41.

37. For an analysis of the precarious economic state of the GDR in fall 1989, see Hertle, *Chronik*, 92–95; Jeffrey Kopstein, *The Politics of Economic Decline in East Germany 1945–1989* (Chapel Hill: University of North Carolina Press, 1997); and Günter Kusch et al., *Schlußbilanz—DDR: Fazit einer verfehlten Wirtschafts- und*

Sozialpolitik (Berlin: Duncker and Humblot, 1991). For a more optimistic view of the GDR's economic health, see Matthias Judt, *Der Bereich kommerzielle Koordinierung: Das DDR-Wirtschaftsimperium des Alexander Schalck-Golodkowski—Mythos und Realität* (Berlin: Links, 2013), 236–237.

38. See the "ungeschminktes Bild" of the dire economic situation in the GDR in "Analyse der ökonomischen Lage der DDR mit Schlußfolgerungen," Oct. 27, 1989, BStU, MfS, HA XVIII 3314, quotation at 5; see also BArch, SAPMO, DY 30/5195, available online on BStU website. The BStU annotator notes that the Politbüro considered, but then deleted, phrasing about working with Bonn to make the Wall "überflüssig" (unnecessary) by the end of the century. See also the interview with Schürer, and "Schreiben von Gerhard Schürer an Egon Krenz," Oct. 27, 1989, both in Hertle, *Fall der Mauer,* 313–321, 460–462.

39. "Schreiben von Alexander Schalck an Egon Krenz, 13.10.1989," reprinted in Hertle, *Fall der Mauer,* 429–430. On Schalck's role and his office more generally, see Frank Schumann and Heinz Wuschech, *Schalck-Golodkowski: Der Mann, der die DDR retten wollte* (Berlin: Edition Ost, 2012); Judt, *Der Bereich;* and Peter Przybylski, *Tatort Politbüro* (Berlin: Rowohlt, 1992).

40. Interview with Schabowski in Berliner Arbeitshefte.

41. "Konzeption: Zum Vorgehen gegenüber der BRD im Zusammenhang mit den vorgesehenen Regelungen im Reiseverkehr," Oct. 23, 1989, BArch, SAPMO, DY 30/IV 2/2.039/342, 113–114; see also BArch, SAPMO, DY 30/J IV 2/2A/3250, 62–63, which reads as follows: "Die BRD-Seite ist darauf hinzuweisen, daß aus der zu erwartenden weiteren Zunahme des Reiseverkehrs für die DDR erheblich Devisenaufwendungen entstehen werden. Gleichermaßen ergeben sich für die DDR aus ständigen Ausreisen enorme Nachteile und Verluste. Es ist in diesem Zusammenhang erforderlich, einen angemessenen Interessenausgleich herbeizuführen (z.B. in Form von Pauschalen für die Erstattung von Ausbildungskosten im Zusammenhang mit ständigen Ausreisen, für die Ausstattung mit Reisezahlungsmitteln sowie von Ausgleichszahlungen hinsichtlich der Beförderungskosten der Eisenbahn)."

42. "Schreiben von Alexander Schalck an Egon Krenz, 24.10.1989" in Hertle, *Fall der Mauer,* 438–443; the original quotation, at 440, is "faktisch unbegrenzten Reiseverkehrs zwischen beiden deutschen Staaten." See also Hertle, *Chronik,* 99–106, and Karl-Rudolf Korte, *Deutschlandpolitik in Helmut Kohls Kanzlerschaft: Regierungsstil und Entscheidungen 1982–1989* (Stuttgart: Deutsche Verlags-Anstalt, 1998), 458–464.

43. "Telefongespräch des Bundeskanzlers Kohl mit dem Staatsratsvorsitzenden Krenz," Oct. 26, 1989, doc. 68, DESE 468–469. In the West German original, Krenz used the word "Wende" to describe what he did *not* want to happen: "Er [Krenz] wolle keine Wende herbeiführen" (468). The East German transcript of the same conversation is in "Gespräch zwischen . . . Egon Krenz und . . . Helmut Kohl," Oct. 26, 1989, BArch, SAPMO, IV 2/2.039/328, and a note attached to the record of this conversation suggests that Mielke and others should start thinking about the practical implications of a new travel law; see "Maßnahmen," Oct. 26, 1989, in same file. Later, at a meeting on Nov. 1, Krenz would hint to Gorbachev about

allowing some travel abroad, although only with a passport, a visa, and sufficient personal funds. See the record of their conversation, Nov. 1, 1989, MG, 240–241; an abbreviated English-language translation of the Russian version of this conversation is available in GC, but it is shorter than the version published by Gorbachev himself; the East German version of this conversation is also available in BArch, SAPMO, J IV 2/2A/3255, and has been published in various locations. See also Süß, *Staatssicherheit am Ende*, 423.

44. Krenz seems to have already thought of some kind of new regulations at that point, but as he was not yet in charge, the idea made little progress at the time. See notes that, according to BArch archivist Sylvia Gräfe, were handwritten by Krenz, Sept. 17, 1989, BArch, SAPMO, IV 2/2.039/77, 54. See also Süss, "Der 9. November 1989," 228–229, 507 n. 7.

45. "2. Oktoberwoche," handwritten, BStU, MfS, Rechtsstelle 101, describes the meeting of the working group under the leadership of Wolfgang Herger. See also note from Krenz to Honecker, Oct. 12, 1989, in BArch, SAPMO, DY 30/IV 2/2.039/342, 77–80; "Zu beachtende Probleme bei der Realisierung der Grundsätze für ein Gesetz zu Reisen von Bürgern der DDR in das Ausland," Oct. 16, 1989, BStU, MfS, ZAIG 7438, 41–43; and Süß, *Staatssicherheit am Ende*, 419.

46. "Maßnahmen im Zusammenhang mit dem am 26.10.1989 geführten Telefongespräch," that is, considerations resulting from the telephone conversation between Krenz and Kohl, Oct. 26, 1989, BArch, SAPMO, DY 30/J IV 2/2A/3252, 62.

47. "Niederschrift über das Gespräch . . . Egon Krenz mit . . . Wolfgang Mischnick," Oct. 25, 1989, BArch, SAPMO, DY 30/IV 2/2.039/328; Momper, *Grenzfall*, 98–105; and BStU, MfS, SdM 664, 34.

48. Stasi documents from both of these meetings are available in "Information über eine Zusammenkunft der SPD-Politiker Walter Momper und Horst Ehmke mit oppositionellen Kräften der DDR am 29.10.1989 im Atelier von Bohley, Bärbel," Nov. 2, 1989, BStU, MfS HA XX/9, 1698, 87–90, and "Information A/043286/31/10/89/01," BStU, MfS Arbeitsbereich Neiber, 194, 72–73.

49. "Information über eine Zusammenkunft," 89; author's interview with Momper; and Momper, *Grenzfall*, 98–109. Quotations at 105 and from author's interview with Momper, respectively. See also *Vier Tage im November* (Hamburg: Gruner + Jahr, 1989), 10.

50. See the correspondence between Dickel and Krenz, Oct. 31, 1989, BArch, SAPMO, DY 30/IV 2/2.039/89.

51. Günter Schabowski, Frank Sieren, and Ludwig Koehne, *Das Politbüro Ende eines Mythos: Eine Befragung* (Hamburg: Reinbek, 1990), 113, discuss how, although East Germany had a state apparatus in name—a minister-president and full set of ministries—they were subordinate to the party organizations, with the Politburo at the top.

52. Author's interview with Lauter.

53. Gerhard Lauter, *Chefermittler: Der Oberste Fahnder der K in der DDR berichtet* (Berlin: Edition Ost, 2012), 48–87.

54. See the evidence about Lauter's service to the Stasi in Hertle, *Fall der Mauer*, 217.

55. Lauter, *Chefermittler*, 11–14.

56. Ibid., 25. On the purging of longtime Communists in the GDR, see Epstein, *Last Revolutionaries*, 2–3.

57. Author's interview with Lauter; and Lauter, *Chefermittler*, 148–152.

58. "Information über die Sitzung des Ministerrates," Nov. 2, 1989, BArch, SAPMO, DY 30/IV 2/2.039/214.

59. "Gespräch mit Gerhard Lauter," in Hertle, *Fall der Mauer*, 326; Lauter, *Chefermittler*, 152; and Florian Huber and Marc Brasse, producers, *Schabowskis Zettel*, video, Spiegel-TV, first broadcast Nov. 9, 2009.

60. "Vorlage für das Politbüro," Oct. 27, 1989, BStU, MfS, SdM 664, 43. See also BArch, SAPMO, DY 30/J IV 2/2/3250, 128; Hertle, *Berliner Mauer*, 189; and Süß, *Staatssicherheit am Ende*, 425.

61. See the television coverage of the refilling of the grounds of the West German embassy in Prague on, among other places, the television news shows *Tagesschau* and *Tagesthemen*, ARD-NDR archive, Nov. 3, 1989.

62. Küsters, "Entscheidung," 42.

63. "Fernschreiben des Staatssekretärs Bertele an den Chef des Bundeskanzleramtes Berlin (Ost)," Nov. 3, 1989, doc. 71, DESE 476–478.

64. Kowalczuk, *Endspiel*, 420; see also "Hinweise auf im Zusammenhang mit der aktuellen Lage in der DDR stehende Aktivitäten in den Bereichen Kunst/Kultur," Oct. 9, 1989, in BStU, MfS, ZAIG 5376, 2–9, also available online.

65. See telegram from Krenz to all leading party officials saying that contacts with the opposition were only to be carried out "so that no official recognition" would be implied: Fernschreiben, BArch, SAPMO, Oct. 31, 1989, DY 30/IV 2/2.039/314. See also "Information 451/89," BStU, ZA, ZAIG 3756, 127–135, and "Hinweise zur möglichen Zulassung des 'Neuen Forum,'" BStU, MfS, ZAIG 7388, 20–22, both available online. On the significance of the New Forum, see Süß, *Staatssicherheit am Ende*, 316.

66. Author's interview with Meckel; FRL 318; see also Markus Meckel, *Selbstbewußt in die deutsche Einheit* (Berlin: Berlin Verlag, 2001).

67. See the concerns expressed about the Nov. 4 demonstration in letter from Kurt Hager to Egon Krenz, Oct. 20, 1989, BArch, SAPMO, DY 30/26269; on the Nov. 4 event itself, see Süß, *Staatssicherheit am Ende*, 385–413.

68. Krenz's comments were also published word for word in all major East German newspapers the next day. See, for example, "Fernseh- und Rundfunkansprache von Egon Krenz an die Bürger der DDR," *Neues Deutschland*, Nov. 4–5, 1989; also printed in *Der Morgen*, Nov. 4–5, 1989, 1, and *Junge Welt*, Nov. 4–5, 1989. On the short notice, see "Amembassy Berlin to Secstate Washdc," Nov. 6, 1989, in CWIHPPC, and Bahrmann and Links, *Chronik*, 76.

69. Egon Krenz, "Befehl 11/89," Nov. 3, 1989, BStU, MfS, ZAIG 14392, 19; and author's interview with Krenz. The original German phrasing says that the

"Anwendung körperlicher Gewalt" is to be used to prevent demonstrators from going "in das Grenzgebiet." However: "Die Anwendung der Schußwaffe im Zusammenhang mit möglichen Demonstrationen ist grundsätzlich verboten."

70. Author's interview with Birthler; see also, at RHG, in Bestand Marianne Birthler (MBi), the various documents related to the Nov. 4 demonstration.

71. "Entwurf: Gesetz über Reisen von Bürgern der Deutschen Demokratischen Republik in das Ausland-Reisegesetz vom . . . ," and "Entwurf: Durchführungsverordnung," *Neues Deutschland*, Nov. 6, 1989, 1–3. Similarly, see "Entwurf: Gesetz über Reisen von Bürgern der Deutschen Demokratischen Republik in das Ausland—Reisegesetz vom . . . ," and "Entwurf: Durchführungsverordnung," *Berliner Zeitung*, Nov. 6, 1989, 2. The symbol ". . ." was to be replaced later with a date for the law to go into effect, but none was given at the time. The notes below refer to the former document as the "Entwurf" and the latter as the "Entwurf, Durchführungsverordnung."

72. For an example of the press coverage, see "Ausreise-Anträge werden schnell entschieden," *Neues Deutschland*, Nov. 6, 1989, 2; see also Süß, *Staatssicherheit am Ende*, 420–421.

73. The draft would, in theory, once it became law, replace both of the legal documents governing travel at the time: (1) "Verordnung vom 30.11.88," *Gesetzblatt der Deutschen Demokratischen Republik*, Teil I, Nr. 25 (Berlin: Dec. 13, 1988), 271–274 (hereafter "Verordnung"); and (2) "Erste Durchführungsbestimmung vom 14.03.89," *Gesetzblatt der Deutschen Demokratischen Republik*, Teil I, Nr. 8 (Berlin: Mar. 28, 1989), 119–120.

74. These provisions are given in the "Entwurf, Durchführungsverordnung," Paragraph 2, Absatz 1, and in Paragraph 5, Absatz 1.

75. "Entwurf," Paragraph 6, Absatz 1.

76. "Entwurf," Paragraph 5.

77. "Reisemittel, Subvention, Besteuerung der Handwerker," *Neues Deutschland*, Nov. 8, 1989, 3.

78. "Information über den Verlauf und die Ergebnisse der öffentlichen Diskussion zum Entwurf des am 06. November 1989 veröffentlichten Gesetzes über Reisen," BStU, MfS, Rechtsstelle 101, 158–160; see also "Reisegesetzentwurf steht zur Diskussion," *Berliner Zeitung*, Nov. 6, 1989.

79. Author's interview with Momper; and Momper, *Grenzfall*, 122–124.

80. Discussion summarized in Hertle, *Chronik*, 106–107. Original: "objektgebunden."

81. Süß, "Der 9. November," 230.

82. "Chronik," *Deutschland Archiv* 22 (Dec. 1989): 1475; Funken, *Das Jahr*, 136–137; Klaus Hartung, "Die Wut in Leipzig nimmt zu," *tageszeitung*, Nov. 8, 1989, reprinted in *DDR-Journal*, 88–89; and Sieren and Koehne, *Politbüro*, 113. See also Egon Krenz, *Wenn Mauern fallen* (Wien: Neff, 1990), 227.

83. "Draft," Nov. 6, 1989, released by my request, 2008-0655MR, from the GHWBPL. Blackwill continued: "Short of that extreme contingency, we should aim

to avert a brutal internal crackdown in the GDR and minimize the risks of spillover into Poland and Hungary."

84. See "Besprechung der beamteten Staatssekretäre, Bonn," Nov. 6, 1989, docs. 74 and 74A, DESE 482–489, esp. 482.

85. "Schreiben, Alexander Schalck an Egon Krenz," Nov. 7, 1989, doc. 12, in Hertle, *Fall der Mauer,* 486–487.

86. "Zwischen Bundeskanzler Kohl, Bundesminister Schäuble, und Bundesminister Seiters am Abend des 6. November 1989 im Kanzlerbungalow abgestimmte Textpassage für den Bericht des Bundeskanzlers zur Lage der Nation im geteilten Deutschland am 8. November 1989 vor dem Deutschen Bundestag," reproduced as a photograph, including handwritten notes, in DESE 491; and "Bericht der Bundesregierung zur Lage der Nation, Erklärung von Bundeskanzler Kohl am 8. November 1989 vor dem Deutschen Bundestag," in Auswärtiges Amt, ed., *Aussenpolitik der Bundesrepublik Deutschland: Dokumente von 1949 bis 1994* (Cologne: Verlag Wissenschaft und Politik, 1995), 609.

87. There were some minor differences between the two older rules and the new draft. For the first time, the new version defined travel to foreign countries as a "right," although precisely what that meant remained unclear. There was also a new "right" added: the "right" to travel back into the GDR at any time. Earlier travelers had not been able to take this for granted; for example, the SED withdrew the citizenship of the prominent singer and dissident Wolf Biermann when he was on a trip in the Federal Republic in 1976 and denied him reentry. Another novelty was the declaration that refusals would be "exceptions" (in "Entwurf," Paragraph 6, Absatz 2, "Die Versagung der Genehmigungen für Reisen in das Ausland trägt Ausnahmecharakter"). Furthermore, if an application was refused, the draft would require the appropriate office not only to inform the applicant but also to explain why. The continuities outweighed the changes, however.

88. The East German ambassador in Prague gave Jakeš's message to the GDR's foreign minister, Oskar Fischer, who in turn passed it to Krenz; see letter from Fischer to Krenz, Nov. 3, 1989, BArch, SAPMO, DY 30/IV 2/2.039/342, 155–156. See also Süß, *Staatssicherheit am Ende,* 425–426.

89. On the phone call to Krenz, see remarks by Lauter, cited in Daniel Küchenmeister, Detlef Nakath, and Gerd-Rüdiger Stephan, eds., " . . . *sofort, unverzüglich": Der Fall der Mauer am 9. November 1989* (Potsdam: Rosa-Luxemburg-Stiftung, 2000) 33–34.

90. "Protokoll Nr. 48 der Sitzung des Politbüros," Nov. 3, 1989, BArch, SAPMO, DY 30/J IV 2/2A/3254, 6; Ilse Spittmann, "Eine Übergangsgesellschaft," *Deutschland Archiv* 22 (Nov. 1989): 1204; www.chronik-der-mauer.de/index.php/de/Chronical /Detail/day/5/month/November/year/1989; and Süß, *Staatssicherheit am Ende*, 425–427. See also "Ein wahrer Treppenwitz der Weltgeschichte," *Die Presse*, Nov. 2, 2013; the author is grateful to Roberto Welzel for a copy of this article.

91. See the file from the Nov. 7 Politburo meeting in BArch, SAPMO, DY 30/ J IV/2/2A/3255, 13–18; and Hertle, *Chronik,* 111–114.

92. A report from Mielke to Krenz indicated that the draft had intensified, not solved, the discontent in the GDR; see "3. Lagebericht," Nov. 7, 1989, BStU, MfS, ZAIG 8266, 9–11, available online. See also Krenz, *Wenn Mauern fallen*, 164, 176–182, and Hans-Hermann Hertle, "'Das reale Bild war eben katastrophal!'" *Deutschland Archiv* 10 (Oct. 1992): 1037.

93. "Document No. 4, Minutes No. 49 of the Meeting of the SED Politburo, 7 November 1989," in *Cold War International History Project Bulletin* 12–13 (Fall/Winter 2001): 153–154.

94. Kotschemassow, *Meine letzte Mission,* 187. As Vladimir Grinin, at the time a junior staffer in the Soviet embassy, recalled in an interview with the author, SED leaders were indeed frequent visitors.

95. Kotschemassow, *Meine letzte Mission,* 17–27.

96. I am grateful to Tim Colton and Serhii Plokhy for information about Kochemasov. See also "Aleksandr Shelepin, 76, Dies," *New York Times,* Oct. 25, 1994; Anna M. Cienciala, Natalia S. Lebedeva, and Wojciech Materski, *Katyn: A Crime Without Punishment* (New Haven, CT: Yale University Press, 2007), 331–333; Igor F. Maksimytchew, "Der Zusammenbruch der DDR," in Horst Möller and Aleksandr Tschubarjan, eds., *Mitteilungen der Gemeinsamen Kommission für die Erforschung der jüngeren Geschichte der deutsch-russischen Beziehungen* (Munich: Oldenbourg, 2008), 51; and Matthew J. Ouimet, *The Rise and Fall of the Brezhnev Doctrine in Soviet Foreign Policy* (Chapel Hill: University of North Carolina Press, 2003), 126.

97. Author's interviews with Burton and Munro. For more on Kochemasov, see Pond, *Beyond the Wall,* 125–127.

98. Author's interviews with Burton, Greenwald, Maximychev, and Munro.

99. "Vermerk über ein Gespräch zwischen Genossen Oskar Fischer und dem sowjetischen Botschafter Genossen W.I. Kotschemassow am 7.11.1989, 11.45 Uhr," 10–11, former DDR Staatsarchiv, Ministerrat, Stoph, DC20-4933; see also Süß, *Staatssicherheit am Ende,* 427–428.

100. "Vermerk über ein Gespräch zwischen Genossen Oskar Fischer und dem sowjetischen Botschafter Genossen W.I. Kotschemassow am 7.11.1989, 11.45 Uhr," Staatsarchiv, Ministerrat, Stoph, DC20-4933; author's interview with Maximychev; and interview with Maximychev in Hans-Hermann Hertle and Kathrin Elsner, eds., *Der Tag, an dem die Mauer fiel: Die wichtigsten Zeitzeugen berichten vom 9. November 1989* (Berlin: Nicolaische, 2009), 20–21; the word "opinion" is at 20; see also Küchenmeister, Nakath, and Stephan, eds., " . . . *sofort, unverzüglich,* " 35–36; and Süß, *Staatssicherheit am Ende,* 427–428.

101. Author's interview with Maximychev; and remarks by Maximychev in Küchenmeister, Nakath, and Stephan, eds., " . . . *sofort, unverzüglich,* " 35.

102. Interview with Maximychev in Hertle and Elsner, eds., *Der Tag,* 20–21, 24–25; Maximychev summary of Shevardnadze quotation at 20.

103. The East German official in Bonn was apparently a "Comrade Glienke." See "Brief vom Oskar Fischer an Egon Krenz," Nov. 8, 1989, Staatsarchiv, Ministerrat, Stoph, DC20–4933; see also "Eine friedliche Revolution," *Spiegel* 46 (Nov. 13, 1989): 18–28.

104. Hertle and Stephan, eds., *Das Ende der SED*, 66.

105. "Referat von Egon Krenz," *Neues Deutschland*, Nov. 9, 1989, 3; Gesamtdeutsches Institut, ed., *Analysen, Dokumentationen und Chronik* (Bonn: 1990), 85; Hertle, *Chronik*, 114–116; and Hertle and Stephan, eds., *Das Ende der SED*, 66–70.

Chapter 5: Failure to Communicate on November 9, 1989

1. Interview with Herger in Hertle and Elsner, eds., *Der Tag*, 22; on Herger's significance to Krenz, see Süß, "Der friedliche Ausgang," 193.

2. Süß, *Staatssicherheit am Ende*, 424–426, cites the relevant documentary evidence, but this is one of the few points on which I disagree with his interpretation. He argues that emigration out of Czechoslovakia in early November represented the actual, unlimited "opening of the Wall," so to speak, since it was, in his view, a form of unlimited travel freedom. It was clear, however, that the Czechs would be putting a stop to this process if the East Germans did not do so themselves, so it was not going to remain unlimited.

3. According to Lauter, as quoted in Küchenmeister, Nakath, and Stephan, eds., ". . . *sofort, unverzüglich*," 46; and author's interview with Lauter; see also Stent, *Russia and Germany*, 93–97.

4. Author's interview with Lauter; Huber, *Schabowskis Irrtum*, 27, 50–55; Küchenmeister, Nakath, and Stephan, eds., ". . . *sofort, unverzüglich*," 46; and Hertle, *Chronik*, 119.

5. Author's interview with Lauter. See also Roger Engelmann and Clemens Vollnhals, eds., *Justiz im Dienste der Parteiherrschaft: Rechtspraxis und Staatssicherheit in der DDR* (Berlin: Links, 1999), 334–339.

6. According to Hertle, *Fall der Mauer*, 217 n. 244; and Süß, *Staatssicherheit am Ende*, 435–437, it appears that Hubrich had been an IM from 1953 to 1984 under the cover name "Roter Matrose"; Lauter, still active in 1989, had been an IM since 1975 in part under the cover name "Richard."

7. Author's interview with Lauter; and Huber, *Schabowskis Irrtum*, 50–51.

8. Author's interview with Lauter.

9. Hertle, *Chronik*, 119–120.

10. BStU, MfS, Sekr. Neiber 553; interview with Lauter in Hertle, *Fall der Mauer*, 328; and Süß, *Staatssicherheit am Ende*, 436–437 nn. 86–93.

11. Author's interview with Lauter.

12. BStU, MfS, Sekr. Neiber 553, 17; and the reprint of the final document in Hertle and Elsner, eds., *Der Tag*, 34–35.

13. BStU, MfS, Sekr. Neiber 553, 27–29; and Süß, *Staatssicherheit am Ende*, 436 nn. 86–90.

14. BStU, MfS, Sekr. Neiber 553, 17–18; author's interview with Lauter; and Süß, *Staatssicherheit am Ende*, 436–438, emphasis added by the author.

15. BStU, MfS, Sekr. Neiber 553, 17–18, emphasis added by the author.

16. Perhaps they added West Berlin as part of the general trend of exceeding orders, or perhaps the fact that the group of four had provided an out for themselves—by indicating that their text was temporary—made them feel better able to add divided Berlin. It is also at least possible that the internal Politburo note calling for more border-crossing options to West Berlin had somehow been communicated to them as part of their tasking, but this is purely speculative; see "Maßnahmen im Zusammenhang," 62. See also Hertle and Elsner, eds., *Der Tag,* 34–35. See also Walter Süß, "Weltgeschichte in voller Absicht oder aus Versehen?" *Das Parlament,* Nov. 9–16, 1990, 9.

17. Author's interviews with Lauter and Maximychev; and Lauter, *Chefermittler,* 155–156; and interview with Lauter in Hertle, *Der Fall,* 328, where he says that he asked an unspecified superior whether his task included West Berlin and was told "yes, yes, also West Berlin."

18. Interview with Lauter, published in Hertle and Elsner, eds., *Der Tag,* 31; and Süß, *Staatssicherheit am Ende,* 440–441.

19. Author's interview with Lauter; and Süß, *Staatssicherheit am Ende,* 437–439.

20. Hertle, *Chronik,* 122–123.

21. Interview with Gerhard Niebling in Hertle and Elsner, eds., *Der Tag,* 30–31.

22. Lauter, *Chefermittler,* 157–158.

23. Author's interview with Lauter; and Lauter, *Chefermittler,* 158–159.

24. Interview with Maximychev, published in Hertle and Elsner, eds., *Der Tag,* 24–25.

25. Author's interview with Maximychev.

26. Notes from the Nov. 9 Politburo meeting, Gorbachev Foundation, Moscow; see also Svetlana Savranskaya, Thomas Blanton, and Vladislav Zubok, eds., *Masterpieces of History: The Peaceful End of the Cold War in Europe, 1989* (Budapest: Central European University Press, 2010), 577–579, and Zubok, *A Failed Empire,* 326–327. Zubok points out that the lack of systematic consideration of German issues continued even after the opening of the Wall.

27. Author's interview with Maximychev; and interview with Maximychev, published in Hertle and Elsner, eds., *Der Tag,* 25.

28. Author's interview with Maximychev; interview with Maximychev in Hertle and Elsner, eds., *Der Tag,* 24–25; and comments by Maximychev in Küchenmeister, Nakath, and Stephan, eds., ". . . *sofort, unverzüglich,"* 40.

29. Kotschemassow, *Meine letzte Mission,* 187.

30. On the composition of the central committee, or ZK as it was known in its German initials, see Hertle and Stephan, eds., *Das Ende der SED,* 22–26.

31. Süß, *Staatssicherheit am Ende,* 439.

32. Kowalczuk, *Endspiel,* 455.

33. Hertle, *Chronik,* 123–127, estimates that about half of the 17 Politburo members were present, and also points out that Krenz and the Politburo members were not the only ones to receive the group of four's text that afternoon. For the sake of appearances, the East German council of ministers—a state entity, as opposed to a

party entity—was charged with issuing the text as their "own" resolution. The ministers' offices received the group of four's text via courier under what was known as the "circulation procedure," according to which ministers would have until 6:00 p.m. that same day to register objections, otherwise the text would go into force. The entire procedure would normally have been just a formality, as it was de facto the Politburo and ultimately Krenz who really held power, but in the chaotic days of Nov. 1989, this represented a chance for someone to raise questions on the afternoon of Nov. 9. Since twenty-nine of the forty-four ministers included in the "circulation procedure" were attending the central committee meeting, however, they would only get back to their offices and see the text before the deadline if the meeting ended on time, which it showed no signs of doing. They did not know that a text to which they had to reply by 6:00 p.m. had just landed on their desks back in their offices while they were sitting unawares in a meeting, and that by failing to respond, they were allowing a radical change to happen. It would seem incumbent upon their staff members to alert them to this problem, but such alerts do not appear to have gone out. See also BStU, MfS, Rechtstelle 101, Nov. 9, 1989; BStU, MfS, ZA, Mittig 30, available online; www.bstu.bund.de/DE/Wissen/DDRGeschichte/Revolutionskalender/November-1989/Dokumentenseiten/09-November_a/09_nov_a_text.html?gtp=1939026_list%253D2.

34. A transcript of the central committee meeting on Nov. 9 is reprinted in Hertle and Stephan, eds., *Das Ende der SED*, 242–379; see also the excerpt "Die Behandlung der Reiseregelung auf der 10. Tagung des ZK, 9.11.1989, 15.47–15.55 Uhr [3:47–3:55 p.m.] (Tonbandabschrift)," doc. 16, in Hertle, *Fall der Mauer*, 492. For Krenz's own summary of this event, see Krenz, *Wenn Mauern fallen*, 179–181.

35. Krenz, *Wenn Mauern fallen*, 181. See also the description of the central committee meeting in Cordt Schnibben, "'Genosse, schlagen die uns tot?'" *Spiegel* 18 (1990).

36. In fact, Meyer would end up looking on in a state of shock as Schabowski announced it instead; see interview with Meyer in Hertle and Elsner, eds., *Der Tag*, 51–52.

37. Since central committee sessions were routinely recorded, it is possible to hear an audio version of this discussion; audio clip for Nov. 9, 1989, 3:47 to 3:55 p.m., in Hans-Hermann Hertle, ed., *Der Sound des Untergangs: Tonmitschnitte aus den letzten Sitzungen des SED-Zentralkomitees Oktober bis Dezember 1989* (Berlin: Links, 2013).

38. For more on this sequence of events, see M. E. Sarotte, "Elite Intransigence and the End of the Berlin Wall," *German Politics* 2 (Aug. 1993): 270–287.

39. For a description of the effects of the emigration on the economy, see Christoph Links and Hannes Bahrmann, *Wir sind das Volk* (Berlin: Links, 1990), 89; and "A Society Deep in Crisis," *Newsweek*, Nov. 20, 1989.

40. For more discussion of how the central committee could have missed the full import of what they were doing, see Süß, *Staatssicherheit*, 438–439.

41. In theory, members of the council of ministers had until 6:00 p.m. to approve or disapprove the text, see n. 33 above, but the party and Stasi offices involved did not bother to wait for that unimportant deadline. Notice went out to the district office of

the Stasi in Karl-Marx-Stadt, for example, by 5:23 p.m. that afternoon, in the form of a telegram from Egon Krenz; see CFS-Nr. 190, Nov. 9, 1989, 17.23 Uhr, in BStU, MfS, BV KMS BdL 503883. Similar notice went out in a telegram over Neiber's name at 8:25 p.m.; see CFS-Nr. 247, Nov. 9, 1989, 20:25 Uhr, in the same file. The time stamp on the latter document answers a question posed by Süß about the timing of its sending; see Süß, *Staatssicherheit am Ende,* 443 n. 120. For relevant party communications, see BArch, SAPMO, DY 30/IV 2/2.039/314.

42. Hertle, *Chronik,* 135–137.

43. Interview with Meyer in Hertle and Elsner, eds., *Der Tag,* 51.

44. Peter Brinkmann has attempted to research Schabowski's whereabouts during his absence from the meeting. As a journalist himself, Brinkmann has tried to find the reporters with whom Schabowski notionally spent the day, but without success. Author's interview with Brinkmann.

45. Among other jobs, he had once served as the editor of the leading party newspaper, *Neues Deutschland.* Information about Schabowski's background from Huber, *Schabowskis Irrtum,* 19–21.

46. Hertle, *Chronik,* 134; interview with Schabowski in Hertle, Pirker, and Weinert, "Der Honecker muß weg!," 39; and Krenz, *Wenn Mauern fallen,* 182.

47. Cordt Schnibben, "'Diesmal sterbe ich, Schwester,'" *Spiegel* 41 (1990); and Schabowski, Sieren, and Koehne, *Das Politbüro,* 136.

48. Interview with Schabowski in Hertle and Elsner, eds., *Der Tag,* 38–39.

49. In his own research into this topic, Peter Brinkmann interviewed Gerhard Beil, who rode over with Schabowski, and Beil said he had no recollection of Schabowski looking at the text while in the car. Author's interview with Brinkmann.

50. Author's interview with Brinkmann; and Peter Brinkmann, *Schlagzeilenjagd* (Bergisch Gladbach: Bastei Lübbe, 1993).

51. Author's interviews with Brokaw, Kusnetz, Lamprecht, and Wheatley.

52. Author's interviews with Brokaw, Gelefsky, Gould, Kusnetz, Neubert, and Walling. For context on the history of US news broadcasters, see Herbert J. Gans, *Deciding What's News: A Study of* CBS Evening News, NBC Nightly News, Newsweek, *and* Time (Evanston, IL: Northwestern University Press, 2004).

53. Author's interviews with Brokaw and Neubert; and Tom Brokaw, "Freedom Danced Before My Eyes," *New York Times,* Nov. 19, 1989.

54. The author is grateful to Peter Brinkmann for sharing, from his personal archive, a complete video recording of the entire press conference (hereafter "Nov. 9 video, Brinkmann Archive"). A typed German-language transcript of approximately the final eight minutes of the press conference, "Internationale Pressekonferenz von Günter Schabowski (in Begleitung der SED-ZK-Mitglieder Helga Labs, Gerhard Beil und Manfred Banaschak), 9. November 1989 (Ton-Abschrift)," is available under the heading "18.00," meaning 6:00 p.m., at www.chronik-der-mauer.de/index.php/de/Start/Index/id/618085. At the same location as this transcript, see also "Hans-Hermann Hertle, 9. November 1989, 18.00 Uhr: Schabowskis Auftritt." Other transcripts and summaries of the press conference are available as well: see, for example,

Albrecht Hinze, "Versehentliche Zündung," *Süddeutsche Zeitung*, Nov. 9, 1990, and Schnibben, "'Diesmal sterbe ich, Schwester.'" See also Schabowski, Sieren, and Koehne, *Das Politbüro*, 136.

55. Author's interviews with Brokaw and Walling; and Brokaw, "Freedom."

56. Nov. 9 video, Brinkmann Archive.

57. Nov. 9 video, Brinkmann Archive; author's interview with Brinkmann; Brinkmann, *Schlagzeilenjagd*; Ewald König, *Menschen Mauer Mythen: Deutsch-deutsche Notizen eines wiener Korrespondenten* (Halle: Mitteldeutscher Verlag, 2014), 184; and Marcus Walker, "Did Brinkmannship Fell Berlin's Wall?" *Wall Street Journal*, Oct. 21, 2009. See also Hertle, *Chronik*, 140–147.

58. The wait could range from hardly anything at all to hours, depending on the whim of the overseer and the Stasi; author's interview with Brinkmann.

59. Author's interviews with Brinkmann, Brokaw, and Neubert.

60. Nov. 9 video, Brinkmann Archive; author's interview with Johnson; and Daniel Johnson, "Seven Minutes That Shook the World," *Standpoint*, Nov. 2009.

61. Nov. 9 video, Brinkmann Archive; see also the summary of these events in Sarotte, *1989*.

62. Author's interview with Momper; and Momper, *Grenzfall*, 129–139.

63. Author's interview with Momper; and Momper, *Grenzfall*, 135–136.

64. Author's interview with Momper; and Momper, *Grenzfall*, 135–140.

65. Author's interview with Maximychev; and comments by Maximychev in Küchenmeister, Nakath, and Stephan, eds., *". . . sofort, unverzüglich,"* 40.

66. Remarks by Maximychev in Huber and Brasse, *Schabowskis Zettel*, video.

67. Interview with Sir Robert Corbett, published in Hertle and Elsner, eds., *Der Tag*, 81.

68. Jaruzelski conveyed Thatcher's words to Krenz; see page 8 of the summary of a conversation between Jaruzelski and Krenz in "An alle Mitglieder und Kandidaten des Politburos des ZK der SED," Nov. 5, 1989, J IV 2/2A/3255, SAPMO.

69. Note from J. Stapleton Roy to James A. Baker, Nov. 9, 1989, Folder 11, Box 108, 8c monthly files, series 8, BP.

70. Bush's schedule for Nov. 9, 1989, is available in Marlin Fitzwater's Press Guidance Files, GHWBPL, organized by date.

71. "Statement to the Press 11/9/89," in Presidential Daily Files, organized by date, GHWBPL.

72. See the press reports in Folder 11, Box 108, 8c monthly files, Series 8, BP; and Tim Russert, NBC News, to the White House, Nov. 9, 1989, stamped "The President has seen," in Presidential Daily Files, organized by date, GHWBPL.

73. Author's interviews with Teltschik and Wheatley.

74. The full visit schedule is available in BArchK, B 136-Anhang, Grüner Ordner 12.

75. This help was scheduled to include 3 billion DM in credit, forgiveness on previous loans, promotion of Polish exports, and advice from experts on various projects, among other things. See letter from Kohl to Mitterrand, Nov. 6, 1989, BArchK, B136-37240.

76. BArchK, B 136-Anhang, Grüner Ordner 12.

77. "Gespräch des Bundeskanzlers Kohl mit dem Vorsitzenden der Gewerkschaft 'Solidarität,' Walesa, Warschau," Nov. 9, 1989, doc. 76, DESE 492–496; and author's interview with Teltschik.

78. Author's interview with Bitterlich.

79. Interview with Eduard Ackermann in Hertle and Elsner, eds., *Der Tag*, 90; see also Andreas Rödder, *Deutschland einig Vaterland* (Munich: Beck, 2009), 133–134.

80. B136-37240, BArchK, contains part of the text of the speeches given at the state dinner in Warsaw on Nov. 9, 1989.

81. Author's interviews with Bitterlich and Teltschik; Eduard Ackermann, *Mit feinem Gehör: Vierzig Jahre in der bonner Politik* (Bergisch Gladbach: Lübbe Verlag, 1994), 310; and Küsters, "Entscheidung," 53–55.

82. Author's interview with Teltschik; and Küsters, "Entscheidung," 53–55.

83. Author's interviews with Bitterlich and Teltschik; Ackermann, *Mit feinem Gehör*, 310; Kohl, Diekmann, and Reuth, *Ich wollte*, 126–127; and Horst Teltschik, *329 Tage: Innenansichten der Einigung* (Berlin: Siedler, 1991), 14–16.

84. Interviews with Albrecht Rau and other participants in this event published in Hertle and Elsner, eds., *Der Tag*, 77–79.

Chapter 6: The Revolution, Televised

1. Author's interviews with Brinkmann, Brokaw, Kusnetz, and Neubert; interview with Brokaw in documentary film produced by Hans-Hermann Hertle and Gunther Scholz, *When the Wall Came Tumbling Down—50 Hours That Changed the World*, 1999; and Ahonen, *Death*, 240.

2. Wire reports, press releases, and broadcast transcripts are reprinted in Hertle and Elsner, eds., *Der Tag*, 54–57, and quoted in Hertle, *Chronik*, 148–151. The two Hertle books have different times for the first Reuters wire report (7:02 p.m. vs. 7:03 p.m.), but an image in the documentary of Hertle and Scholz, *When the Wall*, shows a copy of that report with the time stamp of 7:02 p.m.

3. *Tagesschau*, Nov. 9, 1989, 20:00 Uhr, ARD-NDR video archive.

4. BStU, MfS, HA III 9201. German laws do not allow the release of the names of individuals spied upon without their permission.

5. Audio and video feed from minutes after press conference, Nov. 9 video, Brinkmann Archive.

6. Author's interview with Kusnetz and Neubert.

7. Author's interviews with Brokaw, Kusnetz, and Neubert; video clip from the Brokaw-Schabowski interview on Nov. 9, 1989, available at www.nbcnews.com /id/33590933/#.UmR15lGRP0c; and Hertle, *Chronik*, 146–147.

8. Huber, *Schabowskis Irrtum*, 40, 126–127; and Günter Schabowski, "Wie ich die Mauer öffnete," *Die Zeit*, Mar. 19, 2009.

9. Author's interviews with Brokaw, Kusnetz, and Neubert. Brown, *Rise and Fall*, 537, singles out Schabowski's answers to Brokaw as the ones that succeeded in giving the public impression that East Germans were "entirely free."

10. Author's interviews with Brokaw, Gelefsky, Gould, and Kusnetz. Funken, *Das Jahr*, 199, mistakenly says that Brokaw started broadcasting from the Brandenburg Gate at 7:00 p.m. German time.

11. Author's interviews with Gelefsky and Lamprecht.

12. Author's interviews with Brokaw, Gelefsky, and Gould.

13. Author's interviews with Brokaw, Kusnetz, and Neubert.

14. "Vorkommnisse am 9./10. Nov. 1989 im Grenzabschnitt Brandenburger Tor," Nov. 10, 1989, BStU, MfS, Sekr. Neiber 553, 45.

15. Author's interviews with Kusnetz and Wheatley.

16. A Stasi interview with practical details and statistics from Bornholmer is available in "Auskunftsdokument GÜST Bornholmer Straße, Stand: 01.10.1988," BStU, HA I 3510, 1–22; sketches and photos are in BStU, HA I 2699, 29–34. For numerous photos of Bornholmer on the night of Nov. 9, see Kai Diekmann and Ralf Georg Reuth, eds., *Die längste Nacht, der grösste Tag: Deutschland am 9. November 1989* (Munich: Piper, 2009); for information about border fortifications more generally, see Patrick Major, *Behind the Berlin Wall: East Germany and the Frontiers of Power* (New York: Oxford University Press, 2010).

17. Gerhard Haase-Hindenberg, *Der Mann, der die Mauer öffnete: Warum Oberstleutnant Harald Jäger den Befehl verweigerte und damit Weltgeschichte schrieb* (Munich: Heyne, 2007), 16.

18. Author's interviews with Radomski, Schefke, and Schwarz; and interview with Jäger in Hertle, *Fall der Mauer*, 388.

19. Author's interview with Radomski.

20. Author's interviews with Radomski and Schefke.

21. Author's interviews with Radomski and Schefke; and Funken, *Das Jahr*, 185–186.

22. Author's interview with Hattenhauer.

23. Interview with Hattenhauer, www.zdf.de/ZDFmediathek/beitrag/video/1795 806/; and Pond, *Beyond the Wall*, 118.

24. "Verfügung," Oct. 13, 1989, BStU, Lpz AU 1793-89 Handakte Hattenhauer, 22, says, "die Beschuldigte ist sofort aus der Haft zu entlassen"; and author's interview with Hattenhauer.

25. The Stasi files confirm the birth date; see also Tony Paterson, "The Joy of Freedom," *Independent*, Nov. 10, 2009; and Saunders, "Half a Life Ago."

26. Author's interviews with Hattenhauer, Radomski, and Schefke.

27. Author's interviews with Radomski and Schefke. Funken, *Das Jahr*, 187, reports that the person who spoke to Radomski was Harald Jäger. In an interview, Radomski seconded that statement. However, when I asked Jäger about the accuracy of that claim, he replied that on the night of Nov. 9–10, 1989, he did not speak personally with any of the people on the eastern side attempting to exit to the West; only his subordinates did so. Author's interview with Jäger.

28. Author's interview with Jäger; Haase-Hindenburg, *Der Mann*, 18–21; and Jäger Kaderakte (a kind of Stasi personnel file), BStU.

29. Jäger Kaderakte, BStU.

30. Author's interview with Jäger; interview with Jäger in Hertle, *Fall der Mauer,* 381; and Haase-Hindenburg, *Der Mann,* 15–16, 188.

31. Other staff surveyed the entire border crossing on several television monitors. Various telephones enabled officers to reach their superiors quickly if there were problems. Author's interview with Jäger; Haase-Hindenburg, *Der Mann,* 15–16; and Hertle, *Fall der Mauer,* 381.

32. Jäger's Stasi files, which would include information to show if he had been involved in a killing, are available and show no such evidence; the author is grateful to the BStU staff for confirming this point.

33. As mentioned in the introductory section, the regiments all stood under the leadership of a command in Karlshorst, a location that was also the site of the KGB outpost. Hertle, *Chronik des Mauerfalls,* 157; see also Jochen Maurer, *Dienst an der Mauer: Der Alltag der Grenztruppen rund um Berlin* (Berlin: Christoph Links Verlag, 2011), 22–55, 125.

34. Specifically to the Stasi Main Department VI, run by General Heinz Fiedler; see Hertle and Elsner, eds., *Der Tag,* 81–82, and Maurer, *Dienst,* 125.

35. Author's interview with Jäger; and Hertle, *Chronik des Mauerfalls,* 156–159.

36. Author's interview with Jäger; and interview with Jäger in Hertle, *Fall der Mauer,* 381–386.

37. Interview with Jäger in Hertle and Elsner, eds., *Der Tag,* 86; and Hertle, *Fall der Mauer,* 380 n. 1.

38. Hertle, *Chronik des Mauerfalls,* 160.

39. Interview with Jäger in Hertle, *Fall der Mauer,* 380–382; and Cordt Schnibben, "Die Nacht der Wildschweine," *Spiegel* 45 (2009).

40. "PKE Erfassungsbogen," BStU, MfS, HA VI 15689, 252. The author is grateful to BStU staff member Roberto Welzel for researching the fact that these reports came from Sonnenallee.

41. See the records from Nov. 9, 1989, in BStU, MfS, HA XX 2345.

42. Interview with Peter Leonhardt in Hertle and Elsner, eds., *Der Tag,* 74–75; quotations, 74–75.

43. On the "quick round trip" of the "wild pigs" to the police station and back, see the interview with Jäger in 1990 on the television special produced a year after the opening of the Wall by Georg Mascolo, *9. November 1989/1990,* Spiegel-TV, Magazin 128, broadcast on Nov. 4, 1990; the author thanks Mascolo for a copy of this video. See also interview with Jäger in Hertle, *Fall der Mauer,* 382–383.

44. On Jäger's concern for the safety of his men, see the interview with Jäger in 1990 in Mascolo, *9. November 1989/1990.* On the ambiguity of orders, see Ahonen, *Death,* 219. And on the pressure that West Germany could exert on the East, see Heinrich Potthoff, ed., *Die Koalition der Vernunft* (Munich: dtv, 1995).

45. Author's interview with Jäger; for details of the weapons present at the checkpoint that night, see the interview with Jäger in Hertle and Elsner, eds., *Der Tag,* 99; *Chronik,* 161–162; and Hertle, *Fall der Mauer,* 386.

46. Author's interview with Jäger; and interview with Jäger in Hertle, *Fall der Mauer,* 384.

47. Author's interview with Jäger; and Huber, *Schabowskis Irrtum*, 60–61.

48. Author's interview with Jäger.

49. Ibid. Jäger's description of the "let-off-steam" plan, or in its German name "Ventillösung," matches written evidence from his colleagues at other checkpoints. For example, BStU, MfS, HA VI 15689, 252-253, "HA VI/ PKE, Erfassungsbogen zum Lagebericht," Nov. 9, 1989, according to BStU from the checkpoint at Sonnenallee, notes that at 8:30 p.m. there was a message to this effect from Operational Command, or OLZ, where Ziegenhorn was on duty: "Mitteilung durch OLZ/Anweisung Stv. Ltr. HA, Registrierung der DDR-Bürger die ausreisen" and that the process began about an hour later: "Beginn der Ausreise 21.35." Later that night, checkpoint staff noted that they stopped controls at midnight exactly, "00.00 keine Karten mehr notwendig," "00.17 alles aufmachen," and that they informed Ziegenhorn of this, "Gen. Ziegenhorn + OLZ verst. keine Handlung."

50. Telegram, Nov. 9, 1989, 11:05 p.m., BStU, MfS, HA VI 1735. Video images of East Germans holding IDs thereby rendered invalid, although they did not know it, are in Mascolo, *9. November 1989/1990*. See also Süß, *Staatssicherheit am Ende*, 443 n. 121.

51. Interview with Jäger in Hertle, *Fall der Mauer*, 384.

52. Author's interview with Radomski and Schefke; and Funken, *Das Jahr*, 187.

53. A picture of Schefke's ID with the stamp on his photo is in FRL 498.

54. Author's interview with Schefke; and Funken, *Das Jahr*, 188.

55. Author's interviews with Jahn, Radomski, and Schefke.

56. Author's interviews with Jahn and Momper.

57. Author's interviews with Jahn, Radomski, and Schefke.

58. Author's interview with Jäger; Hertle, *Chronik*, 162; and interview with Jäger in Hertle, *Fall der Mauer*, 386. Both Mascolo, *9. November 1989/1990*, and Barbara Supp, in "'Die machen uns fertig,'" *Spiegel* 45 (1996): 91–96, interview one of the Bornholmer officials called up by this alarm, Bruno Nevyhosteny.

59. Author's interview with Jäger; interview with Jäger in Hertle, *Fall der Mauer*, 387.

60. On the construction of the Wall and the West German practice of paying to free individuals from the GDR, see Harrison, *Driving the Soviets*, and Rehlinger, *Freikauf.*

61. Author's interview with Jäger; and interview with Jäger in 1990 in Mascolo, *9. November 1989/1990*.

62. Video clip from East German television news show *AK Zwo*, 10:30 p.m., Nov. 9, 1989, shown in documentary by Hertle and Scholz, *When the Wall;* see also Hertle, *Chronik*, 168–169.

63. ARD-NDR video archive, *Tagesthemen*, Nov. 9, 1989.

64. Author's interview with Mascolo; Funken, *Das Jahr*, 192; and Hertle, *Berliner Mauer*, 199; and Hertle, *Chronik*, 13. Thanks to video footage from Mascolo's *Spiegel-TV* camera team, which includes a clock, it is clear that the final sequence of events leading to the opening of the wall must have happened shortly before 11:30 p.m., despite comments by some participants in events that it was earlier.

65. Author's interview with Jäger; and interview with Jäger in Hertle, *Fall der Mauer*, 387. Jäger says that he made this call at 10:30 p.m., but, as mentioned in n. 64, video footage shows that it must have been closer to 11:30 p.m.

66. Author's interview with Jäger; interview with Jäger in 1990 in Mascolo, *9. November 1989/1990*; and interview with Jäger in Hertle, *Fall der Mauer*, 387.

67. Author's interview with Jäger; and interview with Helmut Stöss, Fall of the Wall Collection, KCLMA.

68. Video footage from Mascolo, *9. November 1989/1990;* and author's interview with Mascolo. The cameraman was Rainer März and his assistant was German Biester; see Hertle, *Berliner Mauer*, 199, for a still image of the exact moment. Mascolo's footage did not appear on television immediately since it was intended, and used, for a specific television program, not just part of a network's general coverage, but it was the most striking footage filmed that night, and still powerful when it appeared on air. Other camera teams captured images from Bornholmer that night as well, however, and those images did appear quickly, including on the *NBC Nightly News*, as described later in this chapter.

69. Interview with Stöss, Fall of the Wall Collection, KCLMA.

70. Author's interview with Jäger.

71. Author's interview with Hattenhauer; and Tony Paterson, "The Joy of Freedom."

72. Interview with Merkel in Diekmann and Reuth, eds., *Die längste Nacht*, 151; for more on Merkel, see Stefan Kornelius, *Angela Merkel: The Authorized Biography* (Richmond, UK: Alma Books, 2013).

73. Materials on the new organizations that emerged in 1989 are available in RHG; for Demokratischer Aufbruch, see Bestand DA; other organizations have their own collections. For a West German analysis of the new organizations, see PA-AA, BDE, "Bürgerinitiativen in der DDR," Oct. 12, 1989, ZA 140.684E.

74. Schabowski, "Wie ich die Mauer öffnete."

75. Interview with Egon Krenz, Fall of the Wall Collection, KCLMA; on the end of the central committee meeting, see Hertle and Stephan, eds., *Das Ende der SED*, 379.

76. Mascolo, *9. November 1989/1990*.

77. "HA VI/PKE Erfassungsbogen zum Lagebericht," 253; and Hertle, *Chronik*, 168–174.

78. "Vorkommnisse am 9./10. Nov. 1989 im Grenzabschnitt Brandenburger Tor," Sekr. Neiber 553, 45; see also BStU, BV Berlin, Abt. VII 1624, "Rapport Grenzsicherung Nr. 314 vom 10./11.11.1989," 40–41, which says that at 10:35 p.m. wall climbers were still willing to get down.

79. Author's interview with Kusnetz; the opening of the NBC broadcast, showing the clip from the bridge, is at www.nbcnews.com/id/33590933/#.UnEBuFGRP0c.

80. Interview with Carlston Baum, CNN Cold War Collection, KCLMA. The first name is almost certainly misspelled in the KCLMA collection and is probably Carsten or Karsten. The information that the hoses appeared to be leaky, and so not shooting water at full force, comes from this interview.

81. Author's interviews with Gould and Wheatley.

82. Author's interview with Lamprecht.

83. Author's interviews with Brokaw, Gelefsky, and Kusnetz.

84. Author's interview with Brokaw.

85. Author's interviews with Jahn, Radomski, and Schefke; on the disappointment of some dissidents, see Sarotte, *1989*, 53–54.

Chapter 7: Damage Control?

1. Author's interview with Fletcher. For more on the atmosphere in East Berlin in the wake of the Wall's opening, see Garton Ash, *Magic Lantern*, 61–77.

2. From video clips available on NBC, Nov. 10, 1989, www.youtube.com/watch?v=tK1MwhEDjHg.

3. "Vorkommnisse am 9./10. Nov. 1989 im Grenzabschnitt Brandenburger Tor," Sekr. Neiber 553, 45–47.

4. HA VI/PKE Oberbaumbrücke, "Erfassungsbogen zum Lagebericht," BStU, MfS, HA VI 15689, 259, reports that on the night of Nov. 9–10, "um 02.40 gelang es auf der Güst eine normale Lage wieder herzustellen."

5. Interview with Invaliden Stasi official who would only give his initials, S.W., in Hertle and Elsner, eds., *Der Tag*, 151; and "Information über die Entwicklung der Lage an den Grenzübergangstellen," Nov. 10, 1989, BStU, MfS, Sekr. Neiber 553, 32, which reports that at Invaliden checkpoint, "[u]m 3.30 Uhr war die Normallage wieder hergestellt und die Abfertigung der Ein- und Ausreisenden konnte aufgenommen werden." See also Momper, *Grenzfall*, 144–147; and Sarotte, *1989*, 42.

6. BStU, MfS, BdL Nr. 004404, 1.

7. "Diskussionsbeitrag des SdM Genossen Generaloberst Rudi Mittig," Nov. 10, 1989, BStU, MfS, BdL Nr. 005053 Mittig, 3–5.

8. Author's interview with Lauter.

9. Author's interview with Lauter; and Süß, *Staatssicherheit am Ende*, 446.

10. Author's interview with Maximychev.

11. Remarks by Iwan Kusmin cited in Hertle and Elsner, eds., *Der Tag*, 111.

12. Author's interview with Maximychev; and Igor Maximytschew, "Der Fall der Mauer aus russischer Sicht," in Küchenmeister, Nakath, and Stephan, eds., *". . . sofort, unverzüglich,"* 83–87.

13. Ivan N. Kuz'min, "Kurzer Abriss der innenpolitischen Entwicklung in der DDR von 1955 bis zur deutschen Vereinigung," in Horst Möller and Aleksandr Tschubarjan, eds., *Mitteilungen der Gemeinsamen Kommission für die Erforschung der jüngeren Geschichte der deutsch-russischen Beziehungen* (Munich: Oldenbourg, 2008), 98.

14. Helmut Kohl, *Erinnerungen 1982–1990* (Munich: Droemer, 2005), 969.

15. Author's interview with Maximychev.

16. Maximytschew, "Der Fall der Mauer," 84.

17. Kotschemassow, *Meine letzte Mission*, 189.

18. Interview with Grätz in Hertle, *Fall der Mauer*, 390–395; Hertle, *Chronik*, 188–202; and Heinz Keßler, *Zur Sache und zur Person: Erinnerungen* (Berlin: Edition Ost, 1996), 307–312.

19. "Nationaler Verteidigungsrat, Befehl Nr. 12/89," Nov. 10, 1989, reprinted in FRL 503; "Information des Ministeriums für Nationale Verteidigung," Nov. 10, 1989, in Hertle, *Fall der Mauer,* 508–510; Hertle, *Chronik,* 259–260; and Küchenmeister, Nakath, and Stephan, eds., *". . . sofort, unverzüglich,"* 55–82.

20. Hertle, *Chronik,* 205–210, 237; the text of the telegram from Krenz to Gorbachev of Nov. 10, 1989, is reprinted on 237. A similarly inaccurate statement, suggesting that the border was once again secure by 6:00 a.m., appears on a document on the letterhead of the Präsidium der Volkspolizei Berlin on Nov. 10, 1989, so perhaps Krenz took the idea from there, or perhaps he ordered this document to be produced; it is not clear; see "Information vom 10.11.1989," BStU, BV Berlin AKG 20, 28, which reads as follows: "Ab 6.00 Uhr ist der Einsatz von Kräften des Paß- und Meldewesens unmittelbar in den GÜST gesichert." See also Hertle and Stephan, eds., *Das Ende der SED,* 380–437; and James McAdams, *Germany Divided: From the Wall to Reunification* (Princeton, NJ: Princeton University Press, 1993), 178–179.

21. See the Stasi various reports from Nov. 10, 1989, including "Bericht über das Stimmungs- und Meinungsbild der AGT und ZB im Verantwortungsbereich des GK Mitte," and "Lagebericht," among others, in BStU, MfS, HA I 16938, 113–128.

22. "Information," Nov. 10, 1989, BStU, Sekr. Neiber 874, 46–47.

23. Author's interviews with Kastrup and Teltschik.

24. "Remarks and a Question-and-Answer Session with Reporters," Nov. 9, 1989, Public Papers, GHWBPL, http://bushlibrary.tamu.edu/research/public_papers .php?id=1174&. For a US view of the events of Nov. 9, see Timothy Naftali, *George H. W. Bush* (New York: Times Books, 2007); Don Oberdorfer, *The Turn: From the Cold War to a New Era* (New York: Simon and Schuster, 1991); and Philip Zelikow and Condoleezza Rice, *Germany Unified and Europe Transformed: A Study in Statecraft* (Cambridge, MA: Harvard University Press, 1995).

25. Copy in PA-AA, BDE, ZA140.685E, Nov. 10, 1989; see also "Letter from Mr Powell (Nr 10) to Mr Wall," Nov. 10, 1989, doc. 37, DBPO 101–103.

26. "Letter from Mr Wall to Mr Powell (No. 10)," Nov. 10, 1989, doc. 36, DBPO 100–101; and author's interview with Burton.

27. "Minute from Sir P. Wright to Mr Wall," Nov. 10, 1989, doc. 39, DBPO 104–106, esp. 105, n. 5.

28. "Sir R. Braithwaite (Moscow) to Mr Hurd," Nov. 11, 1989, doc. 40, DBPO 106–108, quotation at 106 and 108.

29. Telegram from Moscow to Bonn, AA, Nov. 10, 1989, 4:48 p.m., in PA-AA, BDE, ZA140.711E.

30. Chernyaev diary excerpt, Nov. 10, 1989, MG, 246. See also the NSA online version of the diary; my translation differs from the NSA. For a similar assessment of Gorbachev, see Leffler, *For the Soul of Mankind,* 448; for a critical view, see Lévesque, *Enigma,* 3, and Joachim Scholtyseck, *Die Aussenpolitik der DDR* (Munich: Oldenbourg, 2003), 45. On the larger significance of Gorbachev's actions at the end of the Cold War, see Norman Davies, *Europe: A History* (New York: HarperPerennial, 1998).

31. "Delegationsgespräch des Bundeskanzlers Kohl mit Ministerpräsident Mazowiecki, Warschau," Nov. 10, 1989, doc. 77, DESE 497–500.

32. On the need to coordinate with the three Western allies on all matters relating to West Berlin, see "Gespräch des Bundesministers Seiters mit den Botschaftern der drei Mächte, Bonn," Nov. 10, 1989, doc. 78, DESE 501–502.

33. Transcript, Nov. 10, 1989, 5:32 p.m., BStU, MfS, HA III 8640, 239–241; the names are blacked out in accordance with German laws on Stasi documents, but the conversation is nearly identical in timing, length, and content to the published version, "Mündliche Botschaft des Generalsekretärs Gorbatschow an Bundeskanzler Kohl," Nov. 10, 1989, doc. 80, DESE 504–505. For more on Kvisinky, see his memoir, Julij Kwizisnkij, *Vor dem Sturm* (Berlin: Siedler, 1993).

34. Author's interview with Teltschik; Kohl, *Erinnerungen,* 964–976; Küsters, "Entscheidung," 54–56; Sarotte, *1989,* 50–53; and Teltschik, *329 Tage,* 11–22.

35. See the discussion of Gorbachev's anxious Nov. 10 message in "Letter from Mr Powell (Nr 10) to Mr Wall," Nov. 10, 1989, doc. 38, DBPO 103–104.

36. See, for example, the transcripts of his phone calls with other world leaders such as Bush and Thatcher late on the night of Nov. 10, 1989, in docs. 81–82, DESE, 505–509; see also Sarotte, *1989,* 62–65, and Helga Haftendorn, *Coming of Age: German Foreign Policy Since 1945,* trans. Deborah S. Kaiser (Lanham, MD: Rowman and Littlefield, 2006), 279–281.

37. "Gespräch zwischen dem Generalsekretär des ZK der SED, Genossen Egon Krenz, und dem Bundeskanzler der BRD," Nov. 11, 1989, BArch, SAPMO, IV 2/2.039/328; "Fernschreiben des Staatssekretärs Bertele an den Chef des Bundeskanzleramtes, Berlin (Ost)," Nov. 11, 1989, doc. 88, DESE 517–519; and Süß, *Staatssicherheit am Ende,* 434.

38. Author's interviews with Burton and Momper.

39. Author's interview with Momper; and Momper, *Grenzfall,* 142–146.

40. "Information über die Entwicklung der Lage an den Grenzübergangstellen," 32; and author's interviews with Momper and with Sedlmaier, a West Berliner present at the Invaliden checkpoint, for Momper's remarks.

41. Author's interviews with Momper and Sedlmaier; and Momper, *Grenzfall,* 142–146.

42. Telegram, "'Ouverture' du Mur de Berlin," Nov. 10, 1989, doc. 10, DFUA 101–102.

43. Hertle, *Chronik,* 186–187.

44. Author's interview with Sello; and Kowalczuk, *Endspiel,* 407.

45. Author's interview with Sello.

46. Author's interview with Kusnetz.

47. By the early hours of Nov. 10 alone, the Stasi estimated that close to seventy thousand people had exited for West Berlin on foot and about another ten thousand in some form of vehicle. These are probably underestimates, given eyewitness accounts. "Information über die Entwicklung der Lage an den Grenzübergangstellen," 30.

48. Ibid., 30–39.

49. "Information über die Entwicklung der Lage an den Grenzübergangsstellen," Nov. 11, 1989, BStU, Sekr. Neiber 553, 41–43.

50. "Information über die Entwicklung der Lage an den Grenzübergangstellen," both from Nov. 10 and Nov. 11. It is hard to say how accurate these estimates are in light of the huge numbers involved, but the volume was clearly large.

51. "Aus- und Einreisestatistik," Nov. 20, 1989, BStU, MfS, Sekr. Neiber 618, 272.

52. Spittmann, "Übergangsgesellschaft," 1204.

53. "Opposition: DDR-Behörden von der Reisewelle überrollt," *Tagesspiegel*, Nov. 14, 1989; see also "DDR-Reisebüro beklagt Mangel an Devisen," *Frankfurter Allgemeine Zeitung*, Nov. 10, 1989.

54. Hertle, *Chronik*, 259–260; and Küchenmeister, Nakath, and Stephan, eds., " . . . *sofort, unverzüglich,"* 55–82.

55. Hertle, *Berliner Mauer*, 222.

Epilogue: Violence and Victory, Trust and Triumphalism

1. Durs Grünbein, "Der Weg nach Bornholm," *Zeit Online*, Nov. 9, 2008. Grünbein, born in Dresden in 1962, is one of the most acclaimed writers to emerge from former East Germany. The article from which this quotation was taken appeared as part of a series of essays to mark the nineteenth anniversary of the opening of the Wall. Original in German: "Er war keiner von denen, die sich noch einmal umdrehen, nachdem alles entschieden ist."

2. Robert M. Gates, *From the Shadows: The Ultimate Insider's Story of Five Presidents and How They Won the Cold War* (New York: Touchstone, 1996), 492; Sarotte, "Perpetuating U.S. Preeminence"; and Mary Elise Sarotte, "In Victory, Magnanimity: US Foreign Policy, 1989–1991, and the Legacy of Prefabricated Multilateralism," *International Politics* 48 (Aug. 2011): 482–495.

3. Memorandum of Conversation, "Meeting with Chancellor Helmut Kohl," Feb. 24, 1990, GHWBPL, released due to the author's request, MR-2008-0651 of May 21, 2008. See also George H. W. Bush and Brent Scowcroft, *A World Transformed* (New York: Knopf, 1998), 253. For more on Bush's motivations generally, see Jeffrey Engel, *When the World Seemed New: George H. W. Bush and the Surprisingly Peaceful End of the Cold War* (New York: Houghton Mifflin Harcourt, forthcoming).

4. These issues are one of the central concerns not only of my book *1989* but also of three related articles: Sarotte, "In Victory, Magnanimity"; Mary Elise Sarotte, "Not One Inch Eastward? Bush, Baker, Kohl, Genscher, Gorbachev and the Origin of Russian Resentment Toward NATO Enlargement in February 1990," *Diplomatic History* 34, no. 1 (Jan. 2010): 119–140; and Sarotte, "Perpetuating U.S. Preeminence." For more on the extension of the EC eastward, see Frédéric Bozo, *Mitterrand, German Unification, and the End of the Cold War,* trans. Susan Emanuel (London: Berghahn, 2009).

5. On the history of the Saarland, see www.saarland.de/geschichte.htm.

6. The texts of both Articles 23 and 146 were, however, changed afterward to reassure Germany's neighbors that the process of expanding the FRG's territory would not continue beyond 1990. On the process of unifying the two halves of Germany, see Konrad Jarausch and Volker Gransow, eds., *Uniting Germany: Documents and Debates, 1944–1993* (Providence, RI: Berghahn, 1994); Rödder, *Deutschland einig Vaterland;* Turner, *Germany from Partition to Unification;* Sarotte, *1989,* 119–194; and Ingo von Münch, ed., *Dokumente des geteilten Deutschland* (Stuttgart: Kröner, 1976). On East German efforts to use a roundtable to draft a new constitution nonetheless, see ZRT-WD.

7. Sarotte, *1989,* 162.

8. On the coup and the end of the USSR, see Mark Beissinger, *Nationalist Mobilization and the Collapse of the Soviet State* (Cambridge: Cambridge University Press, 2002); Stephen Kotkin, *Armageddon Averted: The Soviet Collapse, 1970–2000* (New York: Oxford University Press, 2001); Jack Matlock, *Autopsy on an Empire: The American Ambassador's Account of the Collapse of the Soviet Union* (New York: Random House, 1995); and Plokhy, *The Last Empire.*

9. See Sarotte, *1989,* 195–214; Sarotte, "Not One Inch Eastward?"; and Sarotte, "Perpetuating U.S. Preeminence."

10. On Yugoslavia and the lacking European response, see Josip Glaurdić, *The Hour of Europe: Western Powers and the Breakup of Yugoslavia* (New Haven, CT: Yale University Press, 2011), and Brendan Simms, *Unfinest Hour: Britain and the Destruction of Bosnia* (London: Allen Lane, 2001). The lack of any kind of European structure capable of stopping the violence as Yugoslavia disintegrated particularly concerned the former East German dissident leader Bärbel Bohley, who spent much of the rest of her life volunteering in the region; see www.praschl.net/menschen /das-neue-leben-der-baerbel-bohley.

11. Sarotte, *1989,* 187.

12. On the difficulty of converting revolutionary success into a position of post-revolutionary political authority in Germany, see Maier, "Civil Resistance," 276.

13. Author's interview with Hattenhauer.

14. For more on the debate over what to do with the Stasi files saved by activists and how much access to allow to them, see Klaus-Dietmar Henke, ed., *Wann bricht schon mal ein Staat zusammen: Die Debatte über die Stasi-Akten auf dem 39. Historikertag 1992* (Munich: Deutscher Taschenbuch Verlag, 1993). See also Süß, *Staatssicherheit am Ende,* 740.

15. Hertle, *Berliner Mauer,* 222.

16. On some of the debate in 2009 over what to do with the former border-crossing area, see Siobhán Dowling, "Where the Berlin Wall First Fell," *Spiegel Online International,* Nov. 6, 2009.

17. Author's interview with Jäger.

18. Author's interview with Hattenhauer; on one recent film containing a character based on Jäger, see Sven Goldmann, "Brückentage," *Tagesspiegel,* Sept. 29, 2013.

19. Author's interview with Wonneberger; Ralf Geissler, "Der verstummte Revolutionär," *Die Zeit*, Oct. 8, 2009; Mayer, *Der nicht aufgibt*, 144, 148; Peter Wensierski, "Handeln statt Beteln," *Spiegel* 43 (2009): 42–46; see also Pausch, *Widerstehen*.

20. See, for example, the commentary made by state investigators for the new Saxon state government about such stonewalling: "Vorbemerkungen," SS, 21–22.

21. For a scholarly account of this issue, see James McAdams, *Judging the Past in Unified Germany* (Cambridge: Cambridge University Press, 2001); for a popular account, see Rosenberg, *Haunted Land*.

22. Author's interview with Gueffroy; and Ahonen, *Death*, 255–259.

23. Author's interview with Gueffroy; quotation from Rosenberg, *Haunted Land*, 267–268.

24. Ahonen, *Death*, 255–259; and Rosenberg, *Haunted Land*, 345–348.

25. Author's interviews with Gueffroy and Regel.

26. Ahonen, *Death*, 267; Hertle, *Berliner Mauer*, 218–221; and Günter Schabowski and Frank Sieren, *Wir haben fast alles falsch gemacht: Die letzten Tage der DDR*, 2nd ed. (Berlin: Ullstein, 2009), 255–272.

27. Wolfgang Saxon, "Erich Honecker, Ruler of East Germany for 18 of Its Last Years, Dies in Exile at 81," *New York Times*, May 30, 1994; see also Pötzl, *Erich Honecker*.

28. Author's interview with Jahn; and Praschl, *Roland Jahn*, 176–181, quotation at 181.

29. Author's interview with Radomski. On a personal level, Radomski later ended his relationship with his girlfriend of Nov. 1989. As he would later put it, many couples split up after the Wall opened, because once the pressure of living in a dictatorship was removed, many of the "emergency partnerships" that people had formed for support were no longer necessary.

30. His reply showed that he, like so many others, had challenged the dictatorial regime in 1989 for a complex mixture of motives. Author's interviews with Radomski and Schefke.

31. When Hackenberg's boss, the chronically absent Leipzig first secretary, got his wish to be removed from his duties in Nov. 1989, Hackenberg did not succeed him, even though he had long been the leading candidate for the top job. Instead, that top slot went to Wötzel, one of the district secretaries who had cosigned Masur's appeal. Wötzel heard that he owed his success to the fact that Hackenberg could no longer be trusted "to hold together because of his nerves." Hackenberg died in 1999 at the age of seventy-three. See Wötzel, quoted in Niemann, *Die Sekretäre*, 355, and Müller-Enbergs, et al., eds., *Wer war wer*, 468.

32. Author's interviews with Gimln, Lauter, and Maximychev; Lauter, *Chefermittler*, 206–222; and Putin, *First Person*, 80.

33. Durs Grünbein, "Der Weg nach Bornholm"; for more on Durs Grünbein, see Michael Eskin, Karen Leeder, and Christopher Young, eds., *Durs Grünbein: A Companion* (Berlin: De Gruyter, 2013). For more on nostalgia for the former GDR, a phenomenon known as "Ostalgie," see Thomas Goll and Thomas Leuerer,

eds., *Ostalgie als Erinnerungskultur? Symposium zu Lied und Politik in der DDR* (Baden-Baden: Nomos, 2004), and Katja Neller, *DDR-Nostalgie: Dimensionen der Orientierungen der Ostdeutschen gegenüber der ehemaligen DDR, ihre Ursachen und politischen Konnotationen* (Wiesbaden: Verlag für Sozialwissenschaften, 2006).

34. To cite just two of the many examples: (1) Soviet expert Jonathan Haslam could still write that "Krenz . . . instructed that the barriers be raised" (Haslam, *Russia's Cold War* [New Haven, CT: Yale University Press, 2011], 391); and (2) the volume on US foreign policy in the seemingly definitive Oxford University Press History of the United States series could state that, following the ouster of "the recalcitrant hard-liner Erich Honecker," on "November 9, his successor opened the Berlin Wall to passage without visas" (Herring, *From Colony to Superpower*, 905).

35. The gist of this narrative is that when Reagan speaks, "even walls fall down," as summarized in Ratnesar, *Tear Down This Wall*, 195. Ratnesar does acknowledge that factors other than Reagan's speech played a role in the opening of the Wall and acknowledges the contributions of Germans themselves elsewhere in the book, so his book is not the most strident advocate of this view.

36. See, for example, Charles Maier, "What Have We Learned Since 1989?" *Contemporary European History* 18, no. 3 (2009): 253–269.

37. Bloch's interpretation of this phenomenon appears to be the opposite of Tocqueville's. In the opening lines of Part I, Chapter 1, of *Ancien Régime,* Tocqueville argues that events that are in fact inevitable appear to be unlikely before they happen. Bloch's work, however, suggests the opposite: events that are not preordained seem afterward to have been so. This appears to be the definition of hindsight bias as identified by Bloch and described in the introduction.

38. Egon Krenz's email to the author, Oct. 24, 2013. The original two German quotations, given in my translation in the text above, are as follows: (1) "Als am 9. November 1989 Berliner Bürger zu den Grenzübergängen eilten, weil ein Politbüromitglied sie falsch informiert hatte, waren wir einer bürgerkriegsähnlichen Auseinandersetzung näher als das viele heute wahrhaben wollen"; (2) "Am Abend des 9. November und im Verlaufe des 10. November bestand die reale Gefahr einer militärischen Eskalation, in die auch die Großmächte hätten hineingezogen werden können."

39. On the immense size of the Leipzig protest in particular, see Opp, Voss, and Gern, *Die volkseigene Revolution*, 47.

40. For more on this story, see Sarotte, "China's Fear of Contagion," and Ezra F. Vogel, *Deng Xiaoping and the Transformation of China* (Cambridge, MA: Harvard University Press, 2011), 602–694.

41. In hindsight, it is surprising that he did not use even more violence. Honecker's plans for the Oct. 16 march in Leipzig—an aerial assault—suggest that he was moving in that direction. The fact that he had not used such measures already seems to have resulted from a combination of factors: the collapse of cooperation among the member states of the Warsaw Pact appears to have made him uncertain, rightly, about how much support from his allies he would have; and, in addition, there was the awkward

need to extract support from Bonn, and to regard its wishes for a lessening of violence in return. For more on this topic, see Süß, *Staatssicherheit am Ende,* 742–752.

42. Stent, *Russia and Germany Reborn,* 145.

43. A weaker Gorbachev might have given them a greater opportunity to do so had the Wall not opened when it did. The time of day of the Wall's opening was significant as well: that it opened at night during a holiday in the Soviet Union hindered decision making by Moscow until it was too late. On the continued willingness of Soviet military leaders to use force in 1989, despite Gorbachev, see Brown, *Rise and Fall,* 527.

44. Sarotte, *1989,* 188–211.

45. For accounts analyzing the longer-term causes of the end of the Cold War, see, to name just a few, Gaddis, *Cold War;* Harper, *The Cold War;* Judt, *Postwar;* Kotkin, *Armageddon Averted;* Leffler, *For the Soul of Mankind;* Mazower, *Dark Continent;* and Zubok, *A Failed Empire.*

46. Many activist leaders in particular deeply admired Martin Luther King Jr. In their moment of extremity, local leaders such as Wonneberger and Sievers turned specifically to King's example and writings as practical guides on how to manage the situation in which they found themselves. Author's interviews with Sievers and Wonneberger; see also "Notizen des Referatsleiters des Referats XX/7 zur Referatsleitersitzung der Abteilung XX der BV Leipzig des MfS," Oct. 9, 1989, doc. 243, FUF 458.

47. The author is grateful to Jacques Hymans for highlighting this point; see his own work on international relations in Jacques Hymans, *Achieving Nuclear Ambitions: Scientists, Politicians, and Proliferation* (Cambridge: Cambridge University Press, 2012). The question of trust and its role in political action is a major topic among political theorists; see, for example, Brian Rathbun, *Trust in International Cooperation: International Security Institutions, Domestic Politics and American Multilateralism* (Cambridge: Cambridge University Press, 2012).

48. Author's interview with Hattenhauer.

49. Author's interview with Wonneberger.

50. It further suggests that such leaders need to maintain cognizance of the potential impact that a handful of individuals, even those in the middle tier of authority, can have on the future of their country, particularly in times of dramatic change. I am grateful to Chris Miller for this insight. See also Rathbun, *Trust,* 228, who concludes that "overall it seems best to trust in international cooperation."

51. For documents from, and a summary of the history of, the CSCE process, see Jeremy P. Schmidt, *The Helsinki Final Act* (blog), http://cscehistory.wordpress.com/ford.

52. While some writers have started to address this issue, as a phenomenon it remains both important and understudied. Scholars who have started to address it include Brands, *From Berlin to Baghdad;* Falk, "From Berlin to Baghdad"; James M. Goldgeier and Derek Chollet, *America Between the Wars, from 11/9 to 9/11: The Misunderstood Years Between the Fall of the Berlin Wall and the Start of the War on Terror* (New York: PublicAffairs, 2008); Thomas H. Henriksen, *American Power After the Berlin Wall* (New York: Palgrave, 2007); Melvyn P. Leffler and Jeffrey W. Legro, eds., *In Uncertain Times: American Foreign Policy After the Berlin Wall and 9/11* (Ithaca, NY:

Cornell University Press, 2011); Meyer, *Year That Changed the World*, xii; Richard Ned Lebow and Janice Gross Stein, *We All Lost the Cold War* (Princeton, NJ: Princeton University Press, 1994); and Schrecker, ed., *Cold War Triumphalism*. On the impact on relations with Russia, see Stephen F. Cohen, *Soviet Fates and Lost Alternatives: From Stalinism to the New Cold War* (New York: Columbia University Press, 2009), chap. 7, and Angela Stent, *The Limits of Partnership: U.S.-Russian Relations in the Twenty-First Century* (Princeton, NJ: Princeton University Press, 2014), chap. 2.

53. This list of memorials to the opening of the Wall in the United States is not complete; for example, there is also a piece of the Wall in the Reagan Building in Washington, DC. For more information about Wall memorials in the United States and elsewhere, see Bundesstiftung Aufarbeitung, ed., *Die Berliner Mauer in der Welt* (Berlin: Berlin Story Verlag, 2009); I am grateful to Hope Harrison for drawing my attention to this book. Images of the memorials mentioned in the text above are available on the websites of the RRPL and GHWBPL; for an image of the Reagan statue in the US Capitol Rotunda, see the website of the Architect of the Capitol, www.aoc.gov/capitol-hill/national-statuary-hall-collection/ronald-wilson-reagan.

54. The sculptor of the Bush Library statue is Veryl Goodnight; information about the library's statue and the "sister casting" installed in Berlin is available at her website, www.verylgoodnight.com/TheDaytheWallCameDown.html.

55. I am grateful to Hope Harrison for information about the naming of the Platz des 9. November 1989. For more on larger questions about the politics of memory of the Wall, see Hope Harrison, *After the Wall: Memory and the Making of the New Germany, 1989 to the Present* (Cambridge: Cambridge University Press, forthcoming).

56. On the success of a temporary exhibit organized by RHG and consisting largely of information panels on Alexanderplatz in 2009–2010, see Robert-Havemann-Gesellschaft and Kulturprojekte Berlin, eds., *Friedliche Revolution 1989/90* (Berlin: RHG, 2010), and Robert-Havemann-Gesellschaft and Kulturprojekte Berlin, eds., *"Wir sind das Volk!" Magazin zur Ausstellung friedliche Revolution 1989/90* (Berlin: Kulturprojekte, 2009).

57. This foundation's exhibits do mark the fall of the Wall as well, but in the larger context of the history of the Wall, of East German refugees, and of the peaceful revolution. I am grateful to both Axel Klausmeier and Manfred Wichmann, its director and curator of collections, respectively, for their help with my research. For more information about the Berlin Wall Foundation and the memorials that it maintains, see its website, available in English at www.stiftung-berliner-mauer.de/en.

58. On the competition for a bigger memorial to the opening of the Wall in the city center, see Jan Otakar Fischer, "Berlin: The Art of Reunification," Nov. 5, 2009, Design Observer Group website, http://places.designobserver.com/feature/berlin-the-art-of-reunification/11707.

59. Stefan Berg and Steffen Winter, "Going Bats," *Spiegel Online International*, Mar. 6, 2014.

60. For more on the design for the "Freiheits- und Einheitsdenkmal" chosen in the second round, see www.freiheits-und-einheitsdenkmal.de/; see also Apelt, ed., *Der*

Weg zum Denkmal für Freiheit und Einheit. For more on the difficulties of commemo-rating the past in contemporary Germany, see Hope M. Harrison, "The Berlin Wall," in Mark Kramer and Vit Smetana, eds., *Imposing, Maintaining, and Tearing Open the Iron Curtain: The Cold War and East-Central Europe, 1945–1989* (Lanham, MD: Lexington Books, 2013), 173–196. I am also grateful to both Jan Otakar Fischer and Hope Harrison for information about this memorial.

61. Author's interview with Birthler.

Bibliography

Archives and Personal Collections of Participants

Germany

Berlin:
Brinkmann, Peter, personal collection
Bundesarchiv [BArch] and Stiftung-Archiv der Parteien und Massenorganisationen der DDR [SAPMO]
Ministerium für Staatssicherheit [MfS], Bundesbeauftragter für die Unterlagen des Staatssicherheitsdienstes der ehemaligen Deutschen Demokratischen Republik [BStU]
Robert-Havemann-Gesellschaft [RHG]

Bonn/Sankt Augustin:
Konrad Adenauer Stiftung Pressearchiv

Dresden:
Sächsisches Hauptstaatsarchiv

Hamburg:
ARD-NDR Videoarchiv
Mascolo, Georg, personal collection

Koblenz:
Bundesarchiv [BArchK]

Leipzig:
Archiv Bürgerbewegung Leipzig
Sächsisches Staatsarchiv

Poland

Warsaw:
KARTA [Solidarity and opposition materials]

Russia

Moscow:
Архив Горбачев-Фонда [Gorbachev Foundation Archive]

United Kingdom

London:
Cabinet Office [CO] materials, released under the 2005 Freedom of Information law
    [FOI]
Foreign and Commonwealth Office [FCO] materials, released under FOI
King's College Liddell Hart Military Archive [KCLMA]

United States

College Station, Texas:
The George H. W. Bush Presidential Library [GHWBPL]

Princeton, New Jersey:
Jack Matlock, personal collection
James A. Baker III Papers, Mudd Library, Princeton University [BP]
Robert Hutchings, personal collection

Simi Valley, California:
The Ronald Reagan Presidential Library [RRPL]

Washington, DC:
CIA materials released under the US Freedom of Information Act [FOIA]
The National Security Archive [NSA]
State Department materials released under FOIA

Primary Sources Collected and Made Available
at Scholarly Conferences

Cold War International History Project Paris Conference. "Europe and the End of the
    Cold War," Conference, June 15–17, 2006, Paris, organized by the Cold War
    International History Project in collaboration with other research centers, June
    15–17, 2006 [CWIHPPC].
Greenstein, Fred I., and William C. Wohlforth, eds. *Cold War Endgame: Report of a
    Conference.* Center of International Studies Monograph Series No. 10. Princeton:
    Center of International Studies, 1997.

Conferences Organized by the National Security Archive
(in Chronological Order)

"Briefing Book for Cold War Endgame," March 29–30, 1996, co-sponsored by the
    Woodrow Wilson School and the James A. Baker III Institute for Public Policy,
    compiled by the National Security Archive.

Georgia Conference : "End of the Cold War in Europe, 1989," May 1–3, 1998, Musgrove, St. Simon's Island, Georgia [GC].

Prague Conference: "The Democratic Revolution in Czechoslovakia," October 14–16, 1999, Prague, co-organized by the Czechoslovak Documentation Center and the Institute of Contemporary History, Academy of Sciences of the Czech Republic [PC].

Mershon Conference: "US-Soviet Military Relationships at the End of the Cold War, 1988–91," October 15–17, 1999, Mershon Center, The Ohio State University.

Miedzeszyn-Warsaw Conference: "Poland 1986–1989: The End of the System," October 20–24, 1999, Miedzeszyn-Warsaw, Poland, co-sponsored by the Institute of Political Studies at the Polish Academy of Sciences.

Primary Sources Issued by Governments and/or Published

Auswärtiges Amt, ed. *Außenpolitik der Bundesrepublik Deutschland: Dokumente von 1949 bis 1994*. Cologne: Verlag Wissenschaft und Politik, 1995.

———. *Deutsche Außenpolitik 1990/91: Auf dem Weg zu einer europäischen Friedensordnung eine Dokumentation*. Bonn: Auswärtiges Amt, April 1991.

Bozóki, András, ed. *The Roundtable Talks of 1989: The Genesis of Hungarian Democracy, Analysis and Documents*. Budapest: CEU Press, 2002.

Buchstab, Günter, and Hans-Otto Kleinmann, eds. *Helmut Kohl Berichte zur Lage 1989–1998*. Düsseldorf: Droste, 2012.

Bürgerkomitee Leipzig, ed. *Stasi intern*. Leipzig: Forum Verlag, 1991.

DDR Journal zur November Revolution August bis Dezember 1989, vom Ausreisen bis zum Einreißen der Mauer, a compilation produced by the Western newspaper *taz*, 1990.

Die Vereinigung Deutschlands im Jahre 1990: Verträge und Erklärungen. Bonn: Presse- und Informationsamt der Bundesregierung, 1991.

Dietrich, Christian, and Uwe Schwabe, eds. *Freunde und Feinde: Dokumente zu den Friedensgebeten in Leipzig zwischen 1981 und dem 9. Oktober 1989*. Leipzig: Evangelische Verlaganstalt, 1994 [FUF].

Fischer, Benjamin B. *At Cold War's End: US Intelligence on the Soviet Union and Eastern Europe, 1989–1991*. Washington, DC: CIA, 1999.

Fischer, Horst, ed. *Schalck-Imperium: Ausgewählte Dokumente*. Bochum: Brockmeyer, 1993.

Freedman, Lawrence, ed. *Europe Transformed: Documents on the End of the Cold War— Key Treaties, Agreements, Statements and Speeches*. New York: St. Martin's Press, 1990.

Gesamtdeutsches Institut, Bundesanstalt für gesamtdeutsche Aufgaben. *Analysen, Dokumentationen und Chronik zur Entwicklung in der DDR von September bis Dezember 1989*. Bonn: Bundesanstalt, 1990.

Gorbatschow, Michail S. *Gipfelgespräche: Geheime Protokolle aus meiner Amtszeit*. Berlin: Rowohlt, 1993.

————. Отвечая на вызов времени: внешняя политика перестройки–документальные свидетельства по записям бесед М.С. Горбачева с зарубежными деятелями и другим материалам. Москва: Весь Мир, 2010.

————. Галкин, Александр, и Черняев, Анатолий. Михаил Горбачев и германский вопрос: Сборник документов 1986–1991. Москва: Весь Мир, 2006 [MG].

Grenville, J. A. S., and Bernard Wasserstein, eds. *The Major International Treaties Since 1945: A History and Guide with Texts.* London: Methuen, 1987.

Grundgesetz für die Bundesrepublik Deutschland, Textausgabe, Stand: Oktober 1990. Bonn: Bundeszentrale für politische Bildung, 1990.

Grundgesetz für die Bundesrepublik Deutschland, Textausgabe, Stand: Juni/Juli 1994. Bonn: Bundeszentrale für politische Bildung, 1994.

Haines, Gerald K., and Robert E. Leggett. *CIA's Analysis of Soviet Union 1947–1991.* Washington, DC: Ross & Perry, 2001.

Hertle, Hans-Hermann. *Der Fall der Mauer: Die unbeabsichtigte Selbstauflösung des SED-Staates.* Opladen: Westdeutscher Verlag, 1996.

————, ed. *Der Sound des Untergangs: Tonmitschnitte aus den letzten Sitzungen des SED-Zentralkomitees Oktober bis Dezember 1989.* Berlin: Links, 2013.

Hertle, Hans-Hermann, and Gerd-Rüdiger Stephan, eds. *Das Ende der SED: Die letzten Tage des Zentralkomitees.* Berlin: Links, Sept. 1997.

Jacobsen, Hans-Adolf, ed. *Bonn-Warschau 1945–1991.* Cologne: Verlag Wissenschaft und Politik, 1992.

James, Harold, and Marla Stone, eds. *When the Wall Came Down: Reactions to German Unification.* New York: Routledge, 1992.

Jarausch, Konrad H., and Volker Gransow, eds. *Uniting Germany: Documents and Debates, 1944–1993.* Providence: Berghahn Books, 1994.

Jarausch, Konrad H., and Martin Sabrow, eds. *Weg in den Untergang: Der innere Zerfall der DDR.* Göttingen: Vandenhoeck, 1999.

Kaiser, Karl, ed. *Deutschlands Vereinigung: Die internationalen Aspekte.* Bergisch-Gladbach: Lübbe Verlag, 1991.

Kleßmann, Christoph, and Georg Wagner, eds. *Das gespaltene Land: Leben in Deutschland 1945–1990, Texte und Dokumente zur Sozialgeschichte.* Munich: Beck, 1993.

Kowalczuk, Ilko-Sascha, ed. *Freiheit und Öffentlichkeit: Politischer Samisdat in der DDR 1985–1989.* Berlin: Robert-Havemann-Gesellschaft, 2002.

Küchenmeister, Daniel, and Gerd-Rüdiger Stephan, eds. *Honecker Gorbatschow Vieraugengespräche.* Berlin: Dietz Verlag, 1993.

Küsters, Hanns Jürgen, and Daniel Hoffman, eds. *Dokumente zur Deutschlandpolitik. Deutsche Einheit, Sonderedition aus den Akten des Bundeskanzleramtes 1989/90.* Munich: Oldenbourg Verlag, 1998 [DESE].

Lochen, Hans-Hermann, and Christian Meyer-Seitz, eds. *Die geheimen Anweisungen zur Diskriminierung Ausreisewilliger.* Cologne: Bundesanzeiger Verlag, 1992.

Mastny, Vojtech, ed. *The Helsinki Process and the Reintegration of Europe 1986–1991: Analysis and Documentation.* New York: New York University Press, 1992.

Mastny, Vojtech, and Malcolm Byrne, eds. *A Cardboard Castle? An Inside History of the Warsaw Pact.* New York: CEU Press, 2005.

Meißner, Werner, and Anja Feege, eds. *Die DDR und China 1949 bis 1990.* Berlin: Akademie Verlag, 1995.

Mitter, Armin, and Stefan Wolle, eds. *Ich liebe euch doch alle! Befehle und Lageberichte des MfS Januar–November 1989.* Berlin: BasisDruck, 1990.

Nakath, Detlef, Gero Neugebauer, and Gerd-Rüdiger Stephan, eds. *"Im Kreml brennt noch Licht": Spitzenkontakte zwischen SED/PDS und KPdSU 1989–1991.* Berlin: Dietz, 1998.

Nakath, Detlef, and Gerd-Rüdiger Stephan, eds. *Countdown zur deutschen Einheit: Eine dokumentierte Geschichte der deutsch-deutschen Beziehungen 1987/1990.* Berlin: Dietz, 1996.

Nathan, Andrew J., Perry Link, and Zhang Liang [pseud.], eds. *The Tiananmen Papers: The Chinese Leadership's Decision to Use Force Against Their Own People—In Their Own Words.* New York: PublicAffairs, 2001.

Noelle-Neumann, Elisabeth, and Renate Köcher, eds. *Allensbacher Jahrbuch der Demoskopie 1984–1992.* Band 9. Munich: Saur, 1993.

Ostermann, Christian, ed. *Uprising in East Germany 1953: The Cold War, the German Question and the First Major Upheaval Behind the Iron Curtain.* New York: Central European University Press, 2001.

Prados, John, ed. *How the Cold War Ended: Debating and Doing History.* Washington, DC: Potomac Books, 2011.

Salmon, Patrick, Keith Hamilton, and Stephen Twigge, eds. *Documents on British Policy Overseas,* Series III, Vol. VII, *German Unification, 1989–1990.* London: Routledge, 2009 [DBPO].

Saltoun-Ebin, Jason, ed. *The Reagan Files: Inside the National Security Council.* Santa Barbara, CA: Seabec Books, 2014.

Savranskaya, Svetlana, Thomas Blanton, and Vladislav Zubok, eds. *Masterpieces of History: The Peaceful End of the Cold War in Europe, 1989.* Budapest: Central European University Press, 2010.

Schweitzer, C. C., et al., eds. *Politics and Government in the Federal Republic of Germany: Basic Documents.* Leamington Spa: Berg Publishers, 1984.

Schlußbericht des Sonderausschusses zur Untersuchung von Amts- und Machtmißbrauch infolge der SED-Herrschaft, Sächsischer Landtag, 1. Wahlperiode, Drucksache 1/4773 zu DS 1/213, unpublished copy in the collection of the University of Wisconsin–Madison Library [SS].

Stasi-Unterlagen-Gesetz. Munich: C. H. Beck, 1993.

Stephan, Gerd-Rüdiger, and Daniel Küchenmeister, eds. *"Vorwärts immer, rückwärts nimmer!"* Berlin: Dietz, 1994.

Steury, Donald P. *On the Front Lines of the Cold War: Documents on the Intelligence War in Berlin.* Washington, DC: CIA History Staff, 1999.

Thaysen, Uwe, ed. *Der Zentrale Runde Tisch: Wortprotokolle und Dokumente.* Wiesbaden: Westdeutscher Verlag, 2000 [ZRT-WD].

Vaïsse, Maurice, and Christian Wenkel, eds. *La diplomatie française face à l'unification allemande*. Paris: Tallandier, 2011 [DFUA].

Von Münch, Ingo, ed. *Dokumente des geteilten Deutschland*. 2 vols. Stuttgart: Kröner, 1976.

Von Plato, Alexander. *Die Vereinigung Deutschlands—Ein weltpolitisches Machtspiel: Bush, Kohl, Gorbatschow und die geheimen Moskauer Protokolle*. Berlin: Links, 2002.

Weber, Hermann, ed. *DDR: Dokumente zur Geschichte der Deutschen Demokratischen Republik*. Munich: dtv, 1986.

Zimmerman, Hartmut, ed. *DDR Handbuch*. Köln: Verlag Wissenschaft und Politik, 1985.

Autobiographies, Broadcast or Published Interviews, Memoirs, and Other Accounts by Contemporaries and Participants

Ackermann, Eduard. *Mit feinem Gehör: Vierzig Jahre in der Bonner Politik*. Bergisch Gladbach: Lübbe Verlag, 1994.

Anonymous. *A Woman in Berlin*. Trans. Philip Boehm. New York: Metropolitan Books, 2005.

Baker, James A., with Thomas A. Defrank. *The Politics of Diplomacy: Revolution, War and Peace, 1989–1992*. New York: G. P. Putnam's Sons, 1995.

Bernhof, Reinhard. *Die Leipziger Protokolle*. Halle: Projekte Verlag, 2004.

Bloch, Marc. *Apologie pour l'histoire*. Paris: Armand Colin, 1974.

———. *The Historian's Craft*. Trans. Peter Putnam. New York: Vintage, 1964.

Bohley, Bärbel. *Englisches Tagebuch 1988*. Berlin: BasisDruck Verlag, 2011.

Bohley, Bärbel, Jürgen Fuchs, Katja Havemann, Rolf Henrich, Ralf Hirsch, and Reinhard Weißhuhn, eds. *40 Jahr DDR . . . und die Bürger melden sich zu Wort*. Frankfurt: Büchergilde Gutenberg, 1989.

Bohley, Bärbel, Gerald Praschl, and Rüdiger Rosenthal, eds. *Mut: Frauen in der DDR*. Munich: Herbig, 2005.

Boldin, Valery. *Ten Years That Shook the World: The Gorbachev Era as Witnessed by His Chief of Staff*. New York: HarperCollins, 1994.

Brandt, Willy. *My Life in Politics*. New York: Viking, 1991.

———. *" . . . was zusammengehört."* Bonn: Dietz, 1993.

Brinkmann, Peter. *Schlagzeilenjagd*. Bergisch Gladbach: Bastei Lübber, 1993.

Brzezinski, Zbigniew. *The Grand Failure: The Birth and Death of Communism in the Twentieth Century*. New York: Charles Scribner's Sons, 1989.

Brzezinski, Zbigniew, David Ignatius, and Brent Scowcroft. *America and the World: Conversations on the Future of American Foreign Policy*. New York: Basic Books, 2008.

Bush, George H. W., and Brent Scowcroft. *A World Transformed*. New York: Knopf, 1998.

Chernyaev, Anatoly. "Gorbachev and the Reunification of Germany: Personal Recollections," in Gabriel Gorodetsky, ed., *Soviet Foreign Policy 1971–1991*. London: Routledge, 1994.

———. *Die letzten Jahre einer Weltmacht: Der Kreml von innen.* Stuttgart: Deutsche-Verlagsanstalt, 1993.

———. Personal diary, donated to the National Security Archive and posted online at www2.gwu.edu/~nsarchiv/NSAEBB/NSAEBB192.

———. *My Six Years with Gorbachev.* Trans. and ed. by Robert English and Elizabeth Tucker. University Park: Pennsylvania State University Press, 2000.

Cradock, Percy. *In Pursuit of British Interests: Reflections on Foreign Policy Under Margaret Thatcher and John Major.* London: John Murray, 1997.

Darnton, Robert. *Berlin Journal, 1989–1990.* New York: Norton, 1991.

De Maizière, Lothar, and Volker Resing. *Ich will, dass meine Kinder nicht mehr lügen müssen: Meine Geschichte der deutschen Einheit.* Freiburg: Herder, 2010.

Diekmann, Kai, and Ralf Georg Reuth, eds. *Die längste Nacht, der grösste Tag: Deutschland am 9. November 1989.* Munich: Piper, 2009.

Duisberg, Claus J. *Das deutsche Jahr: Einblicke in die Wiedervereinigung.* Berlin: Siedler, 2005.

Eppelmann, Rainer, Markus Meckel, and Robert Grünbaum, eds. *Das ganze Deutschland: Reportagen zur Einheit.* Berlin: Aufbau, 2005.

Falin, Valentin. *Konflikte im Kreml: Zur Vorgeschichte der deutschen Einheit und Auflösung der Sowjetunion.* Munich: Blessing Verlag, 1997.

———. *Politische Erinnerungen.* Munich: Knaur, 1995.

Führer, Christian, Anne Ascher, and Patricia Holland-Moritz. *Und wir sind dabei gewesen: Die Revolution, die aus der Kirche kam.* Berlin: Ullstein, 2008.

Gates, Robert M. *From the Shadows: The Ultimate Insider's Story of Five Presidents and How They Won the Cold War.* New York: Touchstone, 1996.

Genscher, Hans-Dietrich. *Erinnerungen.* Berlin: Siedler, 1995. Abridged English translation: *Rebuilding a House Divided.* New York: Broadway Books, 1998.

German Embassy London, ed. *Witness Seminar: Berlin in the Cold War, 1948–1990; German Unification, 1989–1990.* Unpublished document, distributed by the Foreign and Commonwealth Office, London, 2009.

Gorbachev, Mikhail. *Memoirs.* New York: Doubleday, 1995.

———. *Toward a Better World.* London: Hutchinson, 1987.

Gorbachev, Mikhail, Vadim Sagladin, and Anatoli Tschernjajew. *Das neue Denken.* Munich: Goldmann Verlag, July 1997.

Gorbatschow, Michail. *Alles zu seiner Zeit.* Hamburg: Hoffmann und Campe, 2013.

Grachev, Andrei. *Gorbachev's Gamble: Soviet Foreign Policy and the End of the Cold War.* London: Polity, 2008.

Hanisch, Günter, et al., eds. *Dona nobis pacem: Fürbitten und Friedensgebete Herbst '89 in Leipzig.* Berlin: Evangelische Verlagsanstalt, 1990.

Havemannn, Robert. *Fragen Antworten Fragen: Aus der Biographie eines deutschen Marxisten.* Berlin: Piper, 1970, reprint 1990.

Hensel, Jana. *Zonenkinder.* Reinbek bei Hamburg: Rowohlt, 2004.

Hollitzer, Tobias. "'Heute entscheidt es sich.'" *Horch und Guck* 23 (Feb. 1998): 22–35.

Hollitzer, Tobias, and Reinhard Bohse, eds. *Heute vor 10 Jahren: Leipzig auf dem Weg zur friedlichen Revolution*. Fribourg: InnoVation Verlag, 2000.

Horn, Gyula. *Freiheit die ich meine: Erinnerungen des ungarischen Außenministers, der den Eisernen Vorhang öffnete*. Trans. Angelika and Péter Máté. Hamburg: Hoffmann und Campe Verlag, 1991.

Horváth, István. *Die Sonne ging in Ungarn auf: Erinnerungen an eine besondere Freundschaft*. Munich: Universitas, 2000.

Hutchings, Robert L. *American Diplomacy and the End of the Cold War: An Insider's Account of US Policy in Europe, 1989–1992*. Washington, DC: Wilson Center, 1997.

Jankowski, Martin. *Der Tag, der Deutschland veränderte: 9. Oktober 1989*. Leipzig: Evangelische Verlagsanstalt, 2007.

Jordan, Carlo, and Hans Michael Kloth, eds. *Arche Nova: Opposition in der DDR das "Grün-Ökologische Netzwerk Arche" 1988–90*. Berlin: BasisDruck, 1995.

Keßler, Heinz. *Zur Sache und zur Person*. Berlin: Edition Ost, 1996.

Kiessler, Richard, and Frank Elbe. *Ein runder Tisch mit scharfen Ecken: Der diplomatische Weg zur deutschen Einheit*. Baden-Baden: Nomos Verlagsgesellschaft, 1993.

Kissinger, Henry. *Diplomacy*. New York: Simon & Schuster, 1994.

Klein, Hans. *Es begann im Kaukasus: Der entscheidende Schritt in die Einheit Deutschlands*. Berlin: Ullstein, 1991.

Knabe, Hubertus, ed. *Aufbruch in eine andere DDR: Reformer und Oppositionelle zur Zukunft ihres Landes*. Rowohlt: Hamburg, 1989.

Kohl, Helmut. *Erinnerungen 1982–1990*. Munich: Droemer, 2005.

———. *Erinnerungen 1990–1994*. Munich: Droemer, 2007.

Kohl, Helmut, Kai Diekmann, and Ralf Georg Reuth. *Ich wollte Deutschlands Einheit*. Berlin: Ullstein, 1996.

König, Ewald. *Menschen Mauer Mythen: Deutsch-deutsche Notizen eines Wiener Korrespondenten*. Halle: Mitteldeutscher Verlag, 2014.

König, Gerd. *Fiasko eines Bruderbundes: Erinnerungen des letzten DDR-Botschafters in Moskau*. Berlin: Edition Ost, 2011.

Kotschemassow, Wjatscheslaw. *Meine letzte Mission*. Berlin: Dietz, 1994.

Krenz, Egon. *Herbst '89*. Berlin: Verlag Neues Leben, 1999.

———. *Wenn Mauern fallen*. Vienna: Neff, 1990.

Kwizinskij, J. A. *Vor dem Sturm: Erinnerungen eines Diplomaten*. Berlin: Siedler, 1993.

Lafontaine, Oskar. *Deutsche Wahrheiten: Die nationale und die soziale Frage*. Hamburg: Hoffmann und Campe Verlag, 1990.

Lauter, Gerhard. *Chefermittler: Der Oberste Fahnder der K in der DDR berichtet*. Berlin: Edition Ost, 2012.

Leonhard, Wolfgang. *Die Revolution entläßt ihre Kinder*. Cologne/Berlin: Kiepenheuer & Witsch, 1955.

———. *Spurensuche*. Cologne: Kiepenheuer & Witsch, 1992.

Matlock, Jack F., Jr. *Autopsy on an Empire: The American Ambassador's Account of the Collapse of the Soviet Union*. New York: Random House, 1995.

———. *Reagan and Gorbachev: How the Cold War Ended.* New York: Random House, 2004.

Maximytschew, Igor, and Hans-Hermann Hertle. *Der Fall der Mauer: Vorgeschichte und Hintergründe, eine russisch-deutsche Trilogie.* 2 vols. Berlin: Freie Universität, Zentralinstitut für Sozialwissenschaftliche Forschung, 1994.

Meckel, Markus. *Selbstbewußt in die deutsche Einheit: Rückblicke und Reflexion.* Berlin: Berlin Verlag, 2001.

Mittag, Günter. *Um jeden Preis: Im Spannungsfeld zweier Systeme.* Berlin: Aufbau-Verlag, 1991.

Mitterrand, François. *De l'Allemagne, de la France.* Paris: Editions Odile Jacob, 1996.

———. *Ma part de verité: De la rupture à l'unité.* Paris: Fayard, 1969.

Modrow, Hans, ed. *Das Große Haus: Insider berichten aus dem ZK der SED.* Berlin: Edition Ost, 1994.

Momper, Walter. *Grenzfall: Berlin im Brennpunkt deutscher Geschichte.* Munich: Bertelsmann, 1991.

Neues Forum Leipzig, ed. *Jetzt oder nie—Demokratie! Leipziger Herbst '89.* Leipzig: Forum Verlag, 1989.

Palazchenko, Pavel. *My Years with Gorbachev and Shevardnadze: The Memoir of a Soviet Interpreter.* University Park: Pennsylvania State University Press, 1997.

Poppe, Ulrike, Rainer Eckert, and Ilko-Sascha Kowalczuk, eds. *Zwischen Selbstbehauptung und Anpassung: Formen des Widerstandes und der Opposition in der DDR.* Berlin: Links, 1995.

Putin, Vladimir, with Nataliya Gevorkyan, Natalya Timakova, and Andrei Kolesnikov. *First Person: An Astonishingly Frank Self-Portrait by Russia's President Putin.* Trans. Catherine A. Fitzpatrick. New York: PublicAffairs, 2000.

Reich, Jens. *Abschied von Lebenslügen: Die Intelligenz und die Macht.* Berlin: Rowohlt, 1992.

Robinson, Peter. *It's My Party: A Republican's Messy Love Affair with the GOP.* New York: Warner Books, 2000.

Rusch, Claudia. *Meine freie deutsche Jugend.* Frankfurt: Fischer, 2003.

Sagladin, Vadim. *Und jetzt Welt-Innen Politik. Die Außenpolitik der Perestroika.* Rosenheim: Horizonte, 1990.

Schabowski, Günter, and Frank Sieren. *Wir haben fast alles falsch gemacht: Die letzten Tage der DDR.* 2nd ed. Berlin: Ullstein, 2009.

Schabowski, Günter, Frank Sieren, and Ludwig Koehne. *Das Politbüro Ende eines Mythos: Eine Befragung Günter Schabowskis.* Reinbek bei Hamburg: December 1990.

Schachnasarow, Georg. *Preis der Freiheit: Eine Bilanz von Gorbatschows Berater.* Bonn: Bouvier Verlag, 1996.

Schäuble, Wolfgang. *Der Vertrag: Wie ich über die deutsche Einheit verhandelte.* Munich: Knaur, 1991.

Schultke, Dietmar. *"Keiner Kommt Durch": Die Geschichte der innerdeutschen Grenze und der Berliner Mauer.* Berlin: Links Verlag, 2011.

Schwabe, Uwe. "'Symbol der Befreiung' die Friedensgebete in Leipzig." *Horch und Guck* 23 (Feb. 1998).

Schwan, Heribert, and Rolf Steiniger, eds. *Mein 9. November 1989.* Düsseldorf: Patmos Verlag, 2009.

Shevardnadze, Eduard. *The Future Belongs to Freedom.* London: Sinclair-Stevenson, 1991.

Sievers, Hans-Jürgen. "Brückenschlag zur Demokratie." In *Leipziger Almanach 2011/ 2012.* Leipzig: Leipziger Universitätsverlag, 2013, 343–359.

———, ed. *In der Mitte der Stadt: Die Evangelisch-Reformierte Kirche zu Leipzig von der Einwanderung der Hugenotten bis zur friedlichen Revolution.* Leipzig: Evangelische Verlagsanstalt, 2000.

———, ed. *Stundenbuch einer deutschen Revolution: Die Leipziger Kirche im Oktober 1989.* Göttingen: Vandenhoeck, 1990.

Teltschik, Horst. *329 Tage: Innenansichten der Einigung.* Berlin: Siedler, 1991.

Tetzner, Reiner. *Kerzen-Montage verändern die Welt: Warum die Waffen wirklich schwiegen.* Leipzig: Haus des Buches, 2009.

———. *Leipziger Ring: Aufzeichnungen eines Montagsdemonstranten Oktober 1989 bis 1. Mai 1990.* Frankfurt: Luchterhand, 1990.

Védrine, Hubert. *Les mondes de François Mitterrand.* Paris: Fayard, 1996.

Vier Tage im November. Hamburg: Gruner+Jahr, 1989.

Von Arnim, Joachim. *Zeitnot: Moskau, Deutschland und der weltpolitische Umbruch.* Bonn: Bouvier, 2012.

Wolf, Markus. *Die Troika.* Berlin/Weimar: Aufbau-Verlag, 1989.

———. *Im eigenen Auftrag: Bekenntnisse und Einsichten.* Munich: Schneekluth, 1991.

———. *Spionagechef im geheimen Krieg: Erinnerungen.* Munich: List, 1997.

Wolf, Markus, and Anne McElvoy. *Man Without a Face: The Autobiography of Communism's Greatest Spymaster.* New York: Random House, 1997.

Zelikow, Philip. "The Suicide of the East? 1989 and the Fall of Communism." *Foreign Affairs* 88, no. 6 (Nov./Dec. 2009).

Zelikow, Philip, and Condoleezza Rice. *Germany Unified and Europe Transformed: A Study in Statecraft.* Cambridge, MA: Harvard University Press, 1995.

Index